—BROWN-EYED CHILDREN OF THE SUN—

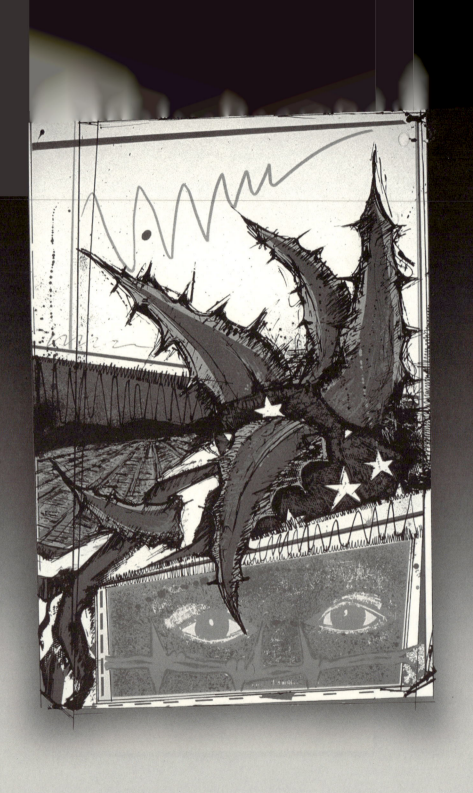

BROWN-EYED CHILDREN
-OF THE SUN-

Lessons from the Chicano Movement,
1965–1975

GEORGE MARISCAL

UNIVERSITY OF NEW MEXICO PRESS
ALBUQUERQUE

11 10 09 08 07 06 05   1 2 3 4 5 6 7

Library of Congress Cataloging-in-Publication Data

Mariscal, George.
Brown-eyed children of the sun :
lessons from the Chicano movement, 1965–1975 / George Mariscal.
p. cm.
Includes bibliographical references and index.
ISBN 0-8263-3805-4 (pbk. : alk. paper)
1. Mexican Americans—Civil rights—History—20th century.
2. Mexican Americans—Politics and government—20th century.
3. Mexican Americans—Ethnic identity.
4. Civil rights movements—United States—History—20th century.
5. Civil rights workers—United States—History—20th century.
6. Political activists—United States—History—20th century.
7. United States—Ethnic relations—History—20th century.
8. United States—Social conditions—1960–1980.
9. Vietnamese Conflict, 1961–1975—United States. I. Title.
E184.M5M3565 2005
305.868'72073'09046—dc22
2005015643

Although every effort has been made to contact copyright holders for the illustrations
in this book, because of the age and nature of the sources it has not always been possible to locate them. The author apologizes for any omissions and welcomes information that would allow him to give proper credit in future printings of this book.

Frontispiece: "Sí se puede" by Malaquías Montoya (silk screen, January 9–13, 1989).
Artist's description: "These images deal with struggle. I use the maguey plant as a symbol of strength. The plant and its power are the manifestation of the poor represented
by the person looking out of the rectangular box." Used by permission of artist.

DESIGN AND COMPOSITION: Mina Yamashita

To my parents, Ralph and Irene Mariscal,
for a lifetime of love and support.
I am so very proud to be your son.

—CONTENTS—

—ACKNOWLEDGMENTS—

THIS BOOK WAS COMPLETED without the aid of fellowships or research assistants. Although I was unable to spend time at the Rockefeller Center in Bellagio, Italy, I did have many useful discussions at the Las Cuatro Milpas, El Comal, and El Salvadoreño in the Barrio Logan district of San Diego. My thanks to Dionne Espinoza, Gail Pérez, and Misha Kokotovic, who joined me at these restaurants and *taquerías* in order to share their friendship, political insights, and the latest *chisme*.

I returned to the final drafts of the book whenever I could find the time during a two-year period when I was leading an effort to reestablish a Chicano/a studies program at the University of California, San Diego. My gratitude goes to my colleagues in the UCSD Chicano/Latino Concilio, especially Patrick Velásquez, Kimberly Jameson, Juan Astorga, Agustín Orozco, and Tony Valladolid. I thank the staff, students, and faculty who helped with that struggle which was undertaken in the spirit of the Lumumba-Zapata students. *Un abrazo solidario* to Olivia Puentes Reynolds for all she does for our *gente*.

Many activists from the Chicano Movement period whom I have had the privilege to know have inspired me. Rosalío Muñoz, Gloria Arellanes, Rudy and Nancy Tovar, Betita Martinez, Ernesto Vigil, and Eliezer Risco have dedicated their lives to La Causa and they deserve a special thank you. Two other militant fighters for justice, María Ana Gonzales and Armando Navarro, did me the great favor of including me in their delegations to Cuba, for which I will be forever thankful. For this Chicano, Cuba was a complex and eye-opening *maravilla*. *Un abrazo bien fuerte* to Herman García, Roberto Bahruth, and Gabriel Gutiérrez, *mis compañeros atravesando las calles de La Habana en busca de la casa del Che*.

In San Diego, the members of Project YANO have my deepest admiration. Their dedication to resisting militarism and intrusive military recruiting in the public schools is unwavering. Carol Jahnkow, Cecila Ubilla, and Vic Mazzarelle in particular have been tireless fighters whose high spirits and energy never cease to amaze me. Rick Jahnkow, director of YANO, is a brilliant grass-roots activist whose courage and commitment are especially remarkable given that his antagonist is the Pentagon itself.

My heartfelt *cariño* to Iris and Carlos Blanco for whom I have the greatest respect. How can we ever repay the countless hours you both have spent educating and mentoring generations of young Raza? To *mi hermana* Alda Blanco, thank you for being my dearest friend.

Shortly after the U.S. invasion of Iraq in 2003, I had the good fortune to meet Fernando Suárez del Solar. Fernando's son Jesús was one of the first Marines killed in the invasion, and Fernando had decided to commit himself to the struggle for peace. I have never met a more intelligent, effective, and fearless activist than Fernando Suárez del Solar. Like César Chávez, Fernando understands the power of militant nonviolence and believes that only our youth can lead us to a better future.

Mis agradecimientos to the following groups and individuals: the students in my courses on the Chicano Movement, especially Cathy Medrano, Denise Pacheco, Jessica Lopez, Ernesto Martinez, Adriana Jasso, Mary Ann Belmontez, Benjamín Prado, Tanya Juarez, Lupe Bacio, Eva Amezola, Laura Gonzales; *mis carnales* John Márquez, Carlton Floyd, and Jerry Rafiki Jenkins; Charlene Martinez and Edwina Welch for taking care of UCSD's students of color; Bob Dorn and his research assistants for their interviews and research on Third (Lumumba-Zapata) College; the staff at UCSD Mandeville Special Collections, specifically Lynda Claassen and Steve Coy; Michael Kelly, Rose Diaz, and Kari Schleher at the University of New Mexico's Center for Southwest Research; my editors at the University of New Mexico Press, Evelyn Schlatter and Maya Allen-Gallegos; Floyce Alexander for his keen eye and committed verse.

Special thanks go to Ignacio M. García for our *pláticas* about the meaning of the Movimiento and to Rudy Acuña and Suzanne Oboler for taking time to read parts or all of my manuscript. A heartfelt *gracias* to Malaquías Montoya for once again allowing me to use his powerful artwork.

To my children Emma and Sam and my wife Elizabeth I can only say you mean everything to me. I love you all very much.

—George (Jorge) Mariscal
San Elijo, Califas
[Cardiff by the Sea, California]

I want young men and young women who are not alive today but who will come into this world, with new privileges and new opportunities, I want them to know and see that these new privileges and opportunities did not come without somebody suffering and sacrificing for them.

—Martin Luther King, Jr.

La Causa for all those blindly involved who do not know
Is the planting of mañanas which will grow
Permitting the faceless Chicanos of that day to go
Like eagles, as high as they can, as high as they want to go.

—Abelardo Delgado, "La Causa"

If we remember those times and places—and there are so many—where people have behaved magnificently, this gives us the energy to act, and at least the possibility of sending this spinning top of a world in a different direction.

—Howard Zinn, *You Can't Stay Neutral on a Moving Train*

Mañana la Raza, la gente que espera, no verá mañana. Our tomorrow *es hoy, ahorita. Que VIVA LA RAZA, mi gente,* Our people to freedom. *¿When? Now, ahorita define tu mañana hoy.*

—Alurista, "When Raza?"

1. Dolores Huerta (far left) with Robert Kennedy, June 5, 1968. Photo by Julian Wasser/Getty Images. Used by permission of Time & Life Pictures.

—Introduction—

"Your children's eyes are smiling, their life
is just begun, and what will you be giving
to your brown-eyed children of the sun?"
—Pedro Contreras, "Brown-eyed Children of the Sun"

IN JUNE OF 1968, on the stage of the Ambassador Hotel in Los Angeles, United Farm Workers union (UFW) co-founder Dolores Huerta stood behind Robert Kennedy as he claimed victory in the California presidential primary. Broadly smiling, Huerta, together with César Chávez and the UFW rank and file, had helped Kennedy win California by mounting voter-registration drives, staging rallies, and leafleting. Due to the UFW's efforts many precincts in predominantly Mexican American areas voted 100 percent for Kennedy. Rather than attending the celebration with Huerta and Kennedy, César Chávez had decided to remain at a party for a local assemblyman in order to avoid the large crowds at the rally.

In the ballroom of the Ambassador, Kennedy concluded his victory speech: "I think we can end the divisions within the United States. What I think is quite clear is that we can work together in the last analysis. And that what has been going on with the United States over the period of that last three years, the divisions, the violence, the disenchantment with our society, the divisions—whether it's between blacks and whites, between the poor and the more affluent, or between age groups, or in the war in Vietnam—that we can work together."[1] Within minutes after he left the podium, Kennedy had been shot several times. He died the next morning. In his novel *Revolt of the Cockroach People*, Chicano attorney and novelist Oscar Zeta Acosta captured the sentiments of the Chicano/a activist community at that moment: "I can feel it in my bones, that the ante has been upped."[2]

A little over one year later, a Mexican born in Tijuana, Baja California, and raised in the San Francisco Bay Area stood at center stage at the event most often recognized as the defining moment of the 1960s generation. Carlos Santana and his multiracial band at the 1969 Woodstock festival delivered its Afro-Cuban and pan-Latino sounds to a half million predominantly middle-class European American youth, at a time when U.S. policymakers and intellectuals still referred to Mexican Americans as the "invisible minority."[3] Few in the audience or media knew that Carlos Santana was a Chicano. Because his music incorporated Caribbean instruments and styles, most North Americans took him to be Puerto Rican. But to young Chicanos and Chicanas across the United States, in the Southwest but also in Mexican communities in Omaha, Chicago, and Portland, he clearly was one of our own and his music was the soundtrack through which we were about to forge our collective identity.

These two iconic moments—Dolores Huerta with Bobby Kennedy and Santana at Woodstock—remind us that the 1960s marked the first time dominant U.S. culture witnessed Americans of Mexican descent on a national stage as self-determined agents rather than subservient and racialized others. As Rodolfo Acuña, the dean of Chicano historians, has written: "The youth and Civil Rights movements of the Sixties provided broader space for Mexican American involvement than other generations."[4] In Chicano communities across the Southwest during the era of the American war in Southeast Asia, this newfound agency would produce a political, intellectual, and artistic movement of unprecedented magnitude.

One of the objectives of this book is to remind us that the so-called Sixties were about more than "sex, drugs, and rock and roll" or middle-class white youth adopting alternative lifestyles or even the African American struggle for civil rights. In ethnic Mexican communities, the period between 1965 and 1975 produced dramatic changes. These changes were influenced in part by the aforementioned developments. But at the same time these charges grew out of local and regional traditions of survival and resistance whose origins lie in the Southwest, in Mexico, and in locations farther south.

It is my hope that the present study will help to restore to the national memory the accomplishments of Spanish-speaking communities in the late 1960s and early 1970s. This restoration of historical memory will be particularly important for young Latinas and Latinos in the United States born after the 1970s and for the thousands of Mexican and Latin American immigrants and their children who have arrived over the last three decades. For students of U.S. history and culture, this book offers an interpretation of several key episodes in the development of Chicano/a activism during the Viet Nam war period.

In the ten-year period surrounding the death of Bobby Kennedy and Santana's historic performance or what has been called the "long

2. Carlos Santana at Woodstock, August 1, 1969. Photo by Tucker Ransom/Hulton Archive/Getty Images. Used by permission of Getty Images.

decade of the 1960s," Mexican American activists developed a complex critique of traditional assimilation and melting-pot discourses in order to transform themselves into Chicanas and Chicanos.[5] Taking a previously pejorative term that had existed along the U.S.-Mexican border for decades, these brown-eyed children of the sun rejected dominant versions of U.S. history, and began the arduous journey toward self-determination and self-definition. A diffuse movement cross-cut by regional, gender, and class issues, the Movimiento (also known as La Causa or La Movida) was a mass mobilization dedicated to a wide range of social projects, from ethnic separatism to socialist internationalism, from electoral politics to institutional reform and even armed insurrection.

For cynical observers of the Mexican American community such as Richard Nixon, who once remarked that "the Mexicans" would never rebel like the Blacks, the Chicano Movement came as a surprising and disturbing development. In 1966, on the eve of the Movement's major events, one scholar suggested that a social movement led by ethnic Mexicans in the United States was highly unlikely: "It is not surprising that Mexican Americans have been unable to put to effective use the tool of the mass voice to promote the common good of their group. They are in fact *not* a group; they do not speak with a common voice; they do not have mutual agreement; they are fragmented first by their heterogeneity and second by the tradition of individualism."[6]

A mere two years later, however, in her 1968 paper prepared for the U.S. Commission on Civil Rights, Helen Rowan described the changes taking place in both the urban and rural areas of the Southwest: "The level of organization, of awareness, and of identity is constantly rising . . . In fact, every aspect necessary to the development and sustaining of a movement is being activated and, most importantly, obtaining financial support. La Raza has become more than a slogan; it has become a way of life for a people who seek to fully realize their personal and group identity and obtain equality of rights and treatment as citizens of the United States."[7] Rowan's recognition that emerging Chicano/a identities were both individual and collective is an important point to which I will return often in this study.

Even social scientists sympathetic to efforts to expose and rectify the historic mistreatment of Mexicans in the United States were unsure of what to make of the emerging militancy. From their perspective, the Movimiento was not congruent with the "typical" Mexican American behavior they had come to expect. Joan W. Moore, for example, who was a faculty member at the University of California, Riverside, and enjoyed close ties to the Southern California Chicana/o community, collaborated with Alfredo Cuéllar for a book in the "Prentice-Hall Ethnic Groups in American Life Series." In the book's final chapter, Cuéllar wrote: "The masses of Mexican Americans in the large cities of the Southwest are politically inert. The very model of Mexican leadership has been the 'quiet fighter,' who does not create any public difficulties. Until the arrival of César Chávez in 1965 and the dramatic agricultural strikes in the San Joaquin valley in California and in the Rio Grande valley in Texas, the 'Mexican way' was quiet and private negotiation, no more. Demonstrations have been few."[8]

Carefully making their way through the calm before the storm, Moore and Cuéllar sensed that Chicana/o youth were about to create something unique in U.S. political history: "The importance of the

Chicano movement as an alternative to pressures from the majority society can hardly be overemphasized. It is a distinctively novel development in the Mexican American community."[9] Surprisingly, even the *New York Times* reported on the transformations taking place. In a front-page story on April 20, 1969, reporter Homer Bigart wrote: "Five million Mexican Americans, the nation's second largest minority, are stirring with a new militancy. The ethnic stereotype that the Chicanos are too drowsy, too docile to carry a sustained fight against poverty and discrimination is bending under fresh assault."[10] Bigart's analysis proved to be prophetic. A little over one year later, Chicanas and Chicanos would organize the largest antiwar demonstration ever staged by a working-class ethnic group in the United States.

The fact that sectors of the Mexican American community had become radicalized did not quite compute for even the most progressive social scientists and historians. It is ironic that thirty years after the most dramatic events of the Chicano Movement, the history of that Movement has yet to be fully integrated into scholarship focused on the 1960s. With very few exceptions, retrospectives on the Sixties do not include the achievements of Chicana/o communities, a fact already recognized by Carlos Muñoz in 1989 when he reported how one conference organizer of a "60s symposium" told him that no Chicano/as were invited because "they were probably not involved in the struggles of the sixties."[11] A full decade after the incident recorded in Muñoz's anecdote, little had changed. At a symposium held in Oakland in 2000 on the Viet Nam war's impact on the state of California, presentations by Muñoz and myself (the only two Chicano participants) were greeted by Caucasian activists from the period with exclamations such as "Oh, I had no idea Chicanos protested against the war." As the bibliography on social movements of the 1960s grows, it is clear that Chicano/a scholars will have to write their own histories in order to carry forward the arduous task of inserting ourselves into a recalcitrant national memory.

As is the case with most social movements, the Chicano Movement did not erupt spontaneously. The Mexican and Mexican American radical tradition can be traced back to a variety of originary moments. According to some Movement intellectuals and artists, the Spanish conquest of the indigenous people of Mexico in general and the Aztec empire in particular mark the initial point of conflict. Others would push the beginnings of that tradition back to the U.S. conquest and subsequent colonization of the Southwest (the preferred origin for most Movement thinkers). In this scenario, the annexation of Texas, the U.S. war against Mexico, and the Treaty of Guadalupe Hidalgo were the decisive moments that marked the beginning of the *longue durée* of Chicano/a resistance. Cultural critic and Movement activist, Tomás Ybarra-Frausto summarized this position in the following manner:

> The Chicano movement of the sixties was a recuperation of a project that had been going on since 1848, with labor strikes and mobilizations and people fighting for justice, dignity, and human rights. The difference between previous social movements and the Chicano movement was one of scope. That is, it was a national mobilization of people in New Mexico, Colorado, Texas, New Jersey, and California. It was a collective. It was also like a mythical movement—it was as if this fire of your identity was slowly going out. . . . It was cleansing at the same time as it was, for some people, destructive. So, the Chicano project of the sixties was the continuation of a long series of struggles of people in the United States. It was different because it was national in scope and also because it had this mythic quality about it.[12]

Many traditional historians have argued that it was the Mexican Revolution of 1910 that gave birth to a modern revolutionary consciousness among Mexicans in the United States, a consciousness that would persist in the trade-union movements of the 1930s and 1940s and the Mexican American civil-rights struggles of the 1950s. More recently, Raúl Fernandez and Gilbert Gonzalez have argued for a stricter separation between the nineteenth and twentieth centuries, claiming that Chicano/a history can only be understood as a corollary to a later and more fully developed capitalist hegemony over Mexico.[13]

Ultimately we need not privilege any one of the hypotheses regarding the origins of the Movimiento. Each functions to produce an historical narrative with specific ideological and political objectives. I would suggest, however, that Ybarra-Frausto's claim that the two factors that distinguish the Movimiento of the Viet Nam war period from other periods were its national scope and "mythic qualities" must be qualified for the following reasons. Much more than the question of geographical scope is the fact that the Movement period produced a complex range of organizing strategies and ideological positions that were unknown at earlier stages of Chicano/Mexicano resistance.

As I hope to show in the following chapters, the complexity of the Movement was the result of national and global developments that included the rise of Third World anticolonial struggles, "national liberation movements" within the United States, the existence of a youth counterculture as part of the new Chicano/a context (especially in the cities), and the multiple U.S. imperial interventions during the period 1965–75. Given the Movimiento's complicated ideological terrain, I would argue that it was qualitatively different from earlier forms of Mexican contestation and that its so-called mythic qualities were in fact necessary elements of a concrete political project which despite the lack of a single ideological focus nonetheless posed a serious challenge to all previous models of citizenship, assimilation, and the role of racialized minorities in the United States.

Whether or not the Chicano Movement constituted a break with the previous generation or was a continuation of earlier political projects is a question that has been debated by a number of scholars.[14] In my opinion, what occurs roughly at the conclusion of the Eisenhower presidency is that Mexican American political activity experiences *an acceleration in a different register*. With the creation of the Mexican American Political Association (MAPA) in 1959, the formation of the Political Association of Spanish-Speaking Organizations (PASSO) and the activism of the Viva Kennedy! clubs in 1960, the appearance of César Chávez's National Farm Workers Association in 1962, Reies López Tijerina's founding of the Alianza Federal de las Mercedes in 1963, and the electoral victories in Crystal City, Texas, that same year, a more militant ethnicity-based politics emerged throughout the Southwest.

Moreover, international and domestic developments such as reaction to the U.S. war in Southeast Asia, the youth counterculture, the Black civil rights, and other radical movements quickened the pace of grassroots political activity across the nation. In March 1966, when several dozen Chicano activists staged a walkout at an Equal Employment Opportunity Commission (EEOC) conference in Albuquerque to protest the exclusion of Mexican Americans from a White House conference on civil rights that was to be held in June of that same year, it was clear that for many activists traditional approaches to change had run their course.

In most of its manifestations, the Chicano Movement participated directly in the Third World critique of Eurocentrism and white supremacy that had its roots in the early twentieth century and exploded in the anticolonial victories after World War II. Whether or not we accept the notion that the Chicano community constituted an "internal colony," there can be little doubt that the Movimiento shared a number of features with anticolonial projects around the world. If, as the ideologues of Manifest Destiny had declared, the United States was an extension, indeed an exceptional form, of European civilization (and according to "scientific racism" a creation of the superior Anglo-Saxon or Nordic races), then Mexicans in the United States were a base mixture of "inferior" southern European (Spanish) and "primitive" Amerindian stock and thus in dire need of salvation.

Represented by traditional U.S. historiography as a people without history, Chicano/as in the 1960s questioned the basic premises of what geographer J. M. Blaut has called "cultural diffusionism," that is, the myths of European superiority and the inevitable march of civilization from east to west.[15] Chicano/a activists and intellectuals reinterpreted the conquest of the Southwest and its aftermath and began to refashion their community's history and to understand their relationship to the histories of other disenfranchised populations. What we shall learn in the following pages is that the Cuban revolutionary experience, the war in Southeast Asia, and even African American radicalism would all have a profound effect on the creation of a sophisticated Chicana/o internationalism.

Another objective of this book, then, is to understand the Chicano Movement not only as a chapter in U.S. history but also as an important consequence of what was a "window of opportunity" for liberation struggles around the world. I understand the term "window of opportunity" to be the thirty year period between the end of the Second World War and the end of the U.S. war in Southeast Asia.[16] What the Cold War and the standoff between the two superpowers facilitated was a series of openings for developing nations and racialized minority groups in the West to attempt to chart an independent course toward greater self-determination and social equality. Such efforts would be limited due to the imperial agendas of both the United States and the Soviet Union. For minority communities in the developed countries obstacles to change arose from structural mechanisms of inequality and direct state repression. Nevertheless, it seemed evident to many in diverse national contexts that a different, more equitable, society was within reach.

One of the most perceptive analysts of this potential for radical and progressive change told a group of students in 1963: "The world is awakening and all the old truths are no longer accepted merely because they have been in place for centuries. What is demanded is evidence for what before was only asserted, the interrogation of what is asserted, and the scientific analysis of what is asserted. And from this questioning are born revolutionary ideas that are spreading around the world."[17] Without exception, the youth subcultures that grew out of and fed back into the international social movements of the late 1960s participated in this new sense of questioning authority and the demand that long-standing promises about social justice and democracy be fulfilled.

At the heart of the diverse collective projects that arose in the United States was a critique of traditional liberalism that exposed the contradictions and the hypocrisies of a system that had promised equality to all groups but had refused to deliver it. Although still embedded in a capitalist framework, Third World and even cultural nationalist agendas in the United States promoted what Samir Amin has called a "social and national" vision that placed the rights and demands of working-class and racialized people at the forefront of political change.[18] While it is true that the achievements of this moment were uneven and often short-lived, it is no less true that significant progress was made on many fronts.

In the present study I am particularly eager to demonstrate the ways in which collective identities at the local level could not be separated from wider global developments. Throughout the 1960s and 1970s, the former colonies of Europe and the United States asserted their self-determination, and national liberation and anticolonial struggles produced a culture of resistance that inspired young people around the world. In a variety of contexts, cultural nationalism, with all its blind spots, was a positive force for both developing nations and racialized minorities in the West. Its ideological power served to bring diverse groups together under the banner of independence from colonial exploitation, economic underdevelopment, and institutional racism. Moreover, for many young activists of the period, local forms of nationalism led logically to international solidarity work.

In Mexican American communities, these utopian and transformative possibilities came together most powerfully in the figure of Ernesto Che Guevara but also through Chicano reimaginings of Emiliano Zapata, Francisco Villa, and the women of the Mexican Revolution—las Adelitas. In its most complex manifestations, the Chicano Movement participated in a global South-West dialectic that drew its inspiration from both the revolutionary traditions of the South (especially Cuba and Mexico) and social democratic reformist agendas in the West during the post-World War II period. Although the Movement did not produce a single ideology that could synthesize gendered, regional, and organizational differences under one banner, Chicana and Chicano activists agreed that a more just and peaceful world was not only possible but also necessary.

It was not long, however, before the most privileged countries decided to close the window of opportunity for the majority of the world's population by reasserting their control over the economies and domestic policies of the former colonies. In a brutal last gasp of this particular stage of U.S. imperialism, the war in Southeast Asia devoured millions of Vietnamese and thousands of working-class American youth. Chicano communities were particularly hard hit. By the late 1970s, whatever gains had been made by the former colonies had been lost to economic downturns and foreign debt. In the wake of the Cold War and with the end of the century approaching, global capital, armed with a technological and military superiority that surpassed even its former imperial glory, reasserted its dominance over the developing world.

The IMF, World Bank, and other agencies offered bailouts but only if formerly sovereign nations submitted themselves to neoliberal programs of structural adjustment, that is, the stripping away of social safety nets and the selling-off of the public sphere to private entities. Backed by the increased willingness of the United States to intervene with force around the world, corporate globalization had arrived. Reactionary media pundits proclaimed the end of history, that is, the end of progressive change and the beginning of the recolonization of the world. With the ascendance of the neoconservative foreign policy of preemptive military action during the George W. Bush administration, U.S. attempts at domination of key strategic areas played themselves out most violently in the 2003 invasion of Iraq and the subsequent occupation of that nation.

On the domestic front in the United States, concerted efforts by conservatives successfully rolled back the meager gains made by disenfranchised groups during the Civil Rights era. In the media and the universities, revisionist historians recast the liberatory moment of the 1960s as foolish and misguided. Many portrayed the Chicano Movement as a flawed and failed experiment. The tremendous transformative potential of the Movimiento became a vague but potent memory for those who had experienced it in their youth. For the vast majority of ethnic Mexican young people growing up in the 1980s, 1990s, and the early years of the twenty-first century and for the thousands of immigrants who had arrived in the United States during that period, the history and the lessons of the Chicano Movement were either poorly understood or completely unknown.

NATIONALIST OBSESSIONS

"Enorme Transformación que de un nopal ya casi moribundo has dado fruto a tan ardiente árbol sin cesar."

("Great Transformation that from an almost dead cactus you have produced fruit from a tree endlessly ablaze")
—raúlrsalinas, *"Enorme Transformación"*

My interest in doing research on the Chicano Movement began when I was teaching introductory courses on Chicano/a literature as well as courses on the Viet Nam war period with a focus on minority experiences of the war. The tremendous achievement of the Chicano antiwar movement, in particular the National Chicano Moratorium Committee, inspired me to learn more about the ways in which other organizations and individuals had challenged liberal and conservative forms of elitism or class racism, the legacy of economic exploitation of ethnic Mexican and other poor people, and recurring racialized media representations of Spanish-speaking communities. As the grandson of Mexican immigrants and the son of a World War II Marine Corps veteran, I had been taught to respect those in authority regardless of my personal opinions. My response to being drafted, therefore, was a passive one, and I soon found myself among thousands of young men sucked into the military in early 1968. Upon my return in 1970 from a tour of duty in Viet Nam, my political education was well under way. But it was not until several decades later that I understood the depth of the Mexican American community's courageous resistance to an imposed status of second-class citizenship during the decade between 1965 and 1975.

I am struck continually by the efforts of many Mexican American professionals to deny any value whatsoever to the Movement period and to cast it in a completely negative light. I began to notice the ways in which at academic conferences and even at the level of everyday community and campus politics something called "Chicano nationalism" had become the *cucui* or bogeyman against which those professionals who had achieved successful careers (a success inconceivable without the Movement's contributions) constructed their public and professional identities. My desire to understand "nationalism" in a Chicano/a context was piqued when a Hispanic bureaucrat repeatedly used the term *nationalist* to discredit a group of Chicano/a staff, students, and faculty committed to contesting elitism and structural racism at their university campus. It was not clear what precisely the term signified for this individual—whether it was the militancy of the advocacy group that frightened him or whether the term was linked in his mind to attitudes like sexism and homophobia, attitudes that were nowhere visible in the group's practices but nonetheless could be invoked in order to discredit one's opponents. In any event, I realized then that the positive contributions of the Movement had become hostage to a scholarly preoccupation with a single ingredient of its complex ideological mixture—the nationalist impulse.

Early in my study of the many forms of nationalism, I found Tom Nairn's definition potentially useful from a Chicano perspective. In his 1977 book, *The Break-Up of Britain: Crisis and Neo-Nationalism*, Nairn suggested that a defining trait of all national struggles, whether they be designed to produce large nation-states, overthrow colonial regimes, or assert the rights of ethnic minorities, was their basic ambiguity. It is not so much a question of "good nationalism" vs. "bad nationalism" but rather, as Nairn puts it, the fact that "all nationalism is both healthy and morbid."[19] Interestingly, a similar analysis had emanated from the inside of one of California's maximum-security prisons in the early 1970s. Writing for a column entitled "*Noticias de la Pinta*" ("News from Prison"), Francisco "Güero" Estrada pointed to the contradictory nature of the nationalist moment: "Of all the political theories that I have been exposed to, I think that Nationalism best expresses my concept of *what is good and bad* for all oppressed people" (emphasis added).[20]

By distinguishing between what he called "reactionary nationalism" and "revolutionary nationalism," Estrada made a convincing case against the most regressive forms of nationalism even as he poignantly explained their origins: "The Pinto who becomes what I define as a 'Reactionary Nationalist' does so principally because the only positive response that he has received from people that he attempted to relate to was from other

Chicanos—exclusively! Consequently, the only people that have molded his life, in terms of ever having done anything to help him, were all Chicanos. . . . He does not care what the troubles of other peoples may or may not be. All he is interested in is doing something for the only people that have ever done something for him, *la raza, nosotros los Chicanos.*"[21]

By extrapolating out from Estrada's analysis, I would submit that the appeal of Chicano cultural nationalism was (is) always greatest for working-class people living in tightly knit urban or rural Mexican communities in the United States. But even in conditions where the potential for class mobility is greater, such as in university social relations, the tendency toward what seem to be narrow nationalist formulations ("*Mi Raza primero*" ["My People first"]) at certain key moments may be a necessary tactical decision in order to organize constituencies with limited resources, to defend the community from nativist or white supremacist attacks, or simply to gain visibility for Chicano/a issues in a context of institutional neglect or hostility.

Looking back at my personal history, I realize that I have had the opportunity to experience both the morbid and the healthy side of the nationalist sentiment. As a graduate student in Madrid in the mid-1970s I witnessed the final throes of the Franco dictatorship. One day in 1974, I was unwittingly caught up in a street demonstration of Falangist youth. Working my way through the crowd on the Gran Vía, I hurried to nearby side streets in order to escape the palpable intensity of extreme nationalist, i.e. fascist, fervor. A full quarter of a century later as a visiting scholar in Havana, I felt the upsurge of nationalist pride as the young Cuban boy, Elián González, who had been held in Miami for several months, returned to his country. Walking through downtown Havana, I watched as Cubans of all ages smiled and embraced one another in an expression of joy and national solidarity.

In his description of nationalism as the "modern Janus," the Roman god with two faces, Nairn reminds us: "In short, the substance of nationalism as such is always morally, politically, humanly ambiguous. This is why moralizing perspectives on the phenomenon always fail, whether they praise or berate it."[22] In other words, it is rarely useful to isolate the nationalist impulse as an abstract category and often more productive to "fill it in" with a specific historical and geographical content. Only then may we be able to judge the effects of a nationalist project and decide whether or not it has served to improve a community's condition.

It is not my intention to either praise or berate, romanticize or dis-credit, the Chicano Movement although I do believe that despite the faults one can attribute to it in retrospect the benefits produced by the Movimiento still outweigh its ideological blind spots. I agree enthusiasti-cally with Robin D. G. Kelley's recent writing regarding African American social movements: "Unfortunately, too often our standards for evaluating social movements pivot around whether or not they 'succeeded' in real-izing their visions rather than on the merits or power of the visions them-selves. By such a measure, virtually every radical movement failed because the basic power relations they sought to change remain pretty much intact. And yet it is precisely these alternative visions and dreams that inspire new generations to continue to struggle for change."[23]

Put another way, the claim that the Movimiento "failed" reduces its scope to an instrumentalist interpretation in the political realm where, as Kelley suggests, relations of power were stacked overwhelmingly against activists demanding rapid change. Such reductionism is cer-tainly one scholarly prism through which to view the past, but in the case of Chicano/a insurgency it blocks out a large part of the ideologi-cal field and erases the Movement's numerous accomplishments.[24] The Movement's successful broadening of a Chicano/a collective and mili-tant identity beyond the narrow confines of isolated groups of ethnic Mexicans where it had resided in previous decades was in itself a major success. On this point I am reminded of William Gamson's claim that "the creation of an ongoing collective identity that maintains the loy-alty and commitment of participants is a cultural achievement in its own right, regardless of its contribution to the achievement of political and organizational goals."[25] Or, as Chicana writer Cherríe Moraga puts it: "What was right about Chicano nationalism was its commitment to preserving the integrity of the Chicano people."[26]

To ask in the first decade of the twenty-first century whether or not the Chicano Movement "failed or succeeded" is a profoundly antihistor-ical question, for it necessarily judges the desire and praxis of a previous moment against the values and conditions of possibility of the present. A statement such as the following—"Though subversive activities on the part of local and federal government agencies hindered the insurgency's attempts to change the status quo, the Chicano Movement also failed to achieve its goals because of its essentialist imaginings of community driven by an ideologically bankrupt cultural nationalism"—vastly oversimplifies the intellectual complexity of the Movement.[27] By reading a rich social movement through the academic critique of a caricatured "nationalism" that dominated elite Chicano/a Studies programs in the 1990s (but interestingly had far less resonance in other locations such as state and community college programs where most working-class youth were found), the potential for historical understanding is diminished.

As we shall see, the dismissal of a mobilizing frame as "ideologically bankrupt" understates the effects of changes in the historical context itself.[28] Moreover, the concept of "bankruptcy" inverts the chain of causality leading to the "decline" of Movement organizations by rhetorically equating a Chicano philosophical "failing" (a blanket concept of "cultural nationalism" essentialized by the historian himself) with the well-orchestrated and violent campaign by law enforcement to destroy the insurgency. Social-movement theorist Alberto Melucci reminds us: "An organization may fail to achieve its objectives for a great number of reasons, both internal and external; but, ultimately, the action (or inaction) of the adversary is always decisive, due to the relative or absolute advantage of its position in the power relationship."[29] From the corporate growers who challenged the UFW to the full force of federal and local law-enforcement agencies, the adversaries who confronted Chicano/a mobilizations wielded a decisive and overwhelming advantage.

In the pages that follow, I will attempt to capture some of the positive aspects of the collective vision created by Chicano/a activists and organizations. We also will see how sectarian forms of nationalism could lead to a wide range of counterproductive attitudes and harmful practices, first and foremost among them sexism and homophobia. As I have suggested, these negative aspects are what most contemporary Chicano/a scholars have chosen to emphasize. But many aspects of cultural nationalism could also produce positive results for women and men, young and old, queers and straights. One of my goals, then, is to elucidate the tension inherent in this double-sided potential and thereby free our understanding of the Movement from the narrow nationalist straitjacket in which it has been placed so that we can begin to reevaluate it in all of its complexity.

In the language of contemporary technology, I understand cultural nationalism to be a networking hub into which diverse input ports feed and from which multiple output ports exit. In other words, cultural nationalism or ethnic pride ("Brown Power") functions as the site of a community's collective identity, organization, and passage into praxis as an historical agent. During the late 1960s and early 1970s, numerous traditions and agendas of ethnic Mexicans in the United States as well as the example of past and contemporary social movements from the Latin American and U.S. contexts entered the hub. Leading out were an array of Movement agendas and political and cultural positions ranging from sectarian nationalism and ethnic separatism to militant reformist programs and coalitions to revolutionary stances on the left espousing strong internationalist solidarity to various forms of socialism. That traditional notions of gender, sexuality, and the family permeated all of these positions should not surprise us given the deep-rooted patriarchal structures that determine U.S., Mexican, and Mexican American social relations. The point is to adapt the lesson of how discriminatory practices debilitated Movement organizations not in order to dismiss the entire period but in order to avoid repeating those practices in the present.

As my anecdote about the Hispanic academic suggests, over the last two decades a professional buffer class has emerged in the academy and elsewhere whose dual purpose is to keep militant activists at bay and by so doing manage their personal success. The shift from Chicano politics to Hispanic politics that began in the 1980s and peaked at the turn of the century is in essence the shift from a grassroots, working-class agenda to a business and professional class agenda. The apparent successes of a relatively small group of Latinos and Latinas means that an individualized and depoliticized version of an ethnicity-based identity (a collective variant of which Movimiento activists had created) can be retained and strategically deployed in order to reap the financial rewards offered by U.S. society. This new "identity" is crafted carefully in order to purge it of the specific demands (self-determination, serious structural reform, access to resources, and inclusion in policy decisions), historical narratives ("Aztlán" or the indigenous past and present), and ideological affiliations (Latin American revolutionary thought) associated with the Movement period.

As one astute Mexican observer put it: "*El hispanismo venía a proponer la aceptación plena del* 'American Way of Life' *como la única posibilidad de 'triunfar' en los Estados Unidos y a desplazar el radicalismo cultural y político del chicanismo. El hispanismo alejó a los méxicoamericanos de una idea del México popular y lo cambió por una relación con quien ofreciera mutuos beneficios políticos, comerciales y financieros visibles a corto plazo*" ("Hispanic identities promoted the full acceptance of the

'American Way of Life' as the only option for success in the United States and the displacement of the political and cultural radicalism of Chicano/a identities. Hispanic identities distanced Mexican Americans from the Mexican grass roots and in exchange offered many visible political, commercial, and financial benefits in the short term").[30]

In its relations with Mexico and Latin America in general, the Hispanic sector cast its lot with ruling parties and powerful elites, and abandoned the Movement's concept of international solidarity with exploited communities. To paraphrase Martin Luther King, Jr., we might say that it is disappointing that the Hispanic professional class had sailed out of rough waters into the relatively calm sea of the mainstream, and in the process had forgotten the storm in which their sisters and brothers were still drowning.[31] Eager to celebrate the surface characteristics of their ethnicity, Hispanics were far less sanguine about taking up the mantle of the struggle for social and economic justice.

In a visionary moment in 1972, the great Chicano educator and organizer Ernesto Galarza wondered aloud about the future of what was then the first large cohort of Chicano/as entering the universities and eventually the professional class:

> The Mexican moving into American urban society is moving into an extremely complicated culture. The community needs people who know their way around in it but if you can learn your way around a complicated culture you can easily be tempted to exploit it on your own behalf and to make a career out of it. Careerism is one of the temptations and pitfalls which faces the Mexican graduate student, he has to make up his mind what his responsibility is. Now if enough such guys come out of the universities who go back well-trained, competent, and capable who use their skills to help the community to find its way through this maze, this meat grinder which is American society, their training will be justified. I will be very interested to see how many men and women [like this] this generation can turn out.[32]

In the early 1980s, the rise of Reaganism marked the beginning of a vicious attack on the public sphere that would continue through the so-called Gingrich Revolution into the new century under the guise of neoliberalism and finally produce the gutting of state and local economies realized by the Bush/Cheney administration under the guise of a "war on terror" without end. Throughout this twenty-year period, a concurrent development was the expansion and solidification of Hispanic markets and identities. Careerism and hyper-professionalization went hand in hand with the adage coined in the 1980s—"Greed is good"—or its later variant popular in the first decade of the new century—"It's all about me."

As early as the late 1970s, it seemed that Galarza's worst-case scenario had come to pass. During the Carter years, a handful of Chicano scholars noted that a Hispanic managerial class already had asserted itself to an extent previously unimaginable in virtually all the major professions. Mario Barrera, in his now classic *Race and Class in the Southwest* (1979), used an internal-colonialism model in order to show how Chicanas/os tended to occupy a separate sector of each class because of racialization mechanisms, gender bias, and other institutionalized discriminatory practices. What Barrera called the "Chicano Ascriptive Class Segments (CACS), Patrick Carey-Herrera jokingly referred to as the "Chicano Ascriptive Class Assimilants" (CACA), that is, Mexicans assimilated into mainstream professions or even the capitalist class but held in check by what in another context would be called the "glass ceiling."[33] Barrera's intuition that there existed the potential for a Hispanic ethos, however, led him to point out that "the various Chicano subordinate segments have certain interests in common, their colonial interests, and certain interests in opposition, their class interests."[34]

Extending Barrera's model to include all Spanish-speaking groups in the United States, it was clear by the 1980s that class interests had superseded whatever cultural commonalities might have existed. Cuban Americans in Miami, as the beneficiaries of special federal programs in place since the early 1960s, were among the first to break through the barriers outlined by Barrera and they actively promoted the new Hispanic identity. The role of Miami-based Cubans as an "Hispanic" front for neo-conservative attacks on multiculturalism as "victimization studies" cannot be underestimated. As one successful Cuban American television executive put it: "I don't even say anymore that I'm Latin, I say I'm Cuban. Because Cubans don't have that woe-is-me-I'm-a-minority thing that keeps other Latinos down. We don't whine."[35]

By the time conservative agendas were repackaged by Bill Clinton and the "New Democrats," even the Mexican American community had a growing number of members convinced that racism and other structural impediments to their success were a thing of the past and that their Chicana/o cousins who continued to advocate for progressive structural change were simply "whiners" and malcontents. About the plight of Mexican and Chicana/o workers who continued to function in the role of exploited labor, the successful "Hispanic Americans" had precious little to say.

The new Hispanic class sincerely believed it was living proof that "bootstraps" and Horatio Alger ideologies worked and that the American Dream was alive and well. As early as 1978, conservative Mexican Americans had articulated what would later become a full-blown Hispanic individualism. In a curious book purporting to be a history of Chicanos, Manuel A. Machado, Jr., a professor at the University of Montana, lamented the fact that he felt obliged to report on the Chicano Movement: "While necessity dictates that we deal with Chicano noise-makers in this section, it should be noted that the Mexican-American who is merely 'doing his own thing' is not very well represented. Why? Simply because he is too busy to become excessively involved in divisive-ness and dissension, two things that would detract from the search for his individual aspiration."[36] By the mid-1980s, a prerequisite for corporate and academic success was a required distancing from collective projects, especially those that appealed to Movement ideologies and principles.[37]

In a 1985 working paper, Renato Rosaldo stated: "Chicano Studies, for the most part, shares in the broader endeavor of combating ideolog-ical, political, and economic forms of oppression confronted by their research subjects."[38] Although elsewhere in the paper Rosaldo unfairly criticizes early activist scholars such as Octavio Romano, he could not have stated more succinctly my view of the past and future mission of Chicana/o studies. But the personal and professional cost of maintain-ing an activist vision of Chicana/o studies is high, for institutions and traditional academic departments most often dismiss as "unscholarly" teachers who are politically engaged beyond campus walls and research that challenges long-standing and racialized disciplinary assumptions. The case of *Dr. Rodolfo Acuña v. the University of California*, for exam-ple, turned on the issue of age discrimination although many people in the Chicano/a community understood that what was really at stake was the University of California system's elitist opposition to a world-renowned, widely published scholar who was fully committed to improving the life chances of his community.[39]

The Reagan-Bush-Clinton-Bush years, then, were triumphalist ones, first for the Cold Warriors who celebrated the demise of the "evil empire" and immediately thereafter for the corporate ideologues, neo-colonialists, and right-wing Christian fundamentalists who assumed power in the George W. Bush administration. Even before the so-called era of globalization and the "new economy" of the late 1990s, however, academic historians and cultural theorists had begun a full-scale revision of the 1960s in order to prepare the groundwork for the final pronouncement by neoconservative thinkers and politicians that mass social movements were a thing of the past and that the end of history had arrived. Newscaster Tom Brokaw's best-seller *The Greatest Generation* (1998), bolstered by such box-office hits as Steven Spielberg's *Saving Private Ryan* (1999), waxed nostalgic over the World War II period and implicitly erased the Viet Nam war period in order to return the nation to a time of unquestioned "unity."

As one commentator pointed out: "Behind the sepia-toned nostalgia for the war years [World War II], one finds a longing to pretend the 1960s never happened, to turn back the clock to a simpler time before Vietnam poked holes in the perceived infallibility of American Empire, before the civil rights movement and feminism ruined everything, back when family, work, god and country formed the four corners of American life."[40] By the time the Supreme Court awarded George W. Bush the presidency in 2000 it was clear to most people that in the new millennium there would be no repeat of Paris, Chicago, or Mexico City 1968 or even of East Los Angeles 1970. The passage of the so-called Patriot Act and other assaults on civil liberties fashioned by Attorney General John Ashcroft and his Justice Department were the structural implements designed to ensure that mass mobilizations would become a thing of the past. The state's desire to make progressive social movements impossible in the new millennium was the practical realization of the philosophical positions promulgated by neoconservative and poststructuralist intellectuals from the 1980s onward.

In 1985, Ernesto Laclau and Chantal Mouffe published an English translation of their *Hegemony and Socialist Strategy*, a book that would have an almost immediate influence in the U.S. academy, especially in departments of literature and ethnic studies. On the opening page of his study, Laclau informs the reader that "an avalanche of historical mutations" have displaced "the evident truths" of progressive thought.

Writing at the height of Reaganism and a few short years before the collapse of the Soviet Union, Laclau argued that this new multiplicity of social struggles held the potential "for an advance towards more free, democratic and egalitarian societies."[41]

From our vantage point a decade and a half later, Laclau's cautious prediction was clearly wrong. Rather than a "long revolution" toward social and economic justice, we have witnessed the increased polarization of poverty and wealth, the imposition of economic arrangements controlled by wealthy nations and backed by U.S. military power, the reemergence of religious fundamentalisms, and the rise of state and free-lance terrorism around the world. In fact, the poststructuralist critique of liberatory projects coincided perfectly with the "end of history" thesis and the loss of hope for a more just social order. That culture critics in the United States posing as radicals bought into Laclau's vision so easily was perhaps predictable but no less scandalous given that they were aiding indirectly both the rise of the New Right and the corporate university. By the late 1990s, history had indeed stopped or so it seemed given the lack of alternative visions of the future and the widespread dismissal of Viet Nam War era social movements for being hopelessly "out of date."

And yet by the end of the first year of the new millennium, there had been massive demonstrations (and police riots that followed) against the World Trade Organization, the International Monetary Fund, and other representatives of a global economic order that judging by contemporary objective conditions had condemned the vast majority of the world's population to poverty and misery. Indeed, on September 11, 2001, the atrocities committed in New York and Washington, D.C., radically jumpstarted history, at least for those self-satisfied Western elites who thought history had come to an end. In December of 2001 in Argentina (Laclau's own country of origin), members of the middle class rioted and looted in the streets of Buenos Aires, victims of four years of recession and the kind of economic restructuring mandated by transnational agencies. In the autumn and winter of 2002–3, as the Bush administration prepared for war against Iraq and a prolonged occupation to follow, large antiwar mobilizations took place across the United States with even larger antiwar protests in Europe. Laclau and his followers, it now seemed, had completely misread their crystal ball.

One of the objectives of the chapters that follow is to map the complex ideological field that was the Chicano Movement of the Viet Nam war era. Given its heterogeneous nature, what I am calling the "Movimiento" is an analytical construct necessary to understand an otherwise disunified discursive and material field made up of diverse practices and agendas. Although the varied sectors of the Movement shared certain characteristics ("ethnic pride" being the most obvious and working-class origins among the most important), they did not constitute a traditional social movement based on a single issue. One theorist of social change has suggested that the empirical reality of most movements is always "messier" than its interpreters would like, and thus exceeds any attempt to categorize on the basis of fixed typologies.[42] This is certainly true in the case of Chicano/a insurgencies in the late 1960s and early 1970s.

Although they contribute more to a cultural than a political history of the period, the studies included here are grounded in the material conditions of Chicano/a communities and the actual practices deployed by activists within the context of multiple and often contradictory agendas. As interpretations of a limited discursive field, therefore, my research does not fully develop every contradiction at play in a social movement that was unusually fragmented by region, gender, and other issues. Rather, I focus on some of the areas that to date have been insufficiently discussed by historians and cultural theorists either because they were thought to be unrelated to what was taken to be the essential thrust of Movement practices or because they contrasted too sharply with a shared common sense (produced primarily in elite universities during the 1980s and 1990s) about the "true nationalist nature" of the Movement.

This book will disappoint those readers interested in a chronological history of the Chicano Movement. My decision to avoid a strict chronological narrative is not due to any "postmodern" approach as one historian colleague suggested to me. It is true, however, that I believe ideological and discursive formations do not march as self-contained units through time. Rather, they constitute noncontinuous systems of social knowledge, at times complementary and often contradictory, that function according to local contexts and needs.

The work of two seminal thinkers guide me here—Raymond Williams and Michel Foucault. From Williams I take the fundamental concept of ideology as "the general process of the production of meanings and ideas."[43] In this view, material conditions produce ideologies even as material effects are produced by ideologies and their discursive manifestations (ideology as both constituted and constitutive). Williams also teaches us that the complex origins of ideological attachments that motivate activists are often beyond the grasp of objective description ("structures of feeling") and therefore cannot always be located in a specific document or archive.[44] Moreover, ideological and discursive fields are intersected by residual, emergent, and dominant traditions that may interact simultaneously in unexpected and unintended ways.

It is on this point that Foucault's contribution is crucial, for rather than imitating the traditional historian's construction of a chain of historical events based on the privileged data of the archive, the cultural "archeologist" attempts to map "systems of dispersion" in which overlapping ideologies and discourses produce figures, practices, and languages functioning under a generalized rubric. In the present study, that rubric is the Chicano Movement. A system of dispersion does not imply chaos and lack of organization in terms of actual practices but does suggest that we will be hard pressed to construct the kinds of linear typologies and periodizations associated with traditional historiography. What post-Movement historians have called a "lack of coherence" in the Movement is in my opinion the natural outcome of the overdetermined centrifugal set of actions and ideas that was Chicano/a militancy in the Viet Nam war period.

Rather than seeking access to "what really happened" during the Movement period construed as a totalized and "objective" historical whole, I am interested in charting the ideological systems that generated a diverse array of organizational styles, political languages, and leaders. The reinsertion of well-known historical figures such as César Chávez or Reies López Tijerina into the rich discursive archive that was the late 1960s and early 1970s will help us to understand the interplay among various sectors of the politicized Chicano/a community. The contrasting agendas and even the apparent contradictions within single organizations on one level suggest "points of incompatibility" (following Foucault's archaeological method). However, what seem to be incompatible historical agents and agendas are in fact all consequences of the same general set of social relations and discursive matrix that I will call the Chicano critique of liberalism.

The fact that diverse Movement figures and organizations assumed different forms in their realization of that critique does not mean there was a "weakness" or "failure" in the Movement. According to Foucault's concept of discursive formations, the relationships among cultural and political objects or statements that appear to be in conflict are not gaps or flaws: "Instead of constituting a mere defect of coherence, they form

an alternative . . . [and] are characterized as link points of systematiza-
tion . . . One describes it rather as a unity of distribution that opens a
field of possible options, and enables various mutually exclusive archi-
tectures to appear side by side or in turn."[45] What is at issue, therefore,
are not historical figures as metaphors or images created by subjective
"perceptions" but rather the manner in which discursive objects participate in political projects and thereby exercise a direct impact on material conditions, in this instance as part of a richly textured social
movement created by ethnic Mexicans in the United States.

Chapter One outlines some of the basic issues that have preoccu-
pied academic commentators. I attempt to contextualize those issues so
that we may understand the contemporary political projects that have
employed the concept of the Movement in order to further specific
agendas in the present. Chapter Two develops the connection between
so-called nationalist practices and a more explicitly internationalist
position in order to argue that the Movimiento cannot be understood
as a simple manifestation of "nationalism," especially in the impoverished definition with which that term is used in current debates within
Chicano/a and American Studies. Chapter Three investigates a crucial
moment in the genealogy of 1960s Chicana/o radicalism—the Cuban
Revolution of 1959—and provides analysis of Chicano/a cultural production having to do with the Cuban experience. The ideological repertoire that underwrote events in Cuba resonated uncannily with certain
key discursive elements of the Movimiento, and coalesced in the figure
of the Argentine Ernesto Che Guevara.

In Chapter Four, I trace the construction of another key figure of the
Movement—César Estrada Chávez. By interpreting the discursive field
that produced Chavez as the "father" of all Chicano/a activism, a field created by Chávez himself but primarily by the entire repertoire of cultural
products that represented him, we begin to better understand some of
the tensions at play in the Movement. Chapter Five outlines the ways in
which some Chicano/a activists sought to make alliances across ethnic
boundaries, specifically with Black militant groups during the late 1960s.
Finally, Chapter Six looks specifically at one attempt to democratize the
system of higher education in California. Led by an impressive coalition
of Chicano/a, African American, and Asian American activists, students
at the University of California, San Diego, for a brief moment challenged
the elitist assumptions of one prestigious university.

CHAPTER ONE

—"THROUGH A SMOKING GLASS DARKLY"—

I am not sure the Chicano movement as a whole wants to go as far as I do because the Chicano movement has older people in it and a lot of them don't want to be as free.

—young Chicana ca. 1970[1]

As WITH EVERY SOCIAL MOVEMENT, the vast majority of people, most of whom stand to benefit from progressive change, feel threatened by the militancy of a few. In the case of Mexican Americans in the late 1960s this was particularly true, for the experience of being perceived as foreigners by dominant U.S. society, the result of over one hundred years of marginalization dating from the 1848 takeover of the Southwest, had driven many to adopt a low political profile in the hope of peacefully assimilating into the melting pot of middle-class comfort and cultural homogeneity.

For the most part, communities retained a limited repertoire of Mexican folkways but rarely if ever displayed their ethnic heritage in public except on specific dates officially sanctioned by the Anglo majority. Cases of "passing" were not unknown and advocacy groups in the early decades of the twentieth century stressed assimilation. The 1929 constitution of the League of United Latin American Citizens (LULAC), for example, included as one of its principal aims: "To develop within the members of our race the best, purest, and most perfect type of true and loyal citizen of the United States of America."[2] Immediately after World War II, ethnic Mexican organizations argued that Mexican Americans ought to be classified as "Caucasian" or chose to call themselves "Latin Americans." As Hector P. García, founder of the American GI Forum, told *Newsweek* magazine: "I resent the term 'brown power.' That sounds as if we were a different race. We're not. We're white. We should be Americans."[3]

The majority of ethnic Mexicans in the United States viewed brash Chicanas and Chicanos demanding the complete overhaul of the entire political system with considerable disapproval. Even after the height of the Movement period, most Mexican Americans would have concurred with the response given to an interviewer in 1975: "Question: Which are the political leaders that you like: Carmichael, King, Guevara, Castro, J. F. Kennedy, Nixon, the 'Young Lords,' the 'Black Muslims,' Chávez? Answer: I think I'd go for Martin Luther King, for John F. Kennedy and César Chávez. The other ones are militants, aren't they?"[4] The "American Dream," the example of a handful of Mexican Horatio Algers, and the bootstraps mentality all contributed to the creation of a powerful mythology of equal opportunity and the good intentions of liberal democracy in the United States. Even César Chávez, who through his organizing activities challenged the century-old exploitation of the Chicano/Mexican farm worker, believed in the fundamentally benign nature of American society. His 1968 telegram to Coretta Scott King, in which he expressed his condolences for Dr. King's death, reiterated a claim that by the spring of 1968 many young people of Mexican descent had already rejected—"despite the tragic violence which took your husband, there is much that is good about our nation."[5]

The sentiment that "there is much that is good about our nation" captured the basic approach of the so-called Mexican American or World War II generation. For Chicanas and Chicanos, however, a new sense of urgency demanded a rethinking of traditional assimilationist narratives. Either the promises of U.S. society would have to be radically renewed and fulfilled, they said, or the entire edifice of racialized economic and social relations in place since 1848 would have to be torn down.

In this chapter, I will begin the process of mapping the ideological field through which the Chicano/a critique of liberalism took shape. From the necessary act of formulating identities based on resistance and collective praxis to the elaboration of accelerated reform agendas and more radical projects rooted in the revolutionary events of the late 1960s, we will see that the Chicano Movement was much more than a narrow nationalist movement limited to ethnic concerns. Regional, national (in the sense of the U.S. nation-state), and even international affinities produced coalitions and solidarity across racial and ethnic lines in ways that historians and cultural critics have yet to elucidate. I will then move to a brief review of how traditional intellectuals and the media understood the Movement in its early years. In a concluding section, I will redefine key terms such as "nationalism" and discuss how competing interpretations of the Movement period continue to have an impact on the academic discipline of Chicano Studies and its potential role as a political force beyond university walls.

IDENTITIES IN MOTION

> What is a movement? It is when a group of people care enough
> so that they are willing to make sacrifices. It is when there are
> enough people with one idea so that their actions are together
> like a wave of water which nothing can stop.
>
> —César E. Chávez[6]

Although the etymology of the term *Chicano* continued to be debated
during the Movement period, those who adopted it as a self-identification
and those who rejected it agreed that in the new context its primary meanings had to do with a political and cultural agenda previously unknown in
Mexican communities in the United States. The attempt to link a militant
identity to the most dramatic episodes of Mexican resistance to colonization and exploitation led one twenty-year-old student activist to invent a
fantastic origin for the term that had little to do with historical fact and a
great deal to do with the spirit of the late 1960s and the status of a community about to experience a tremendous ideological transformation:

> I did a little background work in the origin of the word and the
> way I got it from a couple of grandfathers and ancestors was
> that the word Chicano is derived from an old Aztec word
> meaning rebel and . . . the Spaniards used the word Chicano to
> refer to the Aztecs who never gave up the battle. In other words,
> after the Spanish conquest, there was a group of Aztecs who
> kept fighting the Spaniards, and they were referred to as the
> rebels or the Chicanos . . . So even today, now, the word
> Chicano, could be considered as rebel.[7]

The student's proposed etymology allows us to understand the deeper
meaning of the term for activists at the height of the Movimiento. No
longer content with piecemeal reforms and the broken promises of
North American liberalism, Chicana/o youth contested the status quo
at a variety of locations across the Southwest. The terms *Chicana* and
Chicano became "a litmus test for a political frame of mind," as historian Juan Gómez Quiñones put it, and "an attempt to emphasize not
only a 'life-style' stressing *chicanismo* but also the more widely noted
features of radical personal values of the late sixties."[8]

Carlos Muñoz's assertion that the construction of a new identity was the foundational issue of the Movement is difficult to refute since the necessary precondition for most social movements is the belief that one's place in the world (or "subject position," to use a more academic language) includes the capacity for collective and individual agency.[9] As one scholar of nationalism puts it:

> The whole point of nationalism, it could be argued, is its insistence on the importance of a special cultural group identity as the bedrock of political claims and action. What is more, it frames this insistence in terms of the recovery of some identity which has always been "there" but which has been forgotten or abandoned or threatened. So although it may meet new needs, nationalism claims to do so in terms of an "old" identity. Although it is a novel political doctrine it appears to appeal to precisely that yearning for a firmly rooted identity which is at the basis of its success.[10]

The achievements of every Movement organization, from the United Farm Workers union to the Alianza Federal de Pueblos Libres to the Crusade for Justice to Movimiento Estudiantil Chicano de Aztlán (MEChA), depended on the idea that working-class Mexican Americans could demand and win progressive change. By acting upon this belief, activists broke with earlier identities premised on powerlessness and the tacit acceptance of second-class citizenship and successfully constructed individual and collective sites from which a sustained attack against racialized oppression could be launched.

The experience of writer Gloria Anzaldúa is representative in this regard: "The Chicano movement was a revelation to me because here was a part of myself I could finally accept; it was OK to be Mexican."[11] The Chicana feminist subject that arose in the late 1960s was crucial insofar as it promoted agency on a variety of related fronts—racism, economic inequality, sexism—both inside and outside the Movement. Thus the invention of Chicana/o identities, while not the exclusive goal of activists nor the root cause of political mobilization, was an objective condition necessary for the ongoing elaboration of militant Mexican American political agendas.[12] Whatever the etymology or agreed-upon meaning of "Chicano," on the cultural front the term assumed a third space between dominant U.S. and Mexican identifications. "*Ni de aquí ni de allá*" ("From neither here nor there") was less an expression of personal confusion than it was an emergent sense of a mestizo/a or mixed subjectivity that was empowering rather than debilitating.

Two decades before the postmodern dispensation in Western intellectual circles imposed ideas about de-essentialized subject positions and hybridity, Chicano/a thinkers explored the concept of an identity that was continually "in movement" between the twin poles of traditional U.S. and Mexican national selfhood. An anonymous writer for the Berkeley newspaper *La voz del pueblo*, for example, suggested that the false etymology for the term *Chicano* proposed by some Mexicans obfuscated the fact that the "essence" of the Chicano was that she/he had no essential identity:

> *Nació la palabra chicano de una corrupción, nos dicen los del otro lado. Es una corrupción de mexicano. Chico mexicano? Chicano? Es más bien un nombre sin origen fijo que surgió del pueblo a nombrar una realidad: la intensificación del mestizaje. . . . Pero el chicano es como la marea de un mar histórico, es como una ribera que nunca deja de serlo, está en movimiento perpetuo, se libra del océano mexicano, llega a la playa americana y, aunque algo de ella se quede, lo demás regresa al alto mar, pero antes de que pueda llegar, como en un retorno cíclico, se levanta otra vez. Así es que el chicano, que es inestabilidad (y lo ha sido por más de un siglo) es una anomalía . . . como es el Río Bravo y Grande, la barricada entre las dos Culturas, así el chicano es el "no man's land" humano; la frontera en carne viva.*

(According to Mexicans, the word "chicano" was born from a corruption. It is a corruption of "mexicano." Small Mexican? Chi-cano? On the contrary, the word has no fixed origin and surfaced among the people to name a reality: the intensification of *mestizaje* [mixture] . . . But the chicano is like the tide in the sea of history, like a shore that never ends, in perpetual movement, it frees itself from the Mexican ocean, arrives on the American beach, and although something remains, the rest returns to the open sea but before it can arrive, as in a cyclical return, it rises again. Thus the chicano is an instability (and has been for more than a century), an anomoly . . . like the Rio Bravo and Rio

Grande, the wall between two cultures. Thus is the chicano a human "no man's land," the border in living flesh.)[13]

The metaphors deployed here anticipate the writings of Gloria Anzaldúa and other theorists of "the border" by some fifteen years. Whereas the "American" and the "Mexican" are fixed in their identities, this author asserts, the Chicana and Chicano are contradictions produced by a middle space situated between "two Goliaths." One of the central dilemmas of the Movimiento, therefore, was to imagine political strategies capable of producing political agency out of a diffused and mobile subject position. In most cases, some form of cultural nationalism served as the social glue that held the collective subject in place. But as I will argue throughout this book, the provisional stability provided by cultural nationalist mobilizations was always cut through with a variety of regressive and revolutionary identities and even further complicated for women by a split subjectivity precariously balanced between varying degrees of patriarchal control and an emergent feminist praxis.

Another factor in the complex and often unstable repertoire of Movement identities was regional difference. For activists struggling to create more inclusive agendas, the concepts of Aztlán, la Raza, and *chicanismo* were useful for easing tensions caused by particularities based on region. But diverse local histories often led to divergent approaches despite shared objectives. As one of the key participants in the 1969 Santa Barbara conference on higher education reminded his readers: "There are wide variations between regions and maturity of organizations."[14] *Tejano* essayist Vicente Carranza took a harder stance and argued that because a deep "national" character marked each region of the Southwest, what he referred to as a "School of Thought," there was a need for an umbrella ideology that was inclusive but respectful of regional histories and identities.

For Carranza, however, a hierarchy of types of *mexicanidad* or a continuum of Mexican identities ranging from authentic to less authentic was clearly at play. Casting "California" as antithetical to Texas in terms of its Mexican-origin population's acculturation to dominant society, Carranza claimed: "The closeness of California's School of Thought to the u.s.a.'s philosophy, if not guided properly within the total effort of Aztlán within its crucial development, makes it dangerous to that development."[15] California Chicano/as, it followed, could teach other Chicano/as about "gabacho society" because they were immersed more deeply in it. Left to their own devices, however, they posed a "danger" to the elaboration of an "authentic" Chicano homeland or nation.

In a kind of double cultural nationalism—Chicano and *tejano*—Carranza's text deployed an idealist language of regional essences, e.g. "the phenomenal purity of the history of New Mexico" or "the quietness of Arizona" even as it posited an internationalist program within the structures of La Raza Unida Party. Ironically, thirty years after Carranza's musings, *tejano* cultural critic José Limón reasserted the fundamental difference between Texas and California by arguing not that California Chicano/as were dangerously "gringoized" (Carranza's position) but that they were neither "American" nor "Mexican," but rather stuck in a no-man's-land of cultural stasis.[16] Whereas Texas Mexicans had produced a kind of "marriage" of mutual convenience and desire with their Anglo neighbors, California Chicano/as were simply ignored by Anglos despite an occasional "battering" brought on by nativist hysteria. Unintentionally perhaps, Limón's account resonates with Octavio Paz's infamous claim in *El laberinto de la soledad* that Mexican American youth in World War II–era Los Angeles were devoid of any identity whatsoever and therefore to be pitied.

In his comprehensive history of the Movimiento, F. Arturo Rosales resuscitates the idea of California's essential difference by making a series of generalizations based on national stereotypes about the state ("California was a hot-house for cultivating alternative lifestyles, an atmosphere that also stimulated identity experimentation") and by arguing that California Chicano/as were more alienated from Mexican folkways than their cousins in New Mexico and "less oppressed" than their counterparts in Texas: "In California more than in Texas, for example, much of the motivation for the early student movement participants was derived largely from intellectual perceptions of oppression rather than a personal daily contact with severe discrimination and prejudice."[17] While not wishing to fall prey to a "pity competition" or "oppression Olympics," I would argue that Rosales's characterization of Chicana/o experiences of discrimination and injustice in California as mainly "intellectual" is contradicted by the historical evidence.

Although it is certainly true that the Chicano community was (is) divided by diverse regional histories and objective conditions, it is unclear what is to be gained by recycling regional stereotypes for future generations. One result in terms of possible scholarly projects is the loss of important class-, gender-, and demographic-based distinctions within specific states. As Rosales rightfully points out, the Movimiento in northern California, for example, displayed unique characteristics that were not typical of the Movement in southern California.[18] Another consequence is that the potential for any broad-based political movement in the future is diminished as Chicano/as retreat into their respective locales, viewing their eccentric *primo/as* (cousins) either with suspicion or amusement—southern California Chicano/as at those from northern California, New Mexicans at those from Arizona, everyone at Texans—not to mention our more distant *parientes* (relatives) from Central America, the Caribbean, and other points south. Meanwhile, the structural disenfranchisement and exploitation of the poorest segments of all Spanish-speaking communities in the United States remains intact.

That the Chicano Movement was not a monolithic entity was well understood by contemporary observers of the period and by those historians who over the last twenty years have refused to reduce the diversity of the Movimiento to one of its regional sectors. As one Mexican critic perceptively summarized the issue: "*El Movimiento Chicano no fue desde sus principios homogéneo, con un liderazgo, una ideología y tácticas unificadas. Es más bien una serie de grupos y submovimientos que aún cuando tienen muchos puntos en común de alguna manera difieren en su tipo de miembros, sus líderes, demandas materiales, su conceptualización de nacionalismo, tácticas, etc.*" ("From the beginning, the Chicano Movement was not homogeneous with unified leadership, ideology, and tactics. Rather, it is a series of groups and submovements that, even when they share many interests, differ in their membership, leaders, concrete demands, their conceptualization of nationalism, tactics, etc.").[19]

Given this fundamental premise about the Movement's heterogeneity, the umbrella term *Chicano Movement* becomes a heuristic category of analysis rather than an empirical datum subject to synchronic isolation.[20] In addition to conceptualizing it as an amalgamation of diverse organizations and regional agendas, however, I would suggest that it is helpful to view the Movimiento as a process that underwent substantial changes at both the organizational and individual levels as local, national, and international contexts shifted. In this regard, the Chicano experience was not unlike that of other social movements which recent sociological theory has described as a system of relations and representations. According to

Alberto Melucci: "Collective identity takes the form of a field containing a system of vectors in tension. These vectors constantly seek to establish an equilibrium between the various axes of collective action, and between identification declared by the actor and the identification given by the rest of the society (adversaries, allies, third parties)."[21] By viewing the Movimiento as a system of vectors both in motion and in tension, we can better understand the tremendous achievement realized by activists in their collective creation of a powerful albeit provisional unity as well as the pressures that ultimately contributed to the weakening of that unity.

At the center of virtually all Movement projects was an understanding that the majority of Mexican Americans had been denied access to the promised rewards of liberal democracy and the American Dream. The gap between the expectations generated by U.S. ideologies of upward mobility and the material conditions faced by the Chicana/o working class was simply too great. But by seeking to force the hand of ruling elites to make good on the system's promises, Chicano/as were caught in the ambivalent position of most social movements in the United States—how to improve the community's situation according to the terms already established by dominant groups even as some sectors of the Movimiento critiqued the very idea of "progress" as it had been defined by Anglo society.[22] Tom Nairn writes of nationalist movements: "They had to contest the concrete form in which (so to speak) progress had taken them by the throat, even as they set out to progress themselves." It is on the terrain of that ambivalence where we will see Movement organizations struggling to develop and implement their agendas.

Exhausted by the lack of progress and the inefficacy of working through official channels, astute Mexican American activists of the World War II generation by late 1966 had begun to listen more carefully to Chicana/o militants. When grassroots organizers staged the La Raza Unida conference in October 1967 in El Paso as a protest against the Lyndon Johnson-sponsored Cabinet Committee Hearings on Mexican American Affairs being held in the same city, well-respected voices warned that Chicano demands, if not attended to, could lead to social unrest. Dr. Ernesto Galarza, whose commitment to furthering the cause of equal justice for Mexican Americans was beyond reproach, denounced the hearings and warned: "If the young people are cut off and not listened to, and if the [Johnson] administration keeps trying to suppress the poor, I can predict how they will react."[23]

Long-time Mining, Mill and Smelter Workers Union official Maclovio Barraza was even more direct: "Along with the other disadvantaged people, the Mexican American is growing more and more restless. He's patient but it's running out. He may soon be forced to seek dramatic alternatives to his patience—alternatives that seem to bring more generous responses from government than obedient restraint in face of adversity and injustice."[24] According to Barraza, several cities in the Southwest "could explode into violent riots far more intense than those of Watts, Detroit, or other cities." Just a few months later, on January 28, 1968, Dr. Ralph Guzmán appeared at the American GI Forum meeting in Denver to present a paper entitled "Mexican Americans in the urban area: Will they riot?" Guzmán, a political scientist in the Politics and Community Studies program at the University of California, Santa Cruz, was a longtime activist and educator who had spoken out against police brutality in Los Angeles since the 1950s. Members of Crusade for Justice interrupted the panel and demanded that Corky Gonzales be allowed to address the meeting. Gonzales not only offered an affirmative answer to Guzmán's question but also predicted "guerrilla warfare in the Southwest."[25]

In a variety of ways, then, the diverse sectors of the Chicano Movement pushed beyond a civil-rights agenda in order to challenge the most basic structures of U.S society. As we shall see in the chapters that follow, the tension between radical and reformist agendas produced fractures within the Movement and at times within a single organization. Perhaps the most striking contradiction was the one between the doctrine of nonviolence espoused by César Chávez and the call made for armed insurrection by radical Chicano splinter groups (I address this contradiction in Chapter Four). At one extreme of the ideological spectrum, the revolutionary example of anticolonial struggles served as a model to be imitated even if only at the level of rhetoric. As Adolfo Cuéllar put it: "Whereas the moderates seek to bring major change in American society through nonviolent means, the more militant speak of the need for 'revolutionary activity' though they often leave the details and direction of this revolution unspecified. While they admire the life style and aspirations of revolutionary leaders like Ché Guevara, they have thus far made no systematic theoretical connection between the Chicano movement and the general literature on revolution."[26] Cuéllar's assessment was certainly correct. What "revolution" signified in the actual praxis of the vast majority of Movement groups was a growing impatience with traditional models of social change. This impatience, however, would give rise to fringe organizations that attempted to interpret "revolution" literally.

In early 1971, for example, the Chicano Liberation Front (CLF) claimed responsibility for multiple bombings of banks, schools, and post offices in the Los Angeles area, and boldly stated: "We advocate urban guerrilla warfare. For each Chicano attacked we will cause thousands of dollars of property damage. We believe that every Chicano home should be armed with a shotgun, M-1 carbine, and .357 magnum."[27] Although the CLF proposed to attack property and not people, its stated objective was to drive those whom its members considered to be outsiders, e.g. police, politicians, and Anglo businessmen, out of the neighborhoods: "We hope that the Chicano Barrio will be awakened to the fact that the man with all the machines and atomic bombs can be beaten if you have La Raza behind you." According to FBI documents, the CLF "was composed primarily of hard core Mexican American militants" and operated as "a guerrilla force."[28] The CLF issued communiqués to San Francisco Bay Area newspapers as late as 1974 and was the subject of a dispute between the FBI and Los Angeles police, the latter taking the position that the CLF was not a major organization but a loose band of "terrorists." Law-enforcement investigations into the CLF were continued until June of 1976.

In northern California, a group called the Chicano Revolutionary Party advocated armed revolution even as its literature reproduced the language of the U.S. Declaration of Independence. Their official newspaper, *La Chispa*, was decorated generously with images of assault weapons and Che Guevara, yet its editorials called for full employment and housing reform. The organization's more radical demands, however, called for "a United Nations-supervised plebiscite to be held throughout the Chicano colony in which only Chicano colonized people will be allowed to participate for the purpose of determining the will of Chicano people as to their national destiny."[29] Central to the thinking of this small minority that proposed armed insurrection were the revolutionary models of Cuba and Viet Nam.[30] It cannot be stated strongly enough, however, that the vast majority of Movement activists rejected violence as a viable strategy as they struggled simultaneously to address local issues and construct a coherent agenda for a broader trans-regional movement.

Who are the Chicanos and what do they want?

"En mil novecientos sesenta y ocho
empezaron nuestras avanzadas
pueblo maldecido y bendecido por
sus dioses. Que vivan los mejicanos."

("In 1968, our successes began.
A people both cursed and blessed by
Their gods. Long live Mexicans!")
—Juan Gómez Quiñones, "Ballad of Billy Rivera"

In early 1970, Daniel Patrick Moynihan submitted a 1,650-word memorandum to President Richard Nixon. Moynihan, well known for his controversial 1965 analysis of the "Black family," recommended to the president: "The time may have come when the issue of race could benefit from a period of 'benign neglect.' The subject has been too much talked about."[31] Focusing primarily on the African American community, the memorandum argued, "The American Negro is making extraordinary progress," even as it described the "social alienation among the black lower classes [and] a virulent form of anti-white feeling among portions of the large and prosperous black middle class." Buried in the text of the memorandum as a kind of afterthought, Moynihan wrote: "Greater attention to Indians, Mexican Americans, and Puerto Ricans would be useful."

For most politicians and the mainstream media outside of the Southwest, the Chicano Movement was a distant storm cloud with disturbing similarities to the Black Power movement. The image of rebellious Mexicans did not fit well with Madison Avenue's standard fare of a sleepy brown man under a cactus or the English-deficient immigrant José Jimenez as portrayed on television by comedian Bill Dana. Although César Chávez and the United Farm Workers had received limited national coverage, for the most part the major players in the Chicano Movement were unknown in the late 1960s. By the summer of 1970, however, even the eastern press had begun to take notice of Chicano activities. In a *Wall Street Journal* article entitled "The Angry Chicanos," staff reporter Richard Shaffer presented the Movimiento as a motley conglomeration of violent organizations bent on the "elimination" of the gringo. Displaying a flair for yellow journalism, Shaffer began his report with a description of a "clandestine" San Antonio group called the Mexican American Nationalist Organization (MANO) whose members believe "all whites are racist enemies who should be driven out of the Southwest by force if necessary."[32]

According to MANO spokesman Beto Martinez (who, Shaffer was quick to point out, "served time in Texas prisons for possession of marijuana and for sodomy"), MANO members were primarily ex-cons and Viet Nam veterans preparing for guerrilla warfare. Shaffer quoted sources in the law-enforcement community who had been monitoring Chicano political groups: "One Federal official responsible for gauging the mood of minority groups puts it this way: 'There's an awful lot of ferment among the Mexican Americans, a rising level of militancy among the young, with more demonstrations and more challenging of authority— all the preliminary stages of outright violence.'"[33] Shaffer closed his piece with José Angel Gutiérrez's infamous line "It's too late for the gringo."

Although probably not symptomatic of the kind of generalized "white fear" that surfaced in the late 1990s due to rapidly changing demographics, Shaffer's article did represent well the increasing attention being paid to the Movimiento by federal and local agencies. Outstanding studies by Ernesto Vigil and Edward Escobar have demonstrated the extent to which Chicano/a organizations were the target of widespread infiltration and provocation by the FBI, ATF, and other federal and local law-enforcement entities.[34] Although scholars have yet to gain unlimited access to classified documents relating to Chicano/a activities as they have with COINTELPRO papers on other groups, particularly "New Left" and "Black Nationalist" groups, the existence of a special "Border Coverage" counterintelligence program from 1960 to 1971 is well documented.[35] Within the parameters of this program, virtually all the Chicano/a organizations discussed in the following essays, ranging from early Chicano/a supporters of the Cuban Revolution to Reies Tijerina's Alianza to the United Farm Workers union to Raza student groups on college campuses, were at one time or another the subject of U.S. government covert operations. Outside of the Southwest, federal undercover programs moved against other Latino militants with a special unit aimed at "Groups seeking independence for Puerto Rico" and designed to disrupt the Young Lords and other Puerto Rican political organizations.

Whereas police scrutiny of the Movement was unrelenting from its earliest years, most major newspapers ignored developments in the

Southwest until the August 29, 1970, antiwar demonstration in Los Angeles that resulted in the death of three people including *L.A. Times* reporter Ruben Salazar. In his attempt to explain Chicano activism to puzzled East Coast intellectuals, historian of Mexico John Womack, Jr., offered an account that was less provocative than the one written by Richard Shaffer in the *Wall Street Journal* two years earlier. Womack's article begins with a short history of Mexicans in the United States and an analysis of contemporary developments. After describing the activities of the United Farm Workers, the New Mexican land-grant movement, the high school blowouts, and the demonstration of August 29, he drew the following conclusion: "So altogether the Chicano movement is only another ethnic movement, at its bitterest a threat not to integrate which cannot stop the integration but which can wrest some reparations for the loss of old certainties. Eventually it will win for its surviving professional and amateur chiefs [*sic*] their quota of revenge and power in America, and for its winter and summer members a little better deal than they would otherwise have had for the stakes in their class."[36]

Womack's unsympathetic take on the Movement coincided with a generally hostile tone exacerbated by his repeated use throughout the essay of the rather odd opposition "regular Americans/Mexican Americans." That militant Chicano/as had developed a political project that in many of its key aspects transcended Womack's facile characterization ("only another ethnic movement") was beyond the imaginative capacity of mainstream observers. After all, even after the momentous events of August 29, 1970, "the Mexicans" were thought to be the most pliable and subservient minority.

A more astute observer of Chicano/a activism was Mexican poet Octavio Paz. In a 1971 interview, Paz argued that while the Chicano Movement in the U.S. context might be seen as "only another ethnic movement" (Womack's characterization), in a broader Latin American context it displayed many of the features common to ongoing political changes in the hemisphere:

> *Como todas las cosas, el movimiento Chicano tiene dos aspectos. Por una parte, es un movimiento dentro de la sociedad norteamericana para que los Chicanos tengan el puesto que merecen. En ese sentido es un movimiento absolutamente semejante, con una dinámica parecida al movimiento de los negros y de otras*

minorías. Por otra parte, a diferencia de los negros, los Chicanos poseen una cultura propia, una historia propia. Y eso los liga, evidentemente, a México y la América Latina.

(As in all things, the Chicano Movement has two sides. On the one hand, it is a movement within U.S. society seeking to gain for Chicanos the status they deserve. In this sense, it is absolutely the same as and shares a similar dynamic with the movements of Blacks and other minorities. On the other hand, unlike the Blacks, Chicanos have their own culture and their own history. That is what clearly links them to Mexico and Latin America.)[37]

Given his wide experience with Mexican American culture, Paz was in a position to compare Chicano/a youth in the 1960s with earlier moments such as the 1940s, a period about which Paz had written in his *Laberinto de la Soledad* and his controversial analysis of the *pachuco*. Without modifying his view that pachuco subculture was in a practical sense pre-political, Paz viewed the Chicano as the pachuco's descendant who had become a fully developed collective subject: *"La cosa más importante es que de pronto las comunidades Chicanas empiecen a tener conciencia de sí mismas. No una conciencia pasiva, sino una conciencia activa. Es decir, el pachuco sufría su condición y creaba un mundo imaginario y de violencia en transgresión, nihilista. El Chicano, no. El Chicano asume su condición, reflexiona sobre ella y pretende encontrar una vía"* ("The most important thing is that Chicano communities acquire self-consciousness. Not a passive but an active consciousness. The pachuco tolerated his condition and created an imaginary world of violent transgression and nihilism. Not the Chicano. The Chicano recognizes his condition, analyzes it, and seeks a way out").[38] According to Paz, the Chicano/a was an upgraded and politicized version of the pachuco, a new subject willing to insist on her/his self-determination and prepared to exercise his/her historical agency.

Other Mexican observers of the Movement seconded Paz's assertion that Chicano/as were involved in a project that was more than the creation of a simple ethnic nationalism. Jorge Bustamante, for example, argued that the "nationalist moment" was merely a preliminary step in the Chicano/a community's engagement with injustice:

*Otro error muy difundido en México es el de intepretar en térmi-
nos formalistas el nacionalismo invocado en importantes sectores
del movimiento chicano. El sentido que los chicanos suscriptores
del Plan Espiritual de Aztlán le dieron al nacionalismo tiene una
finalidad práctica. El nacionalismo es definido como un sen-
timiento de orgullo de una herencia cultural que debe difundirse
como "la llave de la organización." Así se declara expresamente,
dando a entender que el nacionalismo será utilizado como medio
de lucha en contra de una situación de opresión. Esta táctica no
es otra cosa que la reafirmación de los valores culturales propios
como la mejor preparación para la lucha en contra de un sistema
cuya perpetuación ha estado cimentada en el rechazo de toda
tradición o valores de la cultura de origen. Este rechazo es la
condición necesaria para la asimilación en una sociedad cuya
estructura fue definida por un grupo anglo sajón para todos los
grupos étnicos que inmigraron a los Estados Unidos.*[39]

(Another mistake that is widespread in Mexico is to interpret in
formal terms the nationalism invoked by important sectors of
the Chicano Movement. The definition of nationalism according to the Chicanos who drafted the Plan Espiritual de Aztlán
has a practical objective. Nationalism is understood to be a
feeling of pride in a cultural heritage that will serve as "a key to
organizing." This is said explicitly—that nationalism will be
used as a weapon against a state of oppression. This tactic is
nothing more than the reaffirmation of one's own cultural values as the best preparation for the struggle against a system
whose reproduction is premised on the rejection of one's original traditions and cultural values. This rejection is the necessary precondition for assimilation into a society whose
structure was established by Anglo Saxons for all ethnic groups
that immigrated to the United States.)

As we shall see in Chapter Two, both Paz and Bustamante understood
that the Chicano Movement could reveal important lessons to
Mexican society by serving as a prism through which Mexico might
view obliquely its own future vis-à-vis the economic and cultural
hegemony of the United States.

CLARIFYING KEYWORDS FOR THE FUTURE

Telling them that we
Must kill the revolutionary soul because it was only
    a magical thing
A momentary thing, a thing outside of time, a sixties thing,
    a sacred thing
A brown beret thing, a grassroot thing, a loud thing,
    a spontaneous thing
A Viet Nam thing, a white radical thing, an Aztlán thing,
    a Cholo thing
A nationalist thing, a for Pochos only thing, a college thing,
    an August 29th 1970
Chicano Moratorium thing, an outdated thing,
    a primitive thing.

—Juan Felipe Herrera,
"Are you doing that New Amerikan Thing?"

A full-generation after the end of the American war in Southeast Asia, the Movimiento has become the subject of historical studies and memoirs written by a wide range of scholars and former activists. Personal accounts by key Movement players such as José Angel Gutiérrez, Ernesto Vigil, and Reies López Tijerina join the classic research of Rodolfo Acuña, Carlos Muñoz, Jr., Mario García, Ignacio García, Armando Navarro, and others. Scholars such as Alma García, Dionne Espinoza, and Maylei Blackwell have undertaken the important work of recuperating and interpreting Chicana feminist writings. In the early years of the twenty-first century, young historians and cultural critics are narrating accounts from their perspective as members of a generation too young to have participated in the dramatic events of the late 1960s and early 1970s.

At the risk of generalizing too quickly, I would argue that the majority of these accounts share a number of characteristics. In contemporary Chicana/o intellectual circles, especially in elite institutions, there exists an accepted "common sense" about the Movimiento that restricts its scope to a limited number of practices typical of 1960s political organizations. Although these practices were important and merit our scrutiny today, contemporary commentators too often use issues such as sexism and homophobia, issues that emerged as points of debate during the Viet Nam war period and with which progressive activists struggled, to either discredit or caricature the Movement. For all intents and purposes, "common sense" about the Movement, especially in elite academic circles, tells us that the Movimiento="nationalism" and "nationalism"= sexism and homophobia.

There can be no doubt that sexism and homophobia existed in all social movements of the late 1960s. What I think we must challenge is not that undeniable fact but rather the facile application of the uninterrogated term *nationalism* to a broad range of ideological practices. If the Chicano Movement was "nationalist" at its essential core, what can we make of Raza activists who participated in the Communist Labor Party, the Socialist Workers Party, and other organizations in which the analytical focus was not the "nation" or "race" but rather the issues of class struggle, imperialism, and international solidarity? Courageous Chicana feminists mounted a powerful critique of patriarchal oppression but nevertheless gained a sense of empowerment through their association with Movement organizations. Are we obliged to exclude the United Farm Workers as part of the Movimiento because it does not fit a narrow nationalist paradigm? What are we to make of Reies López Tijerina who promoted a more properly *territorial* nationalism that deployed an Indo-Hispano identity and had as its principal objective the issue of land recuperation? To what extent are some historians and cultural critics authorizing the very nationalist ethos they condemn when they limit the contours of the Movement to a single ideological pole?

As historian John Breuilly reminds us: "The term 'nationalism' is used too widely and covers many and different kinds of things. It is used to refer to ideas, sentiments and politics, yet these are distinct kinds of things which do not stand in any necessary relationship to one another."[40] Given this conceptual confusion, it is not surprising that some scholars can reduce a complex social movement like the Chicano/a Movement to its more destructive elements while its positive contributions can be bracketed or erased.

My point is that the Procrustean bed of a poorly defined "nationalism" will necessarily distort our understanding of the heterogeneous ideological field that was the Chicano Movement. It is my belief that any discussion of the Movimiento during the Viet Nam war period must cast a wide net to include a variety of organizations that on the surface might seem incompatible. At the same time, we must be attentive to the contradictory ideologies within single organizations and the ways in which positions might shift according to local conditions, unintended consequences, and external pressures. Certainly sexist practices were present throughout all organizations, but rather than dismissing the entire Movement because of its sexism would it not be more productive both for the sake of the historical record and so as to avoid reproducing oppressive practices in our contemporary political work to seek to understand the ways in which women activists negotiated these obstacles? As Tom Nairn outlines the task for students of nationalism in all of its permutations: "It must be to see the phenomenon as a whole, in a way that rises above these 'positive' and 'negative' sides. Only in this fashion can we hope to escape from a predominantly moralizing perspective upon it, and rise . . . I will not say to a 'scientific' one . . . but at least to a better, more detached historical view of it. In order to do this, it is necessary to locate the phenomenon in a larger explanatory framework, one that will make sense of the contradictions."[41]

One of the most critical contradictions in the Chicano Movement arises at the intersection of cultural nationalism and feminism. It is here that the work of Dionne Espinoza is especially enlightening. By subtly rethinking accepted knowledge about so-called Chicano nationalism, especially the way it was characterized in an influential essay by Angie Chabram and Rosalinda Fregoso, Espinoza shows how the myth of a "transcendent Chicano subject" was in reality a subject produced by "the tensions within nationalist discourse, the multiple voices and practices that superseded 'ideal' notions of Chicano subjectivity with 'real' experiences of that subjectivity emerging in social struggle."[42]

Reading Movement practices through the work of British cultural critic Stuart Hall, Chabram and Fregoso had singled out "the Chicano student movement" as the origin of a "static, fixed, and one-dimensional formulation" of Chicano identity. Claiming that "Chicano nationalism" had thrust a heterogeneous community into an ontological space where history no longer existed, i.e. Aztlán, they accused the entire "Chicano movement" of erasing "the complexity of Chicano cultural identity," especially "working-class and women's cultural forms and practices."[43]

There is much to argue with in Chabram and Fregoso's reduction of a complex social movement to its student and intellectual sectors. Their charge that the Movement elided working-class issues is difficult to sustain, and while it is certainly true that "women's cultural forms and practices" did not receive the attention they deserved in masculinist organizations, how can one account for the many formidable Chicana feminist writers and artists who began their work in the late 1960s?

Rather than merely accepting Chabram and Fregoso's assertions about the consequences of Movement gender practices, Espinoza understands Chicana/o agency during the period to be "a dense and contextually resonant social practice" which, although operative within a common "nationalist" discursive field, is in fact an ever-changing series of material conditions and resultant forms of praxis.[44] Even for those groups who otherwise were exploited and relegated to subordinate positions within Movement organizations (such as the women Brown Berets studied by Espinoza), in some settings they were able to construct a political agency they had not previously enjoyed. I would add to Espinoza's argument the fact that the "nationalist frame" within which Chicana/o political practices operated was itself a varied and ever changing network of diverse ideological positions.

Throughout this book I will use the terms *narrow nationalism* and *sectarian nationalism* to signify activist agendas that rejected the use of coalitions, adopted a strict "*Mi Raza primero*" ("My People first") posture, displayed little interest in international affairs, and rejected all forms of socialist thinking as "white man's" philosophy. These forms of regressive or "reactionary nationalism" (Nairn) took the various features of a constructed "mexicanidad" (e.g., language, skin color, etc.) as litmus tests for group inclusion, enforced rigid notions of the family and patriarchal control, and at times could move dangerously close to a separatist program.

I will argue, however, that "separatist" organizations were extremely rare. While some organizations displayed the characteristics outlined above, it was not unusual for the same organizations to manifest at the same time contradictory positions rooted in broader and more inclusive traditions. Less a linear progression from "nationalism" to "socialism," the simultaneous enactment of seemingly opposed ideologies marked Movement practices throughout the period, suggesting that single organizations contained (often under conditions of extreme duress for individual members) not homogeneous but diverse ideological agendas.[45] Put another way, "nationalism" was never a stage in a developmental process but rather a constant and dialectical ingredient within the ideological field available to Movement actors.

By *cultural nationalism* I mean the strategic deployment of key features of Mexican and Mexican American history and culture in order to fashion individual and collective subjects capable of asserting agency and demanding self-determination. Otherwise known as "Brown Pride" or "Brown Power," cultural nationalism was at work to varying degrees within all sectors of the Movement. An ideological frame that could be filled in with additional content drawn from a wide array of sources, cultural nationalism was not determined by a fixed set of political objectives. This was stated succinctly toward the end of the Chicano/a insurgency at the third meeting of the National Association of Chicano Social Science in 1975: "To begin with, Chicano nationalism is not an aggressive or expansive force but has as its rationale the promotion of social cohesion and unity among members of the community; it is not an all exclusive end-in-itself. Thus, other values and interests, such as regional, religious, family, class, are not terminated but continue to function within a nationalist framework."[46] The author here uses the generic "nationalism" to signify what I will take to be cultural nationalism specifically. By asserting that "Chicano nationalism is not an aggressive or expansive force," he alerts us to the distance between negative forms of "political nationalism" and a more properly model of self-determination premised on both political and cultural factors.[47]

In 1978, historian Richard García argued for a specific "era of nationalism" in the Movement lasting from 1965 to 1972, an era superseded according to García by an "era of ideology" (1972–1977) premised on political rather than identity issues. While I agree that by the early 1970s, all forms of Chicano/a activism were inconceivable without the foundation of ethnic pride and empowerment, I argue for overlapping and dialectical structures of experience or "impulses" rather than a linear progression from one ideological formation to the other.[48] As I have already suggested, there was no simple passage in the Movement period from "identity" to "political" agendas since "identity" was always already a necessary precondition for political mobilization. Moreover, the construction of "identity" would be meaningless if not impossible outside of a "political" context. At the same time, the process by which ethnic Mexican and other Latino/a youth became "chicanoized" is an always ongoing process. More important for my argument is the distinction between "cultural nationalism" and the narrow sectarian forms of nationalism I described above. It is my contention that the former is not necessarily condemned to becoming the latter.

Finally, what I call the *internationalist* positions within the Movimiento ranged from simple acts of solidarity embedded in a liberal framework to fully developed critiques of capital's role in U.S. society with an emphasis on the imperial past and present of the United States. Often referred to as "revolutionary nationalism" or "Third Worldism" during the period, this stance actively sought to articulate coalitions with other communities both domestically and abroad. In its anti-imperialist variants, Chicano/a internationalism mounted an antiwar agenda that drew upon earlier traditions and influences (e.g. labor struggles from the 1930s to the 1950s, the Cuban Revolution of 1959, and so on) and extended logically into the domain of labor and women's rights.[49] An uncanny mixture of cultural nationalism and diverse strains of Marxist thought, the language of Chicano/a internationalism could often surface in the rhetoric and actions of individuals and organizations that post-Movement scholars have too often oversimplified as "nationalist."

"Stuck in the Sixties" or Learning from our Elders?

> The most important reason for studying the history of past struggles is that it can help to clarify what strategy we should pursue in the present.
>
> —Alex Callinicos[50]

The widely disseminated cliché about the "bad nationalism" of the Movement is not simply the product of the disagreement between 1960s activists and scholars from the post-Viet Nam war generation. Nevertheless, the issue of "generational conflict" is experienced as real and adversely affects contemporary scholarly and political projects. Alicia Gaspar de Alba, to take one example, begins her important study of Chicano art with the following description of what she perceives to be the tensions that threaten to weaken Chicano/a Studies from within:

> I belong to that generation of Chicano/a scholars who grew up during the Chicano Civil Rights Movement, too young to phys-ically participate in the marches, strikes, boycotts, sit-ins, and blow-outs that characterized el Movimiento during the quak-ing sixties, but old enough to reap the benefits of affirmative action, bilingual education, and "minority" fellowships. I am

also entering the academy at a time when the survival of Chicana/o Studies is threatened as much by the external bureaucratic backlash against anything "multicultural" as by the internecine hostilities of a discipline unwilling to change its ideological and methodological guard.[51]

The sense of "belatedness" is powerful here ("too young to participate") as is what I take to be a non-ironic attraction to a time of her community's revolt ("the quaking sixties"). For a post-1960s generation, the period exercises a kind of parental function insofar as it must be thanked for its efforts yet rejected as a standard against which subsequent generations will necessarily fall short. In effect, "the Movement" is distorted into an obstacle that is perceived as restricting the identities and blocking the agency of those who are younger.

Gaspar de Alba astutely recognizes, however, that her predicament transcends a simple anxiety produced by generational conflict. The historical moment that gave birth to the Movement and Chicano Studies was replaced, she reminds us, with the neoconservative backlash of the Reagan-Bush years and attempts in the university context to strip Chicano/a Studies of its transformative potential even as "minority fellowships" became a cottage industry and elite Chicano and Ethnic Studies programs accelerated the hyperprofessionalization of young scholars. It is this structural and ideological crisis that should concern all of us, I believe, for the complexity that surrounds the contemporary crisis—corporatization of public colleges, privatization and militarization of public schools, explosion of the prison-industrial complex, the planning of an endless "war on terror," the rollback of intellectual freedom after September 11, 2001—becomes more difficult to decipher with each passing year.

In addition to the issue of institutional retrenchment, the passage from Gaspar de Alba points to yet another problem—the refusal of Chicana/o Studies as a discipline to "change its ideological and methodological guard." The reference here is to the unfortunate but perhaps necessary public debate that has taken place between Movement activist/scholars and younger academics trained from the 1980s to the present. Although on the one hand this debate appears to be the kind of generational conflict to which Gaspar de Alba refers, it has been understood by many to be a gendered hostility in which Chicano men in academia (older and tenured) openly criticize Chicana women in academia (younger and untenured) for being insufficiently engaged in political projects or, even worse, insufficiently "authentic" in their ethnic identities. It is a short leap from these oppositions to unproductive manifestations of sexism, homophobia, and ideological litmus tests. More important, the potential for inclusive coalition work in Chicano/Latino communities and for collective scholarship (now a virtually impossible fantasy perhaps given the hypercompetitiveness of academic programs and careers) is lost.

To a great extent, the Movimiento period has become a flashpoint around which one can discern the multiple political positions available to scholars of Mexican descent at the beginning of the twenty-first century. Ongoing debates have less to do with generational differences than they do with shifting understandings of the relationship between scholarship, teaching, and politics. Some of the studies most critical of the Movement and most dismissive of intellectuals associated with the Movement have been produced by historians of the 1960s generation who, for one reason or another, felt excluded by or hostile to Sixties-style Chicano/a activism. Manuel G. Gonzales is interesting in this regard because in the introduction to his study he gestures toward Movement identities (e.g., a self-identified "*indio*" with Marxist training) but nonetheless is critical of the tradition of the activist-scholar in Chicana/o Studies: "Unfortunately, this ideological orientation has worked against the complete acceptance of Chicano historians and other Chicano scholars by their colleagues in the academy."[52]

This is a startling admission given that at its inception the goal of Chicano/a Studies was hardly to please academic colleagues (most of whom fought tooth and nail to keep Chicano/a Studies out of the curriculum) but rather to initiate the complete transformation of the university so that it might serve in a meaningful way the wider Chicano/Mexicano community. But the rush toward the center of the ideological spectrum (i.e. "objectivity and moderation") was symptomatic of political life in the United States at the end of the twentieth century. The complete reorientation of the Democratic Party by Bill Clinton and his Democratic Leadership Council for all intents and purposes erased progressive and left-leaning agendas from the landscape and did so with great success. It should not surprise us, therefore, that many Mexican American scholars would want to rush to the ideological middle without offending those in a position to underwrite their successful careers.

Despite my assertion that the political divide that runs through Chicano/a Studies is not merely a generational divide, in the discipline of Chicana/o history developments during the late 1990s did in fact produce an unfortunate schism between older and younger scholars. This debate was played out in academic journals and formed the conceptual frame for a collection of essays entitled *Voices of a New Chicana/o History* published in 2000. The result of a conference held at Michigan State University in 1996, at which historians were asked to respond to Ignacio M. García's provocative essay "Juncture in the Road: Chicano Studies Since "El Plan de Santa Bárbara," the volume seeks to represent a so-called paradigm shift in Chicana/o historiography in which a "founding stage" comprised of activist/scholars passes into a "developmental stage" made up of scholars with no personal memory of the Viet Nam war period.[53]

In my opinion, Ignacio García's "Juncture" essay was conceived as a good-faith attempt to explain the institutional and theoretical changes of the last thirty years. In order to move Chicana/o studies into the future, García hoped to take what was useful from the Movement agenda in order to refunction it for the present. Due to a series of tactical miscalculations, however, the essay can be read as a hostile attack on certain sectors of the Chicana/o community, an ad hominem criticism of younger scholars' personal histories, and even a backward-looking call to return to the 1960s. The invocation of the 1969 Plan de Santa Bárbara structures the argument and the unfortunate phrase "a return to the plan" is repeated throughout. I say "unfortunate" only because the repetition of the phrase leaves the reader with the strong impression that García is trapped in the past despite repeated indications in the essay to the contrary. At one point, for example, García writes: "The future of Chicano Studies may well rest on the ability of proponents to regain the perspective of the Plan de Santa Bárbara, *or in the development of a new perspective that will facilitate the enhancement of Chicano Studies, while not destroying its heart*" (my emphasis).[54]

It is precisely this "new perspective" that must be conceptualized, for when he is not invoking the "Plan" García admits that any simple return to a document written for a different time and place could not be productive. García writes: "Consequently, it may be unrealistic to assume that Chicano scholars can turn back the clock and put into practice the passionate tenets of the plan. Also, the community has changed significantly in the last twenty-five years."[55] The acknowledgment that the political landscape has been transformed dramatically is crucial here. The fact that Chicano/a Studies finds itself in a radically different historical context ought not be used, however, to claim that the new conjuncture is not as "political" or "radical" as the Viet Nam war period and that therefore scholars ought to strive for "objectivity." I will return to this point below. Rather, scholars would be well served by clarifying keywords and then reentering the Movement-era archive in search of lessons that might be refashioned for the present moment, a moment no less ripe for and in need of progressive interventions than were the late 1960s and 1970s.

Once we accept that neither the "Plan de Santa Bárbara" or the "Plan espiritual de Aztlán" will serve us as a blueprint for the present, we can begin to glean important insights from the documents and adjust them for current conditions. I disagree with Rudy Acuña when he writes that the authors of the "Plan de Santa Bárbara" were "naive" because they failed to understand the coopting power of the university. In my opinion, the inability to foresee the future—in this instance, the rollback of affirmative action, the privatization of public universities, the silent punishment or purging of militant faculty and staff—is not a question of being naive but rather a result of the fact that framers of the "Plan" were products of their particular moment. In the revolutionary atmosphere of 1969, the framers of the Plan could be relatively confident that the radical restructuring of the liberal university was underway and that its complete transformation was a real possibility. As we shall see in Chapter 6, Chicana/o activists throughout the Southwest made serious attempts to accomplish the task of democratizing elitist institutions of higher education. Thirty years later, on the other hand, in a time of neoliberal hegemony and the rise of the corporate academy, few of us if any would be naive enough to even imagine such a transformation despite the persistence of most of the issues outlined in the "Plan."[56]

The acrimony produced by the García article led to a series of responses that attempted to answer in kind. Historian Lorena Oropeza accused García of trafficking in "nostalgia," while María E. Montoya charged him with wallowing in the past and wanting to fight "the old battles of the 1960s and 1970s." Montoya countered García's rhetorical choice ("a return to the plan") with its extreme opposite: "We may have to abandon documents like the Plan de Santa Bárbara."[57] Neither side was willing to entertain the possibility that there might be some middle ground between the act of return and the act of abandonment, a space where one might take the lessons of the Movimiento and rework them for a present moment that was no less hostile to most working-class people than the Viet Nam war era had been. With the terms of the debate misconceived from the opening salvo, the potential for a productive dialogue was lost (in an appendix I will return to the role played by the Movement period in contemporary Chicano Studies).

I conclude this chapter with a poem that captures my belief that the lessons of the Chicano/a Movement can be neither passé nor "defunct" as long as the vast majority of Spanish-speaking peoples in the United States find themselves at the bottom of the economic ladder in a society premised upon continued privileges for the already privileged few. The son of migrant farm workers who migrated from Mexico in 1982, at the height of Reaganism's massive redistribution of wealth upward, Francisco Santana (today a high school principal) reminds us that the race to escape the triple-headed monster of assimilation, racism, and apathy is far from over:

> La carrera continúa
> sí señores y señoras
> la carrera continúa.
> Unos corren con libros de blinders
> otros en el caballo I-Made-It
> y también va el caballo Racism,
> como saben
> casi siempre va adelante;
> pero ahora
> va el Movimiento Chicano.
> Se le empareja Apatía,
> sí señores
> se le empareja.
> Por atrás se le acerca Assimilation.
> El carnalito del Chicano
> se tambalea en Indecision.
> Sí señoras y señores
> la carrera continúa.[58]

(The race continues. Yes, ladies and gentlemen. The race continues. Some run with books as blinders; others on the horse
named "I made it," and the horse named "Racism" runs too; as
you know he is almost always in the lead; but now "Chicano
Movement" catches up to "Apathy." Yes, ladies and gentlemen.
He catches up. From behind "Assimilation" is approaching. The
young Chicano brother tries to keep his balance on
"Indecision." Yes, ladies and gentlemen. The race continues.)

In the following chapter, I will continue the process of charting
Chicano/a forays beyond the objective conditions presented by U.S.
social relations. The race against traditional assimilation and the struggle against racialized economic structures led some Movement activists
to develop global analyses of the community's situation and to understand their relationship to dramatic events taking place far from the
more familiar realities of the Southwest.

CHAPTER TWO

"REVOLUTIONARIES HAVE NO RACE"

The conscience of an awakened activist cannot be satisfied with
a focus on local problems, if only because he sees that local
problems are all interconnected with world problems.

—Dr. Martin Luther King, Jr.

IN 1939, A FULL GENERATION before the rise of the Chicano Movement,
Américo Paredes addressed a poem to the national hero of Nicaragua.
In its final three stanzas, the poem "A César Augusto Sandino" makes
explicit the connection between the plight of Mexican Americans and
anti-imperialist struggles in Latin America:

> *Empuñando el acero ya desnudo*
> *el mañoso sajón volvióse fiera,*
> *quiso que la justicia enmudeciera;*
> *y en el combate rudo*
>
> *tu desdeñaste el yugo. Yo te canto,*
> *yo que he llorado y he sufrido tanto*
> *el yugo colectivo de mi raza.*
>
> *Vives aún y vivirás, Sandino,*
> *más allá del furor del asesino*
> *y del fragor que ya nos amenaza.*[1]

(Grasping the naked blade, the clever Saxon became fierce, wanting to silence justice; but you in harsh combat refused to put on
the yoke. I sing to you. I who have wept and suffered the collective yoke of my people. You still live and will always live, Sandino,
beyond the assassin's rage and the fury that threatens us.)

Despite the consensus in contemporary criticism and historiography
that the Chicano Movement was exclusively a "nationalist" movement,
the pan-Latino agenda of Paredes's text reminds us that Chicano

activism consistently has manifested internationalist tendencies. The potential turning inward of narrow nationalisms has at certain key moments been reversed in order to look outward toward struggles taking place elsewhere in geographical spaces under the heel of "*el mañoso sajón*," that is, U.S. economic and cultural domination.

In this chapter, I want to rethink the Chicano Movement of the late 1960s and early 1970s not as a self-enclosed social movement with historical beginning and end but as one episode in an ongoing narrative of Chicana and Chicano efforts to link domestic struggles to international movements for liberation and self-determination. From this perspective, the origins of the Movement itself extend further back than we have been led to believe, its present is linked to contemporary solidarity and antiwar struggles, and its "conclusion" lies somewhere in the unknown future. By reconfiguring traditional narratives, the pantheon of Movement actors is significantly expanded to include historical agents who have been denied the credit they deserve—Anna Nieto Gomez, Elizabeth Betita Martinez and Enriqueta Longeaux y Vásquez, to name only three of the most committed activist-intellectuals.[2]

The attempt to shift the synchronic focus onto the internationalist moments of the Movement does not negate the significance of the nationalist impulse. In fact, I would argue that in the face of global capital's attempted destruction of the local and the recent resurgence of U.S. imperial ambitions the nationalist insistence on safeguarding cultural and linguistic rights and identities is crucially important. Yet the juxtaposition of the two agendas—internationalist and nationalist—clarifies the potential strengths and weaknesses of both, and may move us toward a revitalization of Chicano and Chicana political agendas. A demystified and grounded revision of the term *Aztlán* is necessary, I would argue, in order to critically engage not only poststructuralist notions of Aztlán as an always receding desire but also the invisible yet well-calculated movements of global capital and "compassionate" neo-imperialism.

I retain the term *internationalism* precisely because of its associations with a socialist project that during the Viet Nam war period posited an alternative and often-utopian model for society that transcended national boundaries and imagined a diverse working-class community. It was this internationalist impulse to make social justice a global project that attracted scores of Chicanas and Chicanos to the ranks of specific organizations despite the fact that few organizations and only a small number of activists considered themselves socialists. I take the term to signify indirect forms of state-sponsored solidarity, as in the example of the Venceremos Brigades (see Chapter Three), but primarily those forms of solidarity work that arose outside the circuits of official state power. Key sectors of the Chicano/a antiwar movement, for example, were based on grassroots coalitions that invoked solidarity with the Vietnamese people but rarely produced statements of support for the government of North Viet Nam or even the National Liberation Front. In my opinion, it is because of its socialist (i.e., borderless and working-class) foundations that the term *internationalism* best captures the various complementary networks of solidarity, at times material but most often ideological, that connected local Chicano/a militancies to liberation struggles around the world.

The tension between what I take to be complementary and dialectically interrelated impulses—internationalism (or "revolutionary nationalism" in some contexts), cultural nationalism, and narrow forms of regressive nationalism—is everywhere present in the artistic production and political positions adopted during the Movement. At times competing impulses are at play at various stages in the career of a single author. Luis Valdez, for example, was capable of expressing solidarity with Cuba and Viet Nam in the long poem "Pensamiento serpentino" and in the Teatro Campesino's antiwar *actos*, but insisted nevertheless that the Chicano political agenda was tied to some autochthonous belief system separate and distinct from the ideologies that confronted U.S. imperialism in those distant countries. "Moctezuma has more to teach us than Marx," a young Luis Valdez once claimed.[3] As Dionne Espinoza has shown, the career of Enriqueta Longeaux y Vásquez exemplifies a more complex and coherent position than that of Valdez by consistently positing a staunch internationalism that strategically deploys nonexclusionary forms of nationalism.[4] Historian Ignacio M. García has argued for a more rigid dichotomy between "barrio and international politics" but agrees that there were some activists who successfully negotiated the two positions.[5]

In his study of internal colonialism in the Chicano novel, Manuel de Jesús Hernández-Gutiérrez describes a three-part spatial and cultural configuration: 1) the Barrio, 2) the Anti-barrio, or dominant U.S. culture, and 3) the Exterior, that is, geographic zones outside the U.S.

mainland. The emplotment of characters in the Exterior signifies what Hernández-Gutiérrez calls an "internationalist element" linking the Barrio to those areas of the world subject to U.S. domination. In Miguel Méndez's 1974 novel *Peregrinos de Aztlán*, for example, the American war in Viet Nam takes the life of Frankie Pérez and has a devastating impact on Chicano and Latino barrios across the country.

By focusing on the war in Southeast Asia, our readings of cultural texts of the 1960s and 1970s and our understanding of the Chicano Movement as an essentially "nationalist" movement becomes more complex. The National Chicano Moratorium Committee, to name only one key organization, drew upon cultural nationalism to organize the community and to mount a critique of U.S. foreign policy but did so without falling into repressive nationalist tendencies.[6] On the artistic front, texts such as Oscar Zeta Acosta's *Revolt of the Cockroach People* make the explicit link between Chicanos and the Vietnamese people, a connection made most powerfully in the Teatro Campesino's actos and the antiwar graphics of Malaquias Montoya and Rupert Garcia.

The issue of the war teaches us that even the best-known "nationalist" leaders were committed to a complementary internationalist agenda. It is important to recall Corky Gonzales's brilliant antiwar speech delivered in August of 1966 (eight months before Dr. King's rejection of President Lyndon Johnson's Viet Nam policy) or the many joint resolutions presented by La Raza Unida Party calling for "the immediate halt of bombing and a withdrawal from Vietnam."[7] While one segment of the Movement of the 1960s may have argued for a political agenda focused almost exclusively on local issues—the "*La batalla está aquí*" position—another segment agreed that there was much to be done on the home front but also understood that conditions in Aztlán were directly connected to events in Southeast Asia, Mexico, and other sites of struggle around the world.

Like Malcolm X who had argued that one could not understand Mississippi without understanding the Congo, the Chicano poet Portilla de la Luz wrote: "Vietnam, Vietnam/*en tu justa y heróica lucha/se decide también el destino de mi lucha*" ("Vietnam, Vietnam/in your just and heroic struggle/the outcome of my struggle is also decided"). Or as raúlsalinas put it in his 1971 poem "Enorme transformación" in which the poet explains the meaning of the Movimiento:

Enorme Transformación
    hoy me das a conocer
que no tan sólo yo . . . soy el que sufro
    El compañero con su piel
obscura, o aquel un poco más pálido
            que yo
        también él sufre
si es oprimido bajo explotación.

Enorme Transformación
    que me hace comprender
que el vietnamita es balaceado
    el negro encarcelado
        el latino pisoteado.[8]

(Great Transformation. Today you make me see that I do not suffer alone. The comrade with dark skin or the one who is lighter than me also suffers if he is oppressed and exploited. Great Transformation that makes me understand how the Vietnamese is shot, the Black incarcerated, the Latino beat down.)

The sentiment invoked in the above verses is representative of many texts written by Chicanas and Chicanos during the Viet Nam war era. The battle may indeed have been "here" on the domestic front but it was not limited to ethnic Mexican communities and could not be separated from global events.

Chicano humanism, which I take to be a much more important principle of foundational Movement documents like the "Plan espiritual de Aztlán" than narrow forms of ethnic nationalism, deployed a variety of tropes, many of them associated with what would become the basis for the environmental movement in the 1970s. Essayist Antonio Gomez, for example, used the language of science and ecology to argue: "Indio Hispanos and Blacks must join with others in eliminating the discrepancies in the standard of living that exist among nations and within any particular country. We must begin to perceive that we do live in a world community, and that all are joined, interdependently and inextricably, in the fabric of life."[9]

The appeal to a prelapsarian nature was especially strong in the writings of Taos, New Mexico, writer Enriqueta Longeaux y Vásquez.

By invoking the wisdom of community elders, she did not look exclusively inward toward her own ethnic group but rather constructed Chicano/a elders as one example of an inclusive concept of human experience and wisdom. She wrote:

> We can all remember some of the things that our viejitos and viejitas taught us, the things they showed us . . . I now realize it was the teaching of humanity, the teaching of life. For in the wisdom of our viejitos we learned about human beings and the universe; we learned about the earth, the land, and we called it: la madre tierra; la santa tierra; la tierra sagrada. Our viejitos taught us about nature and the creatures of the earth.[10]

The origins of the passage were directly linked to local conditions in New Mexico where the land-grant movement dominated all other issues. But for many Chicano/a youth in the urban centers of the Southwest such language resonated with similar effects. By using a discourse of harmony between human praxis and the natural environment, Longeaux y Vásquez critiqued the entirety of capitalist society "because in all of its technology it does not make a place for humans in relation to Nature."[11]

In addition to diverse forms of abstract universalism and an emergent indigenous-based environmentalism, other kinds of solidarity resulted from anticapitalist analyses of concrete objective conditions in specific contexts. Salinas's text above, for example, complicates a narrow nationalist emphasis on "race" as an exclusive category in order to expand its political agenda to include all economically exploited groups ("*aquel un poco más pálido que yo*"). In his essay, Gomez called attention to inequalities of wealth that were the legacy of colonialism and racism: "This implies that poverty, undernourishment, and premature deaths are not the 'fate' of certain people but rather that they are the manifestations of a social inequity that must be eliminated. This small, wealthy minority, throughout the world, is reaping most of the world's blessings because of past and or present policies of exploitation that serve to perpetuate the misery of the world population."[12] At the core of such pronouncements was not "nationalism" understood as a narrowing mechanism but rather a complex Chicano/a critique of the global political economy.

Whether their philosophical base was liberal humanism, indigenous culture, or socialism, Movement leaders, artists, and intellectuals stressed the importance of solidarity with Latin American social movements. Given the linguistic and historical inheritance shared by U.S. Latinos and Latin Americans, it was this area of the world that was often the focus of Chicana/o internationalism (with Southeast Asia as the other major focus as long as the U.S. war there continued). In Chapter Three, I will demonstrate the importance of the Cuban Revolution for emergent forms of Chicano/a activism. The Mexican student movement of the late 1960s also caught the attention of Mexican American youth, especially following the Mexican government's massacre of students in October of 1968. The killings at Tlatelolco were reported in early Chicano Movement newspapers such as Raul Ruiz's *Chicano Student Movement* published in Los Angeles. A few days after the massacre, Chicano/a members of the United Mexican American Students (UMAS) formed a solidarity committee with their Mexican counterparts and demonstrated outside the Mexican consulate in Los Angeles. When Chicano/a student organizations adopted the umbrella name of Movimiento Estudiantil Chicano de Aztlán (MEChA) in 1969, they took their slogan "*Por mi raza habla el espíritu*" ("The spirit speaks through my people") from the centuries-old motto of the Universidad Nacional Autónoma de México (UNAM). Some Chicano leaders, however, imagined that in the future Spanish-speaking peoples in the United States would take on an historical role that would move far beyond simple borrowings.

The day after the assassination of Dr. Martin Luther King, Jr., Reies López Tijerina told an interviewer in Berkeley, California, that the key to future U.S. foreign policy in Latin America was to be found in the Chicano community:

> By the year 2000, there will be 600 million Spanish-speaking people: the giant who has been overlooked by the Anglo neighbor. That's why the Southwest, this brown people, and New Mexico are in a key position. We will be playing a very important role in the future in the relationship of the Anglo and the Hispanic or Latin American countries. And I think that it's time for our government to realize and attend to the cry, the claim, the complaints, the demands of the people of the Southwest, the brown people. Because the time will come when the friendship of the

U.S. and Latin America will be decided on the Southwest behavior. We, who speak the English and Spanish languages, we feel that way, we are no longer thinking in terms of or from a Southwest standpoint, but from a global, universal point of view.[13]

José Angel Gutiérrez voiced similar sentiments in his visits to Mexico where he warned Mexican intellectuals of the seductive power of U.S. cultural imperialism, suggesting that the Chicano experience might provide lessons for resisting that power. In his poem "¡¡Cuídate, Méjico!!," Rodolfo Corky Gonzales advised:

> ¡CUIDATE, MEJICO!
> de los Bank-Americards
> Pepsi-Cola, Woolworths, Hiltons,
> Pittsburgh Paint
> y las colonias Yanquis.
> . . .
> ¡CUIDATE, MEJICO!
> Tus hijos mejicanos
> los Chicanos de U.S.A.
> ya saben vivir dentro
> del estómago del Tiburón,
> ya conocen bien su brutalidad
> su racismo,
> su odio a los mejicanos,
> negros y raza de color.
> No te dejes, Méjico lindo,
> patria de nuestros abuelos,
> tierra natal de toda mi raza
> de bronce.[14]

(Beware, Mexico! Of the Bankamericards, Pepsi-Cola, Woolworths, Hiltons, Pittsburgh Paint and Yankee colonies . . . Beware, Mexico! Your Mexican children, los Chicanos in the USA know about living in the belly of the beast, know well its brutality, its racism, its hatred of Mexicans, blacks, and people of color. Don't give in, beautiful Mexico, homeland of our grandparents, birthplace of all my bronze people.)

In progressive circles south of the border, some Mexican intellectuals agreed. The distinguished poet Octavio Paz, for example, told a Chicano interviewer in 1971: "*Yo creo que los Chicanos en su lucha nos van a ayudar mucho. Por una parte, yo creo que ustedes van a desarrollar formas intelectuales, formas culturales distintas de las nuestras pero que los dos podemos utilizar. Yo tengo una gran fe en el mundo Chicano, en la próxima cultura Chicana*" ("I believe that in their struggle the Chicanos are going to help us a great deal. On the one hand, I believe you are going to develop intellectual forms, cultural forms that are different from ours but that we also can use. I have great faith in the Chicano world, in the future of Chicano culture").[15]

Several years later, Jorge Bustamante suggested to his colleagues: "*Con el más elemental sentido de autocrítica habría que reconocer que tenemos mucho que aprender del movimiento chicano. . . . Seguir de cerca, estudiar sistemáticamente o meterse dentro del movimiento chicano ofrece una oportunidad para la autocrítica de lo mexicano*" ("With even a minimal sense of self-criticism one would have to admit that we have much to learn from the Chicano Movement. . . . To follow it closely, to study it systematically or to join the Chicano Movement provides Mexicans with an opportunity for self-criticism").[16] As we will see in my discussion of the figure of Che Guevara, an emergent pan-Latino solidarity often carried Chicano/a activists beyond the logical connection between Mexican and Aztlán and produced a common identity linked to the rest of Latin America. In his poem "Raíces . . . Raíces" (1974), Corky Gonzales wrote: "Raíces . . . Raíces/of strength/of survival/of love/of power/from Chile to Peru/From Mexico to Guatemala/From El Río Bravo to the Southwest/From the Southwest to the East." In his foundational poem "I Am Joaquin" he had made similar connections.[17]

In the influential treatise *Chicano Manifesto* (1971), Armando Rendón included a section called "The Chicanos of the Américas" in which he invoked the figure of Sandino as the twentieth century's "first national liberator of la raza." Cutting through the Cold War rhetoric of the period, Rendón argued that a Chicano community secure in its own identity might well become a vital link between U.S. policymakers and Latin America: "Through the Chicano, the United States has much to learn about the peoples to the south. The United States may even come to terms with the whole Latin American world, if it will recognize the Chicano as a unique phenomenon of the Americas and assure him the rights and status that are his due. . . . Undoubtedly the United States will maintain its ugly Anglo American attitudes for some time to come. But hopefully, the Chicano will see to it that never again will we offer only gringoismo to the brother nations of the Western Hemisphere."[18]

In the later stages of 1970s Chicano/a activism, Corpus Christi writer Vicente Carranza painted a more realistic and bleaker picture for Latinos in U.S. society:

> If we, the Third Worlders and all the oppressed people do not work toward making these changes that are occurring in favor of the working class, our struggle will be made twice as difficult because these changes are toward a fascist, dictatorial type system. The reason is that the ruling class, using the continental united states to live in, is because of greed isolating itself from the rest of this continent and later the world. And to keep the place where they live safe and secured, will come out with the most unimaginable methods to keep us, the oppressed people, the Third Worlders inside the united states, in line.[19]

A generation later, Carranza's words ring prophetic. While elites in the rich nations enjoy unprecedented luxury and wealth, the vast majority of the world's population, including most U.S. Latinos and African Americans, have witnessed a rollback of civil-rights gains and the intensification of the rigors of daily life.

According to the September 2002 Interim Report of the President's Advisory Commission on Educational Excellence for Hispanic Americans, ethnic Mexicans in the United States fell below every other Latino group "on almost every social and economic indicator." Among all private sector employees in the United States, 41.5 percent are considered blue collar, but 63.5 percent of all Latinos hold blue-collar jobs (U.S. Equal Employment Opportunity Commission 1998). In the year 2000, Latinos made up the fastest growing group in prisons nationwide; between 1985 and 1995 the number of incarcerated Latinos more than tripled.[20] Despite the empirical evidence to the contrary, neoconservative Hispanics either co-opt the languages of social change or dismiss activists of the Movement period for wallowing in "victimization" or being "stuck in the 60s."[21] The "progress" made over the last three decades (presumably for them and their friends), they argue, confirms the basic goodness of U.S. society.

NOT JUST ANOTHER NATIONALIST MOVEMENT

By the late 1960s, there was no defined Chicana ideology. Nor was there a defined Chicano ideology for the total community . . . The expression "cultural nationalism" was not used until later and has never been fully defined in the context of the times.

—Rodolfo Acuña, *Occupied America*[22]

Reduced to its fundamental organizing function, Chicano cultural nationalism was a necessary corrective for ethnic Mexicans in the United States who had either opted for the path of traditional assimilation or felt trapped in an economic and cultural system that positioned them as inferior. At the first Chicano Youth Liberation Conference in March of 1969, Crusade for Justice activists referred to cultural nationalism as "the key to organization [that] transcends all religious, political, class, and economic factions and boundaries."[23] It was this self-assured pronouncement together with Corky Gonzales's epic poem "I am Joaquin," the "Plan Espiritual de Aztlán," and other writings of the late 1960s that marked the entire Movement as "nationalist" for a later generation of scholars who were born after the Viet Nam war period and came of age in the era of Reaganism and triumphant globalized capital. As Rudy Acuña correctly noted, at the turn of the twenty-first century: "[cultural nationalism] has become a popular term after the fact and took on the meaning of an unyielding nationalism that was rooted in patriarchy."[24]

Adding to the negative reevaluation of the Movimiento as essentially sexist was the narrow use by some activists of the term *carnalismo* as "brotherhood." Clearly, individual acts of sexism were widespread throughout the period and varying degrees of patriarchal oppression existed in all Movement organizations.[25] But "carnalismo" was not necessarily a masculinist construct premised on the exclusion of women but rather an overly vague category invoked to promote a collective and militant identity. As Ignacio M. García points out: "*Carnalismo*, like *chicanismo* or cultural nationalism, only made sense in the context of an oppressed people fighting for self-determination."[26] Nevertheless, the centrality of the terms *carnalismo* and *brotherhood* in key documents such as the "Plan Espiritual de Aztlán" left the lasting impression that the future nation was to be for boys only or at least it would have to be based on the unequal relations of the traditional patriarchal family.

Although I would still insist that Chicano cultural nationalism was an ideologically neutral organizing tool, I would add that like most nationalisms constructed around uninterrogated notions of the family, Chicano cultural nationalism always already contained the seed of gender inequality. The assertion in the "Plan espiritual de Aztlán" that "our cultural values of life, family, and home will serve as a powerful weapon to defeat the gringo dollar system and encourage the process of love and brotherhood" was little comfort to Chicanas whose experience of "family" and "home" had not always been a positive one.[27]

Cultural nationalism may have been a necessary strategy for overturning decades of exploitation and cultural loss, but it was always susceptible to conflicting interpretations and appropriations. Once it was transported into the structures of specific Movement organizations, the potential for regressive forms of nationalist practice could increase as traditional patriarchal attitudes were conflated with emergent Chicano subjectivities. As Dionne Espinoza has shown in her study of the Chicana struggle with masculinist oppression in the Brown Berets, the "new" Mexican American male (the Chicano Beret) more often than not displayed the same kind of sexism he had inherited from earlier generations.[28] The complex problem of the Chicano Movement's complicity with reactionary forms of nationalism, I would argue, will have to be studied organization by organization. When scholars are too quick to generalize about "the Movement," that is, when they commit the same error some Movimiento militants had committed—taking an ill-defined "Chicano nationalism" to be the exclusive ideology or philosophy for the entire Chicano/a movement"—the possibility for recuperating positive lessons for the future is squandered.[29]

Thus those interested in understanding the complexity of the Movimiento should be wary of generalizations based on single or partial documents such as the "Plan espiritual de Aztlán." Ernesto Vigil reminds us that the "Plan" was not only the well-known poetic prologue authored by Alurista but that it consisted of two documents, one a utopian declaration (on which historians have tended to focus their attention); the other a three-point organizational agenda for action written by Corky Gonzales and other Crusade for Justice members.[30] In many ways, the language of the programmatic document suffered from the same high level of abstraction that had made Alurista's artistic contribution so powerful.

Calling for "total liberation from oppression, exploitation, and racism," land redistribution, reparations or "restitution for past economic slavery," and "a nation autonomous and free" without specifying exactly how these goals could be reached without significant political and economic resources made the "Plan" an easy target for later critics. Perhaps the most significant disjuncture between the reality of the situation and the rhetoric of the Plan was the invocation of "our revolutionary culture." Although the Mexican Revolution of 1910 still figured prominently in Mexican American historical memory, the cultural practices and traditions for the vast majority of ethnic Mexicans in the United States during this period were far from "revolutionary," and the objective conditions for a nationalist and anticolonial revolution with an independent nation as its goal simply did not exist.

The major contribution of the complete text of the "Plan," therefore, was limited to the mobilizing ideology of cultural nationalism as the "common denominator for mass mobilization and organization."[31] The phrase *"Por la Raza todo, Fuera de la Raza nada"* meant simply that in their daily activities Chicanos and Chicanas ought to focus on how they were working to improve the life chances of their community.[32] As an organizing tool, this appeal to a "national identity" was crucial for both women and men even though, as in any nationalist movement, the attempt to "transcend" differences within the community would lead necessarily to internal contradictions and future critiques as we have seen with regard to gender practices.

In other words, the period following the most intensive organizing of the community or nation will be marked by the return of those differences that had been bracketed during the period of mobilization. As one student of nationalist projects reminds us:

> The nationalist leader often had to invent a unifying culture as well as lead. He played the role of a kind of intellectual version of Lévi-Strauss' bricoleur. A bricoleur was a handyman who, by using bits of machinery or equipment, the original purpose of which had been forgotten or never known, was able to solve immediate mechanical problems. The nationalist leader did something similar with the cultural detritus of the past to create a new national group. In doing so, he pre-empted the choice of others on what the nation was.[33]

All nationalist discourse, then, by creating a "safe space" within a hostile social environment is by its very nature unable to attend to all possible internal differences and divisions.

Tomás Ybarra-Frausto offers the following self-criticism along these lines from the perspective of a former activist: "We were monolithic in thinking about culture. We tried to amalgamate everyone under certain types of strictures. . . . We had to create this imagined community that was whole and holistic, and total and energized. We *had* to do this to struggle against a dominant culture that made you segmented and unaffiliated. The notion that we were united was, in a way, a myth. . . . It was a mistake because we didn't allow for the particularities of experience to come forth" (emphasis in original).[34]

Contrary to Ybarra-Frausto's final assertion here, I have tried to suggest that the project to construct a Chicano/a cultural nationalist identity and related organizational strategies, if only provisional, was not a mistake at all but a necessary component in the dialectical development of the struggle. Less a "moment" or a "stage" to be transcended, the cultural nationalist impulse was a constant to be redeployed or supplemented as objective conditions changed. It is only through the prism of the very different contexts of later historical periods that one might perceive cultural nationalism as a "mistake" (the danger of presentism is self-evident). Ybarra-Frausto admits as much when he writes: "We *had* to do this." In other words, only after the community had coalesced around an identity in opposition to the racialized and racist ones disseminated by the dominant culture could the process of reevaluation take place. Moreover, once the external threat to group cohesion is past (or understood to be less real) identities constructed around issues of gender, class, and sexuality necessarily reassert themselves. This is precisely the process that occurred in Movimiento circles in the decades immediately following the Viet Nam war period.

The cultural nationalist impulse marked the continually recurring site at which Chicano/a activists defined for themselves (over and against dominant stereotypes) their social identities and political objectives in an attempt to mobilize their communities. Before the Movimiento, it was argued, the Mexican American had suffered "an act of self-immolation in terms of a rejection of his heritage and culture, falsely construed as necessarily an infrahuman culture of 'spics' and 'greasers,' since it did not conform to the unquestioned standard of 'civilized' children."[35] The appropriation of selected parts of Mexican history, ranging from Aztec and Mayan mythology to the Revolution of 1910 to the concept of Aztlán itself, determined the basic parameters of the new identity. That some sectors of the community were excluded was an unfortunate yet predictable consequence given the nature of most nationalist projects. This is not to excuse the exclusions that took place but rather to seek to understand them as part of a process not at all unique to Chicano cultural nationalism. The danger was that the results of the act of identity formation become hopelessly narrow and frozen in time. This is precisely the charge leveled at the Chicano Movement during subsequent decades by a variety of groups with diverse agendas.

But the more perceptive activists of the Movimiento period were well aware of the dangers of reactionary nationalism. At the first Denver Youth Liberation Conference in March of 1969, an event often described as the origin of a narrow version of Chicano nationalism, the statement of the Revolutionary Caucus pointed toward an emergent form of humanism: "To us, nationalism is an awareness that we are not caucasian, not Mexican-American or any other label the system puts upon us, but that we are a people with an ancient heritage and an ancient scar on our souls. Because we know who we are, our nationalism becomes an internationalism that does not deny the human dignity of any other people, but accepts them as brothers."[36]

In his summary of the results of the Political Action workshop held at the historic University of California, Santa Barbara, conference in April 1969, Ysidro Ramón Macias recognized cultural nationalism as a "uniting factor" and a "positive factor for political action which is strong enough to build consciousness but not so weak as to be meaningless."[37] More important, he added that the goal of Chicano nationalism was to move toward a more inclusive ideology: "The concept of La Raza can be built up into a more international philosophy . . . [Nationalism] should also be not so strong that it excludes the possibility of coalitions with other Third World groups or whites."[38] According to Macias, there were several dangers in an inflexible nationalist position:

> The primary danger of cultural nationalism is that it is often viewed as an end in itself. In other words, Chicano cultural nationalism is seen as the ultimate ideology or philosophy for the Chicano movement. Chicanos must recognize that cultural

nationalism is not a political ideology but a cultural awareness factor that is useful in uniting our movement; and that if the Chicano movement is going to attain maturity, it must formulate or adopt a political and economic ideology. Chicanos must also guard against becoming so obsessed with cultural nationalist ideas that they start displaying manifestations of racism towards other ethnic groups. Rigidity is something which has historically been inherent in nationalism.[39]

Macías astutely foresees the limitations of sectarian nationalism and its potential for inflexibility once the initial organizing objectives have been achieved. The delicate balancing act sustained by many Chicano/a activists throughout the Movement period demonstrates the richness of Movement thought and belies any simple reduction of the period to a single ideological program (e.g. "nationalism").

Writing in 1971, an anonymous author offered an historical precedent for moving beyond narrow ethnic identities: "But we must be leery of nationalism. At one time it did serve a purpose, that of getting a group of people to realize who the enemy was, but now it can be dangerous in the sense that it can get oppressed people fighting each other, Chicano vs. Asiatic, Asiatic vs. Black, etc. . . . Our spirit of revolution should be like Che Guevara's. He was born in Argentina, became a revolutionary in Mexico, fought in Cuba, and died in Bolivia. In each place he served, he belonged to the people."[40]

Two additional examples illustrate my assertion that many Chicano/a activists understood the weaknesses of a narrow "race-based" movement. Writing in the East Los Angeles College student newspaper *La vida nueva*, an anonymous author advised: "Cultural nationalism may be seen as a transitional stage in the political awakening of our people. However, to make a religion of 'Brown is Beautiful' carries with it a number of dangers."[41] The writer then went on to propose coalition building as a logical next step for a politicized Chicano/a community. A mature nationalism might "open up the way to engage in principled coalitions and alliances both inside and outside of our movement. This analysis will lead us into affirming not only our cultural integrity but will move us to identify with all the struggles of oppressed peoples anywhere. In summary, nationalism is the indispensable driving force of our Chicano movement, but if we haven't got anything to move on to we will end stunted victims of our delusions."[42] Cultural nationalism, then, becomes the necessary precondition and complement to subsequent Chicano/a ideologies and political practices. As a politically "neutral" organizing principle, or what Macías had called "a cultural awareness factor," it has been and continues to be an indispensable factor in every Latino social movement. As an end in itself, it becomes counterproductive and harmful to broader agendas for progressive change.

I have argued that ideological distinctions within and among various organizations had never been clear-cut and by the early 1970s were becoming increasingly blurred. In 1973 at a conference of all University of California MEChAs held on the Riverside campus, the tension between narrow ethnicity-based nationalism and internationalist Marxism broke out into open conflict. According to one participant: "It was felt by many . . . that Mecha's past philosophy of cultural nationalism . . . was contrary to the goal of the liberation of our people." Meeting in separate work groups, the "cultural nationalist" (what I am calling "narrow nationalist") and "class struggle" caucuses hammered out their positions and returned for an eight-hour debate and a final vote that essentially split the organization in two—cultural nationalism, twenty-five votes; class struggle, twenty-one votes. The defeated faction walked out of the meeting in protest of procedural irregularities during the general assembly but circulated their minority position, which seemed to move in the direction of rapprochement. The statement read in part: "By fighting imperialism in the U.S. and by aligning ourselves with the progressive working class movement of this country, we necessarily accomplish a step towards a world solidarity of workers. . . . We also realize the various tools and tactics that currently can be applied to enhance this class struggle analysis. One such tool is cultural identity as a means of organizing and politicizing for an end to class society."

In their closing remarks, the victorious "nationalist" faction reciprocated by making a significant gesture toward an internationalist agenda: "We realize that the Chicano struggle is a part of the international class struggle. . . . We as MECHA members see our role as one of promoting the national liberation of our people stemming from the local to regional to national to international."[43] In effect, the ideology of internationalist solidarity could emerge even in those groups that at specific moments and in specific contexts espoused a regressive form of nationalism.

More than anything else, cultural nationalism was experienced as a "safe space" within a context of over a century of anti-Mexican racism and limited economic opportunity. For some activists, this otherwise defensive posture did not preclude the aggressive use of specific ethnic resources as instruments with which to actively oppose the forces of acculturation and cultural negation. The Spanish language, for example, was both something to be recuperated and protected even as it might be strategically deployed against anglophone hegemony. The writer Luis Pingarrón urged young Chicano/as to not lose their Spanish-speaking ability, and to make a point of speaking Spanish in the presence of non-Latinos if for no other reason than to irritate them: "*Por favor, no se dejen!* Use what we have that he is most afraid of—our language and our culture. Go out of your way to give these sanctimonious bastards the battle they need to put them in their place!"[44] The logic of adopting as a political tool a world language that is spoken in multiple countries necessarily leads beyond local nation-based identities. An important lesson contained in Pingarrón's exhortation, then, is that the "safe space" of Chicano/a linguistic and political self-determination potentially can become a "staging area" from which links to other communities might be constructed.

As a platform or staging area, cultural nationalism was the site from which Chicano/as extended themselves into a variety of struggles for social justice. Even the important place of *el barrio*, that urban space which for many activists provided the core values of chicanismo, could be broadened beyond its physical borders in order to construct an international solidarity that encompassed multiple communities. As longtime activist Frobén Lozada put it in 1968:

> *Nosotros miramos al barrio muy diferente también, no como algo confinado por los arbitrarios límites de una ciudad, que a su vez son determinados por políticos corruptos que desean que tú pienses en los limitados términos de tu propio barrio, para que de esta manera no te molestes en pensar en la gente del Tercer Mundo como tus hermanos. Nosotros miramos a nuestro barrio como no confinado ni restringido a los arbitrarios límites de la ciudad. Nuestro barrio va más allá de esos ficticios límites y se extiende hasta la plaza de las Tres Culturas de la ciudad de México. Nuestro barrio se proyecta hasta las favelas de Brasil. Nuestro barrio se ensancha hasta las montañas de Bolivia y las selvas de Vietnam.*[45]

(We also have a different understanding of the barrio, not as something confined by the arbitrary boundaries of a city which themselves are created by corrupt politicians who want you to think within the limited terms of your own barrio so that you won't worry about people in the Third World who are your brothers. We understand our barrio as not limited by or restricted to the arbitrary boundaries of a city. Our barrio goes beyond fictitious boundaries and extends to the plaza of the Three Cultures in Mexico City. Our barrio extends to the shanty towns of Brazil. Our barrio extends to the mountains of Bolivia and the jungles of Vietnam.)

An anonymous Chicana writer explained the relationship between the cultural nationalist impulse and international solidarity projects in the Movement: "A call for a return to 'Chicano culture' is in itself not reactionary, but simply a way of trying to draw back those who are losing their identity as Chicanos. The other important trend is that of young revolutionaries. They see the futility of relying solely on cultural nationalism, as most of them have been actively working organizing poor people and know that the basis of their problems is economic and not cultural."[46] The gesture toward the issue of class was a crucial one because unfair gender and economic relations potentially created divisions within the imagined totality of "*la familia de la Raza*." Elizabeth "Betita" Martinez would make a move similar to Lozada's redefinition of "el barrio" when she transformed the term *family* into an internationalized solidarity of resistance, what she called "the whole familia of La Raza, the whole family of oppressed peoples."[47]

According to Rodolfo Corky Gonzales, organizing the community through cultural nationalism was only the first stage in a complex process of cultural and political education: "People are starting to identify with themselves and are starting to analyze and recognize themselves and their people. That's just one step. Some people say we're cultural nationalists and that's it. But nationalism is a tool for organization, not a weapon for racism."[48] Cognizant of the fact that the nationalist impulse is by its very nature inward looking and in its narrowest forms exclusionary, Gonzales and other Movement thinkers worried that Chicano/as could fall prey to reproducing the kind of racial prejudice that "Anglo society" had deployed against Mexicans in the Southwest. The irony of course was that whereas many of the most infamous nationalist movements in history had posited racial "purity" as the basis for identity, new Chicano/a identities were premised on the kind of "race mixing" or amalgamation that had horrified racist thinkers since at least the earliest decades of European colonialism. In most contexts, the very concept of "Aztlán," for example, had less to do with an organic territory founded on racial, linguistic, or cultural purity (although the Indo-Hispano nationalism of Tijerina's project often flirted with this idea) than with a "translocal" field in motion produced by migration, multilingualism, and mestizaje.[49]

Any narrow "race"-based political agenda must be understood as a contradiction at the core of the Movement. Nonetheless, racialized strategies could and would be practiced by clever members of the community in order to further personal agendas. As one writer put it: "[Cultural nationalism] may lead into a dead end street while it profits a few at the expense of most Vatos."[50] In other words, a select group trading on its "race" or ethnicity might successfully exploit the limited concessions offered by U.S. liberalism. The potential for the creation of a Chicano/a professional class disassociated from the ethnic Mexican working class in the United States was well understood by Movimiento thinkers. Sensing the possibility that an ethnic buffer class could arise in the future as an unintended consequence of Chicano/a activism, Corky Gonzales warned that the construction of an ethnic or "racial" subject ought not to be used as a screen by opportunistic Mexican Americans who worked against the best interests of the majority of Chicanos/as.

Gonzales feared that a relatively affluent middle class someday might hide behind the cloak of its ethnicity even as it abandoned those in the community who were less fortunate: "It is important that in our own family we cannot allow a class system duplicate of the same society that has stamped us as inferior. The Chicano struggle in relation to the land, culture, and political movement must embrace a collective struggle of the people against individual selfishness, greed, and opportunism."[51] Using their ethnicity to their advantage, calculating professionals would practice what Ysidro Macias called "Tacoism" by deploying their ethnic affiliations in order to build careers upon the sacrifices made by earlier activists even as they attempted to discredit fundamental Movement principles and distance themselves from ongoing working-class struggles for economic justice.[52]

In effect, the "Hispanic success" stories of the late 1980s and 1990s are precisely what astute Chicano/a activists foresaw. Corky Gonzales and other Movement thinkers understood that the logic of reactionary nationalism would lead to irreconcilable contradictions in the future by making it difficult to argue against the resilient ideology of the "American Dream." The demands for more Chicano representation in traditional institutions might well create a small group of Mexican American "success stories" whose mere existence would prove that the militants had been wrong to criticize the status quo. An insistence on a narrow agenda based on "race" alone would lead to the formation of a "Chicano/a" professional class of tokens whose values were aligned with those of already existing elites: "Brown capitalists are still subjected and therefore committed to the continuing exploitation of Chicanos."[53]

With regard to the issue of international solidarity in particular, some Movement thinkers feared that the economic progress made by Latinos in the United States would preclude international solidarity with the poor in Spanish-speaking nations. As John Ortiz put it in 1971, those who made it into the middle class might well argue: "If the system works for our people then it is good despite its actions to the rest of the world."[54] In other words, as long as an identifiable percentage of Latino/as in the United States enjoyed the fruits of consumer culture the desperate conditions of poor people abroad were simply not their concern.

Ortiz viewed internationalism as a necessary corrective both to overly narrow nationalism and uncritical assmilationism. He cited Ysidro Macias who had written: "A Third World mentality can be expressed as an extension of Chicanismo expanded to embrace those ethnic minorities who are also suppressed and are victims of Anglo exploitation."[55] Solidarity would extend not only to other countries, then, but also to other historically exploited groups in the United States, a strategy employed several years earlier by Reies López Tijerina, as we will see in Chapter Five. For Ortiz, Chicano nationalism and internationalism were not rival but complementary projects:

> Cultural nationalism and Third World concepts are not con-
> flicting ideologies. Nationalism speaks to the political develop-
> ment of a community by realizing it as a separate entity. Third
> World concepts speak to the relationship of that community to
> the rest of the Third World. These are not conflicting ideas and

should not be understood as such. They should not work against each other but in conjunction and co-ordination to serve the Chicano community.[56]

In this sophisticated political statement, Ortiz avoids presenting the "nationalist moment" as an immature stage on the way to a more mature internationalist moment. Rather, he understands that the two positions could and should coexist if the Movimiento was to realize its goals of mass mobilization and a critique of U.S. liberalism in both its domestic and foreign-policy manifestations.

As we will see in subsequent chapters, the tension between sectarian nationalist and so-called Third World activists formed a fissure through which law enforcement sought to break down progressive alliances. In the African American community, such divisions demanded the constant attention of organizers. Eldridge Cleaver, for example, explained: "I don't think there is necessarily a distinction between . . . nationalism and proletarian internationalism because it's been shown many times that if you can't love those around you, which is a form of nationalism, relate to those within your own entity, then you can't relate to those beyond you."[57] But the divide between extreme Black nationalists and internationalists, exacerbated by the provocation of government agents, became a fundamental cause of the decline of radical movements in the United States during the Viet Nam war era.

Más allá del barrio/Beyond the barrio

Mentalmente el Tercer Mundo se puede expresar como una extensión del chicanismo.

(Intellectually, the Third World can be understood as an extension of chicanismo.)

—Anonymous, *¡Es tiempo!* (June 1972)

As I suggested in the Introduction, the potential for pan-Latino solidarity has always been strong in Chicano/a activist circles. The continual influx of Mexican immigrants has brought with it the variety of Mexican political agendas, and shared linguistic and cultural traditions ensured that Mexicans in the United States would look south in moments of crisis.

During the Movement period, Latin American liberation struggles ignited the imagination of Chicano and Chicana youth who found themselves engaged in their own fight for self-definition and human rights.

Early contacts with the Puerto Rican Young Lords, for example, provided the National Chicano Moratorium Committee with a pan-Latino potential that was never fully developed. By the early 1970s, several Chicano/a student activists in California had joined the Young Lords because they were attracted to the organization's internationalist agenda.[58] The Young Lords, whose origins lie in the mixed-race neighborhoods of Chicago and New York, had developed great skill in the kind of coalition building that factored in issues of "race" even as they looked beyond local conditions in order to practice an international solidarity along class lines.

On the issue of cultural nationalism as an end in itself, the Young Lords' position was quite clear: "Our feeling is that nationalism is important—that we have to be proud of our nation, our history and our culture—but that pride alone is not gonna free us, the ability to play congas is not gonna free us, the ability to speak Spanish fluently is not gonna stop landlords, the ability to run down Puerto Rican history like it was right from the beginning is not gonna stop the exploitation of our people on their jobs and every place else. We know that just going back to our culture is not gonna make it in and of itself."[59]

According to the chairman of the Young Lords: "Every group works separately in their community and we come together every so often and rap about what's happening. We try to keep close contact with each other. We feel that we're revolutionaries and revolutionaries have no race. The system is the one that's using the tool to divide us."[60] Like Los Siete de la Raza in the pan-Latino Mission District of San Francisco (see Chapter Five), the Young Lords understood the long-term political liability of restricting the Movement to any one Spanish-speaking group or even to people of color. "Siete" defendant Tony Martinez explained: "Most of the young people on the block think that the enemy is the regular white guy on the block too. They try to blame their oppression on him. So we try to make them see that he's not the enemy. We think we're really getting someplace by educating them through different methods to see who their enemy really is."[61]

The Young Lords' "13 Point Program" was especially sophisticated on the issue of coalitions and international solidarity. Point 2 was titled "We want self-determination for all Latinos"; and Point 4 declared "We know that Washington, Wall Street, and City Hall will try to make our nationalism into racism, but Puerto Ricans are of all colors and we resist racism." Point 11 explained the group's internationalist focus: "Our people are brainwashed by television, radio, newspapers, schools and books to oppose people in other countries fighting for their freedom. No longer will we believe these lies because we have learned who the real enemy is and who our real friends are. We will defend our sisters and brothers around the world who fight for justice and are against the rulers of this country. QUE VIVA CHE GUEVARA!"[62]

Preliminary attempts at pan-Latino organizing, however, ran up against an entrenched lack of knowledge about groups other than one's own and an inability to produce a coherent agenda. As early as October 1971 at the Unidos Conference in Washington, D.C., Chicano/a, Puerto Rican, and Cuban activists attempted but failed to establish the solidarity they all desired. The conference was noteworthy, however, in that it attracted many prominent Latino elected officials to a gathering of primarily grassroots activists, including Reies López Tijerina. Senator Joseph Montoya and Representative Manuel Luján of New Mexico, Representative Edward Roybal of California, and Representative Herman Badillo of New York spoke to the approximately one thousand attendees at the Hospitality House in Arlington, Virgina.[63] The conference adopted more than one hundred resolutions, many of which echoed the demands of Chicano Movement organizations, e.g., formation of a Latino third political party, abolition of the draft, and an end to the war in Viet Nam. Although the conference did not lead to further pan-Latino organizing, it initiated the slow process by which Chicano communities educated themselves about the complexities of other Latino groups in the United States.[64]

Alliances with the Pilipino community also survived throughout the Movement period. The most notable of these coalitions had begun in 1965 when Pilipino farm workers in California had gone on strike against grape growers and were joined a week later by César Chávez's National Farm Workers Association (NFWA). Labor leaders Larry Itliong, Andy Imutan, and Philip Vera Cruz were instrumental in the early successes of what would become the United Farm Workers union. Their relationship with Dolores Huerta had begun in the 1950s in the Agricultural Workers Organizing Committee (AWOC), a AFL-CIO-sponsored entity that eventually merged with Chávez's NFWA in 1966.[65]

The Chicano student movement, especially on college campuses where there was a Pilipino presence produced coalitions that owed their ideological base to "Third Worldism" but developed according to local contexts and issues. The most famous example may be the one at San Francisco State College where a Third World Liberation Front included a Chicano organization called El Renacimiento, the Filipino-American Students Organization, and other ethnic-based organizations.

At San Jose State College in California, an anonymous writer invoked the example of the farm workers and called for alliances between people of color: "Personally, I am convinced that Chicanos and Filipinos can forge a united front dedicated to bringing about the changes for the needs of both our peoples as well as bringing about a brotherhood of the skin that Third World peoples can look to as the beginning of a new era. Our racial and cultural characteristics are more alike than different. The blood of the hated Spanish conquistador runs in my veins as well as yours. Our brown skin puts us in the same boat as far as the white man is concerned. By personal experience we are all greasers. If this be the case, then let us raise a defiant fist together, for together we are unstoppable. Viva la Causa! Mabuhay!"[66] The shared experience of Spanish colonialism is deployed here as a distant link between the Chicano and Filipino communities, a link that curiously does not lead the author of this piece to a discussion of the shared experience of U.S. invasion and conquest.

The relationship between the Movimiento and predominantly Caucasian political organizations was strained throughout the Viet Nam war period. Too often Chicana/o activists were faced with white radicals who displayed a strong sense of entitlement or at best a patronizing attitude toward young working-class people of color. In a November 5, 1967, appearance in Los Angeles at a fundraising event for the "People's World," a pre-New Left organization of U.S. Communist Party regulars and fellow travelers, Corky Gonzales challenged what he perceived to be the group's lack of understanding of racial issues and their essentially middle-class prejudices. "I'm looking at a sea of old Anglo faces," Gonzales reportedly said. In a speech that kept white radicals at arm's length even as it petitioned them for their support, Gonzales explained that Chicanos would not allow themselves to be used by any group as political window dressing:

The Anglo always wants to be the leader, but he cannot lead today's Mexican and black movements. The liberals and radicals of this country must now leave the minorities alone. We need your financial and moral support, but in the end it is the Mexican or the Negro who will determine whether your help has been good or bad. There is a new movement coming. . . . The Mexicans have the bodies and blood to give for their revolution but the Anglos have only dollars. . . . Are the old radicals of today once-a-year radicals? Are they living off past glories? These are questions that need answers.[67]

In the immediate wake of the assassination of Martin Luther King, a group of concerned whites on the University of California, San Diego, campus formed a Tuesday the Ninth Committee (TNC) that quickly disintegrated because of what students of color perceived to be "charitable" and "superior" attitudes on the part of whites: "The vast majority of TNC people never realized that a fight against racism was not only in the interest of blacks and browns, but also was in their material interest."[68] On the antiwar front, Chicana/os had raised similar issues. Rosalío Muñoz and other organizers, for example, had encountered what they felt was a lack of understanding of working-class Mexican issues among antiwar groups. The unacceptable treatment they received at the San Francisco Mobilization in 1969 confirmed their sense that there was a need for an all Chicano/a Moratorium committee.[69] Chicana feminists throughout the Movement period were faced with class- and ethnic-based differences that made alliances with Caucasian feminists difficult if not impossible.

San Diego, California, activist René Nuñez (whom we will meet again as a key player in the 1969 Plan de Santa Bárbara conference) spoke at a March 23, 1971, rally for Angela Davis, and directly confronted what some Chicano activists considered to be the problem of white arrogance and the fundamental cultural and economic differences between them and Mexican American youth:

Today we see a basic contradiction in the relationship between the White radical movement and the Chicano. I am told that the Chicano is on a Nationalist kick and that it is counter-revolutionary. That to save himself the Chicano must join a third world front led by the radical white man—coalition, alliance seems to be the password. Yet these same radicals whole heart- edly support nationalist movements in North Viet Nam [sic], Cuba, Chile, etc. . . . Your paternalism and self-righteousness is not different than when it confronts us from the liberals of America—it's just as devastatingly one-sided. You've got so much to learn, white friends. We are not of Europe. . . . We do not need the religion of Marx, Lenin, Trotsky. We have thinkers of our own. We have Zapata, Flores Magón, we have Che, we have our literature, we have humanistic aspirations. We do not need your western European philosophy.[70]

Although later in the speech, Nuñez suggested that the Movimiento might use Western political theory as a tool to be discarded when no longer appropriate to the specific circumstances of the Chicano, the overall rejection of "white" allies was uncompromising. Comparing white radicals to the "Catholic Spaniards" and "European Puritanism" that had destroyed the indigenous people of the Americas, Nuñez invoked Mexican writer José Vasconcelos's notion of "La raza cósmica" in order to posit a virtually unbridgeable divide between Chicanos and radical white youth.

The irony was that even as Movement thinkers distanced them- selves from what they perceived to be the white counterculture there was an uneasy intersection of ideas given that both groups rejected fun- damental aspects of U.S. capitalist society. In its most "spiritual" mani- festations, Movimiento rhetoric sounded remarkably like the utopian language of those who urged young people to simply "drop out" of con- sumer culture. The basic difference of course was one of class since many if not most "hippies" had enjoyed middle-class upbringings whereas the vast majority of Chicano/a activist circles consisted of first- generation college students whose families made up the bulk of the Mexican and Mexican American working class. Nonetheless, the view that Chicano culture stood for an essentially alternative set of values that was opposed to materialism and careerism linked some Chicana/o writers to countercultural agendas.

Drawing inspiration from Octavio Paz, Frantz Fanon, and Abraham Maslow, for example, essayist Thomas Martinez insisted upon a hard dichotomy between "Chicanismo" and "Anglowhiteism," that is, spirituality vs. materialism. For Martinez, Chicanismo meant "spiritualism, honest self-examination, complete love of life, and a consciousness of here and now," the latter characteristic assuming an almost Buddhist-like "involvement in the present."[71] More important, Martinez's essay represented one of the more extreme forms of the Movement's humanist tendency in which political solidarity passed over into a generic love of all living things: "To the Chicano who adheres to Chicanismo, all humans are part of one family. There is a humanistic tradition inherent in the Chicano culture. It embodies an identification with all that is living. Needless to say, humanism is not a part of traditional mainstream America."[72] Because for Martinez the "Chicano way of life" is intrinsically superior to Anglo lifestyles (once again a racialized claim that owes much to Vasconcelos), Chicano pride ought to grow naturally out of la Raza's essential goodness. Not unlike the hippies themselves, Martinez offered an alternative philosophy to what he and others considered to be a decadent and morally sick culture.

For many militant Chicano nationalists, the "hippie" and "yippie" subcultures as well as most positions on the left were antithetical to traditional Mexican American concerns. In 1970, less than two months before the antiwar demonstration of August 29, a writer identified only as "El Gavilán" imagined a dialogue between a Chicano activist and a white radical. With the provocative title "Honkyism: A Satire," the piece mounted an implacable rejection of not only "white" middle-class solidarity with anticolonial struggles (represented in the text as "El Gava," i.e., *el gabacho* or Whitey) but also any concept of "Third Worldism" that might accompany it: "You're white and I'm brown and I do not know anything about your third world [sic]. I want your money, your institutions and if necessary your life. I owe you nothing and I do not need your honky rhetoric."[73] Although the thrust of the piece is satirical with characters representing the extremes of both the Chicano regressive nationalist and non-Chicano positions, it captures in an exaggerated form the tension felt in many Movement organizations around the issues of coalition building and internationalist politics. Unspoken here was the equally divisive problem created by the behavior of some "white leftists" who approached Chicano organizations with commissar-like attitudes that were arrogant and disrespectful.

The suspicion of agendas from the left emerged for a variety of reasons and often exacerbated tendencies leading toward narrow nationalism.

The extreme stance adopted in the above quotation resonates with Luis Valdez's proclamation early in the Movement period that Chicanos had "nothing to learn from Marx." It is also reminiscent of the narrow nationalist/Third World division negotiated by Chicano/a students on college campuses, the declaration made in the "Plan de Santa Bárbara" that the Chicano/a possessed an "essentially different life style," and the Brown Berets' suspicion of any alliance with non-Chicano organizations.

Created in 1967 as a community self-defense organization with paramilitary trappings and a diverse set of political influences, the Brown Berets quickly became one of the most visible groups in the Movimiento. As I have argued with regard to the Movement in general, it would be misleading to paint any one organization with a single ideological brush. While some sectors of the Berets espoused sectarian nationalist views, others voiced an internationalist Third Worldism that contradicted the tendency to "turn inward" toward exclusionary organizing practices. As Rudy Acuña has taught us: "[Beret Prime Minister] David Sánchez himself remained anti-communist. . . . Another faction of Berets had a revolutionary focus such as La Junta, led by Cruz Olmeda, who were influenced by the writings of Mao Tse-tung. Olmeda broke away from the Berets in July 1968, and subsequently collaborated with a local leftist organization such as the Los Angeles Committee for the Defense of the Bill of Rights."[74] The Beret organization would eventually fall prey not only to internal political divisions but also to gendered conflicts that led to the decision by some Beret women to leave the organization.[75] While attempting to negotiate what were perhaps inevitable fissures, the Berets as a collective were also subject to intense law-enforcement infiltration at a level perhaps only surpassed by the deliberate government effort to eliminate the Black Panthers.

On the one hand, the Berets closed off avenues for a popular front with non-Chicano progressives; on the other hand, they invoked the names of Che Guevara and Mao Tse-tung as positive influences. Dionne Espinoza has argued: "Beret ideology—while uneven in its adaptation and thoroughly conflicted at each step of its evolution—nevertheless, in general rapidly accelerated from a vague self-understanding as a defense unit and reformist organization of community organizers to a radical denunciation of U.S. global capitalism and its local effects on Chicanos."[76]

Espinoza's assertion is important because it captures the internal and often conflictive logic of a number of Movement organizations that, as I have tried to show in the preceding pages, were rarely "nationalist" in their totality and almost never "frozen" in any one particular political agenda. In the vast majority of cases, local political pressures and rapidly changing national and international developments during the Viet Nam war period would necessitate an ongoing transformation of ideologies and practices. To reiterate one of this book's basic assertions—because the basic forms of cultural nationalism never disappeared from the discursive field of the Movimiento, the development of complementary ideological positions that were more expansive and inclusive was often difficult.

On the issue of coalition building, the extreme nationalist position espoused by some sectors of the Brown Berets meant that while white and Black radicals might express solidarity with the Chicano Movement they could not consider Chicanos as part of an "American" radical agenda since, according to the philosophy of one group of Berets, Chicanos constituted a separate nation. What concerned these Berets was what concerned many other activists in ethnic Mexican communities, that is, the risk of entering into a coalition in which Chicano/as were forced too often into secondary roles premised upon the same racialized stereotypes so prevalent elsewhere in U.S. society. One essayist in the Beret newspaper, *La Causa*, put it this way:

> The Revolutionary stance of non-Chicanos assumes that since we all have a common oppressor we must consider each other as brothers. After all, none of us can do it alone. However, this ignores some very essential points. Part of the problem is reflected in the non-Chicano's contention that Chicanos are too "conservative," "religious," "obstinate," "racist." Calling us those things show an ignorance of who and what we are, of our history and of our essential worth as children of the earth. This kind of talk by black or white so-called revolutionaries is, in short, patronizing. It is another way of saying, "Those Mexicans just don't want to do things OUR way." These kind of "Revolutionaries" want the kind of equality of relationship that is shown between a horse and its rider—with the Chicano being the horse.[77]

At the core of the dispute between white middle-class activists and most sectors of the Movimiento were stark class differences that produced misunderstandings on both sides. Narrow nationalism's focus on ethnic and "racial" differences exacerbated these class distinctions and diminished the potential for collaboration. As we have seen in the comments by Luis Valdez and René Nuñez, any cultural product identified with "the West" could be automatically cast under a cloud of suspicion. The essay in *La Causa* therefore asserted: "White nationalism, then, means reactionary support of the Western European system in America, and it is the basis for White revolutionary pronouncements that 'not all Whites are bad' and that Marx and Lenin and even Jefferson had things to contribute."[78] According to the most regressive nationalist position, even Black radicals on the left were considered to be "tainted" by "foreign ideologies."

Black leftists came in for harsh treatment by the author of the *La Causa* essay because of their identification with what he considered to be "European ways of struggle": "They are in danger of being swallowed up by the very culture that robbed them of their own atavistic rites and replaced them with psalm-singing."[79] The racist implications of such statements were painfully obvious to most activists and not widely shared. Despite such narrow conceptions of a radical Chicano agenda, many of the founding members of the Brown Berets established close ties with Black militants in Los Angeles as early as 1967 (see Chapter Five). Carlos Montes, for example, recalls working closely with a variety of Black groups.[80] Those efforts and other alliances between Chicano/a and African American activists were either forgotten or rejected by authors like the one quoted above who, in his mixed message of putative support for other groups couched in a language of distrust and rejection, drew a rigid ethnic nationalist boundary around the concept of Chicano liberation.

Perceived by many Chicano youth as a "foreign" or "white" ideology, socialism had never been well understood in Spanish-speaking communities in the United States. When editor Agustín Gurza of the Berkeley, California, *La voz del pueblo* asked Corky Gonzales whether or not the socialist tradition had influenced his own thinking, he replied:

> If you take the definition of socialism or communism, or any one of those "isms," they are defined by white Western European ideology. The only difference is that your definition can be the same if you go back to "communism" or "familyism" or "tribalism" because it relates to the same thing. It relates to sharing. It relates to the people controlling the state and not the state controlling the people. . . . If you want to relate what we're doing, Chicanismo, as socialism—fine. But if you said it today,

you'd lose 90 percent of the Movement. We realize these things. We have to take certain steps at certain levels.[81]

Gonzales's imprecise definitions of specific ideological programs were to be expected given his focus on practical grassroots organizing. Broadly speaking, however, confusion about the meaning of socialism was symptomatic of much of the Movimiento. Gonzales's fear—that large numbers of Mexican Americans would abandon the Movement were it to declare a socialist agenda—was certainly well founded in a community deeply implicated in Cold War common sense about a perceived communist menace.

According to historian Richard García, at the third Chicano Youth Liberation Conference in Denver (June 1971), Gonzales "gave a speech that de-emphasized his usual themes, the family and nationalism, and emphasized a more 'socialist' approach."[82] Later that year, at a Mexican Independence Day celebration at the University of California, San Diego, he delivered a similar speech that focused on the war in Southeast Asia and social injustice at home. García's interpretation of the diverse ideological positions adopted by leaders like Gonzales is harsh. He writes:

> Gonzales's socialism was somewhat similar to Malcolm X's socialism: it emanated more from experience and emotions than from philosophy and reason. . . . Thus, even when reality intruded into his mythical world view, the concepts of "socialism," freedom, and equality were still oriented toward fulfillment within the "nation" of Aztlán rather than within the United States. Gonzales's "nationalist heart" was always in conflict with his "socialist head"; he could not fully accept a fusion of socialism and nationalism.[83]

In my opinion, García's dissection of Gonzales's "head and heart" is less productive than understanding the multiple discursive options at play in the cultural field in which Gonzales and other Movement leaders developed. It is not so much that activists "vacillated" among political stances (a charge leveled by García against Bert Corona) but that the pressures of practical organizing in an unusually volatile political climate (i.e., the Viet Nam war period) demanded a tactical flexibility that did not compromise shared strategic objectives in the long term.

Unfortunately, not every activist group was adept at devising principled strategies for collective action. Already in the early 1970s, ideological debates in Chicana/o communities between narrow nationalist and socialist factions erupted into divisive infighting. In the Houston newspaper *Papel Chicano*, for example, accusations were made against four Chicano members of the Socialist Workers Party and the Young Socialist Alliance, all from Texas and two of them founders of the Houston Mexican American Youth Organization (MAYO), of "bringing foreign ideologies into the Chicano community."[84] The article, entitled "Socialist Workers Party invades Aztlán," asserted "Chicanos do not need to endorse or accept any foreign ideology" and contained veiled threats against the four activists should they attempt to organize in Houston barrios because they were "controlled by Anglos."[85]

In their spirited responses, the accused argued: "Ideas are not bound by race, color, or nationality. They must be judged on their own merits." One of the four, Pedro Vásquez, a native of Segundo Barrio in Houston and organizer of the "*Raza contra la guerra*" committee, stated that his political beliefs were not foreign imports but were the products of his direct experience in Movimiento organizations: "My ideas developed from the struggle demanding Chicano control of the Chicano community, politically, economically, and culturally. I, like other carnales and carnalas in the movement, began to realize that the question of liberation was more than one of just our own Raza. I was one who began to realize that it was this whole system that needed not be overhauled but to be replaced."[86]

At a Chicano/a high school conference at San Diego State University in 1974, tensions between sectarian nationalist groups and a socialist contingent reached a breaking point. A reporter for the local *Prensa Popular* wrote: "Many people tried to undermine the conference by using those same ideas of the past such as Chicanismo. These differences led to a minor physical confrontation in the conference. One wonders now how those ideas ingrained in Chicanos about their cultural heritage, their being descendants of the Aztecs, their building the nation of Aztlán, about education, about being Chicanos could ever have been thought to be the solution to lower food prices, capitalism, exploitation of workers, and unemployment."[87] Five years after the first Denver Youth Conference where the basic elements of a cultural nationalist agenda had been articulated, many Chicano/a youth were supplementing that agenda with a broad critique of the global political economy.[88]

Chicana/o Internationalism in Practice

It was so gratifying to learn how important these people in other lands thought we were. Even we don't think as highly of ourselves as they did.[89]

—José Angel Gutiérrez

Within the framework of La Raza Unida Party, José Angel Gutiérrez pursued a conscious strategy of placing Chicano-related issues at the doorstep of Mexican politicians such as President Luis Echeverría who as Secretaría de Gobernación had met with Chicano leaders and who as president of Mexico demonstrated an interest in Mexicans in the United States as part of a Third World solidarity agenda. According to Gutiérrez: "*Hemos logrado . . . que México finalmente ha reconocido que los chicanos son una colonia dentro de los Estados Unidos y que son parte del Tercer Mundo. Esto ya se ha publicado y Echeverría admitió que hay algo llamado chicano y que nosotros somos oprimidos*" ("We have succeeded in making Mexico finally recognize that chicanos are a colony within the United States and that they are part of the Third World. This has been acknowledged publicly and Echeverría admitted that there is something called chicano and that we are oppressed").[90]

Gutiérrez's miscalculation was that he chose to deal primarily with elite groups in Mexico as opposed to grassroots organizations struggling to democratize the Mexican political system. Although throughout the late 1970s he arranged several meetings with the Partido Socialista de Trabajadores, that party itself was for the most part under the domination of the ruling Partido Revolucionario Institucional (PRI) and many of its members adopted a dismissive attitude toward Chicano delegations and La Raza Unida Party.[91]

Within the Chicano/a community, Gutiérrez's rivals began to accuse him of establishing personal ties with Mexican politicians that did not necessarily benefit the Movement as a whole. Mario Cantú, for example, argued: "*Es aquí que por su necesidad José Angel manipula y compromte los intereses del movimiento Chicano para beneficios que favorecen solamente a Crystal. . . . En el caso del apoyo al presidente Luis Echeverría, 500 libros para la biblioteca de Crystal, una estatua de Juarez y 17 becas a Chicanos seleccionados por él [Gutiérrez]*" ("Here is where José Angel selfishly manipulates and compromises the interests of the

Chicano Movement in order to receive benefits that only favor Crystal . . . . In the case of President Luis Echeverría's support the benefits include 500 books for the Crystal library, a statue of Juarez, and 17 scholarships for Chicanos hand picked by him [Gutiérrez]").[92]

Mexican presidents who succeeded Echeverria showed increasingly less interest in Chicano issues until Carlos Salinas de Gotari moved the PRI's focus on to the emerging Hispanic corporate class, effectively abolishing ties to working-class and militant Chicano organizations. Gutiérrez also led a delegation to Cuba in 1975 while other MAYO and Raza Unida Party members traveled to Nicaragua to demonstrate solidarity with the Sandinista revolution, met with *quebecoise* separatists and Spanish socialists, and even entered into "diplomatic arrangements" with the PLO (meeting for three hours with Yasir Arafat in 1980).[93]

As a trade-union leader with internationalist ties, César Chávez regularly had received delegations from around the world and traveled abroad to meet with labor groups. In its later incarnation, CASA (Centro de Acción Social Autónomo) sent delegations to Puerto Rico in 1975, Cuba in 1976 and 1978, and Cyprus in 1977. According to historian David G. Gutiérrez, CASA corresponded regularly with the Puerto Rican Socialist Party (PSP) throughout the 1970s, a fact that earned CASA the rebuke of the Socialist Workers' Party (SWP) and some of its Chicano/a members.[94]

As we will see in Chapter Five, Reies López Tijerina created a movement for New Mexican Hispanos around the land-grant issue and the Treaty of Guadalupe Hidalgo but also forged alliances with a wide range of African American and American Indian organizations. In a 1971 interview, Tijerina articulated a broadly humanist position: "I think every human being who really wants to do good in this world immediately begins to feel the responsibility towards all mankind, not just his own people. Naturally, I have to begin with my own people because if I can't help my own people, how can I help others? I have closer ties to my own people than to anybody else—physical ties. However, intellectual and human ties I do have with the whole world."[95] The cultural nationalist impulse, then, originates in the desire to "help one's own people." In no way, however, even for those leaders most associated by contemporary historians with regressive nationalism (e.g., Tijerina), did cultural nationalism preclude the elaboration of an expansive and internationalist agenda for progressive social change.

Unfortunately a majority of commentators on the Movement have yet to investigate the complex meanings of a widely reproduced terminology, a lamentable scholarly practice described by Rudy Acuña: "The term 'cultural nationalism' . . . has never been fully defined in the context of the times. It has become a popular term after the fact and took on the meaning of an unyielding nationalism that was rooted in patriarchy."[96]

Juan Gómez Quiñones has argued that the Movement's "nationalism" was not nationalism at all (in the sense of being revolutionary and anticolonialist) but rather a form of culturalism within an older liberal project of petitioning the dominant system for access to resources. Early commentators on the Movement's ideological repertoire recognized the contradiction outlined by Gómez Quiñones insofar as the stated objectives of most organizations awkwardly juxtaposed the rhetoric of "decolonization" and revolution with the appeals to economic and cultural inclusion. In his 1975 book, Edward Muguía questioned the future of any anticapitalist agenda for Chicana/os:

> It is unclear whether the Mexican American youth will attempt improvement of their socioeconomic status by means of a group communal effort, for example, by means of co-ops, community owned factories and shops—or individualistically by means of competitively participating in the present capitalistic system. Because of the size and force of the latter, and the increasing opportunities for the group in the larger system, it is much more likely that the Mexican American youth will continue to be absorbed into our present system than they are likely to create a new system.[97]

Even at the height of the Movimiento, the idea of a socialist Aztlán, which took revolutionary Cuba as its primary model, did not attract a significant segment of the Chicano/a community. In a real sense, Murguía's prognostication was correct. Capitalist hegemony in the United States had never allowed space for a large-scale leftist movement, and there was certainly no reason to think that even the most radical Chicano/as could successfully counter the seductive power exerted by consumer society upon most Mexican Americans and virtually all newly arrived Mexican and Latin American immigrants.[98]

A slightly different view of Movement ideologies is the one put forward several years ago by historian David Gutiérrez in his study of CASA. Attempting to soften the strict opposition between nationalist and socialist currents, Gutiérrez traces a progressive shift in one organization from an ethnic-based *mutualista*-style agenda to one based on Marxist principles of class conflict. According to Gutiérrez, it was not until the 1975 reorganization of CASA that a properly class analysis dominated the group's philosophy: "The contradiction which had been submerged in the rhetoric of the movement since the First National Chicano Youth Conference now more and more became the focus of the movement's internal debates."[99]

Gutiérrez points out that by 1976 and 1977 "a scathing critique of the Chicano movement" appeared in *Sin Fronteras*. CASA argued that the ideology of Aztlán provided only a "narrow and chauvinistic nationalism which excluded anyone not born in the United States."[100] Gutiérrez's phrasing—"a scathing critique of the Chicano movement"—reduces the entire Movement to its regressive nationalist sectors even though it is not clear that the CASA ideologues were painting with such a broad brush. As I have tried to demonstrate, "narrow and chauvinistic nationalism" certainly existed in many Movement organizations but its meaning was widely disputed and its predominance rarely unchallenged so that it often was forced to compete with the inclination to build international and domestic coalitions.

To what extent can we transfer the CASA model as outlined by Gutiérrez to the Movement at large? In many ways, CASA stands as a unique entity whose ideological faultlines are difficult to trace, given that one of its key founders, union organizer Bert Corona, had been sympathetic to international socialist causes consistently from the 1930s (*cardenismo* in Mexico) through the 1950s (July 26th Movement in Cuba).[101] As we have seen, few of the young Movimiento activists in the late 1960s studied Marxist texts early in their political careers. The majority of those who by the mid-1970s espoused some form of socialist or communist thinking had come to those positions after a passage through other ideological frames, in most instances cultural nationalism since cultural nationalist appeals had been the magnet that had drawn many into activism in the first place.

It would be misleading, however, to extrapolate the changes in CASA to other Movement organizations and thus to the Movimiento in its entirety. For my own study, Gutiérrez's analysis is useful insofar as it undermines the notion that socialist thought was "foreign" to Chicano/a political culture. But by suggesting that a "socialist moment" was a belated development that only arose late in the 1970s, Gutiérrez's account makes the existence of a Chicana/o internationalism that was present at the Movement's very origins, e.g. solidarity with socialist Cuba and Viet Nam, more difficult to discern. In subsequent chapters, I trace some of these early internationalist currents within Chicano/a activism.

Towards a Renewed Chicana/o Internationalism

Ay Raza Vieja
Raza nueva y orgullosa
Sun-bronzed and arrogant
Con el Espíritu de Che y Sandino
Con el ardor de Malcolm X y Zapata.

(Ah, Ancient People, proud and renewed, sun-bronzed and arrogant, with the Spirit of Che and Sandino, with the courage of Malcolm X and Zapata.)
—Roberto Vargas, "Segundo Canto" (1969)

In the twenty-first century, international economic and cultural developments are not easily separated from the local conditions in which Spanish-speaking communities struggle against the rollback of civil-rights advances only a generation old and significantly limited life chances for the majority vis-à-vis other sectors of U.S. society. Globalization theory reminds us that the chain of causality for what may appear to be a local problem is linked most assuredly to international corporate agendas.

I say that contemporary theory has only "reminded" us of this fact because intellectual workers with a keen sense of the totalizing capacity of capital have always understood it. In the early 1960s, for example, Malcolm X declared: "Today, power is international, real power is international; today, real power is not local. The only kind of power that can help you and me is international power, not local power. Any power that's local, if it's real power, is only a reflection or a part of that international power. . . . If your power base is only here, you can forget it."[102] Writing out of different circumstances, Chicano essayist Antonio Gomez pointed out: "Indio-Hispanos and Blacks living in the United States cannot be satisfied with improving their economic and social position but must affirm their willingness to work for the elimination of social oppression and economic exploitation of all people throughout the world. This affirmation must be based on the observation that people throughout the world are inextricably united and living in a world community."[103]

Given that texts such as Gomez's were not unusual in the Movement period, I believe the following analysis by Tomás Ybarra-Frausto is misleading. Although it correctly acknowledges Chicano/a internationalism, like so much scholarship of the last twenty years it once again reduces the Movement to the imprecise category of "nationalism," this time in order to contrast it with contemporary discourses of globalization:

A last critique has to do with nationalism. The Chicano movement based its ideology in the ideals of the Mexican revolution, the Cuban revolution, and Third World struggles. We were very conscious of what was going on in Africa, Vietnam, and South Africa. But essentially, ours was a nationalist project. The new project of the nineties is a global project. People are seeing and making connections with Latinos in Latin America and Europe, asking how exiled communities belong in the continental project, the national project, or the local project. The project for the nineties no longer is localized in a nation but is a transnational global project.[104]

The first half of Ybarra-Frausto's remarks belies his assertion that the Movimiento was at its "essence" nationalist, for if thousands of Chicana/os were engaged in an internationalist politics there is certainly no reason to limit our understanding of the Movement to a narrow nationalist agenda. As I have attempted to show throughout this chapter, Chicano/a cultural nationalism functioned as an organizing tool that could point either to sectarian forms of regressive "nationalism" or toward coalition building, solidarity projects, and even socialism. Chicana/o internationalism, then, existed in a complementary and at times conflictive relationship with narrow nationalisms throughout the Viet Nam war period. How that relationship played out depended on specific organizational structures, local conditions, and a rapidly evolving political context.

In 1978, Mexican intellectual Jorge Bustamante foresaw the potential inherent in the internationalist sectors of the Chicano Movement as well as the dangers of a revitalized discourse of assmilationism:

> *Lo que sí es difícil predecir es el camino que seguirán los chicanos después de haber conquistado posiciones de poder, ya no a nivel individual sino de grupo. La alternativa de llegar a obtener una mejor porción en el reparto de la riqueza norteamericana podría llevarlos tanto a una mejoría de sus condiciones materiales de vida como a un reformismo conformista con el sistema existente. Por otro lado, su creciente acceso al poder podría significar para los chicanos un papel preponderante en las luchas del Tercer Mundo y ciertamente de América Latina.[105]*

(What is difficult to predict is the direction Chicanos will take once they have attained positions of power, not only as individuals but as a group. The option of attaining a larger portion of North American wealth may lead them to an improvement in their material conditions but also to a conformist relationship with the existing system. On the other hand, their increasing access to power may mean that Chicanos will play an important role in Third World struggles, especially in Latin America.)

Bustamante's vision of an international role for Chicano/as has yet to be realized. To the extent that the notion of Aztlán was premised upon a progressive global politics as opposed to regressive nationalism, however, we can trace a continuity from the late 1960s to the present. The transnational activist agendas of the late 1990s such as solidarity with the EZLN (Zapatistas), transborder labor movements, and Chicano/a opposition to the U.S. invasion of Iraq in 2003 were less an epistemological break with the Movement agenda than they were an elaboration of its internationalist thrust in a new historical conjuncture.

What was self-evident to Chicano/a organizers in the Viet Nam war era was no less obvious thirty years later—the vast majority of Spanish-speaking people in the United States stood to gain little from North American notions of exceptionalism and empire, the slashing of local and state budgets, and the creation of vast federal deficits for a militarized economy. Although the administration of George W. Bush openly promoted reactionary domestic and foreign-policy agendas, it was during the Clinton presidency that neoconservative ideologues explicitly mapped out a cultural agenda for globalization. Myron Magnet, for example, invoked the hoary notion of "universal civilization" to explain the West's divine mission: "That universal civilization is part and parcel of the globalism toward which the world is irresistibly moving. It is globalism with a Western, not a multicultural, twist. As we increasingly find our fortunes linked to those of the Japanese, the Chinese in Hong Kong, Singapore, and Taiwan, the Koreans, the Latin Americans, the Indians, they become more like us, subscribing to the Western values that underlie Western democratic individualism."[106] Even more fashionable than Magnet's musings, at least in the liberal media and academy, were the writings of philosopher Richard Rorty in which he argued for the superiority of "American" ethnocentrism and "our way of life."[107]

In the wake of the atrocities committed by Saudi Arabian terrorists in New York and Washington, D.C., on September 11, 2001, the echoes of Manifest Destiny resounded even louder. In his 2003 State of the Union speech, President George W. Bush declared: "Americans are a free people, who know that freedom is the right of every person and the future of every nation. The liberty we prize is not America's gift to the world; it is God's gift to humanity."[108] The implication here is clear enough. God gave liberty to humanity. The United States is the interpreter and agent of God's will on earth. The president went on to say: "America is a strong nation and honorable in the use of our strength. We exercise power without conquest, and we sacrifice for the liberty of strangers." Surely the people of Latin America and Iraq would have a different view of the matter.

In a poem written a full fifty years after Paredes's ode to Sandino with which I began this chapter, Cherríe Moraga called for "the dissolution of self, the dissolution of borders" and warned us: "but it is not safe. Ni for me, ni for El Salvador." Moraga's linking of her own identity to that of the embattled Central American nation opens her book *The Last Generation*, one of the most eloquent statements of Chicana internationalism of the last thirty years. In the essay "Art in América con acento," Moraga meditates on the fall of the Sandinista government: "I don't blame the people of Nicaragua. I blame the U.S. government. I blame my complicity as a citizen in a country that, short of an invasion, stole the Nicaraguan revolution that el pueblo forged with their own blood and bones. After hearing the outcome of the elections, I wanted to flee the United States in shame and despair."[109]

Writing at the end of the 1980s, Moraga was compelled to abandon the heroic language of Paredes's poem. Despite the fall of the Spanish republic in 1939, Paredes's poetic voice was underwritten by a still powerful socialist internationalism, and thus was able to dream of a revolutionary future for both Nicaragua and Aztlán. Trapped in the post–Cold War era of Reaganism, Moraga's character could no longer share that dream. When the character accidentally wanders into a pro-Bush, anti-Sandinista demonstration in San Francisco, she can only wonder "*Dónde stá mi pueblo?*"—where are the Chicanos and Chicanas who support anti-imperialist movements in Latin America?

Despite differences of historical context, both the Moraga and Paredes texts share the realization that Latino/as in the United States are often complicit with, and in some cases actively support, U.S. imperial adventures. Moraga's character feels the urge to "flee the United States in shame and despair," a sentiment well known to those who would rather see the most powerful nation in the world adhere to its own enlightened principles. But an immigrant recently arrived from Mexico or Latin America may sense no disconnect between the reality and the promise of "American democracy." On the contrary, he or she may be anxious to assimilate into what is an infinitely better situation than the one they have left behind. Thus the many "green card" (noncitizen) or recently naturalized immigrants who join the U.S. military in order to demonstrate their "gratitude." The complex heterogeneity of ethnic Mexican communities does not allow for the easy formulation of a coherent Chicano/a political agenda. Given the massive influx of Latino/a immigrants during the decade of the 1990s and the radical turn to the right of U.S. political culture, the prospects for a new phase of radical Chicano/a internationalism seem distant.

Nevertheless, Chicano/a internationalism continues to function as a pedagogical device for understanding our own situatedness in relation to other communities of color within the United States. At the same time, our understanding of movements against corporate globalization in other parts of the world allows us to rethink battles considered to be already lost in the U.S. context. Here I am thinking, for example, of the

1999 strike at the National Autonomous University of Mexico (UNAM) in which courageous high school and college students faced head-on the issues of privatization in public institutions, government corruption, and the exclusionary consequences of standardized testing.

The example of the UNAM strikers reflects back to many of us our own passivity as Chicano/a faculty and graduate students in the increasingly corporate and elitist North American university. Have we been active enough in opposing attacks on affirmative action, unfair tuition hikes, or supporting staff and student struggles for unionization? Because the vast majority of university faculty will avoid local activism for a variety of self-serving reasons, it is often appealing for them to make abstract gestures toward events taking place elsewhere in the world. What I am calling international solidarity is not a comfortable cosmopolitanism but rather an active engagement with local struggles understood within a progressive analysis of global conditions. Or, to put it in a more precious academic language, a multivalenced politics of location that recuperates the much maligned idea of totality.

Moraga's *Last Generation* is a literary testament to the kind of international solidarity that will be needed in coming years if the Chicano community wants more for itself than cell phones, e-trading, and token celebrity role models. I conclude this chapter, however, by insisting that the language of Moraga's argument leads us down a precarious path that I will call "The Possessive Investment in Race." Moraga writes: "We must learn to see ourselves less as U.S. citizens and more as members of a larger world community composed of many nations of people and no longer give credence to the geopolitical borders that have divided us, Chicano from Mexicano, Filipino American from Pacific Islander, African American from Haitian." So far so good. Moraga continues: "Call it racial memory. Call it shared economic discrimination. Chicanos call it 'Raza'—be it Quichua, Cubano, or Colombian—an identity that dissolves borders."[110]

A term like *racial memory* may indeed dissolve national borders as Moraga claims, but it does not in any way attack the problem of economic stratification and inequality. As teachers and activists, we need to be cautious about recycling terms from a racializing language most closely associated with nineteenth-century scientific racism or those thinkers like José Vasconcelos who reacted against scientific racism but remained dangerously within its terms. What undesirable baggage does a concept like "racial memory" bring to contemporary debates? What precisely is a "racial memory" in the context of Moraga's proposed internationalism? How will a "people of color" solidarity withstand the divisions between Chicanas and right-wing Miami Cubans, Chicanos and the Mexican ruling class, Chicanos and conservative Hispanics?

Moraga has the courage to name economic discrimination. One ought not efface that issue by granting it equal status with the metaphysical concept of "racial memory" but rather insist that economic justice on a worldwide scale be part of every discussion about Latino politics in the next century. This must occur especially in the educational sphere where working-class youth have limited access to university educations and too often are tracked into low-tech futures, hazardous military duty, or prison.

At the same time, tenured Latino/a faculty who enjoy a generalized class privilege (in large part due to the successes of the Movimiento) ought to be attentive to hierarchies of labor within the university— part-time and junior faculty in relation to endowed chairs; to inequalities based on gender and sexuality; to the unequal distribution of symbolic capital—the so-called star system; to a still uninterrogated elitism—research institutions versus so-called teaching colleges. In short, our analytical tools must be turned onto the ways in which academic programs created thirty years ago by mass social movements, e.g. Chicano/a Studies, today either participate in or challenge capitalist structures of exploitation and market values.[111] An internationalist agenda for Aztlán would seek to understand local struggles for and within Chicano/a Studies in their widest possible context, remembering the inescapable fact that the unequal distribution of symbolic and material resources will not be the only problem but surely one of the fundamental problems of the twenty-first century.

In the next chapter, we will see how one of the major events of twentieth-century Latin American history resonated throughout the barrios of the Southwest. The example of the Cuban Revolution and more specifically the figure of Ernesto Che Guevara ignited the sense of urgency I have described and drove many young Chicanos and Chicanas to throw off their apathy and join in the pursuit of dignity and equality. More important, it sowed the seeds of a broader political vision that looked beyond the barrio to struggles taking place around the world.

CHAPTER THREE

—"TU QUERIDA PRESENCIA"—

Che is fairly intellectual for a Latino.
—Central Intelligence Agency Information Report
(February 13, 1958)

It was indeed fitting that the 1960s should be ushered in by an event that not only went on to contribute to later global radicalism but also foretold, in its early euphoria, the rebelliousness of that decade.

—Antoni Kapcia

IN CHICANO PERFORMANCE GROUP Culture Clash's brilliant 1992 comedy skit, "The Return of Ché!," the figure of Che Guevara miraculously appears in the Berkeley apartment of Chuy, the part-time activist and full-time *vato loco*. With a massive reproduction of the classic 1960 Korda photograph of a stern and ominous Che as a backdrop, Chuy explains to the *comandante* that he is not a Mexican but a Chicano. A puzzled Che inquires: "Chicano? What is a Chicano?"[1]

In an ironic twist of history, the figure of Ernesto Che Guevara would become from the mid-1960s to the present a powerful sign in the ideological repertoire of Chicano art and politics. That the real-life Guevara knew very little about Mexicans in the United States should not surprise us given that the Chicano/a community did not emerge as a self-determined historical agent until the mid-1960s. It was precisely at that moment when the Chicano Movement appeared on the stage of world history that Guevara undertook covert guerrilla operations in the Congo and later Bolivia, where he was eventually murdered in October of 1967.

Culture Clash's portrait of Guevara (as performed by Herbert Sigüenza) builds upon the Korda photograph's representation of a severe Guevara by making him a Mexican revolutionary wrapped in bandoleras of ammunition who shouts loudly and wildly waves a rifle (figs. 3–4). As we will see, it is this defiant and threatening image, what Mario Benedetti called in his poem "Che 1997" "*la rabia embalsamada*" ("embalmed rage") that dominates all others in the Chicano iconography of Che.[2] A figure

3. Original photograph by Alberto Díaz Gutiérrez ("Korda"), March 5, 1960. Used courtesy of Museo Ken Damy, Brescia, Italy.

4. "Che Guevara" played by Herbert Sigüenza of Culture Clash. Photo by Craig Schwartz. Used by permission of photographer.

that embodied the Chicano community's collective frustrations and anger, the visual image of the "Chicano Che" would gather to itself a relatively limited but fundamental set of cultural and political meanings.

But the image of Guevara was only the most visible sign of Chicano/a activism's relationship to what had been accomplished in Cuba in 1959. In the final years of Chicano/a militancy in 1979, San Antonio poet Alfredo de la Torre condensed the general sense of what revolutionary Cuba had meant for many young Chicana/os:

> **EL GRITO**
> *y dicen que Fidel*
> *es comunista,*
> *porque no les tiene*
> *miedo a los gringos*
> *pos aunque*
> *sea comunista*
> *QUE VIVA*
> *la revolución*
> *Cubana.*

> ("**THE SHOUT**" And they say Fidel is a communist because he's not afraid of the Americans. Well, even if he is a communist, LONG LIVE the Cuban Revolution)[3]

As ethnic Mexicans raised and educated in the United States, Chicanos and Chicanas of the 1960s generation found themselves deeply immersed in the Cold War ideologies of the period. De la Torre's poem suggests, however, that for some the appeal of revolutionary Cuba held the potential to trump any "fear" of communism that exacerbated the reluctance shared by a vast majority of Mexican Americans to challenge U.S. policymakers. For a small minority of ethnic Mexican youth on barrio streets and the very few found on college campuses in the early and mid-1960s, an admiration for Che and the entire Cuban experience signaled a new questioning of Cold War common sense.

It was not so much that these young men and women were committed socialists or that they possessed even the most rudimentary understanding of the history of Cuba and the complex meaning of events there in 1959 and after. Part of a global phenomenon in which progressives in the "First World" projected their utopian desires for a more just society on to the fledgling Cuban experiment (with the best-known examples ranging from Jean Paul Sartre to C. Wright Mills), some Chicano/as saw in Cuba an alternative model to the North American system in which they no longer believed. In most cases, however, the attraction to the Cuban Revolution and to Che emerged from less complicated reactions. According to one of my activist friends: "*Son los únicos que le dieron en la madre al gabacho*" ("They're the only ones who gave hell to the Americans").

A statement such as this leads us to delve deeper into the reasons behind the Chicano/a identification with Che instead of with some other revolutionary figure of the period. Any attempt to sort out the multiple origins of the Chicano/a appropriation of the Che figure is destined to be incomplete. That incompleteness, however, does not diminish the evocative power and historical importance of the "Chicano Che." It should not surprise us that the assassination of Guevara on October 9, 1967, coincided with the period in which new Chicano/a identities were taking shape and the emergence of an urgent radicalism was spreading across the Southwest. The Los Angeles Brown Berets (formerly the Young Citizens for Community Action and Young Chicanos for Community Action) adopted the beret precisely in the autumn of 1967. In New Mexico, key members of Reies López Tijerina's *Alianza* (see Chapter Five) and the Black Berets organization understood enough about what Cuba signified in the context of U.S.-Latin American relations to know that the status of Latinos in the United States was part of a related historical process. A small group of activists/scholars in southern California such as Rodolfo Acuña, Carlos Muñoz, Jr., and Juan Gómez Quiñones were students of Latin American history and had studied with Marxist faculty in Los Angeles and San Diego. By the time of the first Chicano Youth Liberation Conference in March of 1969, the image of Che had become a staple at most Movimiento gatherings.

If the legacy of the Mexican Revolution and leaders such as Francisco Villa and Emiliano Zapata formed the foundation of the new Chicano history, for some Che and Fidel stood in as younger and contemporary exemplars of the Latin American revolutionary tradition. Unlike the Mexican example, the Cuban model was seen (rightly or wrongly) as immune to institutionalization, more flexible, and more open to the challenges and expectations of a new generation. The youth and style of Che in particular, including his legendary status as a *guer-rilla* but also his long hair, beard, and beret, offered young Chicano men a prototype for an alternative masculinity that contrasted sharply with the one practiced by their fathers and grandfathers. At the same time, the image of Che in the edited version of the famous 1960 Korda photograph that had been circulated around the world by an Italian publisher became one of the first international glamour photographs of the 1960s and a requisite accessory for every political demonstration.[4]

I am certainly not suggesting that Chicano/as adopted and customized the Che image merely as a fashion statement even though it is true that Mexican American youth might never have known about Che if not for the posterized version of the Korda photograph. Below the surface of subcultural appearances and romanticized affinities one finds more substantial correspondences between the emergent Movimiento and the Cuban revolutionary experiment. It is not so much that these correspondences were fully articulated by Movement thinkers, although in this chapter we shall see many artistic and philosophical manifestations of a strong affective relationship. Rather than direct influences, we must speak about a diffuse ideological kinship composed of multiple discourses that were shared by progressive social movements during the Viet Nam war period.

Central to this discursive field in the Chicano context were the images of individual leaders—César Chávez but also Zapata, Villa, Sandino, and Che Guevara—that far from being the frozen icons they may have become in later decades were living signifiers for the utopian desire of many young people around the world. Moreover, Cuba stood as the foremost Latin American example of decolonization and anti-U.S. imperialism at an historical moment in which some sectors of the Movement were moving toward a "Third World" position (as I discussed in the previous chapter). While the case of Viet Nam was the most urgent, for many Chicano/as it was logical that the example of Cuba would become even more important. If the founders of the New Left, for the most part white and middle class, adopted Cuba and Che as symbols from the "South" to be emulated in the "North," Chicano/a youth who understood their community's historical predicament took Cuba and Che to be signs of resistance taken from the "South" to be deployed by the "South" in the "North" (i.e., Chicano communities "*en las entrañas del monstruo*" or "belly of the beast").

More specifically, it was at the level of ideology that Chicano/a activists encountered important parallels. At the core of the Cuban revolutionary process, for example, was an anticolonial discourse that historian Antoni Kapcia has called "a code of moralism."[5] As a sign for a renewed and secularized moralism designed to purge Cuban society of corruption and dependency, socialist Cuba signified for many progressives around the world a restoration of dignity for a formerly colonized nation, an unyielding commitment to self-determination, and the practice of service and sacrifice directly linked to the *pueblo* or common people.

Nowhere was this discourse more fully embodied than in the figure of Che, particularly after his death. Cuban philosopher Cintio Vitier has written that Cuba's long tradition of "revolutionary ethics," with its origins in José Martí, combines an insistence on sovereignty with the proposed transformation of the individual accomplished through a commitment to a larger social good. According to Vitier, the greatest contemporary expression ("*máxima expresión contemporánea*") of that ethic is Ernesto Che Guevara who had written in his *El socialismo y el hombre en Cuba* (1965): "*Todos los días hay que luchar porque ese amor a la humanidad viviente se transforme en hechos concretos, en actos que sirvan de ejemplo, de movilización*" ("One must struggle every day so that the love of living humanity can be transformed into concrete deeds that serve as a model and contribute to activism").[6] This statement, standing alone and placed in the appropriate context, might just as easily be attributed to César Chávez himself who at the same moment was mobilizing one sector of the Mexican American community with a similar message.

In fact, dignity, self-determination, and service either to the working class or to an abstract notion of "la Raza" were key concepts in a majority of Chicano organizations. These ideals would be enacted through a variety of hybrid practices depending on location and under the pressure of North American capitalist and "Anglo" hegemony. On one level, the armed nature of the Cuban Revolution as it was represented by the figure of Che stood in direct contrast to the pacifist César Chávez. But what other leader in the Chicano context better represented the discourse of moralism as it had been elaborated around the figure of Che?

Although Chávez's role in the Movimiento was (and continues to be) controversial for some activists, it was widely accepted that his role as a moral compass for an array of Chicano political agendas was decisive (see Chapter Four). Despite the vast historical and material differences that separated Cuba and the U.S. Southwest and the dissimilar social movements that produced Guevara and Chávez, powerful ideological resonances would flow directly from the "idea" of revolutionary Cuba into Chicano/a radical art and writing and in the process give birth to the Chicano Che.

Rooted in discourses of anticolonialism, youth culture, and what I am calling moralism, the Chicano Che was not merely a "symbol" but a charged sign for emergent Chicano political struggles. It not my intention in this chapter to write a political history of Chicano/a contact with socialist Cuba. The fact that Maoist and Trotskyite doctrines competed for the attention of Chicano/a activists is less important for the present study than the function of the image of Che at the level of discursive practices. Although I will refer to the actual experiences of the small number of Mexican Americans who visited Cuba during the Viet Nam war period, these visits formed only one part of the subtext for the elaboration of Movement ideologies. No less important were the multiple cultural objects drawn from poetry, the visual arts, and especially muralism that concretized the meaning of Che and Cuba for Chicano/a activists.

As we shall see, it was through cultural production that the Che image was "mexicanized" and finally "chicanoized" in a process of "customization" typical of "politico-historical myths."[7] According to Kapcia, such mythic figures "distil what is a complex, and often necessarily contradictory, system of beliefs in comprehensible form—comprehensible because it is expressed in a single figure, event or symbol with which the collectivity can identify itself readily, since the subject of the myth is seen to express the core value, or values, that constitute the agreed ideology."[8] In the case of the Chicano Che, the role of culture will be central since as I have already noted actual contact between Cuba and Chicano/as was limited to a very small number of activists.

The impulse on the part of some Chicana/o activists to discover direct links between Che and the Movement, however, was at times so strong that it produced spurious writings such as the "Letter to the Youth of the United States," published in New Mexico in 1973 with an attached note from the editor: "The following is a letter said to have been written by Ernesto 'Che' Guevara. How it reached the movement in the U.S. and whether it was really written by Che cannot be verified. But it is so much in El Che's spirit, that we present it." Calling North American youth to contribute to international revolutionary projects, the letter states: "To achieve that world revolution you, the children of the Yankees, must lend a hand."[9] Although clearly not written by Guevara, the letter was symptomatic of the strong affective ties that had been forged between militant Chicano/as and el Che. More important for my argument here is that the letter was suggestive of the Movement's pan-Latino genealogy in which for some activists the Cuban Revolution played a key role.

In his 1974 poem, Roberto "Che" Luera, theater director for the Crusade for Justice's Escuela Tlatelolco, narrated the history of the Cuban Revolution for a Chicano/a audience, taking literally the example of armed struggle:

CUBA: TIERRA DE LIBERTAD

Los gritos de la gente de Cuba
se oían por todo el hemisferio.
Gritos de angustia!
gritos de hambre!
gritos de opresión!
Ayúdame! Ayúdame!
las voces decían.
Y el títere Batista riéndose
y el gusano encajado en la tierra
      Sí mi gente. Yo las oigo.
Y en México hombres se juntan
un abogado, un doctor y varios más
Entrenamiento de guerrillas
y la "Granma" sale a Cuba
      Sí mi gente. Yo las oigo.
Sangre derramada en la playa
y doce siguen la pelea
Ya no abogado ni doctor
pero comandantes con valor
Los tremendos siguieron a los dos
Fidel y Che peleadores con honor.
      Sí mi gente. Yo las oigo.
Ni ejército ni imperialista
es fuerza contra la gente
y la gente grita "Libertad!"
y la gente toma el poder!
      Sí mi gente. Yo las oigo.

Y Batista ya no es
el títere ya se fue
en la tierra gusanos ya no hay
pero en Miami sí los hay
y en Denver también
En Cuba ya no hay gritos de tristeza
pero gritos entusiasmados
y el yanki encabronado
y el OEA en el lado
El embargo no mata
a la gente preparada y armada
Ahora Cuba escucha
los gritos del hemisferio
y Che murió en Bolivia
Comandante Fidel llevas la pelea
más Cubas habrán
        Sí mi gente. Yo las oigo.
Y sus angustias jamás serán.

Gente de Aztlán
sus gritos de odio se oyen
sus esfuerzos de pelea se sienten
y el yanki no escucha
pero sí siente.
Sí Cuba, Tierra de Libertad
tu ejemplo se tiene que tomar
ni imperialista, ni gusana, ni vendido
nos puede parar.
        Sí mi gente. Yo las oigo.
con fusil en mano yo las oigo
Y Aztlán será tierra de Libertad! (Luera 1974, n.p.)

("Cuba: Land of Liberty." The cries of the Cuban people are heard across the hemisphere. Cries of anguish! Cries of hunger! Cries of oppression! Help me! Help me! The voices say. And Batista the puppet is laughing and the maggot is hidden in the earth. Yes, my people. I hear them. And in Mexico men gather, a lawyer, a doctor, and others. Guerrilla training and the

"Granma" sails for Cuba. Yes, my people. I hear them. Blood
spilled on the beach and the Twelve continue fighting. No longer
lawyer or doctor but brave Comandantes. The great ones follow
the pair, Fidel and Che, warriors with honor. Yes. My people. I
hear them. Neither army or imperialist can defeat the people and
the people cry "Freedom!" and the people take power. Yes, my
people. I hear them. And Batista is no longer, the puppet is gone,
maggots no longer in the earth but now in Miami and in Denver
too. In Cuba no more cries of sadness but enthusiastic cries. And
the yankee furious and the OAS cast off. The embargo cannot kill
those who are armed and prepared. Now Cuba hears the cries of
the hemisphere and Che died in Bolivia. Comandante Fidel continues the fight; there will be more Cubas. Yes, my people. I hear
them. And the anguish will end. People of Aztlán, your cries of
hate are heard, your struggles are felt and the yankee cannot hear
but feels. Yes, Cuba, Land of Liberty, your example must be followed. Neither imperialist or maggot or sell-out can stop us. Yes,
my people. I hear them. And Aztlán will be a land of liberty!)

Luera's call to create "more Cubas" echoes Guevara's widely circulated
remarks on the need to create "more Viet Nams," and the poem suggests
that the rifle will be taken up against counter-revolutionary forces in
both Miami and Denver.[10] For the vast majority of young Chicanas and
Chicanos, however, the significance of Guevara and Cuba for the
Chicano Movement had little to do with reproducing the revolutionary
process inside the United States but rather with the indirect and
immeasurable ways the man and the revolution inspired some Mexican
Americans to shed decades of colonial inhibitions in order to struggle
for dignity and self-determination.

Revolutionary Cuba and the Chicano Movement

Having no real leaders of our own, we accept Fidel Castro."
    —Luis Valdez and Roberto Rubalcava, "Venceremos

In this chapter, I continue the process of rethinking the Chicano
Movement of the late 1960s and early 1970s not as a self-enclosed
"nationalist" project with historical beginning and end but as one

episode in an ongoing story of Chicano/a efforts to link domestic and international struggles for social justice. From this perspective, the origins of the Movement itself extend further back than we have been led to believe and its "conclusion" lies somewhere in the unknown future. In the same way that early Mexican American ties to radical Mexican and Central American struggles in the 1940s and 1950s are the antecedents of the Movement's support of revolutionary Cuba and Viet Nam, so too does Chicano/a internationalism of the Movement period point forward to the experiences of young Latino/as in Central American solidarity groups in the 1980s, Zapatista support networks in the 1990s, and anti-war organizing during the 2003 U.S. invasion and occupation of Iraq.

In this longer view, then, the Movimiento was far more than simply a series of isolated "militant particularisms" mired in sectarian nationalism and divided by issues of region, gender, and class. The delicate equilibrium sustained by many Chicano/a activists throughout the late 1960s and early 1970s demonstrates the richness of Movement thought and belies any simple reduction of the period to a narrow ideological agenda (e.g. "*Mi Raza primero*" or "*La batalla está aquí*") although activists may have deployed such agendas at the appropriate time and place.

Writing in 1971, an anonymous student at the University of California, San Diego, urged Chicano/a youth to move beyond identities based solely on ethnic difference and offered an historical precedent: "We must be leery of nationalism. At one time it did serve a purpose, that of getting a group of people to realize who the enemy was, but now it can be dangerous in the sense that it can get oppressed people fighting each other, Chicano vs. Asiatic, Asiatic vs. Black, etc. . . . Our spirit of revolution should be like Che Guevara's. He was born in Argentina, became a revolutionary in Mexico, fought in Cuba, and died in Bolivia. In each place he served, he belonged to the people."[11]

Although it is not my intention to write a political history of the "Chicano left," one key episode from the Cold War period involving Mexican American progressives is noteworthy. Among the earliest contacts between participants in the Cuban Revolution and activists later associated with the Chicano Movement occurred in San Francisco in the mid-1950s when longtime labor organizer Bert Corona and members of the Asociación Nacional México-Americana (ANMA) participated in fund-raising events for the July 26th Movement attended by Camilo Cienfuegos, one of the future heroes of the Cuban Revolution.[12]

Cienfuegos originally had traveled to New York for economic reasons in the summer of 1953, where he worked at a variety of odd jobs under the assumed name "Ramón Ruiz" in order to evade immigration officials. After one month in Chicago, he made his way to San Francisco where he met and married *salvadoreña* Isabel Blandón and came into close contact with Mexican immigrants and Mexican American workers. In a letter to his family dated October 4, 1954, Cienfuegos wrote: "*Este papel está regado no más, pero mire usted mano, ya me enmejicanisé, aquí hay creo 90 millones de mexicanos que, por cierto, sí son buena gente, es una big diferencia a la canalla de New York. Tengo que terminar para ir a comerme unos tacos o unas enchiladas, pues estoy delgadísimo*" ("This paper is lousy but look here bro' I'm already mexicanized, there are some 90 million Mexicans here, and for sure they are good people, it's a big difference compared to the bums in New York. I have to sign off so I can go eat some tacos and enchiladas 'cause I'm super skinny").[13] Eventually detained by immigration authorities, Cienfuegos would spend thirty-nine days in close contact with undocumented Mexican immigrants in the INS detention facility in Chula Vista (San Diego) before being deported. He returned to San Francisco ("San Pancho, Califas," as he wrote in one letter) in the spring of 1956 where he participated in the political events in support of the July 26 Movement. By September of that year, Camilo was in Mexico City where he belatedly joined Fidel Castro, Che Guevara, and others who had just completed preparations for the *Granma* expedition.

After the defeat of the Batista dictatorship in January of 1959, revolutionary Cuba would come under continual attack from U.S. government agencies. By October, the Eisenhower administration already was supporting exiled Cubans in their efforts to overthrow the new government. In January of 1960, the CIA established Task Force WH/4 (chaired by the same agent who had organized the overthrow of the democratically elected Guatemalan government in 1954) with the specific goal of removing Castro from power. After over a year of extensive U.S.-backed training in Florida and Guatemala, a mercenary force was considered ready. On April 14, 1961, President Kennedy authorized the first air strikes, and the Playa Girón (Bay of Pigs) invasion began. Six days later, the Cuban military had defeated the last remnants of the "expeditionary force." The following day, Kennedy assumed responsibility for the fiasco.[14]

Latino responses to the Bay of Pigs invasion varied widely. As strong supporters of Kennedy, Mexican Americans were not eager to criticize him in public.[15] But in every Latin American country, anti-U.S. demonstrations denounced the U.S. attempt to invoke the Monroe Doctrine and impose its will on Cuba. In Mexico, for example, massive protests continued throughout the week of the invasion; on the third day after the initial landings, twenty-five thousand demonstrators filled the Zócalo in Mexico City. From El Paso/Juarez, *Los Angeles Times* reporter Ruben Salazar filed a report on a large protest against the Cuban invasion.[16] In the San Francisco Bay Area, University of California students marched in support of revolutionary Cuba. Although we cannot know for certain how many Chicanos and Chicanas of the Movement generation were initiated into political activism at these events, many of them sponsored by local Fair Play for Cuba committees, U.S. aggression against Cuba resounded widely in Chicano communities.

In Los Angeles in 1959, New Mexican Delfino Varela, who had moved to southern California in 1955, was interrogated at hearings held by the Committee on Un-American Activities. According to official intelligence reports, Varela was an active member of the so-called Zapata section of the Communist Party, whose mission was to recruit Mexican Americans.[17] Whether or not such charges were true and whether or not such a CP program existed, it was a fact that Varela was one of the most dedicated Chicano activists throughout the Movimiento period. At the other end of the ideological spectrum, the Bloque Anti-comunista Latinoamericano, a group of recently arrived Cuban exiles and former Batista supporters, attempted to recruit members in Los Angeles to join the rapidly failing invasion. Mexican American World War II hero Guy Gabaldón, who had founded what he called the "Drive Against Communism" and reportedly had once exclaimed "I'd gladly give my life if I could personally assassinate Fidel Castro," offered his services. But Gabaldón's views were too extreme even for the anticommunist Cubans and they soon distanced themselves from him.[18]

The summer of 1964 marked a turning point in the thinking of several young Chicano students from San Jose State College in California who in the coming years would exercise a powerful cultural influence on the Chicano Movement. Upon returning from a visit to Cuba organized by the Progressive Labor Party, Luis Valdez and Roberto Rubalcava issued a "Mexican American statement on travel to Cuba" in which they made the connection between the colonized status of the Chicano community and the U.S. imperial presence in Latin America:

The Mexican in the United States has been, and continues to be, no less a victim of American imperialism than his impoverished brothers in Latin America. In the words of the Second Declaration of Havana, tell him of "misery, feudal exploitation, illiteracy, starvation wages," and he will tell you that you speak of Texas; tell him of "unemployment, the policy of repression against the workers, discrimination . . . oppression by the oligarchies," and he will tell you that you speak of California; tell him of U.S. domination in Latin America, and he will tell you that he knows that Shark and what he devours, because he has lived in its very entrails.[19]

Narrating the conquest of the Southwest from 1838 on and invoking José Martí's famous "belly of the beast," Valdez and Rubalcava situated Chicano issues within the larger context of Latin American history, and argued that "the example of Cuba will inevitably bring socialist revolution to the whole of Latin America."[20]

The implication, of course, was that the revolution would extend north of the U.S.-Mexican border to include the Spanish-speaking populations of the Southwest. Although the revolution did not come to pass, the Valdez/Rubalcava statement on Cuba was one of the first radical Chicano proclamations that broke decisively with the World War II generation's more accomodationist stance with respect to U.S. foreign policy. Indeed, historian Carlos Muñoz, Jr., has argued: "the manifesto represented a radical departure from the political thought of the Mexican-American Generation and a harsh critique of its political leadership."[21]

Within a year, the exuberance of Valdez and Rubalcava would be redirected away from Cuba and toward the emerging Chicano Movement as it was taking shape in the activities of the United Farm Workers, the Crusade for Justice, the Mexican American Youth Organization (MAYO), and other militant organizations. A handful of Chicano/a activists who had preceded Valdez and Rubalcava to Cuba continued to visit the island. Elizabeth Sutherland Martinez, for example, had been in revolutionary Cuba as early as 1959.

A former UN researcher, book editor for *The Nation* magazine, organizer for SNCC, and publisher of *El Grito del Norte* newspaper, "Betita" Martinez found in the Cuban experiment a series of lessons for U.S. Latinos and other people of color. Her 1961 report in *The Nation* on the first National Congress of Cuban Writers and Artists outlined the tensions between a democratic socialist cultural policy and a more rigid Soviet-style approach.[22] In July of 1967, she accompanied Stokley Carmichael and other members of SNCC to Havana to attend the meeting of the Organization of Latin American Solidarity.[23] The book that resulted from that experience is today one of the most perceptive analyses of Cuban society ever written by a U.S. intellectual. If the vast majority of emerging Chicano leaders and artists acted upon a relatively superficial identification with the revolution, often limited by an attraction to hypermasculinist and militarized figures of Fidel and Che, Martinez fully engaged the complex issues of race, class, and gender as they were being transformed in socialist Cuba.

Martinez's book, *The Youngest Revolution: A Personal Report on Cuba*, published under the name Elizabeth Sutherland, is a brilliant combination of ethnographic research, travel writing, and cultural-political analysis. Openly sympathetic to the revolution, Martinez nevertheless introduces the reader to the multiple contradictions facing Cuban society in 1967. Whereas some advances had been made, much remained to be done, and the book's overall tone is one of a commitment to progressive change and hope for the future. According to Martinez, Che's theory of the "New Man," who would be more interested in the collective good than his own comfort, would eventually be joined by a "New Woman" who would function as an equal partner in building a more humane society. Martinez wrote: "Along with all the theories and institutions, there were individual educators in Cuba whose humanism and strength made it seem possible for a new consciousness to evolve."[24]

In the chapter "Colony within the Colony," Martinez describes in nuanced fashion the issue of race relations since the revolution, and explains how changes in official policy would not be enough to eliminate centuries of racial bias produced by colonization. While some orthodox Marxists continued to subordinate the question of race to that of class, Martinez found in the Cuban experience the potential for a more complex model:

Although a class analysis may work better for Cuba than other nations, it still misses the mark. It fails to take into account the long-range effects of the double colonization of blacks, the variety of exploitation from one race to another, the fact that racism cuts across class lines. . . . Only a combination of the two analyses can explain the total reality of racism and point the way to full liberation. This would be a truly dialectical, revolutionary analysis.[25]

In her next chapter, "The Longest Revolution," Martinez further refines her argument by introducing gender relations as a site of struggle in Cuban society. The *testimonios* of young Cuban women gives Martinez's account the sense of reality that was often lacking in U.S. writings in support of Cuba. The reader can almost feel the energy of the Cuban women as they grapple with the promise of their new situation and with obstacles from the past: "These two young women recognized that women had been oppressed both culturally and economically; that, as in the case of racism, the cultural factors had acquired a force of their own so great that their automatic disappearance under socialism should not be taken for granted. But socialism provides the only basis for true liberation, they believed."[26]

As a complex representation of a specific historical moment, *The Youngest Revolution* stands as unquestionably the most sophisticated Chicano/a response to what was taking place in Cuba and what Mexican Americans and progressives in general might learn from it. But Martinez's study of Cuba was not well disseminated in Chicano Movement circles.[27] For the relatively few Chicano/a college students and faculty during the late 1960s, a book like C. Wright Mills's *Listen, Yankee: The Revolution in Cuba* (1960) might have been better known. In retrospect, however, it is clear that it was Martinez's book that prophetically announced many of the issues that would concern Chicano/a studies scholars from the 1970s well into the 1990s, in particular how to devise a method for understanding culture and politics that might negotiate the intersections of class, race, gender, and sexuality without reducing the analysis to a single axis.

For Martinez, the Cuban experiment was much more than a national independence movement. It was both nationalist and internationalist, and dared to propose a system of social relations completely outside capitalism. The Cubans' attempt to eradicate structural racism resonated strongly with a Chicana who had begun her activist career as a young woman by traveling to Monroe, North Carolina, in order to join the Robert Williams Defense Fund. Like the Mexican Revolution before it, the example of the Cuban Revolution could remind Chicano/as that Washington, D.C., would attempt to crush any and all struggles for self-determination by Latino peoples.[28]

The collaboration between Martinez, Beverly Axelrod, Enriqueta Longeaux y Vásquez, and other progressives connected to the *El Grito del Norte* newspaper in northern New Mexico led to consistently internationalist editorializing in support of the Cuban Revolution. Longeaux y Vásquez's own experience in Cuba in 1969 produced a two-part report in which she expressed her enthusiasm for what she had witnessed, from educational policy to literary campaigns to the concept of *"el hombre nuevo"*: "The idea of the new man (and new woman) is the realization that human beings have no limit for development. They have great capacity. They can be unselfish, and without *envidia* [envy]. They can all work together for the common good. They can be freed from the pressure of getting money, and become real humans instead of work-machines."[29] The Cuban struggle to build an open socialist society made ideological sense to many Chicano/a Movement activists who themselves were engaged in a political project for self-determination and the reimagining of relations of gender, "race," class, and their own relationship to U.S. liberalism and capitalism.

Eight months after the first National Chicano Youth Liberation Conference organized in Denver by the Crusade for Justice, the Cuban government initiated a project that would bring numerous young people from around the world to the island—the Venceremos Brigades. Departing from Mexico City on November 28 and December 1, 1969, and from New Brunswick, Canada, on February 13, 1970, the first groups of *brigadistas* included several Chicanos and Chicanas, among them Beatriz Pesquera, Leonor de la Cruz, Ernesto Collosi, Ron Uriarte (all from California) and Roberto Contreras of New Mexico.[30] The Cuban insistence upon having equitable gender and ethnic distribution in the brigades meant that African Americans, Asian Americans, and U.S. Latinos would learn not only the specifics of Cuban socialism but also would have to confront their own cultural biases and blindness. Issues of sexism and racism at times pitted Brigade members against one another, even as they labored with international contingents in the sugar harvest and citrus groves. As the recruitment brochure for the 1971 Brigada stated:

La Brigada Venceremos is an organization of solidarity with the Cuban Revolution and the Third World struggles around the world as well as within the U.S. We know that in their struggle to liberate themselves, our revolutionary brothers and sisters in the Third World are in fact liberating us; and that by building up our struggle here, we become part of the worldwide effort to defeat imperialism and to guarantee the right of self-determination of all people.[31]

Central to Brigade activities were the so-called Third World Seminars in which Chicano/as were exposed to representatives from Viet Nam and other developing countries in Africa and Latin America who, in turn, learned about Chicano history and contemporary events. The seminar presented by the Chicano caucus in the 1970 Brigade spoke about the Denver Youth Conference, high school blowouts across the Southwest, the New Mexico land-grant movement, the December 1969 and February 1970 Chicano Moratorium Committee antiwar demonstrations, and the distinction between "cultural nationalism and nationalism within a political and revolutionary context." The seminar ended with the following declaration: "Our political activities have now transcended reformist demands. Now the U.S. government knows that before it tries another Bay of Pigs, it will first have to contend with the Southwest. Chicanos will help bring the struggle of liberation home to Latin Americans within the United States."[32]

Once the more utopian rhetoric subsided, North American brigadistas found that the Cuban emphasis on collective agency in a revolutionary context challenged their deep-seated individualism and previous identities. As one of the first Chicano brigadistas, Ron Uriarte, later recalled: "It filled my heart with love to know that I could meet the Cubans through the brothers and sisters on the trip—love, hope, and aspirations for the whole Brigade, the whole movement, and the whole expression of internationalism."[33]

For these Chicanas and Chicanos, the Cuban Revolution signified an act of self-determination and collective agency, the lessons of which could be used to construct a radical Chicano/a consciousness: "The Cuban people are on their legs. They stand erect, you know, and they have a lot of pride. But people back home are still, you know, still doubtful about what they are. They're still talking about color, talking about status and position. We have to keep in mind that there are people back home that have to be liberated and this is where we have to go—back home, to liberate our own."[34] Returning to San Diego after his experience in the 1970 Brigada, Chicano activist Carlos Calderón told the University of California, San Diego, newspaper *Third World*: "The capitalists, in essence, are afraid that Chicanos and Cubanos will not only relate to one another on the basis of common heritage but also on the basis of common problems and common solutions."[35]

Out of his experience as a brigadista in 1975 and again in 1977, poet raúlrsalinas composed a collection entitled *Simplemente, Cuadernos Cubanos*. The poems chronicle salinas's reaction to the Cuban socialist project, which he had witnessed firsthand at the Campamento Julio Antonio Mella and which he had explored in discussions with Cuban intellectuals. Having spent a great deal of his youth in prison and as a key player in Chicano and Native American social movements, salinas understood Cuba to be a model for Chicano/as with which they might analyze their own predicament: "Bajo Cuban skies/those yanqui-fabri-cated lies/will penetrate our social state/(of mind!)/no more."[36]

By the mid-1970s, a variety of Chicano political organizations were operating throughout the Southwest. The Raza Unida Party struggled to build upon its considerable achievements as a third party after its divisive national convention in 1972. Its primary leader, José Angel Gutiérrez, had been thrust into the media spotlight in 1969 when he asserted that radi-cal Chicanos intended to "remove the base of support" of Anglo domina-tion. Known as his "Kill the Gringo" speech, Gutiérrez's comments led national politicians like Congressman Henry B. Gonzalez to raise the spectre of "Cuban infiltrators" and "Castroite influences." On the floor of the House of Representatives, Gonzalez argued: "He [Gutiérrez] is simply deluded if he believes that the wearing of fatigues and a beard makes his followers revolutionaries, or that the genius of revolution is in slogans," and added that "these young men are trying to fashion a miniature Cuba in southern Texas."[37] The charges were ridiculous, yet there was no doubt that the Cuban experiment fascinated many young Latinos.

Like other Movement organizers and thinkers, Gutiérrez's agenda often could shift between narrow nationalist and internationalist positions. In a letter published in *La Gente* in 1973, for example, he outlined what on the surface seems to be a rather rigid "Mi Raza Primero" stance:

> In the last few months we have seen declarations from California and Colorado that defend the struggle for a free

Puerto Rico, in support of Lucio Cabañas, Angela Davis, Cuba, Africa, etc. . . . It would be better to defend one's own first. The reality is that our people comprehend very little and care even less about Cuba, Cabañas, Africa or Puerto Rico. Our people want relief here and now. Capitalism begins its dehumanizing process here with us. When we struggle here, we weaken the enemy over there. . . . If they want an international movement let them continue to meddle in other parts of the world. For my part, I have no need to concern myself with them.[38]

Despite the apparent dismissal of an internationalist solidarity agenda ("let them continue to meddle in other parts of the world"), Gutiérrez's own language reveals the link between foreign and domestic struggles: "When we struggle here, we weaken the enemy over there." The rivalry between Gutiérrez and Rodolfo Corky Gonzales for control of La Raza Unida Party produced a hardening of positions that, as we have seen, need not have been mutually exclusive. Only two years after Gutiérrez's statement cited above, he led a delegation of nineteen Chicano/a leaders to Havana at the invitation of the Casa de las Américas and the Cuban government. Although Gutiérrez's attempt to interest César Chávez and Reies López Tijerina in the trip failed, the ten-day encounter was highly publicized and upon his return Gutiérrez incurred the wrath of red-baiting politicians, the south Texas media, and even members of his own party.[39]

The phantom of "Cuban subversion" in the United States contributed to the close attention paid by governmental agencies to Chicano statements about Cuba. As Ernesto Vigil has shown, in 1972 the FBI was advising its offices throughout the Southwest to be "particularly alert for activities by Chicano groups . . . on behalf of the Cubans in the United States."[40] FBI files on La Raza Unida Party were cross-referenced with those on "Cuban subversion," and the Crusade for Justice's interest in Latin American solidarity groups such as the "Committee of Solidarity with Latin America (COLAS)" and "Latin American Pro-independence Movement, known in California as Instituto de Investigación México-Aztlán (PIM-IIMA)" drew the attention of federal agents. A document from the Bureau's San Francisco office spoke openly about the potential for "urban guerrilla warfare" waged by domestic organizations should the United States invade Cuba.[41] For government officials, the omnipresence in Latino youth communities of the image of Che Guevara contributed to the fear that a guerrilla war at home was a real possibility.

THE FIGURE OF CHE IN THE CHICANO/A IMAGINATION

> I will help the rest of the working people regardless of race and color. I am ready to give my life for this cause because my blood is the same as that of Che Guevara, Pancho Villa, Chicanos, who died to give people their freedom.
> —Anonymous, *El Grito del Norte* (June 5, 1971)

At the marriage of Nita Gonzales, the oldest daughter of Corky Gonzales, during the 1969 Denver Youth Conference, the attending priest blessed the couple "in the name of the God of Che, the God of Reies Tijerina, and the God of Cesar Chavez."[42] Later that year, the inaugural issue of the Oakland, California, journal *El Pocho Che* (with the dedication "A Fidel en el espíritu del 26 de julio") featured a Malaquias Montoya drawing of the revolutionary (fig. 5). In their recording of political songs, the Denver *conjunto* "Los Alvarados" included a poster portraying "five brave men who gave their lives for the Chicano Movement, our people, and the Revolution: Ricardo Falcón, Ernesto Che Guevara, Luis 'Junior' Martínez, Emiliano Zapata, Francisco 'Pancho' Villa."[43] In February 1970, the women members of the Los Angeles Brown Berets, ended their letter of resignation with a simple "Con Che!"[44]

I list these examples (and one could catalog many more) to show that by the 1970s many Chicano/a artists and activists had incorporated the image of Che into their discursive repertoire. As the above epigraph suggests, some even had converted the Argentina-born and honorary Cuban Guevara into a Chicano and so the image of the mestizo head with three faces that was widely distributed in Raza communities at times featured Che as its central figure (fig. 6). Ernesto Che Guevara, the revolutionary icon par excellence, had ascended together with Pancho Villa and Emiliano Zapata into the pantheon of Mexican American and Mexican heroes.[45]

In his introductory essay to Che's Bolivian diary, published in the United States by *Ramparts* magazine in the July 28, 1968, issue, Fidel Castro referred to the tremendous impact the "idea" of Che was having around the world less than one year after his assassination: "Right in the United States, members of the Negro movement and the radical students, who are constantly increasing in number, have made Che's figure their own. In the most combative manifestations of civil rights and against the aggression in Vietnam, his photographs are wielded as emblems of the struggle. Few times in history, or perhaps never, has a figure, a name, an example, been so universalized with such celerity and passionate force."[46]

More than likely unaware of the importance of Che in U.S. Latino communities, Castro's government since its earliest days had made a special effort to connect with African Americans. From Richard Gibson's role in the Fair Play for Cuba committees to LeRoi Jones's essay "Cuba libre" to the radical activities of Robert F. Williams to Castro's famous weeklong stay in Harlem in September 1960, progressive African Americans played a critical role in fostering support for revolutionary Cuba. On the island, the newspaper *Revolución* declared a "Solidarity Week with the Negro Peoples of the United States," and a September 21, 1960, *New York Times* article announced "Castro is Seeking Negroes' Support."[47] Throughout the late 1960s, Black Panthers and other African American radicals were welcomed in Havana. Eldridge and Kathleen Cleaver named their son after Cuban independence leader Antonio Maceo, and the Panther newspaper declared: "We wish the Cuban people victory in their struggle against the blockade and may the Cuban people achieve their goal of 10,000,000 tons in the 1970 sugar cane harvest."[48]

As we have seen, Chicano/a experiences in Cuba during the first half of the decade of the 1960s were limited to individual visits and lacked the official encouragement on the part of the Cuban government that was afforded African Americans. For many Movement activists and artists, therefore, the identification of Che Guevara with Chicano political issues was premised on thinly drawn analogies between the conditions that had produced the revolution and the plight of Mexican Americans in the United States. But whereas Guevara was the foremost proponent of armed insurrection in Latin America during the mid-1960s, the vast majority of Chicano Movement activists did not promote anything approaching Guevara's version of socialism and certainly did not support the taking up of arms or *foquismo*.[49]

During the early years of the Movement in one region of the Southwest, however, some observers believed that Mexican Americans indeed had adopted Guevara's tactics. In his struggle to reclaim the lands of northern New Mexico for Hispano residents, Reies López Tijerina and his followers carried out a series of armed actions. In 1966,

5. Malaquias Montoya, "El Pocho Che." Used by permission of artist.

6. Anonymous, "El Che mestizo." Author's collection.

after the takeover of the Echo Amphitheater section of the Carson National Forest, the leader of the Alianza Federal de las Mercedes told the press: "Fidel Castro has what he has because of his guts. Castro put the gringos off his island and we can do the same."[50]

Although we can only speculate on what Che Guevara's opinion of such sentiments might have been, it is interesting that in an inscription to his book *La guerra de guerrillas* presented to visiting U.S. student Maurice Zeitlin he wrote: "The lessons in this book are not intended to apply to the Rocky Mountains."[51] Nevertheless, in the wake of the June 1967 Tierra Amarilla courthouse raid young radicals from across the country began to descend upon northern New Mexico speaking about a "Sierra Maestra" in the United States. Following the assassination of Guevara in October of that year, members of the Alianza proudly disseminated the slogan: "Che is alive and hiding in Tierra Amarilla."[52]

According to one account, New Mexico state officials took Tijerina's activities to be a credible threat. Clark Knowlton reported in *The Nation*:

> The northern mountains, so close to the state capital, suddenly became ominous. A mass Spanish-American uprising was rumored to be slaughtering the Anglo-American population in the north. Guerrilla bands, secretly trained and led by Cuban army officers, were said to be marching on Santa Fe. Other guerrilla forces were believed, in the hysteria, to be establishing bases in the remote mountain areas, and revolutionary urban cells of the Alianza were planning to set fire to Santa Fe and Albuquerque.[53]

It is not clear the extent to which law-enforcement agencies truly believed that there was a mini-Cuban revolution about to take place in the "Land of Enchantment." Writers recognized by the mainstream media as authorities on the Southwest, such as Frank Cullen Brophy, claimed to have irrefutable knowledge about the nature of Tijerina's actions: "Reies Tijerina, with his limited education, yet undeniable facility for inflammatory Spanish, is leading a Castro-style revolution based upon the most transparent sort of hoax—and with the full support of the Communists."[54]

Brophy's article reproduced one of the favorite tactics of conservative commentators, that is, the expression of concern for "decent Mexican Americans" who might be misled by the Chicano militants. According to this view, Mexican Americans were a compliant population under the sway of outside agitators. Brophy invoked his family history as landowners in Arizona and confidently predicted the demise of the Movimiento:

> Since I was born along the Mexican Border towards the end of the last century, and since my father before me had been closely associated with Mexicans in their own country, and those who, like him, had emigrated to this country, I have had a long and happy association with many strata of Mexican-Americans, whom I have known intimately throughout an active lifetime. These are among the best citizens we have in the United States of American [*sic*] today, and that is why I raise my voice to protest efforts to deceive and seduce them in the interests of Communist revolution. They will *not* long be deceived![55]

One anonymous Chicana writer dismissed these ideas as the product of official red-baiting, yet corroborated the idea that at least some organizers in this particular sector of the fledgling Chicano Movement were paying close attention to developments in Cuba:

> The present influx of influences also includes that of Cuba. Anyone with a cheap short-wave radio can get Radio Havana, loud and clear, in English and Spanish, seven days a week. Many listen to it. Recently, several local movement activists have traveled to Cuba. The Cuban influence turns people on to the idea of socialism, being built by fellow Latinos. It shows them that when the people take things into their own hands, quick progress can be made. This is strongly positive.... Ever since the Courthouse Raid, there have been rumors that Cuban guerrillas were training in the mountains, that "Reds" were arming the people.... Cuban influence is there, although Cubans aren't.[56]

Alianza leaders such as Felix Martinez had spoken openly about the need for armed revolt in the months following the Tierra Amarilla courthouse raid. In a 1968 interview with Los Angeles counterculture newspaper *Open City*, Martinez had warned: "We could always retreat to the mountains which are nearly impregnable.... We could do exactly what Fidel and Che did in Cuba when they retreated to the Sierra."[57]

Ramón Tijerina, brother of Reies, reportedly told a reporter for the Santa Fe *New Mexican* that "in thirty or forty years a vast monument would be built" in northern New Mexico dedicated to Che.[58]

In fact there was little likelihood of a socialist revolution in northern New Mexico or anywhere else where small groups of leftists in the Chicano Movement struggled with sectarian nationalisms and a vast majority of ethnic Mexicans who were still very much invested in the American Dream. Certainly Tijerina's thinking had never included a well-thought-out analysis of the political economy although his emphasis on retaking the land struck at the very root of capitalism's insistence that property be kept out of the hands of the poor. Despite the fact that the specter of a Cuban/Chicano socialism haunting local and federal authorities was a figment of their imagination, the example of revolutionary Cuba in fact had led many Chicano/a activists to complicate their political thinking and reinvigorate their praxis. More important, it sustained the internationalist tradition that had always informed key sectors of Chicano/a and Mexican American activist communities.

EL CHE: REPRESENTATION OF A UTOPIAN PRAXIS

Vengo a traerte un recado
de mi pueblo que es tu pueblo.
Dice el pueblo Che Guevara
Que es mentira que hayas muerto.

(I come to bring you a message
from my people who are your people too.
The people say Che Guevara
That it is a lie you have died.)

— Carlos Puebla, "Un hombre"

At the center of José Antonio Burciaga's mural "The Last Supper" sits the classic image of Che Guevara in the position of Christ. Directly behind him stand a *calaca* (skeleton) and the Virgin of Guadalupe. To his right we see Zapata, César Chávez, and Sandino; to his left Ricardo Flores Magón, Carlos Santana, Benito Juárez, and Martin Luther King (fig. 7). That the pacifism of Chávez and King, for example, were ideologically incompatible

7. José Antonio Burciaga, "Last Supper Of Chicano Heroes." Used by permission of Mrs. Cecilia Burciaga y familia (with the assistance of Jim Prighott and Robin Dunitz).

with the revolutionary agendas of Zapata, Sandino, and Che was a tension for the most part left uninterrogated by artists and activists. More important, the fact that a non-Chicano should take center stage in the pantheon of Chicano heroes underscores Che's importance as the embodiment of the borderless and pan-ethnic internationalism that informed key elements of the Chicano Movement.

In his *Chicano Manifesto* published in 1971, Armando B. Rendón wrote: "It is quite logical that the Viva Zapata element—along with traces of Che Guevara—is present most vehemently among Chicano youth; every demonstration, school walkout, or rally is sure to include one or more signs bearing the Zapata legend. (The Che look, often in evidence and growing strongly in the Brown Beret youth groups, reflects a searching, emotional attachment to the Cuban revolutionary but rather unclear ideological ties)."[59]

Despite the hazy political genealogy that connected Che to Chicanos, there is no question that Che's figure was widespread in the cultural practices of young Mexican Americans engaged in the invention of a new collective identity. The Colegio Jacinto Treviño in

Mercedes, Texas, for example, offered Christmas cards of Zapata, Che, and Villa, and his image appeared on all publications of New Mexico's Black Beret organization (fig. 8). The literature of the Black Berets in particular combined Guevara-like language with the rhetoric of 1960s youth culture: "We realize that to save our people we must be motivated, not only by the hatred for the *marrano racista* [racist pig], but by the great emotions and feelings of love that we have for our Raza and the Third World peoples."[60] San Francisco poet Roberto Vargas saw the vitality of the entire Chicano Movement as being inspired by Che and a select group of martyred heroes. He wrote: "*Ay Raza vieja/Raza nueva y orgullosa/Sun-bronzed and arrogant/Con el Espíritu de Che y Sandino/Con el ardor de Malcolm X y Zapata.*"[61]

José Rendón developed a similar sentiment in his poem "Ernesto, Emiliano y Doroteo":

Ernesto, Emiliano y Doroteo
foreign to an english mouth
but not my half-bastard tongue

these lyrics glide past it
with the ease of a machete through *caña* [sugar cane]

Images that I see by these sacred words
live in my soul
        buried deep
        never to be destroyed by white-wash

Images running through me
taking the place of mortal blood
leaving me inhuman strength
bestowing upon me a frame of mind
that will conquer a sick earth
and be gentle to children y abuelitas.

Ernesto, Emiliano y Doroteo
your hand will steady my gun
your eyes will re-enforce mine
        guide my bullets at white oinkers

8. Christmas cards from Texas.

> you will teach me to hide, teach me to become rivers,
> trees and mountains, teach me to fight with the fury
> of a mother protecting her young, and with skill only you can possess
>   teach me to be brave
>   teach me to have respect
>   teach me to be loyal
>   teach me to be loved
>   teach me to be you.[62]

Rendón's poem reproduces the image of the tenderhearted warrior who fights courageously but also displays deep feelings of love for his people. The extent to which such reimaginings of masculinity constituted a challenge to traditional Latino patriarchy is unclear. The historical record and subsequent accounts of the Movement by women activists show that the vast majority of Chicano men did not significantly reform their masculinist practices. To a great degree, Chicano artists and intellectuals focused exclusively on Che the revolutionary warrior and military hero.

Nevertheless, Che's famous statement about love as a prime motivation for revolutionary action is undeniably at work in Rendon's text, reminding us that the potential for ethical renewal inherent in the concept of the "New Man" resonated with other moral codes at play within emergent forms of Chicano masculinity. Guevara's elaboration of the concept of the "New Man," outlined in his 1965 essay "Socialism and Man in Cuba," invoked an agency based upon collective identities (vs. capitalist individualism), agrarian-based cultural formations, and international solidarity. With its origins in the earlier notion of the "New Soviet Man," Che's reworking found fertile ground in Cuba but also among young people around the world. For many Chicano/as especially, Che's self-sacrifice and service to a larger cause resonated with their own aspirations and with activist and ethical models closer to home such as César Chávez.

Although Guevara's "revolutionary love" and moral commitments coincided to a certain extent with Chávez's ideal of egoless service to the people, militant Movement activists necessarily viewed the two men quite differently (see Chapter Four). The tension between Chávez's nonviolence and Che's idea of armed revolt captured in Nephtalí de León's play *¡Chicanos: The living and the dead!* (1972) first appeared in Guadalupe Saavedra's 1968 acto *Justice*. Founder of the Teatro Chicano of East Los Angeles, Saavedra addressed the issue of police brutality and urged barrio residents to answer violence with violence. In reaction to the exploitation of farmer Honkie Sam ("I am the whitest dude in the universe, and you know that White is all pure") and his dogs (representing the police), la Madre and el Compadre begin to defend themselves by killing the dogs. The figure of Justice embraces the barrio residents, and a voice proclaims, "Justice belongs to the people. In the final analysis, it is the people who administer it." In a short coda, a local woman goes into labor and miraculously delivers a child: "Everyone forms a stage picture of the Nativity scene with the woman who just gave birth cradling a picture (as Mary held Jesus) of Che Guevara."[63] The play concludes, then, with the symbolic birth of the New Man transported to a Chicano context.

Tejano poet David García revisits Che's messianic stature by linking Guevara and Christ through the categories of revolution and "brownness" in his poem "A Tribute to Che":

> Che is alive and well
> *aquí en Aztlán.*
> We saw him again today,
> on a poster
> and on a button,
> *y también en nuestros libros.*

Each working day, the sunrise
is greeted by images of "the
bearded one,"
and we remember his advice.
"Constant mobility"
"Constant wariness"
And "Constant vigilance"
Sound advice from the Revolutionary
doctor.
He who is the Cristo image
of this people revolution,
constantly engaged
in battles with many enemies.
Christ also was brown
and too, he led a revolutionary life.
Just as Christ was
the Che of a religious revolution,
Che is our Christ
of this political people's revolution.[64]

If for García and Saavedra Che was the long-awaited messiah, other Chicano writers stoically contemplated his life as a bright but fleeting moment in the otherwise dreary march of traditional societies mired in the feudal structures Guevara had fought to abolish. Historian and activist Juan Gómez Quiñones drew upon the trope of Che as Nature in order to suggest the never-ending struggle for justice:

OCTUBRE 1967, A CHE
los arrieros
se ven
cruzando el monte
son llagas en el sol
ayer pasó
la sangre por la tierra
Perú-Bolivia
donde se contaba
con nudos
el tiempo, el dinero y el espacio.

(The mule trains can be seen crossing the mountain, they are wounds in the sun. Yesterday blood ran on the ground. Peru-Bolivia, where time, money, and space are counted with knots.)[65]

The images of blood and wounds ("*llagas*") reasserts the transformation of the historical Guevara into the Christ-like figure that would be fortified by the graphic photographs of his body released by the Bolivian government after his murder. For Chicana poet Dorinda Moreno, Che's death would lead eventually to his rebirth as a youthful symbol of hope and freedom:

CHE—REENCARNE EN ALAS DE JUVENTUD
Voló la esperanza en alas de la muerte con el Che.
A un lugar muy retirado
y lloré con orgullo y tristeza
Con solo ver su cara tan angélica
y estoy esperando con ansias el
día de la gloria
en que reencarne en un pajarillo pequeño
precioso Che renacido
arrancando sus alas al vuelo
Como la verdad y solo la verdad
es necesario sacrificio de lucha
"No hay otro camino"
Canta, canta Che
Canta tu canción
por la juventud
de tristeza, de esperanza
de la libertad.

(Che—be reborn on the wings of youth: Hope has flown with Che on the wings of death to a distant place, and I cried with pride and sadness just seeing his angelic face. And I am anxiously awaiting the day of glory when he is reborn as a small bird, precious reborn Che, spreading his wings in flight like truth and only truth. Sacrifice in the struggle is necessary, "There is no other path." Sing, Che, sing. Sing your song for the youth, of sadness, of hope, of freedom.)[66]

9. Gonzalo Placencia and Victor Ochoa, "Chicano Park Che." Used by permission of Victor Ochoa.

Moreno's hopeful conclusion converts the tragedy of Guevara's assassination into a vague yet better future. The poetic voice is both saddened and proud ("*orgullo y tristeza*") as it implicitly invokes the infamous photograph of the dead revolutionary, suggesting the circuitous yet powerful ways in which the figure of Che facilitated the Chicano Movement's construction of "Brown Pride" and a self-determined and militant agency. Beautifully captured in Malaquias Montoya's 1973 poster, Guevara had become for U.S. Latino/as "*una flor que brota en tiempos duros*" ("A flower that blooms in hard times").

The Chicano appropriation of the Che as Christ or Che as Nature tropes was closely linked to a series of images that insisted that his legacy led logically to Chicano/a political praxis. Whereas Gonzalo Placencia Ochoa transforms the Korda matrix figure into a ferocious and somewhat frightening image (fig. 9), the stoic voice in Luis Omar Salinas's "Guevara . . . Guevara" is that of a collective "we" who scours the American landscape in search of the fallen Che only to find the persistence of the poverty and suffering he had fought to eliminate:

Guevara . . . Guevara
we have come to claim your body
       undertakers of a huge America
cutting through shrubs of a
              silent heaven
       saddened
by your blood that flows from
          darkened leaves
on the Bolivian hills

we plunder through the world
in search of you
     and find you
        a child
passionate and hungry
(the passion of your mother Che)
your eyes form avenues
for dusty withered skulls
        through grass
           blood
           and more blood

Guevara . . . Guevara wake up
        it is raining in Bolivia
        and the campesinos
        with voices of lead
        are talking with putrid suspicion
(sinews and flesh from Argentina Che)

and secretive Gods with sharpened axes
       look for your body
    as cocaine
          smolders
   from the windows
   making disguises
   in the huge Bolivian sky
(the landing Che . . . the landing)
   Guevara . . . Guevara

there is hunger in Bolivia
and children mumble on the hilltops
with your lips
(the river is strewn with dead communists
Guevara)

and that mystery that talks of you
on that damp earth
waiting for that troubled sea
to chant
Guevara . . . Guevara
we have found you
your blood fills our throats
our lungs
our belly
with a smell as fresh
as yesterday's fallen snow.[67]

In the end, "Guevara" is found in the face of a poor child and ultimately is recognized as that force which animates the struggle for justice and dignity. The recurring image of the blood of Che as life-giving and eternal links him to the image of Christ as clearly as did Burciaga's "Last Supper" and David García's "A Tribute to Che." Roberto "Che" Luera reiterates the call to political action and links the Chicano struggle to the process begun by the Cuban Revolution:

Che, santo, fuiste grande y poderoso
Hombre con humor y dignidad
Estás vivo siempre Che; es tu espíritu

Guerrillero eras y serás entre nosotros
Unidos en vida y muerte ganaremos
Estamos peleando lo que tu odiabas
Venceremos con tu filosofía y táctica
Andale Che, levántate que ya es tiempo
Revolución ya es y venceremos
Andale Che, levántate que ya es tiempo.

(Che, saint, you were great and powerful, a man with humor and dignity. You will always live, Che; it is your spirit. You were a warrior and will continue to be among us. United in life and death we will win. We are fighting what you hated. We will win with your philosophy and tactics. Hurry up, Che, it's time to rise up. It is revolution and we will win. Hurry up, Che, it's time.)[68]

In his 1971 poem "Zambo," Elias Hruska y Cortés had employed imagery taken from the natural world, yet emphasized the social dimensions of Che's meaning for Latinos and other disenfranchised communities in the United States. Extending from the Mission District of San Francisco to Harlem, the cry of resistance to capitalist exploitation takes on a pan-ethnic and internationalist thrust:

> . . . *y tú que desde las entrañas de la selva saliste*
> *desde los barrios de la misión y de harlem*
> *con el nombre de Sandino grabado*
> *y el de Ernesto y de Camilo grabados*
> *y el de Martin y el de Malcolm y el de Lumumba*
> *mártires grabados en el alma*
> *como imanes de profetas oscuros*
> *nombres esculpidos en la piedra*
> *de un océano que golpea*
> *en los costados de tu verde grito de León*
>
> . . .
>
> *y la pantera*
> *y la pantera negra*
> *y la pantera bronce de montombo*
> *la que se llama Che*
>   *y Sandino*
>   *y Lumumba*
> carries black velvet claws
>   /silent/
>   into the jungle
> where she lives & bides the hours
> until the blackbird flies
> and the blue cat roars
> and the mockingbird sings the sound of war

and the brown and the black and the red and the yellow and the white
become one
        become one
until the brown and the black and the red and the yellow and the white
seize the hour & the minute & the second
to lay mumble jim on a marble slab
the red   the white   the blue
              & to unload the dice
                      & to unload the dice
                      and win.

(. . . and you who emerged from the depths of the jungle, from the
barrios of the Mission and Harlem, with the names of Sandino,
and Ernesto, and Camilo, and Martin, and Malcolm, and
Lumumba engraved, martyrs engraved on your soul like magnets
of lost prophets, names sculpted on stone, like an ocean that
pounds the shore of your green lion's roar . . . and the panther,
and the black panther, and the bronze panther of Montomobo
who is named Che and Sandino and Lumumba . . .)[69]

Dr. King not only joins Malcolm but also Guevara, Cienfuegos,
Sandino, and Lumumba as prophetic magnets around which the people will coalesce. The image of the panther, based in part on the Black
Panther Party but given an expanded meaning here to include Latin
American and African revolutionaries, moves against the red, white,
and blue of U.S. imperialism and announces a universal solidarity of
the exploited and dispossessed. The final verses posit the overturning of
a system that has perpetuated inequality. In the new world of social justice, the capitalist-controlled dice will no longer be loaded and those
who for centuries have been forced to lose will win.

The presence of Ernesto Che Guevara within Chicana and Chicano
political and artistic languages would outlive the revolutionary moment
of the late sixties and early seventies. San Diego-based muralist Mario
Torero's "We are not a minority!" took Che's image into the barrios of
East Los Angeles in order to assert pan-American solidarity and call
attention to the demographic future of Chicano/Latino people as a new
majority and, according to projections, by 2050 the third largest
Spanish-speaking population in the world (fig. 10). In 1987 *tejano* poet

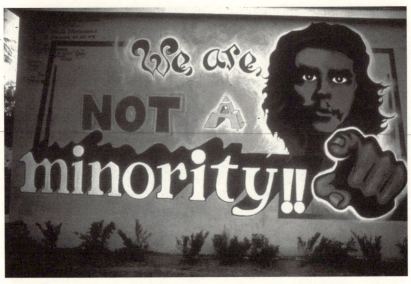

10. Mario Torero, "We are not a minority!" Mural located at the Estrada Courts, East Los Angeles. Used by permission of artist.

raúlrsalinas, who as we have seen was a member of one of the first Venceremos Brigades, dedicated the poem "Short Rap with Che" to Guevara on the twentieth anniversary of his execution:

> i've never written you a poem
> before, because . . .
> i felt others had said it
> All.
>
> Yet, striving to exemplify your life,
> become
> El Hombre Nuevo,
> is to
> Me
> rendering
> You
> my
> Ultimate Poem.[70]

The concept of "el hombre nuevo," which we saw at work in the earliest Chicano writings about Cuba, resurfaces here as a still unfulfilled project. The passage of years did not dilute the power of Che as an inspiration for young Latinos and Latinas although thoughtful poets understood the impossibility of reproducing the heroic deeds of earlier historical moments in their own time and place. Reyes Cárdenas cautioned: "If we praise the Aztecs/or Zapata/we praise something/too far removed/if we embrace Guevara/we must realize/that revolution/works only/on rare occasions."[71] As the twentieth century came to an end, many young Latino/as would adapt the fundamental meanings of Che's legacy for their own historical moment. In 1995, Chicana/o high school students in San Francisco, protesting California governor Pete Wilson's anti-immigrant policies and cuts in the state education budget, moved through city streets chanting "¡Wilson, Wilson, *a la chingada*! ¡*Viva, viva* Che Guevara!"[72]

COMANDANTE GUEVARA EN EL SIGLO XXI

I was never the Che Guevara-type but there's nothing wrong with revolution.
—Reyes Cárdenas, "I was never a militant Chicano"

In a post–Cold War era of conservative triumphalism, renewed forms of U.S. imperialism, and the ongoing effort by establishment historians and media talking heads to discredit progressive movements of the 1960s, no small amount of courage is necessary to invoke the name of Che Guevara in a public setting. French journalist Viviane Forrester points out that to use terms such as *exploitation, classes,* and especially *socialism* in North American and European intellectual circles is to be met with "brows not frowning angrily, but raised in incredulous amazement mingled with pity. 'You surely don't mean . . . You can't be still . . . The Berlin Wall came down, don't you know? So you liked the USSR? Stalin? But what about liberty, the free market . . . No?' And a helpless smile is bestowed on the poor retarded fool, so corny as to be endearing."[73] In the United States, liberals and conservatives alike react to any positive description of socialist Cuba with "But Castro is a dictator" or "They're still communist, aren't they?" In some circles, similar expressions of surprise greet anyone seeking to find a useful historical lesson in the Chicano Movement: "Are you a nationalist?," "Don't you know they were sexist?," "We're over all that protesting stuff," "You're stuck in the 60s, carnal."

In the current climate such responses are not surprising. Fifty years of corporate public relations have produced an Orwellian language in which "community" now means wealthy CEOs and their lackeys, "freedom" is reduced to consumer choice, and the "end of racism" means the abolition of social programs like affirmative action that had attempted to remedy racism's effects. Throughout the so-called post-Movement period, the appropriation and refashioning of the radical tradition's key terms and figures proceeded quickly and ideological confusion reigned. For one bizarre moment in the late 1990s, right-wing ideologues labeled Bill Clinton a socialist and novelist Toni Morrison declared Clinton to be "the first African American president." Never mind the fact that Clinton sat atop the economic bubble of the 1990s like some giant Elvis impersonator performing a parody of traditional liberal values even as he did more to cut away the social safety net for the poor and working poor than any of his predecessors. In short, the values, language, and common sense of Viet Nam war-era mass mobilizations for progressive change have been turned on their head. In this Oz-like reality, to speak of economic justice or call one's self a Chicano or Chicana was to mark oneself as hopelessly "old school," "divisive and cranky," a whiner, or simply out of touch.

In Chicano/a studies circles, the effects of two decades of Reaganism, Clintonism, poststructuralism, and sundry deradicalizing ideologies have produced a suspicion of Movement agendas despite the fact that Chicano Studies programs would not exist if it were not for the activism of the early 1970s. Younger scholars have been taught a parody of the Marxist tradition, many have swallowed large doses of poststructuralist mystification, and the vast majority knows nothing of Latin American history or political traditions. Outside the academy, Chicanos and Mexicanos made up a community comprised in part of an unbroken line of immigrant seekers of the "American dream" and therefore never particularly attracted to political arguments from the left as well as second- and third-generation urban youth who grew up seduced by hip-hop culture's imitation of consumer culture's worst features. Any attempt to resurrect Chicano/a radical traditions, especially the internationalist and anti-imperialist traditions, will face overwhelming obstacles. All indications are that Che Guevara's most cherished ideals have been consigned to the dustbin of history.

11. Alex Donis, "Che and Cesar." Non-extant image destroyed by vandalism at Galería de la Raza, San Francisco, in 1997. Used by permission of artist.

But if we have learned anything from the last forty years we know that every time Che's potency as a symbol of radical change is declared defunct, it reappears wherever people have had their dignity trampled and their lives endangered. In the 1993 short film *Cholo Joto* by Augie Robles, we meet the gay character Valentín who mines the potential for agency residing in Gonzalo Placencia Ochoa's Che Guevara mural in San Diego's Chicano Park. At first confused by Che's notion of revolutionary love, Valentín eventually reclaims it for his own struggle for equal rights: "Then I realized, yeah, that's right. That I'm not going to fight out of anger but because I love myself and I love my community." According to critic José Esteban Muñoz's reading of the film: "In this video performance, Guevara stands in for all that was promising and utopian about the Chicano Movement."[74]

Perhaps the most stunning appropriation of the Che figure in a contemporary Chicano context was the installation created by Los Angeles queer artist Alex Donis in 1997 (fig. 11). Portraying César Chávez and

Che in a homosexual embrace, poised as if about to kiss, the painting was briefly exhibited at San Francisco's Galería de la Raza. The artist, who held both men as personal heroes, explained: "I created this work to try and melt down the stoicism in male Latino heroic figures and address the fear in feminizing masculinity. . . . I realized that joining these two almost cult figures in Latino culture, positioned them on the frontline of a very different cause, subverting and redefining the rhetoric to which they had historically been so entrenched."[75] If, as I have argued in this chapter, the figures of Chávez and Guevara converge somewhere in the Chicano/a imaginary as models of revolutionary commitment, sacrifice, and love for the common people, the now lost painting by Alex Donis stands as a fleeting but powerful glimpse into that realm of correspondence.

Throughout the Americas, the relevance of Guevara persists through the anti-globalization movement and recurring attempts to retain some form of self-determination. In July 2001, three thousand students from the Universidad de El Salvador, for example, marched against neoliberalism dressed in red and white t-shirts bearing Che's image. In North America at the turn of the century, Che may seem to be nothing more than a pop icon used by musicians and artists. But by exposing Chicano/a and Latino/a youth to the image of Che, groups such as Rage Against the Machine may lead some young people to investigate further the values he espoused. The political commitment displayed by the young people who gathered in Seattle in 1999 to protest the World Trade Organization or who denounced the U.S. invasion and occupation of Iraq in 2003 is heartening and suggests a renewal of alternative visions of what a just world might be.[76]

More than any other figure from the Movement period, Che reminds young Latinas and Latinos that their local surroundings cannot be separated from other areas of the world where injustice reigns. As Latin American scholar James Petras has written: "Probably the most significant contribution of Che to the contemporary revolutionary movements was his internationalism. His recognition that imperialism was everywhere organizing the exploitation of every crevice on earth's soil, intervening militarily in the most remote villages, undermining the most cherished cultural practices."[77] Although the intensity with which capital restricts human potential may vary from the remote villages of developing countries to the abandoned inner cores of U.S. and

European cities, the dire conditions contested by Che's life and later by his image are equally destructive.

In his attempt to refashion Che's thought for a contemporary critical pedagogy, Peter McLaren reminds us that capital's domination of those regions Che had sought to liberate is stronger than ever. The utopian power of Che's figure, however, remains undiminished: "To retrieve the memory of Che is to break the trance of inevitability by mocking the blatant exploitation that marks the present capitalist moment. It is to dislodge what appears to be the intractable hegemony of commonsense, quotidian reality, and to describe and ultimately change it."[78] Just as the ideas of Che and the original utopian promise of revolutionary Cuba contributed to the rise of Chicano/a militancy in the 1960s, so too will they reappear in any new attempt to challenge inequality and injustice as it is suffered by U.S. Latino and Latin American working people.

I began this chapter with Culture Clash's parodic send-up of the Che figure because despite its deconstruction of certain leftist ideologies associated with the 1960s, it retains a high degree of respect for progressive values. As Chuy tells the pizza delivery boy in his attempt to explain Che's significance: "The vato was always on the side of the underdog, Frankie." Given that the majority of Mexican and Latino people in the United States have yet to achieve full social equality and economic justice, the question posed by Che to Frankie and Chuy is the question all Chicana/os must answer no matter what heights of class privilege they attain—"Are you ready to struggle for the rights of the less fortunate?"

In the next chapter, we will investigate further the impact of César Chávez on the Chicano/a struggle for the rights of the disenfranchised. Rapidly transformed into a sign for a militant and ethical commitment to progressive social change, Chávez in many ways complemented the image of Che Guevara even as his pacifist principles contrasted sharply with the reality of armed insurrection. As icons of the Movimiento, the figures of Guevara and Chávez maintained an uneasy coexistence.

CHAPTER FOUR

"NONVIOLENCE IS THE ONLY WEAPON"

That is what it takes to bring change in America today. Nothing less than organized, disciplined nonviolent action that goes on every day will challenge the power of the corporations and the generals.

—César Estrada Chávez

IT IS AN IMPRESSIVE HISTORICAL FACT that the Chicano Movement's discursive and ideological field was able to accommodate the fiery rhetoric of Reies López Tijerina, the charismatic leadership of Rodolfo Corky Gonzales, the paramilitary formations and styles of the Brown and Black Berets, and even the ubiquitous image of Ernesto Che Guevara and the idea of armed struggle. But unless we are willing to exclude the figure of César Chávez from the ranks of the Movimiento, we are hard pressed to reconcile his philosophy of nonviolence with the languages and practices of other Movement leaders.[1] Armando Navarro writes: "The militant actions of Tijerina and Gonzales, coupled with the nonviolent direct action of Chavez, provided role models for both students and barrio youth."[2] Navarro is surely correct, yet in retrospect we are struck by the incompatibility of the different leadership styles practiced by *los jefes*. F. Arturo Rosales notes as much when he points out: "Interestingly, the leader of the farmworkers, César Chávez, contrasted sharply with other Chicano leaders. The former farmworker . . . did not possess an imposing figure; he did not swagger or project a tough persona as did many militant activists of the era. Chávez's short stature and soft-spoken, quiet demeanor was often mistaken for the stereotypical look of passivity rather than forceful leadership."[3]

For some contemporary observers of the Movimiento, Chávez was the necessary complement to the more traditional "warrior" styles of Corky Gonzales and López Tijerina. Three weeks before he was assassinated by law-enforcement agents on August 29, 1970, *Los Angeles Times* reporter Ruben Salazar offered this analysis of the Chicano Movement: "César is our only real leader. . . . [Gonzales and Tijerina] rant and rave and threaten to burn the establishment down. That's good because most people won't listen unless you rant and rave. But this provides the community with little more than emotional uplift; nothing palpable."⁴ In retrospect, Salazar's assertion that Gonzales and Tijerina produced no concrete gains for their communities and functioned merely as a rhetorical sideshow is open to debate. Ironically, even as moderates like Salazar authorized Chávez as the only authentic Chicano leader, young activists criticized him for being too narrowly focused on one issue and too conciliatory vis-à-vis traditional liberal organizations such as the Democratic Party.

In this chapter I will trace the complex and often contradictory relationship between César Chávez and the various sectors of the Chicano Movement in the crucial period of the American war in Southeast Asia.⁵ As I have done in the previous chapter with the figure of Che Guevara, I will draw upon the entire field of discursive practices that contributed to the construction of multiple images of Chávez and the ways in which these images were put to political use. Chávez's own self-fashioning, then, his public statements and actions, will make up one area of inquiry but so too will journalistic, artistic, and literary representations of the leader as well as critiques from both the political right and the political left.

By mapping the broader cultural field in order to understand what the figure of César Chávez signified for various groups, I do not adhere to the naive empiricist notion that so-called historical sources (archival documents, testimonials, etc.) are somehow more authoritative (i.e., "real") than cultural materials. A passage in a novel or a poem dedicated to La Causa, for example, may have had as much to do with the construction of Chavez as a powerful sign of the Movimiento as did the actualized practices of the fast and the march, themselves to a great extent political and artistic interventions rooted in Mexican cultural traditions.

By the time of the Delano Grape Strike in late 1965, the political, cultural, and economic project that was the National Farm Workers Association (NFWA) and later the United Farm Workers Organizing Committee (UFWOC) and the United Farm Workers union (UFW) had already established the groundwork for the multiple forms of Chicano/a activism that emerged in the final years of the decade. Years before the full-blown Movimiento burst onto the historical stage, the NFWA had become a classic version of what Raymond Williams called a "militant particularism."⁶ A group of workers in a specific geographical locale, faced with intolerable conditions, organize to change those conditions for the better. But the particularities of the farm workers' struggle spoke to a wide range of related issues that affected virtually every Mexican American community in the United States during the Viet Nam war period.

As other militant particularisms developed across the Southwest, the UFW functioned as an affective link and practical training ground for Movement organizations with diverse agendas. In a dialectical and often contradictory process, the union's project fed into an emergent cultural nationalism in the urban barrios and provided Chicano/a organizations with a repertoire of symbols and tropes. At the same time, however, the unique membership of the UFW meant that key issues associated with the more insular aspects of nationalism, e.g., identity, language, and ethnic "authenticity," were simply less important. As one Mexican observer wrote: "*Es interesante destacar que este movimiento presenta menos características nacionalistas que los otros submovimientos chicanos . . . No trata en forma específica de definir la identidad del mexicano-norteamericano, identidad que no parece ser problemática*" ("It is interesting to point out that this movement presents fewer nationalist characteristics than other Chicano submovements [organizations] . . . It is not a specific question of defining a Mexican-American identity since the issue of identity is not viewed as problematic").[7]

In 1971, Carlos Blanco Aguinaga astutely argued that few, if any, of the farmworkers (approximately half of them Mexican nationals in the early 1970s) felt compelled to construct a new ethnic identity since they understood themselves to be *mexicano/as* and workers: "They know exactly where they stand in terms of their Mexicanidad and of their working-class condition and, therefore, of their relationship to the ever-present and clearly definable bosses . . . The Chicano aspect of the struggle, the Mexican 'identity' of the 'causa' did not even have to be alluded to for the simple reason that the talk [by César Chávez] was given in Spanish."[8] Traditional trade union practices also worked against the construction of a sectarian ethnicity-based identity by insisting on multiethnic coalition building and international solidarity with workers around the world.

By both underwriting and destabilizing a "resistance identity" designed to create a collective subject based on shared cultural traits ("our essentially different life style" invoked in the Plan de Santa Barbara), the UFW indirectly assisted in the formulation of a more radical Chicano/a "project identity" that critiqued the entire structure of U.S.

capitalism at home and abroad.[9] One of my assertions in this chapter, therefore, is that just as the overall impact of the Movimiento is inconceivable without the UFW the most dramatic successes of the UFW are inconceivable without the Movimiento in its emergent stages within the broader radicalized condition of U.S. society, especially among youth.

For many non-Latino activists, the efforts of the UFW embodied a utopian project composed of diverse ethnic groups and classes. As one participant put it:

> Something remarkable has happened in the town of Delano, something that a scant few months ago no one foresaw. A pattern for a New America has emerged out of the chaos of a bitter labor dispute, the pattern of people of all races and backgrounds working and living together in perfect and unprecedented harmony. Idealistic people in other parts of America talk about this ideal; in Delano today it is working. When the strike began last September "Huelga" meant only that: "Strike." But something has happened along the way; "Huelga" has come to mean something more than "Strike"; it has come to mean cooperation, brotherhood, Love.[10]

The distance between this statement, written in 1965, and the subsequent Summer of Love in 1967, the youth counterculture, and the antiwar and Third World people's movements is not terribly far. The connection between César Chávez and the revolutionary period of the 1960s was perhaps best captured in the title of Peter Matthiessen's classic book published in 1969—*Sal Si Puedes (Escape If You Can): Cesar Chavez and the New American Revolution*. According to Matthiessen's ambivalent characterization, this new "American Revolution" was an "American renaissance" led by young radicals whose "philosophical poverty and abrasive attitudes should not obscure the fact that these people are forming the front line in a *necessary* revolution."[11]

But how exactly did César Chávez fit into the panorama of 1960s radicalism? As we shall see, Chávez's unconventional leadership, drawn from religious and pacifist traditions, placed some Chicanos in the Movement in the uncomfortable position of balancing the admiration they held for him with a preference many of them held for warrior models of manhood. One of the more militant Chicano writers unfavorably compared

Chávez to Che Guevara. Nephtalí de León's play, ¡Chicanos!: The Living and the Dead! places Che in direct confrontation to Chávez's philosophy (represented by the character Manuel) and argues that nonviolence is of no use to Chicanos:

> Manuel: Yet there are many of us who had and still have faith. César Chavez has faith and look how far he has advanced.

> Che (somewhat exasperated): And how far is that hermano? Don't our people still do stoop labor? Only it's by contract now. Now they are really true slaves, for they have told the yankee farmers: "We will sell our bodies and our souls to you, but only if you promise us you'll buy them!" He should have asked not for contracts to pick grapes or lettuce, but for contracts for an education and a preparation to cope with the technical-industrial age that now governs the world—an age that still enslaves him and his people. How different are California's farm laborers from the Chinese peasants who sweat their lives away stuck in their rice paddies? No, Manuel, my heart has bled for Cesar, a giant of a man, stuck by his children into that earth that enslaves him and his people. While America basks in plenty, our dear brown Saint starves with his brothers and sweats his life out for a contract that has chained them.[12]

The criticism voiced by Che, who as we have learned was one of the more pervasive signifiers for Chicano/a aspirations, is harsh but captures some of the tensions that existed in left-leaning activist circles with regard to the objectives of the UFW. Elsewhere in his writings, however, de León praises Chávez (without sarcasm) as a "modern prince of peace," "a very human man," and "one of those rare happenings that occur every time a people are oppressed and every time the universe and man join hands to yield us such a being."[13] The contradiction in de León's writing underscores the dilemma Chávez presented to Movement militants. What many of them did not understand well were the origins of Chávez's spiritual praxis and its function in a time of revolutionary rhetoric, police brutality in the barrios, and massive military aggression in Southeast Asia.

In a curious column that appeared in an issue of the UFW newspaper El malcriado, it was announced that the paper's official logo would

Don Quijote
and
his
creator

Don Quijote

12. Graphic of Don Quixote with UFW Eagle. Used by permission of United Farm Workers of America, AFL-CIO.

be Don Quixote (fig. 12). Wearing a UFW button on his lapel and with the union eagle on his shield, this farmworker version of Cervantes's knight errant would be "a Quixote who represents accurately the spirit of our struggle, always in good humor in spite of the risk." According to the anonymous author:

> Quixote symbolizes the spirit of man which always believes in human strength; in defense of the weak; in protection of women and children; in sacrifice for one's fellow-men; in the struggle against evil; in the fight against the powerful in favor of the disinherited; he represents these and many similar things, in the spirit of battle even when there are not enough resources for it, in the great causes in which man has involved himself.[14]

What is interesting about this attempt to link the traditional image of Don Quixote to the farmworker movement is that it invokes both idealism and militancy at the same time.[15] Although Cervantes's character never killed anyone, his actions were at times quite violent, and at one point in the 1605 novel he is denounced by another character whose leg he has broken. The column in *El malcriado* develops the theme of militancy by devoting some space to Cervantes himself. It specifically emphasizes his career as a soldier and participant in the battle of Lepanto, the 1571 naval conflict in which Catholic forces defeated the Muslim Ottoman Turks. According to the UFW author, Lepanto was "the first act in the establishment of what we now call 'Western Civilization.'"

Cervantes and Don Quixote, then, represented both the defense of traditional Catholic/Western values and the idealistic struggle to defend the disenfranchised. Whatever the traces of Eurocentrism that informed this interpretation of Don Quixote, the emphasis for the UFW writer fell primarily upon the call to service and social activism. The key ideological link, therefore, was to be found in the idea of "militancy," a concept Chávez himself had written about in reference to Dr. Martin Luther King, Jr.: "His nonviolence was that of action—not that of one contemplating action."[16] Chávez's distinction is between the "philosopher of nonviolence" and the active practitioner of nonviolence in the pursuit of justice. It was this latter idea that would inform Chávez's entire career.

HYBRID AND HYPER-MASCULINITIES

We must respect all human life, in the cities and in the fields and in Vietnam. Nonviolence is the only weapon that is compassionate and recognizes each man's value.
—César Estrada Chávez

In terms of his political persona, Chávez presented urban Chicanas and Chicanos with a form of masculinity virtually unknown outside the Catholicism of their *abuelitas*.[17] At its very core was the principle of "militant nonviolence." Seemingly an oxymoron, the phrase retains a commitment to social change but disassociates that commitment from aggression against other individuals or groups by incorporating a strong Christian empathy for the oppressor. Nonviolent change, therefore, is to be sought not only at the level of institutions but in the very attitudes of the antagonist. In their practical effects, Chávez's actions constructed a hybrid form of masculinity that combined "passive" elements most often linked by Western patriarchy to "feminine" subjectivities with a fearless determination that traditional gendered representations have reserved exclusively for "masculine" practices.

At the core of this hybrid agency is the belief that the political activist, by resorting to physical violence, is actually admitting his or her own weakness. A nonviolent approach requires a deeper and more sustained engagement. According to Chávez, "In some instances nonviolence requires more militancy than violence. Non-violence forces you to abandon the shortcut in trying to make a change in the social order."[18] This is essentially what Martin Luther King, Jr., had advocated consistently throughout his career. Shortly before his death, Dr. King told an interviewer: "To be militant merely means to be demanding and to be persistent, and in this sense I think the nonviolent movement has demonstrated great militancy. It is possible to be militantly nonviolent."[19]

In one of his most succinct definitions of nonviolence as he practiced it, Chávez articulated a similar view: "Our conviction is that human life and limb are a very special possession given by God to man and that no one has the right to take that away, in any cause, however just. . . . Also we are convinced that nonviolence is more powerful than violence. . . . We operate on the theory that men who are involved and truly concerned about people are not by nature violent. If they were violent they couldn't have that love and that concern for people."[20] As he would many times during his public life, Chávez argued that those who resort to violence do so because of their inability to organize their constituencies in an effective way.

Although neither Chávez's nor King's concept of nonviolence was as deeply wed to an elaborate religious and philosophical framework as was Gandhi's method of *satyagraha* ("holding to truth") in which the spiritual soul force of existence triumphs over material reality, both men drew freely from Gandhi's practical methods.[21] Chávez's use of the fast, for example, combined Catholic practices with Gandhian ideas about self-purification. According to Gandhi's reading of the *Gita* and *Upanishads*, fasting ought not be used to produce direct political effects but rather to cleanse the sensory perceptions and strengthen the moral resolve of the subject and potentially facilitate a spiritual change of heart in the adversary.

In the Gandhian view, fasting as coercion designed to force specific political concessions was itself a form, albeit a lesser form, of violence and ultimately could only produce a violent reaction.[22] Upon ending one of his more famous fasts on March 10, 1968, Chávez explained his use of the fast: "Some of you still wonder about its meaning and importance. It was not intended as a pressure against any growers. For that reason we have suspended negotiations and arbitration proceedings and relaxed the militant picketing and boycotting of the strike during this period. I undertook the fast because my heart was filled with grief and pain for the sufferings of farmworkers. The fast was first for me and then for all of us in this Union. It was a fast for nonviolence and a call to sacrifice."[23]

Three years later, in an informal talk in which he elaborated on the negative consequences produced by the combination of large financial contributions and unions, he argued that the fast was an organizing tool of greater value than traditional fund-raising. The fast modeled the sacrifice demanded of all supporters: "When you sacrifice, you force others to sacrifice. It's an extremely powerful weapon. When somebody stops eating for a week or ten days, people come and want to be part of that experience. Someone goes to jail and people want to help him. You don't buy that with money. That doesn't have any price in terms of dollars."[24]

While Chávez modeled a Mexican American variation on Christian asceticism and studied the works of Gandhi, Aquinas, and St. Paul, young Chicano militants were reading Fanon and Che Guevara.[25] Nonetheless, Chávez's rhetoric at times intersected with that of leaders elsewhere in the Movement. In what seems an unlikely pairing, two photographs that shared the wall of Chávez's office at UFW headquarters were those of the pacifist Mahatma Gandhi and the armed revolutionary Emiliano Zapata. The word *revolution* had appeared in UFW documents as early as Chávez's letter written before the March to Sacramento in 1966 and in the "Plan de Delano": "We shall pursue the REVOLUTION we have proposed. We are sons of the Mexican Revolution, a revolution of the poor seeking, bread and justice. Our revolution will not be armed, but we want the existing social order to dissolve, we want a new social order."

The concept of a "nonviolent revolution" held two traditions in an uneasy tension that was difficult to negotiate for many young activists. Chávez constantly reminded his followers that armed struggle was incompatible with his project:

Let me give you an example: the armed revolutions we have. What happens? Once you set up an army or militia to gain independence you have to maintain that army. You know against whom? Against your own people . . . In Latin America, who gets killed in case of a revolution? The poor people, the workers. Who gets nothing but crumbs when another force comes into power? Take the Mexican Revolution, take any revolution—the people of the land are the ones who give their bodies, who get killed, and they really don't gain that much from it. I think it's too big a price to pay for not getting anything.[26]

To many in the Movement such as those who looked to the Cuban model for inspiration, such remarks were disappointing since it was unclear to them how a "new social order" might be installed through the use of traditional trade-union tactics. In terms of the rhetorical presence of "revolution" in the Plan de Delano and other texts, we can only conclude that the language of many Movement documents exceeded the actual expectations of those who deployed it.

What the Plan de Delano and Chávez's 1966 letter emphasized was the fact that Mexican Americans were the heirs to a tradition of insurgency, and that the U.S. Southwest was a conquered land whose original inhabitants had been colonized by foreigners: "Delano is his [the farmworker's] 'cause,' his great demand for justice, freedom, and respect from a predominantly foreign cultural community in a land where he was first. The revolutions of Mexico were primarily uprisings of the poor, fighting for bread and for dignity. The Mexican American is also a child of the revolution. Pilgrimage, penance, and revolution. The pilgrimage from Delano to Sacramento has strong religio-cultural overtones. But it is also the pilgrimage of a cultural minority who have suffered from a hostile environment, and a minority who means business."[27] Chávez would claim that the religious underpinnings of his beliefs did not diminish the radical nature of his political objectives. The phrase "means business" invokes a more traditional form of masculinity premised upon the threat of physical action but links it to religious practices associated with saintliness. The hybrid nature of Chávez's masculinity maintained these tensions in a precarious balance throughout the various stages of his public life.[28]

To "mean business" nonviolently was precisely what Dr. King had proposed in his use of the term *nonviolent gadflies* to describe militant activists. Taking the "gadfly" image associated with Socrates, King argued that to mean business, at least in the initial stages of a social movement, was to demand the attention of the powerful in order to shine light on the problems of the disempowered. According to the "Letter from the

Birmingham Jail" (1963), rather than a passive act, nonviolent militancy was designed to create a crisis of consciousness within the ranks of the ruling majority: "Nonviolent direct action seeks to create such a crisis and establish such creative tension that a community that has constantly refused to negotiate is forced to confront the issue. It seeks so to dramatize the issue that it can no longer be ignored."[29]

Less than two years later, he elaborated on the pedagogical goals of mass mobilization: "Our nonviolent direct action program has as its objective not the creation of tensions, but the *surfacing* of tensions already present. We set out to precipitate a crisis situation that must open the door to negotiation. I am not afraid of the words 'crisis' and 'tension.' I deeply oppose violence, but constructive crisis and tension are necessary for growth.... To cure injustices, you must expose them before the light of human conscience and the bar of public opinion, regardless of whatever tensions that exposure generates."[30]

César Chávez understood that the strategy of nonviolent militancy would expose to the light of day not only the plight of the invisible farmworker but the conditions of the vast majority of ethnic Mexicans in the United States. In the 1969 "Good Friday Letter" addressed to a California grower who had accused the UFW of using violent tactics, Chávez presented a brilliant analysis of not only the farmworker's situation but also the demands and aspirations of Chicanos and Chicanas in urban centers across the Southwest. Three sections in particular suggest the ways in which Chávez's analysis participated in the discursive field I have called the Critique of Liberalism. Given these correspondences, Chávez's occasional reluctance to refer to himself as a Chicano Movement leader was unfortunate given his profound understanding of what the Movimiento, in all of its diverse sectors, took to be its principal issues and political objectives:

> The color of our skins, the languages of our cultural and native origins, the lack of formal education, the exclusion from the democratic process, the numbers of our slain in recent wars—all these burdens generation after generation have sought to demoralize us, to break our human spirit. But God knows that we are not beasts of burden, we are not agricultural implements or rented slaves, we are men.
>
> · · ·

While we do not belittle or underestimate our adversaries, for they are the rich and the powerful and possess the land, we are not afraid nor do we cringe from the confrontation. We welcome it! We have planned for it. We know that our cause is just, that history is a story of social revolutions, and that the poor shall inherit the land.

. . .

We advocate militant nonviolence as our means for social revolution and to achieve justice for our people, but we are not blind or deaf to the desperate and moody winds of human frustration, impatience and rage that blow among us. Gandhi himself admitted that if his only choices were cowardice or violence, he would choose violence. Men are not angels and the time and tides wait for no man. Precisely because of these powerful human emotions, we have tried to involve masses of people in their own struggle. Participation and self-determination remain the best experience of freedom; and free men instinctively prefer democratic change and even protect the rights guaranteed to seek it. Only the enslaved in despair have need of violent overthrow.[31]

If Che Guevara had dreamed of a society in which "new men and women" would fundamentally transform the nature of capitalist social relations, Chávez saw the union as a means to decolonize the farmworker's subjectivity and sufficiently improve surrounding conditions, albeit without addressing the farmworker's place in the relations of production. Chávez argued that farmworkers, with their "natural dignity" restored, would no longer be at the mercy of the corporate bosses: "Workers whom they previously had treated as dumb members of a forgotten minority suddenly are blooming as capable, intelligent persons using initiative and showing leadership."[32]

But the newfound agency of the farmworker would not necessarily be shaped by the dominant ethos of capitalist individualism, which led necessarily to self-interest and personal rivalries, but rather by the idea of community solidarity and service. Speaking on the occasion of the historic contract signings in the summer of 1970, Chavez said of his union members: "They found that only through dedication to serving mankind—and in this case to serving the poor and those who are

13. Robert Kennedy and César Chávez, March 10, 1968. Photo by George Ballis © 1976. George Ballis/Take Stock. Used by permission of Take Stock Photos.

struggling for justice—only in that way could they find themselves."[33] It is here, at the intersection of selfless commitment and militancy, that figures who at first glance seem to be incompatible—César Chávez and Che Guevara—are linked in the Chicano/a imagination.

The influence of the Cuban Revolution and leftist thought on Chávez himself, however, was minimal and indirect, coming through younger associates such as Luis Valdez, Eliezer Risco, and others. Much more important were the religious underpinnings of Chávez's project that resonated with the tenets of liberation theology as they had been formulated in the 1960s in Latin America. Pope John XXIII and Vatican Council II had shifted the role of the Catholic Church toward service to the poor, and liberation theologians drew upon thinkers in both the Christian and Marxist traditions in order to formulate a powerful concept of religious activism or "orthopraxis" as opposed to abstract orthodoxy.[34]

In fundamental ways, both the Vatican II reforms and Chávez's project embodied traditional forms of Mexican Catholicism in which the role of the indigenous poor took precedence over institutionalized religion. One of the earliest treatises on the Virgen of Guadalupe, for example, depicts a scene in which Juan Diego, the indigenous man who had seen the Virgin on the hill at Tepeyac, complains that because he is a commoner (*macehual*) he is ill suited to carry the Virgin's message to the bishop. The Virgin replies: "Do listen, my youngest child. Be assured that my servants and messengers to whom I entrust it to carry my message and realize my wishes are not high-ranking people. Rather it is highly necessary that you yourself be involved and take care of it. It is very much by your hand that my will and wish are to be carried out and accomplished."[35] The idea that it is the poor who carry out God's work was at the core of Chávez's public style and it resonated with the foundational working-class membership and principles of the majority of Chicano/a Movement organizations.

Because of his conscious decision to draw upon Mexican Catholic iconography and rituals, Chávez would soon find himself in a position he had not anticipated and certainly did not seek. For some of his followers, Chávez became less a Don Quixote than a Christ figure who incarnated the saintly virtues of humility and service to the poor in a corrupt and immoral world. The beatification of Chávez coincided with the ways in which the figures of the murdered Kennedy brothers functioned in the Mexican American imaginary.

Chávez's association with Robert Kennedy, martyred in June of 1968, seemed to increase each man's stature, and indeed Bobby Kennedy's indirect role in the development of Chávez's national reputation cannot be underestimated. His ties to the UFW leader were captured most dramatically perhaps in the widely circulated account and photographs of RFK feeding Chavez a piece of bread and conversing with him as he ended his fast on March 10, 1968 (fig. 13).[36]

Although Chávez had met Kennedy for the first time in 1960, the two men actually spent very little time together over the ensuing years. Kennedy had traveled to Delano in 1966 for congressional hearings, but according to Kennedy biographer Evan Thomas that meeting with Chávez initially held little appeal for Kennedy: "His involvement followed a familiar pattern: at first, he grumbled, he didn't want to fly to California to meet with some striking Mexicans. . . . But reluctantly, as a favor to his liberal activist friends in the United Auto Workers, he flew out to Delano, California, in mid-March."[37]

By the time of his second trip to Delano in 1968, however, Kennedy had become a staunch supporter. In a press release announcing his visit, Kennedy wrote:

This is a historic occasion. We have come here out of respect for one of the heroic figures of our time—Cesar Chavez. But I also come here to congratulate all of you, you who are locked with Cesar in the struggle for justice for the farmworker, and the struggle for justice for the Spanish-speaking American. . . . The world must know, from this time forward, that the migrant farm worker, the Mexican American, is coming into his own rights. . . . And when your children and grandchildren take their place in America—going to high school, and college, and taking good jobs at good pay—when you look at them, you will say, "I did this. I was there, at the point of difficulty and danger." And though you may be old and bent from many years of labor, no man will stand taller than you when you say, "I marched with Cesar."[38]

The second half of the statement was a brilliant description of the importance of nonviolent activism and efforts to legislate federal protection for farm laborers. After Kennedy was assassinated just a few months later, the support of the nation's best-known Democrat politician was gone but the symbolism linking Chávez to the Kennedy brothers took on an enhanced power.

THE ELABORATION OF A LEADER

Instrumental in the earliest representations of Chávez as the leader for whom la Raza had been waiting was playwright and Teatro Campesino founder Luis Valdez. In 1970, he told the Berkeley, California, newspaper *La voz del pueblo*: "*Pero allí teníamos al líder esperando y no nos dábamos cuenta. Era César Chávez, y estaba allí consumiéndose a fuego lento, pobre como nosotros y hablándonos, sugiriéndonos lo que debíamos hacer—nunca ordenando—y poco a poco nos fuimos reuniendo en torno suyo . . . un hombre, en fin, que había sufrido en carne propia las vicisitudes de toda la Raza en los Estados Unidos*" ("But without realizing it we already had the leader we were waiting for. It was César Chávez, and he was there slowly burning, poor like us and telling us, suggesting to us what we should do—never ordering us—and little by little we began to organize around him . . . a man, in short, who had suffered in his very being the trials of all Mexican people in the United States").[39] By this time, as the Delano Grape Strike was coming to a successful conclusion, the identification of Chávez with earlier holy figures was so great that California poet Ricardo C. Pérez could compose the following:

> Con un libro de Gandhi en la mano
> Cual héroe en un mundo putrefacto
> Buscando la justicia en un pacto
> Anda con alta frente el chicano.
>
> Sufre como un hereje el desprecio
> Sufre como un Cristo el martirio
> Sufre por sufrir que es el precio
> Del que ama la llama de amor, el lirio.
>
> Pero grande en su humilde aspecto es
> Y por todo lo que sinceramente cree
> Porque es suya la única vía que
>
> Es tocada por la redentora fe
> Que hará todo humilde a la vez
> Tan grande en heroísmo cual los Andes!

(With a book of Gandhi in his hand, like a hero in a decadent world, searching for justice in a contract, the Chicano walks proudly. He suffers disdain like a heretic, suffers martyrdom like Christ, suffers for suffering which is the price for he who loves the flame of love, the lily. But he is great in his humility and in all he truly believes because his is the only way that is touched by redeeming faith, that will make every humble person a hero and in that heroism as immense as the Andes.)[40]

At once a Chicano "Everyman" and Christ himself, Peréz's Chávez is linked in the final stanza to all of Latin America and by implication to the struggles of Spanish-speaking communities throughout the hemisphere. The religious language of the poem ("*la llama de amor, el lirio*") taken from the Catholic mystic tradition, together with the reference to Gandhi, produce a tone of holiness, and establish Chávez as less a union organizer than a twentieth-century saint.

Other Movement writers contributed to the canonization process. San Francisco poet Elías Hruska-Cortés, for example, wrote:

. . .

> Delano the strategy and César
> César and Cristo and Victory
> César and filipino hall and victory
> Delano and Solidarity and People
> Delano the boycott and victory
> Delano the strike and César
> the strike and victory
> *huel-ga huel-ga huel-ga*[41]

Shortly after he ended his career as a Movement attorney, candidate for sheriff of Los Angeles county, and all-around *vato loco*, Oscar Zeta Acosta solidified for the Chicano/a imaginary the image of Chávez the saint. Early in his 1973 novel, *Revolt of the Cockroach People*, Acosta's literary alter ego makes a pilgrimage to Delano. As the character of the Brown Buffalo approaches the room in which Chávez has been fasting for twenty five days, an air of otherworldliness permeates the scene: "I enter and close the door behind me. It is very dark. There is a tiny candle burning over a bed, illuminating dimly a wooden cross and a figure of La Virgen on the wall. My ears are buzzing. There is a heavy smell of incense and kerosene. I don't move. I hear nothing. I no longer have any idea of why I have come or what I will say, 'Is that you, Buffalo?' The voice is soft, barely audible."[42]

Seeking spiritual and political guidance, Buffalo is surprised to learn that Chávez is aware of his activities in Los Angeles: "In the darkness, I think again of his words. The Father of Chicanos, Cesar Chavez, has heard of me."[43] For Acosta, then, the figure of Chávez functions as a powerful touchstone against which all other agendas and practices will be measured. Not only a saint, Chávez in Acosta's hands becomes the moral and ethical core of the Movimiento in stark contrast to the depravities of the Brown Buffalo and his associates. By giving his blessing to Acosta and "the Militants" in L.A., César Chávez assumes his role at the symbolic center of Movement history.

In a concluding section of the novel the figure of Chávez reappears as a character witness for Corky Gonzales who had been detained after the Chicano Moratorium antiwar demonstration that took place on

August 29, 1970. Chávez's stature is intact, according to the narrator, who tells us: "They [Chávez and Gonzales] are number one and two in the Nation of Aztlán."[44] But the Brown Buffalo himself has moved away from the ideal of nonviolence: "I have not seen Cesar since I first began in L.A. He is still my leader, but I no longer worship him. I am pushing for Corky because when things go political, I will push for the more militant of the two. Corky laughs at me. He tells me that Cesar's work is more important than both of us combined. Speak for yourself, I tell him."[45] Given Acosta's real-life role as a Movement participant, we must read this statement as more than a mere declaration made by a fictionalized character. The passage captures well the tension between Chávez's militant nonviolence and alternative Movimiento practices that viewed insurgency as necessarily linked to hyper-masculine acts of physical aggression.

Even as sectarian nationalist and leftist groups in the Movement mounted critiques of the strategies preferred by the UFW, right-wing attacks on Chávez proliferated as the union continued to achieve moderate success. Ironically, what bothered conservatives more than anything else was Chávez's public image as a Gandhi-like pacifist. In a vitriolic book aimed at discrediting Chávez, conservative writer Ralph de Toledano wrote: "A small man with an oversize messianic complex has put his mark on Delano. He has been able to do so by mobilizing in this small town the raw power of organized labor, the hysteria and psychosis of the New Left, and the pressure apparatus of the clergy."[46] Toledano, the son of Spanish immigrants to the United States, had made a career in Republican Party circles by writing laudatory biographies of J. Edgar Hoover and Richard Nixon. As an early incarnation of a "Hispanic intellectual" in the service of corporate and law-enforcement interests, Toledano made it his business to represent the growers as the victims of the UFW's evil intentions.

Other writers inclined to follow Toledano's lead sought to portray Chávez as just another corrupt union boss: "Chávez has been depicted as an almost Gandhiesque character, loving his fellow man, eschewing violence, calling for peaceful resolution of human problems. His detractors view him as a conniving labor czar who deliberately defrauded the grape pickers in order to aggrandize his labor union. Generally, this latter view seems more accurate and to the point, for it dwells on the ability of one man to manipulate others and to use what can best be described as shady tactics to achieve his ends."[47] Such attempts to cast Chávez as a thug were doomed to fail despite a well-funded, grower-sponsored public-relations campaign. The right-wing and anti-Mexican John Birch Society ran a small cottage industry throughout the Viet Nam war period whose sole objective was to produce attacks against Chávez and the UFW in books such as *Little Cesar and His Phony Strike* or *The Grapes: Communist Wrath in Delano.*[48]

One of the more hysterical efforts to link the UFW to a communist conspiracy was produced by Orange County, California, reporter John Steinbacher: "The young who follow a Chavez are not unlike the Narodniks, those bearded beatnik young of the Czarist regime, who helped to bring on the blood bath that led to the Red takeover of Russia ... The young follow a Hitler or a Stalin or a Kennedy—or a Chavez—in a mad lust for power through the darkling bye-ways of America."[49] Rhetorical flourishes such as this, the product of an almost irrational hatred of liberalism, remained on the margins of public discourse in the 1970s. Even conservatives could only view the implication that Chávez was somehow equivalent to Hitler and Stalin as extreme.

Not only conservative Birchers, Republicans, and their hired "Hispanic" writers criticized Chávez. As I have demonstrated, activists within the various sectors of the Movimiento itself were at times at odds with several of Chávez's political positions throughout the Movement's militant period. Undoubtedly, the most contentious point had to do with the UFW's public statements with regard to undocumented labor. Advocating strict immigration controls and a closed border policy, Chávez, Dolores Huerta, and other union leaders hoped to deprive growers of a vast pool of potential strikebreakers. In his 1969 testimony before the congressional subcommittee on labor, Chávez referred to "illegals" and "green carders" as "natural economic rivals of those who become American citizens or who otherwise decide to stake out their future in this country."[50]

From the union's perspective, the logic of their position made sense. As Chávez told a union audience: "Brothers and sisters, we know that right now in California there are at least sixty to seventy thousand illegals from Mexico breaking strikes and working elsewhere. . . . If we were able to remove the illegals from California, at least from the strike fields, we would win the strike overnight."[51] But many Movement activists viewed the UFW's official position on undocumented workers as misguided and complicit with reactionary and anti-immigrant rhetoric and legislation.

By the mid-1970s, the criticisms of Chávez and the union on this issue had reached a breaking point, primarily due to threats from the Department of Justice to begin the deportation of undocumented workers. Chávez, sensing the growing discontent among many of his supporters, published a defense of "illegal aliens" in a 1974 letter to the *San Francisco Examiner*. Tensions on the issue continued unresolved, however, and Chávez himself angrily told an interviewer in *El malcriado* that "most of the left attacking us has no experience in labor matters. They don't know what a strike is. . . . And they don't know because really they haven't talked to the workers."[52] Beyond the specific issue of immigration, however, other differences of opinion emerged from within a Movement that increasingly encompassed diverse ideologies and agendas.

As early as 1965, members of Tijerina's Alianza Federal de las Mercedes had declared the philosophy of nonviolence to be less desirable than the actions taken by the Black community in Los Angeles during the Watts riots. Alianza member Felix Martinez had visited both Watts and Delano in 1965, and upon his return to New Mexico he reported: "revolution speeds up evolution."[53] In this view, Chávez's reformist agenda lacked the necessary intensity that drove insurgent Chicano political programs. In his 1970 poem titled "Los caudillos," therefore, tejano poet raúlrsalinas could write:

> In rich Delano vineyards
> Chavez does his pacifist thing
> "lift that crate
> and pick them grapes"
> stoop labor's awright—with God on your side.
> Small wonder David Sanchez
> impatient and enraged in L.A., dons a beret
> . . .
> Tijerina, Indo-Hispano
> you're our man.[54]

From a more strictly leftist position, activist Frobén Lozada complained: "And the pacifists want us to preach morality to them who have none!"[55] One labor and antiwar activist took a more pragmatic position with regard to Chávez's perceived pacifism: "They [the UFW] have been able to win broad public support by demonstrating that it is their enemies who are violent. But in elevating nonviolence to an absolute principle, the union's leadership has unfortunately given up the right of the union to physically defend itself in any circumstances."[56] For many Chicanos, self-determination would never be realized without the right to self-defense, given the high degree of racialized violence and economic exploitation that characterized institutional practices in the United States.

Other sectors of the Movement found themselves in disagreement with UFW strategies. Chicano organizers struggling to create a third political party were particularly critical of Chávez for his unwavering allegiance to the Democratic Party. The union newspaper *El malcriado* had stated repeatedly that John F. Kennedy would "always be our president," and as we have seen, Robert Kennedy had given the union his support in public statements and appearances. For some of the founders of La Raza Unida Party (LRUP), therefore, Chávez's efforts to keep Chicanos in the Democrat camp were counterproductive if not outright "treason":

> [Chávez] would be doing a disservice to people about the crying need to break with the Democratic Party. He would be miseducating people, and it's a lot harder to educate people after they've been miseducated about what is necessary. . . . It would make it harder for us to talk about a Chicano party if Chavez was at the same time campaigning and registering people in the Democratic Party. And the truth of the matter is that this has already been tried again and again and nothing has come from it. Malcolm X made a very strong statement on this. He said, "Anyone who supports the Democratic Party after its record of oppression, and what it has done to our people, is not only a fool, but a traitor to his race."[57]

The exaggerated rhetoric of the attack was certainly divisive and the use of Malcolm X's remark misleading and out of context. In practical terms, the tensions between LRUP and Chávez produced serious signs of disunity. Filmmaker Jesús Treviño reports that Chávez turned down an invitation to attend the LRUP convention in 1972 because both José Angel Gutiérrez and Corky Gonzales had made it clear to him that they were displeased with the union's endorsement of Democratic candidate George McGovern.[58] According to one account, several LRUP officials in the Texas delegation saw the break with Chávez as a necessary step in the eventual displacement of older organizers considered to be too accepting of the status quo by younger, more radical, leaders.[59]

The criticisms of Chávez by some members of LRUP precluded potential alliances that could have furthered Movement agendas. Historian Juan Gómez Quiñones has summarized these unfortunate developments:

> For all his visibility and connections, La Raza Unida viewed Chavez negatively; absurdly, they felt he was negligent in pursuing broader Chicano issues or in demanding political concessions for Chicanos. To LRUP, Chavez was simply an arm of the Anglo political establishment; and allegedly he represented the traditional negotiating posture in politics, one that clashed with La Raza Unida's rhetorical emphasis on Chicano "self-determination." LRUP, however, overlooked UFW strength in California and the fact that they were seeking electoral office in the system for themselves. La Raza Unida was weakened by the inability to incorporate support from a prominent Chicano organization.[60]

The question of whether or not the UFW was a "Chicano organization," however, depended on how the latter term was defined. On various occasions Chávez himself declared that he was a union leader, not a leader in the Chicano Movement. Some activists observed early on that Chávez was conspicuously absent from important Movement events such as the Poor People's Campaign in 1968 or the August 29, 1970, Chicano Moratorium antiwar demonstration in Los Angeles.[61] Had they been readers of *The New Yorker*, young Chicano/a activists would have been surprised by Chávez's comments in Peter Matthiessen's 1969 essays. Stressing the need to avoid the narrowest forms of regressive nationalism, Chávez seemed to attack several of the basic principles of emergent Chicana/o identities:

> "I hear more and more Mexicans talking about *la raza*—to build up their pride, you know," Chavez told me. "Some people don't look at it as racism, but when you say '*la raza*,' you are saying an anti-gringo thing, and it won't stop there. Today it's anti-gringo,

tomorrow it will be anti-Negro, and the day after it will be anti-Filipino, anti-Puerto Rican. And then it will be anti-poor-Mexican, and anti-darker-skinned Mexican . . . *La raza* is a very dangerous concept. I speak very strongly against it among the chicanos. At this point in the struggle, they respect me enough so that they don't emphasize *la raza*, but as soon as this is over they'll be against me, because I make fun of it, and I knock down machismo, too."[62]

Matthiessen's conversation with longtime UFW organizer LeRoy Chatfield about Chavez's attitude toward the Movement might have added fuel to the fire. Chatfield remarked: "Everyone should be proud of what he is, of course, but race is only skin-deep. It's phony, and it comes out of frustration—the *la raza* people are not secure. They want to use Cesar as a symbol of their nationalism. But he doesn't want any part of it. He said to me just the other day, 'Can't they understand that that's just the way Hitler started?' A few months ago, a big foundation gave some money to a *la raza* group—they liked the outfit's sense of pride, or something—and Cesar really told them off."[63]

It was moments like these that held the potential to strain the otherwise strong links between Chávez and younger Chicano/a radicals. Reflecting more than just a "generation gap" or even ideological differences, tensions arose around issues of leadership style and organizational structures. Veteran organizer Bert Corona, for example, recalled an argument between University of California-Santa Barbara student militants and Chávez in which the students complained about a lack of consultation despite the fact that they had provided the manpower for recent union pickets.[64]

When asked whether or not the organizing strategies of the Crusade for Justice were in conflict with those of the UFW, in particular with regard to coalition building, Corky Gonzales replied that there was no disagreement between the two but insisted that Chicanos ought not enter into alliances as "junior partners": "There's a difference between that [Chávez's] and my philosophy. He feels that maybe it's the only way he could do it, that is, to get this outside help and make this outside alliance in order to remain autonomous. That's quite a contradiction, but it's an irony that's true. In order to have autonomy he had to have financial support. We work differently. We feel that no matter how long it takes, we have to develop our own leadership. We don't want those alliances. We'll take their support, but they can't make any decisions for us. They can't influence us."[65] Differences of opinion continued to separate the organizing strategies of major Movement leaders despite joint appearances and public pronouncements as to shared objectives.

In the end, however, the most astute commentators of the period understood that the activities of the UFW and of Chávez himself served as crucial points of reference for the Movimiento as a whole. At its core the Movement was a working-class project and who else but the farmworker, after all, was more exploited? As the poet Abelardo Delgado put it: "Many movement people charge that Chavez may be one hell of an organizer, but not a leader in the Chicano movement in that he fails to embrace many other areas of concern affecting millions of other deprived Chicanos. Whether the charge is a valid one or not, the fact remains that we can rally behind our national leaders, and whether movement Chicanos claim Chavez owes them something or whether Chavez himself acknowledges the movement, the fact remains that he is a Chicano whose immense contribution cannot be ignored or belittled."[66]

Delgado's sentiments were widely shared by Movement activists. At the same time, some activists argued that the UFW's successes themselves were inconceivable without the mass mobilizations organized by various Movement organizations. In a period in which the trade-union movement was not particularly strong and the number of farmworkers relatively small, Chávez's efforts, they believed, depended on the popular base created by the Movimiento.[67] Even *chavistas* like Peter Matthiessen, who in his book had constructed a subtle division between Chávez and what he called "la raza Mexicans," that is, Movement activists, understood the strong ties that bound the various groups together. For Matthiessen, however, the source of "Brown Power" identities could be traced directly to the founder of the UFW: "The newborn pride in being chicano, in the opinion of most people, is due largely to Chavez himself."[68]

By the 1970s, with the exception of revolutionary groups like the August 29th Movement, which accused Chávez of reformism and class collaborationism, the artificial division between "Movement people" and Chávez to a large extent had been repaired. After the arrest of Corky Gonzales on a concealed-weapons charge at the August 29, 1970, Chicano Moratorium antiwar demonstration, Chávez agreed to serve as a character witness for Gonzales at the Los Angeles trial. In response to questions from attorney Oscar Zeta Acosta, Chávez testified that Gonzales's "general reputation for truth, honesty, and integrity is excellent."[69] Even Chicano socialists were rethinking the role of the UFW within the overall Movimiento. Writer and activist José G. Pérez, for example, who had covered Chávez for the *Young Socialist* newspaper, argued in 1973: "Because the UFW is part of both the Chicano Movement and the labor movement, both must rally to its defense—otherwise both will be weakened and the way will be cleared for further assaults by the employers and their racist government."[70] As the American war in Southeast Asia came to an end, Chávez became less critical of the concepts of "Aztlán" and "La Raza" in his public speeches although he always subordinated them to the discourses of trade unionism.

El legado de César

Attempts to organize farmworkers in California had met with failure in every decade of the first half of the twentieth century. The relative success of the UFW was the product of an historical conjuncture in which grassroots mobilizations around a variety of issues affecting Mexican Americans, the ascendancy of the liberal wing of the Democratic Party, Pope John XXIII's shifting of the Catholic Church's agenda toward the poor, the general politicization of U.S. society caused by the Viet Nam war, and an emerging Chicano/a consciousness created a context in which it was possible to extract long-sought concessions from political and economic elites. At the end of this extraordinary historical moment, capital continued to treat labor as a commodity, but at least working conditions had improved and the discourse of the worker's inherent dignity had achieved a temporary prominence. The Chicano/a Critique of Liberalism had forced liberal democracy in the United States to deliver on some but not all of its promises.

As I have argued in this chapter, two characteristics of the UFW unique among Movement organizations was the fact that from its inception the union consistently practiced coalition and internationalist politics and the fact that its most celebrated leader deployed a nontraditional form of masculine leadership that contrasted sharply with other forms of the period.[71] Understood in its original context, La Causa was at once a union movement, an ethnic Mexican movement, and a result of the more generalized social transformation known as the 1960s. As one astute student of farmworkers's movements wrote: "The United Farm Workers story is significant for three reasons. In general terms, the UFW exemplified the basic goals and strategies of the social movements of the stormy 1960s. The major social movements of the period were insurgencies, that is, organized attempts to bring the interests of previously unorganized and excluded groups into the centers of economic and political power. By organizing farmworkers, the UFW took up the interests of one of the more disorganized and marginal segments of American society."[72]

By the mid-1980s, the conservative counterattack against progressive social movements was winning on many fronts. In California, Governor George Deukmejian, backed by affluent corporate growers, brought the "Reagan Revolution" to the farmworkers by gutting the Agricultural Labor Relations Act that had been passed in 1975. Chávez reacted to these rollbacks with anger: "There is a shadow falling over the land, brothers and sisters, and the dark forces of reaction threaten us now as never before. The enemies of the poor and the working classes hold power in the White House and the governor's office. . . . They have created a whole new class of millionaires while forcing millions of ordinary people into poverty."[73] At this moment perhaps more than previous ones, Chávez understood that the early activities of the UFW had been inextricably linked to a broader movement having to do with the construction of a new and collective identity that challenged the racial and economic status quo. In a speech to the Commonwealth Club of California, he said:

> The UFW's survival—its existence—was not in doubt in my mind when the time began to come—after the union became visible—when Chicanos started entering college in greater numbers, when Hispanics began running for public office in greater numbers, when our people started asserting their rights on a broad range of issues and in many communities across the country.
>
> The union's survival—its very existence—sent out a signal to all Hispanics: that we were fighting for our dignity, that we were challenging and overcoming injustice, that we were empowering the least educated among us, the poorest among us.
>
> The message was clear: If it could happen in the fields, it could happen anywhere—in the cities, in the courts, in the city councils, in the state legislatures. I didn't really appreciate it at

the time, but the coming of our union signaled the start of great changes among Hispanics that are only now beginning to be seen.[74]

The criticism of a "Brown Power" agenda voiced by Chávez in his 1969 *New Yorker* interviews was now tempered by the recognition that the UFW had been an integral part of a multifaceted social insurgency with disparate sectors loosely linked together under the rubric of the Movimiento.[75]

During the same period, Chávez made explicit the connections between the shift to the right in U.S. domestic politics and U.S. support for reactionary groups abroad. Referring to events in El Salvador, Guatemala, and Nicaragua, he told union members: "Our enemies are responsible for the brutal murder of thousands of dark-skinned, Spanish-speaking farm workers through their military support of blood-thirsty dictators in Central America. The men, women, and children who have been slaughtered committed the same crimes we have committed: they wanted a better life for themselves and their families, a life free from hunger and poverty and exploitation."[76] A full decade after the high point of the Movement, Chávez articulated the basic principles of what had always been a strong and too often forgotten current of Chicano internationalism.

As the decade of the 1990s began, Chávez reflected upon the legacy of Dr. King. In a speech delivered in January of 1990, his critical analysis of the current state of affairs wove together the critical language of the Movement with fundamental messages about coalition building and nonviolence:

My friends, as we enter a new decade, it should be clear to all of us that there is an unfinished agenda, that we have miles to go before we reach the promised land. The men who rule this country today never learned the lessons of Dr. King, they never learned that non-violence is the only way to peace and justice. Our nation continues to wage war upon its neighbors, and upon itself. The powers-that-be rule over a racist society, filled with hatred and ignorance. Our nation continues to be segregated along racial and economic lines. The powers-that-be make themselves richer by exploiting the poor. Our nation continues to allow children to go hungry, and will not even house its own people. The time is now for people, of all races and backgrounds, to sound the trumpets of change. As Dr. King proclaimed, "There comes a time when people get tired of being trampled over by the iron feet of oppression."[77]

Throughout the years of the Bush Sr. and Clinton admininstrations, the conservative reaction Chávez had warned about during Reagan's presidency gained momentum. This was particularly so in California, where ballot initiatives attempted to destroy the social safety net for undocumented workers, eliminated affirmative action, and gutted bilingual-education programs.

Although the UFW grew in membership in the 1990s and carried out large organizing campaigns such as the one in the California strawberry industry, victories were few and far between. On the over four hundred farms where the union had won elections since 1975, less than half the growers agreed to sign contracts. The problem of unsafe transportation for farmworkers, an issue captured in Tomás Rivera's brilliant novel set in the 1950s, *Y no se lo tragó la tierra*, had been responsible for numerous deaths over the previous thirty years. Despite Chávez's personal efforts to win reforms on this issue, it was not until 2002 that the California state legislature finally passed a law mandating that growers provide safe vehicles.[78] Also in 2002, after a well-publicized march on Sacramento to force the hand of Governor Gray Davis, the union won the right to have outside mediators and the Agricultural Labor Relations Board decide disputes between workers and growers.[79] Not unlike his disembodied voice that speaks from beyond to all those who visit the UFW's official website, the image of Chávez hovers over these victories and all contemporary acts of Chicano/a activism.

Today, Chávez enjoys widespread admiration throughout Mexican American and Latino communities and even within Hispanic corporate culture. For progressive Chicanas and Chicanos, of course, he continues to be the major historical icon, and it would be difficult to imagine a contemporary Chicano/a rejection of Chávez's legacy like the backlash Michael Dyson records in his book on Martin Luther King. Dyson reconstructs a conversation in which a thirty-something African American scholar vehemently denouces King for being upper middle class, accomodationist, an Uncle Tom, and implicitly not "man enough."[80] Unlike earlier critiques of Chávez from within some

Movement sectors that raised doubts about his political alliances and tactics, contemporary Chicano/a intellectual projects have refrained from such a harsh reinterpretation perhaps because many ethnic Mexican professionals have rejected outright the more contestatory aspects of the Movimiento. In the context of a generalized dispersion and fragmentation of progressive forces in the United States, the image of Chávez has become one of the safer ones associated with a revolutionary period, a period that still frightens many in both the corporate art world and the corporate university.

The death of César Chávez in 1993 solidified his position as a historic Mexican American leader and by 2001 the state of California had instituted an official holiday in his honor. Although neoconservatives in their attempts to block the holiday continued to represent Chávez as a union mafioso, for the majority of Americans Chávez had become a somewhat romanticized and nonthreatening figure that was less associated with unions and social movements than he was with nonviolence or religion or dot-comer "creativity." The commodification of Chávez's image proceeded along the lines of that of Martin Luther King, Jr. Featured in the Apple Computers "Think Different" series, Chávez joined his ally Robert Kennedy as one more pitchman for corporate gain.

Even as the depoliticization of Chávez moved forward, the general public's understanding of the plight of contemporary farmworkers in the United States improved only slightly, if at all, from what it had been in 1962 when Chávez, Dolores Huerta, Larry Itliong, and others created the UFW. At the turn of the century, conditions in the fields were still deplorable with Mexican farmworkers reporting significantly higher rates of cancer than other Latinos in California, a higher risk of contracting HIV/AIDS, 63 percent with only six years of school or less, and 75 percent without health insurance.[81]

In contemporary Chicano/a culture, Chávez continues to fulfill a number of functions not the least of which is that of a spiritual force at one with the powers of nature. Novelist Rudolfo Anaya, for example, has written:

> Our César has not died!
> He is the light of the new day.
> He is the rain that renews parched fields.
> He is the hope that builds the House of Justice.

He is with us! Here! Today!
Listen to his voice in the wind.
He is the spirit of Hope,
A Movement building to sweep away oppression!
His spirit guides us in the struggle
Let us join his spirit to ours![82]

In a process not unlike the one that transformed Che Guevara into a revolutionary saint, the mythologizing of Chávez removes him from the historical reality in which he lived and worked and effaces his militant critique of economic inequality in order to construct a figure for the ages.

In its weakest form, then, the image of Chávez becomes one more petrified icon deployed to demonstrate the virtues of American pluralism and liberal democracy—an aestheticized image on a postage stamp. Poet César Cruz brilliantly captured the contradiction between this assimilated figure and the radical pursuit of social justice to which Chávez devoted his life:

I am wearing a
César Chávez t-shirt
driving a car with
César Chávez stickers
on César Chávez Boulevard
passing by
César Chávez school
on César Chávez Day
hearing
César Chávez commercials
on the local radio
and seeing
César Chávez billboards
announcing a
César Chávez march
sponsored by multinational
corporations
wondering
if
we praise you

or curse you
when farmworkers are still underpaid
under-appreciated
when immigrants
are scapegoated
when nothing you stood for
is respected ...[83]

And yet even as the historical reality of Chávez recedes into the distant pantheon of "American" heroes there can be no doubt that his name may still be invoked as a catalyst for ongoing struggles to end exploitation and to win full political rights for working-class people. In 2001, recently organized janitors and service workers, made up overwhelmingly of Latina/o immigrants, marched through the streets of San Diego, California, chanting "*Sí se puede*" ("Yes, we can") as they locked arms behind the image of César Estrada Chávez.

In my next chapter I will explore some of the lessons to be learned from the fact that historical actors who on the surface appear to be inward-looking and exclusionary Chicano "nationalists" often actively pursued alliances with other communities, most notably the African American community. If, as I have advocated, we refuse to reduce the Movimiento to its most regressive ideological expressions we may be better able to rethink the tactics and philosophies of Movement organizations and leaders in order to strategize for future struggles.

CHAPTER FIVE

—"BROWN AND BLACK TOGETHER— (AS LONG AS THE SUN AND THE MOON SHALL SHINE)"

"I've heard about what you guys are up to . . . It isn't much different than the blacks."
"Bullshit! The Chicano thing is different."
"Yeah, it's different . . . but from two thousand miles away it looks just the same."[1]

FOR TWO DAYS IN LATE AUGUST OF 1970, world-renowned anthropologist Margaret Mead and famed author James Baldwin participated in what they called an informal conversation on race. The transcripts of the meeting were published in 1971 as *A Rap on Race*. At one point in this fascinating exchange between two highly articulate spokespeople for progressive causes, Mead asks Baldwin the following question: "Have you learned to say Chicano?" Baldwin's response is both a heartfelt admission of ignorance and a symptomatic expression of the historic erasure of Mexican Americans from the national consciousness:

Mead: Have you learned to say Chicano?
Baldwin: No, not really. It is absolutely new for me. I don't even know where it came from and I don't even quite know what it means!
Mead: It means Mexican, in the United States; Mexican on the Pacific Coast, at present.
Baldwin: That's right, that's where I picked up the expression. I didn't know how to use it. I didn't know whom to ask. Do you know what I mean? It really is kind of frightening, because you don't want to use it. I hate people—hippies, for example—who pick up various black phrases and use them to death and don't know what they are talking about. I never want to be caught in that bag myself. So I have become rather tongue-tied, too. I don't know what to say. I don't know what Chicano means.[2]

Mead's incomplete definition of the term *Chicano* limits its usage to the West Coast and ignores its widespread dissemination throughout the Southwest, especially by 1970. Baldwin's attitude reveals his intelligence and cultural sensitivity—he will not use the term *Chicano* until he has investigated its origins and cultural meanings. What is discouraging in retrospect is to learn that one of the country's leading African American figures of the civil-rights era found himself completely disconnected from another community of color participating in related struggles, a community that several years earlier had played a key role in a broad coalition for economic justice during the Poor People's Campaign in the nation's capital. Three days after the Baldwin-Mead dialogue, on August 29, 1970, the Chicano community would stage a massive antiwar demonstration in Los Angeles that was the first such event in the United States to be organized by a significant sector of the ethnic minority working class.

In this chapter I will trace only some of the relationships between Chicano and African American organizations during the Viet Nam war period. As I stated in Chapter One, my hypothesis is that once the Movement's ideological complexity is unpacked it becomes more difficult to reduce the Movement to narrow forms of sectarian nationalism, a reduction perpetrated by a number of contemporary historians and culture critics. Despite the relative popularity of the slogan "Mi Raza primero" ("My People first"), large numbers of Chicano/a militants were able to negotiate between their commitment to serving local communities and a broader understanding of national and global economic and race relations. It was this understanding that allowed them to forge alliances with Puerto Rican and Black groups and express solidarity with anticolonial movements in the developing world.

In some cases, such as that of Reies López Tijerina, coalitions were a tactic designed to heighten the degree of Indo-Hispano militancy and garner greater public attention for the issue of land rights. For many in the student-activist sector of the Movimiento, coalitions grew naturally out of their sense that the fundamental component of their collective identity was their working-class origins. Although the social consequences of racializaton and anti-Mexican racism in the United States clearly marked their experience and that of their families, the effects of class privilege and economic exploitation led these activists to various forms of Marxist analysis and participation in the trade-union, antiwar, and international solidarity movements.

For the vast majority of African Americans whose political education had taken place in regions of the country where there were few Latinos, Mexican Americans were an unknown quantity. According to some Black leaders, Chicanos were just another kind of white people speaking a different language. As early as 1965, however, Martin Luther King, Jr., had noted a broadening of the Black community's political agenda in order to include other groups outside of the United States who had endured the legacy of colonialism and white supremacy. When asked by an interviewer if solidarity with Africa was on the rise, he answered: "Consciously or unconsciously, the American Negro has been caught up by the black Zeitgeist. He feels a deepening sense of identification with his black African brothers, and with his brown and yellow brothers of Asia, South America and the Caribbean. With them he is moving with a sense of increasing urgency toward the promised land of racial justice."[3]

On the domestic front, Dr. King met with Chicano activists late in his career, but he continued to rely in his final speeches and writings upon a black/white vision of U.S. race relations. His planning of the Poor People's Campaign, cut short by his assassination, had moved him haltingly toward a wider perspective: "We must not overlook the fact that millions of Puerto Ricans, Mexican Americans, Indians and Appalachian whites are also poverty-stricken."[4] Despite Dr. King's hope that a united "rainbow coalition" against racism could be built, for a variety of reasons throughout the late 1960s and early 1970s such alliances would be tentative at best. As we shall see, where multiracial coalitions were indeed successful, law-enforcement agencies moved in quickly to disrupt them.

The influence of African American popular culture in the Viet Nam war era followed a pattern set decades earlier in large U.S. cities. Spanish-speaking youth, racialized and marginalized within mainstream social practices, had looked to other communities of color for support and inspiration. The pachuco phenomenon of the 1940s, for example, drew heavily on Black subcultural styles, and at its peak was the hybrid product of Mexican American, Filipino, Black, and "white" influences. In the late 1960s, the Civil Rights Movement and the cultural icons surrounding it provided young Chicano/as with models at a time when Mexican-origin public figures were few and often in the ethnic closet.[5] In California in particular, where redlining and real estate covenants had produced cross-ethnic contacts and cultural exchanges throughout the urban centers, the impact of Motown, Aretha Franklin, and for young Chicano men especially, Muhammad Ali, was undeniable. Even the most sectarian nationalists, who might accuse more open-minded Chicano/as of being *mayateros*, were hard pressed to conceal their attraction to African American performers and sports icons.

Despite the undeniable influence of African American politics and culture on Chicano/a youth during the Viet Nam war period, it would be inaccurate to claim that the Chicano Movement took Black activism as its primary inspiration. I have outlined in a previous chapter on the Cuban Revolution how one episode in Latin American history played a key role in the complex genealogy of the Movimiento. The claim that "Chicanos were copying Blacks," an assertion made by some scholars during the Movement and a number of post-Movement historians, was the same charge made by conservative critics of the Movement during the Viet Nam war period.

Celia Heller, for example, a professor at Hunter College in New York had conducted fieldwork in East Los Angeles among Mexican American youth in the mid-1950s. Her opinion of emerging Chicano/a identities a decade later was that they would harm the image of the majority of youth who simply wanted to assimilate ("the new converts to the American Dream"). The Chicanos, she claimed, were capturing the headlines by copying the "black militants": "By focusing attention on the incipient Mexican-American militancy and not bringing to light the beginning 'success story,' the mass media may play a part in the development of Mexican-American militancy (that emerged in the emulation of blacks) and in the extinguishment of the embryonic achievement orientation."[6] Another academic asserted in 1970 that Chicanos merely had borrowed their political language from African Americans: "A direct translation of 'We shall overcome' is the slogan 'Venceremos."[7] Although such a translation certainly was possible, the assertion was misleading insofar as it erased the specific Latin American origins of the latter term.

For many activist Chicana/o youth, the beret of Che Guevara had preceded by several years that of the Black Panther, and for them "Venceremos" had more to do with revolutionary Cuba than it did with Oakland or Selma. Figures such as Malcolm X, Martin Luther King, and the Panthers certainly played important roles in the radicalization of some sectors of the Movement, but one would be hard pressed to explain the political agendas and styles of diverse Chicano/a organizations through the exclusive prism of Black activism. As one close observer of the southern California Movement scene wrote in the late 1970s: "Although the black movement clearly influenced the Chicano upsurge of the 1960s, this upsurge undoubtedly did not, as sometime it is simplistically stated, derive basically from the black movement. Rather it tended to continue and to renew long-established patterns of struggle for change and for justice, whether social or economic, whether urban or rural."[8]

This important point had been stated several years earlier at the conclusion of one of the most complete studies of Mexican Americans published during the Movement period: "The new militancy is not just a simple imitation of Negro protest; it can be seen also as a resurgence of the historic conflict between Mexican Americans and Anglos in the Southwest. Tijerina's rebellion in New Mexico represents a modern counterpart of earlier guerrilla warfare and border clashes."[9] Or as one of the more knowledgeable students of the Mexican American community wrote: "Basically eclectic, *chicanismo* draws inspiration from outside the United States and outside the Mexican American experience. The Cuban Revolution, for example, exerts some influence, as do the career and ideas of Che Guevara. For instance, the Brown Berets (a Chicano youth group) affect the life style of this revolutionary. Black Power also offers something of a model. Most recently, Chicanos have resurrected the Mexican revolutionary tradition."[10] In his 1971 essay for *Trans-Action* magazine, UC Berkeley sociologist Bob Blauner offered a succinct critique of the copycat hypothesis:

> There is a common belief—to a great extent misleading—that Chicanos have been following in the footsteps of the black movement, though perhaps ten years behind . . . Yet Chicano intellectuals and working people had been living their version of cultural nationalism long before black militants brought the term to public attention a few years ago. Therefore we must be skeptical about the idea that the brown political dynamic is recreating the black's—the similarity of Brown Beret dress and rhetoric to the Black Panthers' notwithstanding. For the historical and sociocultural context of Mexican-American life has been unique—it cannot be fitted into the pattern of black-white relations, nor to the model of European ethnic group immigration, for that matter.[11]

An overemphasis on the impact of Black liberation models leads to distorted representations of both the Chicano/a and the Black Power movements. In his caricature of the Movimiento, for example, Ramón A. Gutiérrez argues: "Since so much of the ethnic militancy that Chicanos articulated was profoundly influenced by black nationalism, it is important to recall one of the truly poignant insights in the *Autobiography of Malcolm X*."[12] Gutiérrez uses Malcolm's comments on Black masculinity in order to reduce the Chicano Movement to issues of "social emasculation." In a like manner, cultural critic José Limón writes: "Those of us who participated largely took our inspiration from the Southern African-American civil rights movement, and later from the Black Power movement. We attempted to emulate these movements in our own, often militant protest."[13] In a similar vein, historian Manuel G. Gonzales portrays the Movimiento as a kind of aftereffect created by an exhausted Black struggle: "The black civil rights movement, though, left a powerful legacy. One of its most momentous consequences was the stimulus it provided for other people of color to stand up for their rights. These included Mexicans, who now initiated their own movement of self-awareness."[14] What Gonzales ignores is the fact that for a period of time sectors of the two movements overlapped and often collaborated.

While there is no doubt that African American organizations and leaders during the Sixties had a profound impact on all progressive young people, I take the "copycat hypothesis" to be a gross oversimplification of the genealogy of the Chicano Movement. The effect of that oversimplification is the representation of Chicano/a activism as derivative and secondhand. Whether intentionally or not, such arguments reassert the black/white opposition that structures U.S. political history and erase both the long history of Mexican American political resistance in the Southwest and other Latin American influences such as the Mexican and Cuban revolutions. Chicano/a activists learned much from African American social movements. But it would be a mistake to claim that in their rejection of white supremacy, anti-Mexican racism, and the unfulfilled promises of liberal democracy they opted to become "Black."[15]

Another somewhat misleading argument is that because Blacks and Chicanos were in competition for resources generated by federal programs in the 1960s their primary relationship was one of competition, antagonism, or indifference.[16] Although it is true that major African American civil-rights leaders were slow to understand the historical similarities between their community and Latinos and therefore slow to incorporate Mexican American agendas into their movement, grass-roots contacts between Brown and Black activists were commonplace throughout the Viet Nam war period. SNCC (Student Non-Violent Coordinating Committee), for example, had provided financial support for two of its members, Marshall Gans and George Ballis, in their activities with the United Farm Workers union in California.

While some narrow forms of Black nationalism cast Latinos as overly passive and subservient to white domination, organizations like the Black Panthers came to the aid of Los Siete de la Raza in San Francisco, and as we shall see, Reies López Tijerina signed a mutual-defense treaty with Black groups as early as 1967.[17] At "Free Huey" and "Free Angela" rallies throughout the period, Chicano/as were present. Dr. King's meeting in Atlanta, shortly before his death, with major Chicano activists signaled an important shift in the thinking of the mainstream Black civil-rights leadership. But the death of Dr. King, the ensuing chaos during the Poor People's Campaign, and perhaps more important the concerted effort on the part of law-enforcement agencies to destroy Brown/Black alliances precluded the development of sustained and strong coalitions.

The issue of coalition building had always been a difficult one for Mexican Americans. In an environment of Black vs. White, ethnic groups outside the strict dichotomy or those that participated in both "extremes" at the same time often found themselves excluded from national discussions about race relations. In 1971, Bob Blauner pointed out: "The distinctive features of racism directed against yellow, red, brown, and Spanish-speaking have not been explored in a society many of whose unconscious cultural assumptions and patterns of thought polarize around the white-black axis. Thus liberals and radicals alike in America tune in on the black thing; the intermediary colors strike a weak chord."[18] The challenges were painfully evident to those Chicano/a activists who had attempted to work in coalition settings: "In the past coalition with blacks has meant playing a secondary role to blacks. Furthermore, in a coalition where all three groups are involved (blacks, Chicanos, and whites), white liberals tend to support blacks over Chicanos."[19]

The question of why white liberals were (are) more "comfortable" appointing African Americans to positions of authority than they are Latino/as has plagued Chicano/a activists for decades. The powerful legacy of slavery and Reconstruction, in effect, locked Blacks and whites into a permanent dance of interdependence, guarded cooperation, and white guilt. In the Southwest in particular, institutional traditions in higher education have wedded Black and white interests in a mutually sustained relationship that creates a small African American buffer class often unwilling to challenge structural obstacles for the majority of working-class people of color. The effects of class difference are crucial here since the existence of a small but articulate Black intellectual class had no counterpart in the Latino community in the Viet Nam war period, and it was not until the 1980s that a Hispanic professional class akin to what Manning Marable refers to as the Black petite bourgeoisie came into being.[20] Caught in this class-inflected binary of black and white, Chicano/as nevertheless have at times been able to form bonds of solidarity with those Blacks who were (are) capable of seeing the ways in which the "racial" status quo does little more than perpetuate white hegemony.

THE POSSESSIVE INVESTMENT IN RACE

> Our struggle while distinct in many ways from the Black and Indian struggles is, at the same time, at one with them. I see dangerous fighting going on among these groups; fighting that is being gleefully watched by the enemy.
> —Manuel I. López, "The Role of the Chicano Student" (1971)

As we have seen in earlier chapters, the power of cultural nationalism resides in its ability to mobilize an oppressed community so that it may reenter history as a self-determined agent. The construction of new collective identities is a key factor in this mobilization, and at the heart of many of those identities during the Movimiento period was the concept of "race." The ubiquitous image of the "Mestizo Head," a visual representation of the centuries-long process of European and indigenous transculturation in the Americas, signified the links between the new Chicano/a subject and other peoples on the "Bronze Continent."[21]

If mestizaje or "racial" mixture was central to the individual identities of many Movement activists, notions of race-based separatism or "racial purity" simply did not make logical sense. Nevertheless in the writings and speeches of leaders such as Rodolfo Corky Gonzales and Reies López Tijerina we find curious examples of racialized language that produce less than clear messages and leave the mistaken impression

that the entire Movimiento practiced the most regressive forms of ethnic nationalism. Already in the final stanzas of Gonzales's "I am
Joaquin," for example, an emphasis on inherited "blood" links the
Chicano/a experience to both the Visogothic inhabitants of the Iberian
peninsula and the indigenous nations of preconquest America: "Part of
the blood that runs deep in me/could not be vanquished by the Moors/I
defeated them after five hundred years, and I endured/The part of
blood that is mine/has labored endlessly five-hundred /years under the
lustful Europeans/I am still here!"[22] Although it is not explicitly stated,
the implication here is that the Muslim "Moors" (i.e., Muslims) who
invaded Spain in the eighth century and were finally expelled in 1492
are analogous to the Spaniards who destroyed indigenous America just
a few decades later. This suggests that Chicano/a "blood" somehow
remained "untainted" at two or even three distinct historical moments
despite the intrusion of "outsiders" (Iberia in 711, America in 1492, and
presumably Aztlán in 1848). Adding to the conceptual confusion is the
poetic voice's assertion in the final verses that "My blood is pure."

Tijerina's Indo-Hispano project wavered in a similar fashion
between a rejection and a glorification of a mixed genealogy and a
European/Catholic heritage. Speaking to an interviewer in 1967, he
stated: "It wasn't by chance that the Spanish people crossed the Atlantic;
it was God that selected them. . . . We were born as a new breed—not
Mexicans, not Indians. . . . The Indians had blood of the ten lost tribes
of Israel. The Spanish had Jewish and Arab blood. A new breed was
born here from two great bloods. A *santa raza* [holy people] who would
find justice was created."[23]

The extent to which the thinking of Gonzales and Tijerina was
influenced by the works of Mexican writer José Vasconcelos, author of
La raza cósmica (1925), has yet to be fully investigated.[24] At the height of
the Movement, one young historian attempted to draw a distinction
between the Chicano concept of "La Raza" and that of Vasconcelos.
Basing his argument less on Vasconcelos's actual texts than on a single
secondary source, Mario T. García asserted: "Quite clearly, Vasconcelos's
'cosmic race' is not a racist idea."[25] A close reading of *La raza cósmica*,
especially its treatment of Asian and African peoples, would belie such
an assertion. But the more interesting point is that García chooses to
argue for the superiority of the Mexican people over "the Anglo" and
criticizes Vasconcelos for not doing the same:

Vasconcelos' "cosmic race" is at odds with the Chicano concep-
tion of La Raza. The latter's exhalation [*sic*] of La Raza is noble,
for it gives pride to a people long trampled upon by a racist
society. One cannot help but feel, however, that this view in
itself contains elements of racism, but this is unavoidable, for
the crisis of the moment demands that Mexican-Americans be
instilled with racial pride; without it, they would be left
defenseless against the encroachment of the Anglo "melting
pot," one of the most racist hoaxes ever perpetrated upon the
world. To offset this, La Raza holds to the superiority of the
Mexican way of life over the Anglo. This stands in contrast to
Vasconcelos, who held that no race or culture—not even the
Mexican—is superior to another.[26]

Moving dangerously close to a regressive and race-based nationalist
position, García rejects Vasconcelos's thought until some future
moment "when racial and cultural harmony comes to this nation." In
the meantime, he argues, the concept of "la raza cósmica" is simply not
racialized enough.

García's repudiation of Vasconcelos grows out of an extreme position that was not widely held in Movement circles. Elsewhere in the
Movement archive there is little evidence that activists seriously
engaged Vasconcelos's ideas or that Vasconcelos exerted a major influence. In my opinion, among key documents of the period only
Tijerina's writing reveals traces of Vasconcelos's thinking. In his long
personal account, *Mi lucha por la tierra* (1978), Tijerina wrote: "*El mestizo de Norte, Centro y Sudamérica debe unirse como una familia.
Algunas razas están moralmente más perdidas que otras. Algunas ya no
tienen remedio moral. Han rebasado el punto de esperanza y se burlarían
de la armonía fraternal. Pero el pueblo nuevo mestizo, y los pueblos del
oriente, todavía tienen grandes reservas de dignidad humana.*" ("The
mestizo of North, Central, and South America should come together as
a family. Some races are more morally lost than others. For some, there
is no moral solution. They are beyond hope and they would make a
mockery of fraternal harmony. But the new mestizo people and the
peoples of the east still have great reserves of human dignity.").[27]

Not unlike Vasconcelos himself, who had elaborated his theories in
response to nineteenth-century European "scientific racism" and its

depiction of "Southern peoples" as inherently inferior, Tijerina struggled to counter North American traditions of white supremacy and the
fear of "racial mixing." In terms of creating a broad and effective social
movement, however, an over reliance on racialized categories and "la
familia" could only hamper Chicano/a attempts to achieve ideological
clarity and break away from the traditional terms of racial and patriarchal thinking.

Insofar as some isolated sectors of the Movement emphasized a narrow race-based nationalism, those sectors revealed themselves to be quin-
tessentially "American," i.e., the product of social relations in the United
States where social injustice was almost always identified as primarily a
"racial" problem. Because the analytical category of "class" has been virtually nonoperative throughout most of the history of the United States,
economic and cultural inequality are too often reduced to issues of "race"
rather than being construed as the intersection of racializing and gendered practices, economic stratification, and other structural hierarchies.
Although armed with a powerful critique of anti-Mexican racism, some
Movement thinkers were hard pressed to challenge in a significant way
what Omi and Winant have called the racial state, a racial order premised
on black/white histories and relationships. By the end of the Movement
period, therefore, the dominant system's ability to absorb Chicano/a
insurgencies had produced "a cloudy mirror . . . reflecting their demands
(and indeed their rearticulated identities) in a distorted fashion."[28] In
other words, it would be a relatively easy passage from "Chicano Power"
to "Hispanic Pride" or from a radical rejection of liberalism and assimi-
lationism to an enthusiastic acceptance of liberalism's tokenism and well-
monitored rewards for the few.

Despite internal contradictions and a lack of clarity about
Chicano/as as a "race," and given the potential for cultural nationalism to
transmute into sectarian nationalist projects, many Movement activists
refused to insulate themselves from other groups engaged in similar
struggles. This was no easy task given the ability of governing elites in the
United States to devise ways for pitting minority groups against one
another. As one social-movement theorist puts it: "In multiracial societies
such as the United States, there is always the potential for racial resistance
to be diverted from a vertical challenge to the power structure into a hor-
izontal struggle with other racial minorities over artificially scarce
resources. . . . Hence, struggles around racial formation become two

degrees more complex in societies with multiple racial groups and multiple structures of power."[29]

Even those sectors of the Movimiento most associated with narrow nationalism at one time or another actively pursued coalition building. In urban centers across the Southwest, Chicano/a and African American youth came together in a politically charged context in which revolutionary explosions had already taken place in Watts, Detroit, and Newark. The famous Los Angeles coffee house La Piranya, founded by the Brown Berets in September of 1967, hosted meetings with Black Panther H. Rap Brown, SNCC's Stokely Carmichael, and United Slaves (US) leader Maulana Ron Karenga.[30] With funding received from the Episcopal Church in 1968 for an initiative called the Afro-Mexican proposal, a group called the Acción de Bronce Colectiva joined with the Los Angeles Black Congress in order to stage a variety of events dealing with educational and police-brutality issues. On June 2, 1968, Karenga, together with Walter Bremond of the Black Congress, appeared at a rally for the Chicano 13, the young men who had been indicted for the high school blowouts three months earlier.[31] As we shall see, the problematic figure of Karenga would move in and out of contact with Chicano activists throughout the Viet Nam war period.

Although not as well known as Carmichael and the Black Panthers, Karenga would become a highly visible and controversial actor in the Black Power movement. His organization espoused a sectarian form of nationalism that stood in opposition to the Panthers' broader internationalist and, in some cases, Marxist-Leninist analysis of U.S. society. The ideological divisions that divided the Panthers from US would be exploited by the FBI and local law-enforcement agencies and led to a number of murders of Panther members, the most infamous being at UCLA's Campbell Hall where Bunchy Carter and John Huggins were killed. Whether or not some US members were willing or simply unwitting agents of the invidious COINTELPRO agenda is still a question debated by historians. But for the Panthers in California there was little doubt that US was not an ally.[32] By the summer of 1969, Bobby Seale and the organizers of the Panther-sponsored United Front Against Fascism Conference to be held in Oakland pointedly excluded US.[33]

In the Mission District of San Francisco, the case of Los Siete de la Raza brought together a pan-Latino movement with strong African American support. Six young men (one of the original seven escaped) were charged with shooting police officer Joseph Brodnik on May 1, 1969, and held for eighteen months without trial. Two of those charged were not even in San Francisco at the time. Two others were not on the street where the incident took place. The group included four Salvadorans, one Nicaraguan, and one Honduran, all of whom had been radicalized in the local Latino and African American youth group the Mission Rebels (founded in 1965 to stress education) and in pan-Latino organizations such as the Brown Heritage Club, later COBRA (Confederation of Brown Race for Action), the Brown Berets, and especially the College Readiness Program at the College of San Mateo. In December of 1968, College of San Mateo administrators had threatened to eliminate the College Readiness Program. Students reacted with demonstrations, and police occupied the campus for the remainder of the school year. It was in this volatile environment that Officer Brodnik was killed.

Poet Sonia Sánchez taught a variety of subjects to the Mission Rebels, including the writings of Ernesto Che Guevara. As *hondureño* Danilo Bebe Meléndez recalled, "She gave me *Che Speaks*, some other works of Che, *Black Boy*, and some other literature. I took them home and read them all. After that you wouldn't see me without a book of Che in my back pocket."[34] Latino youth in the Mission also received copies from the editors of *Ramparts* magazine of their July 27, 1968, issue devoted to Che's Bolivian diaries.

The defense committee for Los Siete transformed itself into a vibrant community organization called La Raza Workers Collective that provided breakfast programs, operated the Basta Ya! restaurant, published the newspaper *Basta Ya!*, recruited high school students for college, and staffed free medical and legal clinics. Although the Collective received minimal support from Chicano organizations across the Southwest and was often at odds with Trotskyite groups, it found committed allies across the bay in Oakland, where Black Panther Party members Bobby Seale and David Hilliard made resources available.[35] Support also came from the internationalist Puerto Rican Young Lords Party and the Red Guards. On November 7, 1970, the six young men were acquitted.

The political positions espoused by Los Siete were decidedly pan-Latino and internationalist and therefore often critical of narrow forms of Chicano nationalism. Los Siete defendant *salvadoreño* Mario Martinez stated in a 1969 interview: "One problem especially is with the Chicano Movement which is just strictly from Mexico. With Chicanos, you know, if you're white, sometimes you can't talk to them guys. All they see is people from Mexico and nobody else. This is bad because they are alienating themselves. That's where this term 'brown people' came about where you can unite all the people of brown color, that includes the people of Hawaii, Samoa, the Islands. We see too that it can't just be brown people—it has to be all the oppressed classes—whether they be white or whatever color they be."[36]

The move toward a more complex form of racial politics that included a rigorous class analysis distinguished the activists involved with Los Siete de la Raza from Movement organizations that espoused more sectarian positions. Yet at no time was the issue of race ignored, as Los Siete's close alliances with African American groups indicated. According to defendant Tony Martinez:

> The struggle is a class struggle of oppressed people. Black people and brown people are both oppressed—maybe not in the same ways, but the system uses the same tactics. The young people have finally, little by little, overcome the man's divide and conquer game. We have learned a lot from the black people. We have learned from the many tactics they have used in the struggle. The Black Panthers have helped the movement for Los Siete a lot. . . . We have to build an ideology so that all people can be united—not just brown people but black people too. We have had to overcome a lot of problems within brown people before we got the stage we're at now. Before the movement used to be just Chicano—so-called Mexican Americans—they were leaving a lot of brown people out. Finally, we overcame that when the "brown" term came about, everybody of brown descent became united. Then the next step was to move to get united with black people.[37]

The demographic composition of San Francisco's Latino population compelled Los Siete to broaden the idea of the Chicano Movement a full decade before the influx of Central Americans into Los Angeles and other urban centers in the late 1970s forced a rethinking of Chicano/a identities and Chicano/Latino coalitions. Martinez's desire for a "Brown Movement" based on shared somatic and cultural features would find only limited acceptance in other parts of the Southwest, yet one poet understood the story of Los Siete to be the story of all Raza: "*Son los siete de la Raza/En sus vidas hay un cuento/De la historia de la Raza/Y de todas que se aman./De la gente vienen/Y a la gente devuelven*" ("They are the People's Seven/in their lives is the story/of the People's history/and of all who love/From the People they came/And to the People they will return").[38]

By the early 1970s, Brown/Black encounters were somewhat less commonplace but now included figures that had won high public visibility. On April 28, 1973, for example, Angela Davis was in Denver for a Crusade for Justice rally that drew approximately twelve hundred activists. Together with American Indian leader Clyde Bellecourt and Crusade leader Corky Gonzales, Davis told the crowd: "When they see the revolutionary face of the Crusade for Justice, they, the rulers, the criminals, feel that their system is being threatened. Now I think that everyone who is here today and has experienced the tremendous presence and inspiration of the Crusade, everyone who has experienced this, can say that brothers and sisters they are quite right—their system is being threatened."[39] As we will see in the case of Reies López Tijerina, this kind of political dialogue stretching across ethnic and "racial" lines under the rubric of "revolutionary praxis" was at work in the earliest days of the Movimiento and forces us to abandon both the "copycat" hypothesis and the reductive rubric of "nationalism" as gross simplifications of the historical record.

Tijerina y los negros

This urge, this growth, for unity of la raza with the Negro people cannot be resisted. It will come because it must.

—Reies López Tijerina

Thirty years after the peak of his celebrity, it may seem logical to view Reies López Tijerina as a regional leader with little more than a single-item agenda. The land-grant issue in northern New Mexico initially was difficult to understand for Chicano/as elsewhere in the Southwest, particularly in urban settings, and Tijerina's personal style owed more to local religious traditions than it did to the trade unionism of César Chávez or the grassroots community organizing of Corky Gonzales. As we have seen in the chapter on Cuba, however, Tijerina's rise to prominence in the Movimiento grew out of his audacious rhetoric and his willingness to challenge the federal government "by any means necessary."

The legend of "el Tigre" and Tierra Amarilla continued beyond the high point of Chicano/a activism in the Viet Nam war period. When asked by German researcher Wolfgang Binder in 1975 which Chicano Movement leader they most respected, a group of tejano college students unanimously replied: "Reies López Tijerina."[40]

Born in 1923 near San Antonio, Texas, to a farmworker family, Tijerina as a child followed the migrant routes from Texas to the upper Midwest picking crops. He eventually graduated from an Assembly of God Bible School where he learned a particular kind of fiery evangelism typical of the border region. Throughout his youth, his family experienced violence and persecution including the burning down of their home. When he visited northern New Mexico in 1959, the centuries-old issue of land claims by heirs of original Spanish settlers resonated strongly with him. In late 1962, he created the Alianza Federal de las Mercedes (Federal Alliance of Land Grants) in order to contest the federal government's abrogation of the Treaty of Guadalupe Hidalgo.[41] The Alianza's first official meeting was held north of Albuquerque in the town of Alameda on February 2, 1963, the anniversary of the treaty's signing.

The Chicano/Mexicano struggle for land lost to conquest and colonization can most assuredly be traced to the 1830s in what is now the modern state of Texas or to 1848 and the conclusion of the U.S.-Mexican War. But for many Chicano Movement activists the primal scene of theft and violation was the arrival of Europeans in the Americas, in particular the destruction of indigenous lives and culture in central Mexico.[42] The construction of a new Chicana/o political agency drew upon the resistance mounted by indigenous people in the early sixteenth century, taking as their models not only male warriors such as Cuauhtémoc but also the rebellious indigenous women who attacked the Spaniards during the corn riot of 1692: "*Vamos con alegria a esta guerra y comoquiera Dios que se acaben en ella los españoles, no importa que muramos sin confesion! ¿No es nuestra esta tierra? Pues ¿qué quieren en ella los españoles?*" ("Let us go joyfully into battle. If God wills that the Spaniards be wiped out, it won't matter if we die without confession. This is our land isn't it? What business do the Spaniards have here?").[43]

The issue of the land surfaced in dramatic fashion in northern New Mexico in the early 1960s, and echoed across the Southwest as the symbolic foundation for a wide array of local struggles. It is important to note that Tijerina's "nationalism" was not so much a "Chicano nationalism"

as it was an Indo-Hispano nationalism founded on the cultural particularities of New Mexican culture and history. For Tijerina, as for César
Chávez, there was no need to invoke "Aztec" or Maya ancestors and culture as key elements of a new collective identity. If Chávez and the farmworkers represented the most exploited Mexican workers, Tijerina's
movement reminded Chicano/as of what was understood by many to be
the original scene of loss. If Chávez and the UFW deployed the iconography of traditional Mexican nationalism even as the activities of the
union contributed to the formulation of a new Chicano/a cultural
nationalism, Tijerina and the Alianza, far from the major urban centers,
promoted an Indo-Hispano identity that coincided with and indirectly
contributed to an emergent Chicano/a militancy in the cities.

In the late 1950s, Tijerina had made a series of trips to Mexico where
he began to formulate the outlines of a self-fashioned subjectivity and an
attendant political project. It was then that he began his intense study of
the Treaty of Guadalupe Hidalgo as well as visiting historical archives and
pre-Columbian sites such as Teotihuacán. According to his own account,
it was on his third visit to the pyramids outside Mexico City that he began
to link the ancient Mexican past to the plight of Mexican Americans in
the United States: "One time I climbed to the summit of each [pyramid].
And I stayed there a long time, thinking about the sad history of my people in New Mexico, Texas, and California. . . . Something intuitively told
me that I had to study and learn many things so that I could understand
the rights of my people and how I could help them."[44] The trope of the
"return to Mexico," so familiar in Chicano/a narratives of identity, makes
an early appearance in Tijerina's personal trajectory a decade before the
height of the Movimiento.

By 1966, the Alianza claimed a membership of some twenty thousand
people (law enforcement said three thousand; historians estimate ten
thousand). On July 4 of that year, its members staged a march from
Albuquerque to Santa Fe in order to present its demands to the governor.
On October 22, the Alianza conducted a symbolic takeover of the
600,000-acre San Joaquín land grant by taking control of the Echo
Amphitheater Park. The impact of these actions on local Chicano/a
youth was especially strong. Tijerina wrote: "This awakening in our children affected us all throughout the state. In the schools, our young people had acquired inferiority complexes and learned an incorrect history.
Now, our children were beginning to remove the yoke of ignorance that

the Anglo had placed on them."[45] It was at the intersection of the militant pursuit of the community's rights and the shaking off of the legacy of white supremacy that Indo-Hispano cultural nationalism set an important precedent for other forms of radicalism invented by young Chicanos and Chicanas who pursued the struggle in other locations.

By this time Tijerina had begun to travel extensively throughout the Southwest and would soon become one of the most recognizable figures associated with the Movimiento. While the land-grant issue was always foremost on his agenda, he increasingly spoke on broader questions of cultural and political self-determination and against the U.S. war in Southeast Asia. As the lyrics of one *corrido* (border ballad) put it, Tijerina was no longer simply a local leader but was fighting and making personal sacrifices for the entire Chicano/a community:

> *Tijerina no es bandido*
> *Ni tampoco comunista*
> *Es hombre de gran talento*
> *Que defiende la justicia.*
>
> *Tijerina no es bandido*
> *Ni anda de robabueyes*
> *El sacrifica su vida*
> *Para proteger la de ustedes. . . .*[46]

(Tijerina is neither a bandit nor a communist. He is a man of great talent who defends justice. Tijerina is neither a bandit nor a cattle rustler. He sacrifices his life in order to protect your life. . . .)

As we saw in Chapter Three, the discursive correspondences between the Cuban Revolution and the actions of Tijerina's organization were strong by 1967. The charge that the Alianza was a "communist front" appeared regularly in conservative publications, and the *aliancistas* themselves would often cultivate their image as revolutionaries by sprinkling their media interviews with references to Che and Fidel Castro. The extreme right-wing John Birch Society seemed convinced that Cubans were hiding in northern New Mexico, and they compared the Tierra Amarilla courthouse raid to Castro's 1953 assault on the Moncada barracks (the symbolic origin of the Cuban Revolution).

Writing in the Birch Society journal, *American Opinion*, Alan Stang analyzed Tijerina as part of a "communist conspiracy" and attacked liberal newspapers for supporting him:

> The point once again is that Tijerina isn't trying simply to transfer property from American to American. He is trying to use this dead issue to begin a guerrilla operation in the United States. "Reies Tijerina isn't interested one iota in the land grant situation," says the high police official cited before. And since Tijerina is trying to destroy the United States, the national news media, as you know, have naturally advanced his cause—just as they early advanced the cause of the Black Power revolutionaries . . . and of another Spanish-speaking revolutionary named Fidel Castro. . . .
>
> What will certainly happen now is that Tijerina, like Castro, will strike again with his revolutionary gang; that like Castro he will be hailed as a "Robin Hood" by the same national Press which so hailed Castro . . . and that, if he and the people behind him are successful, the same Communist dictatorship Castro established will descend over all Americans, Spanish and Anglo, "from Colorado to California," as [Corky] Gonzales said.[47]

Despite the claims of his right-wing critics, Tijerina's ideological position was neither socialist nor Cuban inspired. At most, the Alianza promoted a premodern form of communalism and rejected Marxism as a European import. As Tijerina would write in his autobiography, Chicano/a leftists were: "*Confundidores* [*que*] *enseñan ideologías importadas*" ("Those who confuse by teaching imported ideologies").[48] Nevertheless, Tijerina's public notoriety depended to a great degree on his name being associated with armed rebellion and on the Cold War rhetoric that distorted the true nature of all progressive social movements during the Viet Nam war period.

A lesser-known fact is that Tijerina's visibility was due in part to his willingness to make alliances with a variety of groups pursuing civil rights and radical agendas. Historian Ignacio M. García reminds us: "He [Tijerina] became the first Mexican American activist to seek out alliances with Native American and African American leaders. First with established mainstream black leaders and eventually with black-power advocates, Tijerina saw this partnership as a way to radicalize Hispanos into direct action, something that he saw the black community heading toward. Even before [César] Chávez and his union became the darlings of the liberal left, Tijerina represented the radical Mexican American activist."[49]

More than any other Chicano leader of the period, Tijerina actively sought out American Indian allies. This was a natural connection since most of the land Tijerina and his followers claimed had once belonged to local indigenous groups. As early as 1964, the Alianza had supported the land claims of the Taos Pueblo people, and in his interviews and writings Tijerina insisted: "We have not robbed the Indian, as some accuse us, nor do we seek harm for the Indian. The Indian is our brother."[50]

The contact with African American militants was less predictable, and it demonstrated Tijerina's broad vision for radical change. That vision would put him in close contact with every major Black leader of the late 1960s and earn him the close scrutiny of the FBI and other government agencies. According to Tijerina's own account, his initial collaborations with poor Blacks had begun early in his career as a preacher in the Valley of Peace colony outside Phoenix, Arizona. By 1960, he had traveled to Chicago and had conducted a weeklong series of discussions with the Honorable Elijah Muhammad, the founder of the Nation of Islam (NOI), in which the two leaders imagined a unified front made up of "Arabs and Africans and Latino peoples of the Americas."[51] Tijerina's contact with the NOI continued throughout the decade, and his ability to create ties to other African American civil-rights organizations was sustained and impressive.

The day after the assassination of Dr. Martin Luther King, Jr., Tijerina told an interviewer: "I think the black people are here to stay and their cry is a holy cry. No matter if they are divided into hundreds of organizations, the time will come when only the color will count, and the black people will decide their destiny and their friends and their course on base of color. . . . We can speak about combining colors . . . and bring harmony between colors and it's a good time to start. We select and take from all these various colors and peoples just like Martin, Dr. King, was doing in his last moment, bringing all the colors together, to fight together."[52] In fact, Tijerina's first contact with Dr. King had taken place two years earlier when the Alianza invited the civil-rights leader to speak at its 1966 convention.[53]

As I described in Chapter Three, Tijerina and the Alianza had been implicated in the events surrounding the Tierra Amarilla courthouse raid and the land takeover at the Carson National Forest. By mid-February of

1967, Tijerina was out of jail and in March he attended a meeting with Dr. King in Atlanta. In July, he reportedly said: "Our people are forced by the same circumstances, and the same fight, irresistibly towards the Negro people and their fight."[54] The following month, Tijerina accepted an invitation to the "New Politics" convention in Chicago. Julian Bond asked Chicana and longtime SNCC activist Maria Varela to escort Tijerina, and in Chicago he met briefly again with Dr. King, Rodolfo Corky Gonzales, and other African American and Puerto Rican leaders. One report described Tijerina's impression of Dr. King in the following manner: "[He is] sort of a philosopher. He is a slow-spoken man, who weighs his words very much before making his statement."[55]

According to Tijerina, it was he who suggested to Dr. King the idea of a coalition between poor people of every color.[56] But in a preview of what would transpire several months later at the Poor People's Campaign in Washington, D.C., Latino leaders soon found themselves excluded from planning committees for the Chicago convention. An Executive Board of twenty-six members was elected with a half white and half Black composition, and a perfunctory gesture was made toward "the just aspirations of the Mexican-American national minority."[57] Despite the inability of convention organizers to seriously rethink the black/white paradigm, Chicano activists maintained a tenuous relationship with the "New Politics" group. More important, Corky Gonzales and Crusade activists began planning for an all-Latino meeting. That meeting would eventually become the first National Chicano Youth Liberation Conference held in Denver in March of 1969.

For his part, Tijerina continued to speak of the need to broaden the coalition while distinguishing among group differences: "The situation of the Mexicans and Puerto Ricans is similar to that of the Negro people, but it is not the same. We have to fight for the right to speak our language. Even the demand of the Puerto Rican for independence is different from the Mexican's demands. But we must unite all these with the Negro, the Indian, and the 'good Anglos,' in order to change our condition."[58] Tijerina's inclusive language created hope among many activists that a broad coalition might be formed in order to challenge the traditional political parties and their brokers. On September 10, 1967, just one month after the Chicago conference, Tijerina told a meeting of Alianza members that he planned to invite Black leaders, including Dr. King, to the next Alianza convention.

14. From left to right: Tomás Ben Yacya, Ralph Featherstone, Maulana Ron Karenga, Reies López Tijerina, Albuquerque, October, 1967. University of New Mexico, Peter Nabokov Collection.

In late October of 1967, members from a variety of Black organizations boarded buses for the two-day inaugural convention of the renamed Alianza Federal de Pueblos Libres (Federal Alliance of Free City-states) in Albuquerque (fig. 14). Tijerina's experience in Chicago had convinced him of the importance of coalitions, and he invited members of CORE (Congress of Racial Equality), SNCC, US, The Black Panther Party, and the Black Congress to come to New Mexico in order to forge a coalition with the Alianza and other Chicano organizations, including the Crusade for Justice and MAYO. Among the attendees were Corky Gonzales, José Angel Gutiérrez, Bert Corona, Maria Varela, Brown Beret Prime Minister David Sánchez, Eliezer Risco, and Hopi leader Tomás Ben Yacya. African American leaders included Ralph Featherstone (who was mysteriously killed by a bomb in 1970), Ethel Minor, and Willie Ricks (SNCC), Ron Karenga (US), James Dennis (CORE), Anthony Akku Babu (Black Panther Party), and Walter Bremond (Black Congress). Dr. King did not attend.

Although many of the speeches were in Spanish, African American activists nodded their approval of the proceedings. According to several accounts Ralph Featherstone of SNCC led a chant of "*Poder negro*" ("Black

15. SNCC member Ralph
Featherstone, Albuquerque,
October 1967. University of
New Mexico, Reies López
Tijerina Collection.

power") and held up a bumper sticker that read "Che is alive and hiding
in Tierra Amarilla" (fig. 15). The controversial leader of United Slaves (US),
Maulana Ron Karenga, received a thunderous ovation when he told the
audience in passable Spanish: "*Somos juntos, somos hombres de color . . .
Tenemos una nueva misión . . . ¡Viva Tijerina! ¡Vivan los indios! ¡Vivan los
hombres de color!*" ("We are together, we are men of color . . . We have a
new mission . . . Long live Tijerina! Long live the Indians! Long live men of
color!").[59] At the conclusion of the meeting, on October 22, representatives
from all groups signed a seven-part "treaty" of "Peace, Harmony, and
Mutual Assistance." According to the organizers, "the important thing is
that for the first time the old myth of coalition for mutual self-interest is
exploded and we move into the area of mutual respect."[60]

The treaty document itself is a fascinating mixture of Tijerina's
prophetic thought and hard-nosed political pragmatism. The opening
sections resonate with a messianic ideology filtered through the
ambiguous category of "race." Today, the treaty strikes us as being very
far from the secular and revolutionary language of leftist movements
during the Viet Nam War period:

IN THE NAME OF GOD ALMIGHTY
ART. I

Sec.(A)   Both peoples (races) will consider this TREATY as a SOLEMN agreement, and subject to the Divine Law of the GOD of JUSTICE.

Sec.(B)   Both peoples solemnly promise to respect the Faith, the CULTURE of each other, and every RIGHT and LIB-ERTY that GOD has given to the HUMAN RACE.

Sec.(C)   Both peoples do promise not to permit the members of either of said peoples to make false propaganda of any kind whatsoever against each other, either by SPEECH or WRITING.[61]

In the concluding articles, the apocalyptic tone of the document intensifies as the specter of an atomic apocalypse arises like some biblical plague: "In case a Nuclear War should erupt upon the earth, the two peoples SOLEMNLY promise to assist each other." According to the logic of the treaty, the proposed coalition was to serve no earthly ideology but Divine Providence itself. Article 7 makes clear that it is God who ultimately will be the agent of social justice; the human actors are merely witnesses: "The two peoples agree to take the same position as to the CRIMES and SINS of the Government of the United States" (Sec.A). "Neither of said both peoples shall intervene in the holy JUDGMENT of GOD against the United States of America" (Sec.B).

Whether or not the Alianza's attempted coalition with other militant groups contained the potential for a viable political movement, the sheer fact that Black and Brown radicals were meeting was enough to motivate law-enforcement agencies to step up their activities. All speeches at the October event were illegally recorded, and New Mexico Senator Joseph Montoya denounced the meeting: "Spanish Americans will make no alliances with black nationalists who hate America. We do not lie down in the gutter with Ron Karenga, Stokely Carmichael, and Rap Brown."[62] Hispano middle-class organizations in New Mexico reacted bitterly as well, reportedly distributing leaflets that attacked Tijerina as an outsider and his Black allies as "reds": "We true Spanish are white, and we are Catholics. We fight communists. We don't care for foreigners, Negro or White, to come and lie about our race. The only race problem is the one brought in by dirty communists who try to pass as Spanish to get our land grants."[63]

As activists returned to Los Angeles from Albuquerque, federal marshals stopped and searched the buses carrying members of US and SNCC. In Los Angeles, plans began for the founding of a Brown-Black Unity Council described as "a council of leaders in the Black and Mexican American communities of Los Angeles aiming at coordinated programs against the Man, and for the mutual welfare and self-determination of both peoples."[64] Back in New Mexico, Tijerina went on trial for contempt of court. When the U.S. attorney asked him why militant Blacks had been invited to Albuquerque, Tijerina responded: "There is no reason why peoples who are both oppressed should fight each other. I thought it wise to make a treaty with them. The white people must now face up to the consequences of bringing them here in chains."[65]

In February 1968, Tijerina was in southern California where he appeared at East Los Angeles College and other campuses at the invitation of the United Mexican American Students (UMAS). On February 18 in Los Angeles, he spoke on a program for the Huey Newton Defense Fund that included Rodolfo Corky Gonzales, H. Rap Brown, Maulana Ron Karenga, Stokely Carmichael, Bobby Seale, and other prominent African American leaders.

FBI and alternative press reports estimated that between four thousand and five thousand people attended the meeting. The *L.A. Times* did not cover the event but reported in a short note that "a formidable array of militants" had met at the Sports Arena.[66] According to the Los Angeles counterculture newspaper *Open City*, the meeting brought together many activists who previously had embraced only the most unyielding forms of regressive nationalism. Now they attempted to form a powerful multiethnic coalition: "It was the kind of union which the establishment has feared for years, has constantly propagandized against, has had nightmares over. If fully integrated, the already violent black revolt and the explosive chicano rights drive would bring to bear a force of more than 20 million blacks and nearly four million chicanos. And this is a fighting, not a talking, alliance."[67] Angela Davis, who had helped to organize the rally, recalled in her autobiography that many of the speakers threatened widespread violence should Newton be convicted.[68]

Open City reporter John Bryan noted that Tijerina hugged Rap Brown and Stokely Carmichael and "not only hugged Ron Karenga but lifted him bodily in the air in a gesture of brotherhood and joy which far surpassed the ability of any of the thousands of words spoken that day to demonstrate the rapidly tightening unity between the black and chicano revolutions."[69] Exposing the links between police brutality directed against the Black Panthers in Oakland and violent acts perpetrated by U.S. federal agents in New Mexico, Tijerina reportedly stated: "The brown and black are here to fight the same enemy, and this enemy, the U.S. government, is trying to oppress the whole world. But they are losing all their friends, its time is running out. . . . The black, brown, and Indios have been selected by the forces of nature to march together, fight together, and even die together."[70] With generous quotations from the Bible, Tijerina slipped easily into the apocalyptic mode for which he had become famous: "The nuclear age is forcing things to a showdown. . . . And the last war on earth will be decided on the basis of color and race, . . . The millionaires have tried to keep our cry for unity of the black and brown and the red man from being heard and read in the newspapers, on the radio, and television stations they own. But Stokely Carmichael and Rap Brown have spread the word everywhere. We will be heard."[71] Ron Karenga followed Tijerina to the podium and stressed that Black radicals would only form "permanent alliances" with people of color, not with whites. In what was a rousing finale to what may have been the high point of black-brown coalition building, Carmichael asserted: "Communism and socialism are not ideologies for black people."[72] As we have seen in Chapter Two, it was this kind of narrow nationalism that plagued both African American and Chicano/a political projects throughout the Viet Nam war period.

One month later, Tijerina was in Atlanta to meet with Dr. King and other organizers of the Poor People's Campaign. News stories reported that, in the face of militant gatherings such as the one at the L.A. Sports Arena, Dr. King saw the march on Washington, D.C., as a final attempt at nonviolent politics. According to most accounts, Dr. King took the idea of organizing a poor people's march on Washington from Marian Wright Edelman, then an attorney for the NAACP. Dr. King soon began planning for a series of massive and escalating acts of civil disobedience to be carried out in the nation's capital in the summer of 1968.[73]

From Tijerina's perspective, Dr. King's position was approaching that of the Alianza. His enthusiasm for the upcoming Campaign was sincere: "This is one of the greatest plans that Martin Luther King has come out with, something fantastic, beautiful."[74] In the same interview in which he described his March 14 meeting with King at the Paschals

Motor Inn in Atlanta, Tijerina claimed: "Yes, his philosophy had changed. His last speech, a closed-door speech, was plain. He said this march would not represent civil rights, but human rights. For the first time the black people would ask for land. Would demand land, not just jobs, education, and housing, but land. Just like the people in New Mexico are demanding land."[75]

Whether or not Dr. King had opted for a politics of land reform is unclear, although many in the main civil-rights organizations such as SNCC understood the land issue to be central to the future of African Americans. Chicana SNCC activist Maria Varela recalls: "In Mississippi towards the end of SNCC's work in rural communities, we were beginning to realize that loss of black-owned land would economically equal the political disenfranchisement of black people in the region. I also learned how ownership of land affected the way a people organized themselves. . . . I began to feel that owning land was a key requirement for defeating poverty and taking control of community and culture."[76] If in fact Dr. King was about to propose a program of land redistribution for African Americans, his position would have shifted ironically toward the stance that both the Alianza and the Nation of Islam had been espousing for several years.

There is no doubt, however, that the original concept of the Poor People's Campaign as conceived by Dr. King was an audacious break with previous civil-rights strategies. The official campaign description disseminated by the Southern Christian Leadership Conference (SCLC) emphasized the disparity between rich and poor and the issue of underemployment: "Poor people are kept in poverty because they are kept from power. We must create 'Poor People's Power'. . . . Most poor American adults work hard every day but are not paid enough for a decent life for their families. . . . There is a great contrast in the lives of rich and poor people in America. . . . America spends more money in one month to kill in Vietnam than it spends in a year for the so-called 'war on poverty.'"[77]

By stressing the connection between economic justice and the war in Southeast Asia, Dr. King in effect alienated his base of support that relied so heavily on financial and moral assistance from white liberals. As his political stance shifted to the left, he reportedly said: "In a sense, you could say we are engaged in a class struggle, yes. It will be a long and difficult struggle, for our program calls for a redistribution of economic power."[78] In the face of such statements, Democratic Party politicians and the national media began to withdraw their support from King. Even established labor unions were divided as to whether or not to actively support the Campaign. César Chávez, who was invited to participate in the initial planning session in Atlanta on March 15, 1968, declined due to pressing issues in California that included an ongoing fast, but sent a representative and subsequently spoke in favor of the Campaign in Los Angeles and elsewhere.[79]

Following the assassination of Dr. King, Tijerina had been in Atlanta to attend the funeral. There he met with Corky Gonzales, Stokely Carmichael, Bobby Seale, and others in order to discuss what he called "the destiny of the people and the downfall of this criminal government."[80] Organizers for the Poor People's Campaign proceeded with their planning but without the sense of solidarity among groups with which the project had begun.[81]

On April 24, Rev. Ralph Abernathy named Tijerina as Southwest Coordinator for the Poor People's Campaign. Ironically, Abernathy's aggressive style was more akin to that of the Chicano leaders than was Dr. King's style. As Tijerina told a large rally in D.C.: "Under his [Dr. King] leadership we were only going to shake America . . . until it fell into line. But under Ralph Abernathy's leadership we're going to turn it upside down and right side up."[82] Such rhetoric appealed not only to more militant African Americans but to militant Chicano/as as well. Two days after being selected by Abernathy, Tijerina was arrested. The charges stemmed from an earlier incident and had already been dismissed at a previous hearing.

Studies of FBI activities during this period reveal a massive covert operation to disrupt the Campaign. According to Gerald McKnight, a COINTELPRO was aimed specifically at key participants, D.C. police were said to have mobilized ten thousand officers, and the Pentagon readied twenty thousand regular army troops in preparation for the arrival of the demonstrators.[83] In the wake of the numerous urban riots that had erupted after Dr. King's death, official Washington was terrified that an army of radicals was descending on the capital. A Johnson administration task force warned: "We must be prepared for guerrilla-type warfare, incidents in the suburbs, use of children, Castro-trained commandos, and various other possibilities."[84] Tijerina's arrest and the subsequent failure of the Campaign must be understood in the context of a vast government project to neutralize radical leaders.

Within a week after his arrest, Tijerina had been released and he traveled to Memphis where the inauguration of the Campaign took place May 2 and included a memorial service at the Lorraine Motel where Dr. King had been killed on April 4, 1968. On May 17 and 18, a banquet and march were held in Albuquerque to raise funds for the Campaign. In attendance were Rev. Ralph Abernathy, various representatives of the American Indian Movement (AIM), and diverse celebrities including actor Marlon Brando. At the nearby University of New Mexico campus, folksinger Joan Baez and her husband David Harris addressed a draft-resistance meeting. Former SNCC activist Maria Varela served as liaison between the Alianza and organizers for the events planned for Washington, D.C.

Chicanos began to complain that the SCLC leadership had excluded them in the decision-making process, and protested at various meetings on the way to Washington, D.C. Tijerina later said that his biggest difference with the Black leadership was their unwillingness to place American Indian issues in the foreground of their agenda. By early June, dissent was widespread because of an editorial by Bayard Rustin in the *Washington Post* that aggravated the feeling that non-Black delegations had been excluded from the planning sessions, a feeling that had surfaced early on during stops in Kansas City and St. Louis. In his editorial Rustin had described what he called "realistic goals" for the campaign. Unfortunately, Rustin neglected to mention a single issue specific to Chicano/a, American Indian, and Puerto Rican agendas.[85]

Once in the nation's capital, Chicano/as took up lodging at the Hawthorne School instead of the main encampment of Resurrection City.[86] From the school they participated in various demonstrations at institutional sites. At the Department of Education, for example, Corky Gonzales demanded bilingual education and a school curriculum relevant to Mexican Americans. A multiethnic coalition held a press conference at the Department of Justice to present a list of demands, and a Puerto Rican Day rally took place on June 15.

The confusion and despair caused by the assassination of Robert Kennedy in early June had put additional stress on organizers, and at one point Hosea Williams publicly questioned Tijerina's motives and clashed with Corky Gonzales. Although some African American leaders argued that Tijerina was too narrowly focused on the land issue, Abernathy attempted to hold the coalition together and Coretta Scott King intervened to ensure that Tijerina and American Indian and

Puerto Rican activists be allowed to speak at the June 19 "Solidarity Day" or "Juneteenth Day" rally. As patience ran out and tempers flared, internal differences over strategy also arose between Gonzales and Tijerina. By the time Abernathy was arrested and Resurrection City destroyed by government agents, the coalition had broken down and Corky Gonzales headed home to Colorado.

In the wake of the Poor People's Campaign, which Tijerina called the worst confusion he had ever seen, leaders attempted to establish a permanent and more democratic coalition. With Resurrection City gone, remaining activists moved to Mexican American headquarters at the Hawthorne School where Tijerina was selected as spokesman for what remained of the Chicano/a delegation. It was here that Tijerina employed a rhetoric charged with the issue of class struggle and relatively free of the religious overtones for which he was known: "The poor is the only sector of the country which has the right to question the legitimacy of the rich. I feel the poor, if well organized and properly directed, can bring the rich and the establishment machine to their knees."[87] This remark contrasted in important ways with statements made earlier in the campaign when Tijerina's language had revealed a slippage between weakly defined concepts of "race" and class.

In April, for example, he had spoken to the same reporter about his opinion of Robert F. Kennedy who was pursuing the Democratic Party presidential nomination. Tijerina said: "I have never supported him and I don't feel I will ever support him. I feel he belongs to the self-proclaimed angels and when it comes to deciding between his people and my people I don't think he will decide to support my people because eventually I think these races, these classes, will clash. We are on the side of the working class, the poor people and he is on the side of the rich people. We stand in completely opposite positions."[88] Tijerina's imprecise use of the terms *people*, *class*, and *race* made his agenda more difficult to understand for activists outside his immediate circle. At the same time, his tendency to fall back on racialized divisions complicated his ability to sustain viable coalitions.

Despite these obstacles, Tijerina's collaboration with Black militants continued through the end of the decade. On July 29, 1968, he was in Oakland where he attended another "Free Huey" rally sponsored by the Black Panther Party and the Peace and Freedom Party. Flanked by an escort of Oakland Brown Berets, Tijerina told the assembled crowd at Defremery Park that there was a continuing need for coalitions among Black and Brown militants. One report quoted Tijerina as saying: "There is no need for us to fight among ourselves. We both have a common enemy. You need me and I need you."[89] On December 13, Tijerina was acquitted on charges of kidnapping, false imprisonment, and assault related to the Tierra Amarilla raid. In June of 1969, members of SNCC joined Tijerina for a four-day "San Joaquin Liberation Seminar" in New Mexico, where Alianza activists voted to attempt a citizens' arrest of Republican Governor David Cargo.

It is a great irony that contemporary historians have reduced Tijerina's role in the Movimiento to the issue of the land grants and downplayed his innovative attempts at coalition building with African American and American Indian groups. Having been portrayed as a "one-issue leader" and the irrational head of a "nativistic cult," Tijerina has not fared well with those who would control our collective memory.[90] While it is true that his rhetoric was often inflated and bombastic, I would argue that this was in part the result of several factors—Tijerina's personal formation, the ideological complexity of the Alianza agenda, and the fact that in a social group with very limited material resources and virtually no cultural capital rhetoric may be the only tool available for collective mobilization.

As Tom Nairn argues, in most nationalist struggles "all that there *was* was the people and peculiarities of the region: its inherited ethnos, speech, folklore, skin-colour, and so on. Nationalism works through *differentiae* like those because it has to. . . . In the archetypal situation of the really poor or 'underdeveloped' territory, it may be more or less all that nationalists have going for them. For kindred reasons, it had to function through highly rhetorical forms."[91] Indo-Hispano cultural nationalism, then, found its voice in the transplanted preacher from Texas. Its cadences indirectly influenced and complemented the primary instrument for collective mobilization—cultural nationalism—that was assuming diverse forms elsewhere in the Southwest.

In terms of political objectives, however, Tijerina's project contained strong ethnocentric tendencies, the logic of which eventually would have isolated Indo-Hispanos from all other groups in some utopian space called "Justicia." Tijerina's ambivalence about the term *Chicano*, for example, was indicative of this tendency. His preference was always for the term *Indo-Hispano*.[92] His spirited defense of Spanish-language rights both inspired Chicano/a youth and at the same time potentially alienated those ethnic Mexican youth who had lost Spanish as well as those supporters who were not from Spanish-speaking backgrounds.

But Tijerina at various times throughout his activist career also deployed a "polycentric nationalism" (to use Anthony Smith's designation) that posited the kind of mutual cooperation among groups that in the 1980s came to be called multiculturalism and in the political sphere the "rainbow coalition."[93] When the Alianza declared in their 1969 convention that it would petition the federal government for the establishment of a sovereign Hispano nation, Tijerina (who was incarcerated at the time and did not participate in the convention) reacted angrily, denounced the move toward separatism, and threatened to resign.[94] For many Chicana/o activists, it was this tension between a strong focus on their own community and a belief in cross-ethnic progressive struggles that informed their philosophy and their praxis.

ACTIVISM ACROSS RACIAL LINES

Within the rank and file of grassroots activists during the Movement period, there existed a small group of ethnic Mexicans who ventured forth to contribute to social struggles in communities not their own. Perhaps the best-known Chicana with civil-rights and social-justice credentials is Elizabeth "Betita" Martinez whom we have met in earlier chapters. Whether it be pan-Latino/a organizing, women's rights, solidarity with revolutionary Cuba, or working with African American progressives, Martinez stands as a beacon for a cross-ethnic and internationalist Chicana/o ethics.[95] But she was not alone.

In his study of the Student Nonviolent Coordinating Committee (SNCC), Clayborne Carson refers briefly to a Chicana in charge of the Alabama literacy campaign.[96] In her account of the origins of contemporary feminism, Sara Evans tells us: "Mary Varela was one of the most important activists in both her participation in SDS and later in SNCC."[97] In fact, Maria Varela had deep roots in the Civil Rights Movement that stretched from religious organizing for social justice in the North to SNCC's Mississippi Summer Project to the New Mexican land-grant movement. The story of Maria Varela is another astounding tale of personal commitment and extraordinary courage.[98]

The daughter of a Mexican father who had immigrated to San Antonio during the Mexican Revolution and an Irish-German mother,

Varela grew up in a variety of areas stretching from New Jersey to Chicago. In 1962, she was a field-worker for the Young Christian Students organization and had recently attended the first meeting of Students for a Democratic Society (SDS) in Michigan. It was at the Port Huron conference that she met Sandra Cason (Casey) Hayden who invited her to work in the Atlanta office of SNCC. By October of 1963, she had joined a literacy project in Selma, Alabama, initiated by Father Maurice Oulette, the local Catholic priest. Varela's responsibilities included developing educational materials for SNCC's growing number of organizers in an area now expanded to include four southern states. In January of 1965, she relocated to Tougaloo, Mississippi, but returned to Alabama for the historic Selma to Montgomery march.

Varela was one of the five SNCC representatives who attended the October convention in Albuquerque organized by Reies López Tijerina. When she received a letter from Tijerina inviting her to join his efforts in New Mexico, she agreed rather than accepting other offers she had received from the United Farm Workers in California and activist groups in South Texas. The issue of land ownership now became central to her thinking, leading her eventually to leave her career as a photojournalist in Albuquerque in order to dedicate herself full-time to the development of non-profit organizations in rural areas of northern New Mexico. Working with key members of the Alianza, Varela managed a medical center, La Clínica del Norte, and founded a farming cooperative.

For those young people identified as Chicana or Chicana during the Viet Nam War period but who were of mixed heritage, the crossover to other communities took a less circuitous route. I want to mention briefly two activists of Mexican and African American ancestry who moved freely among the various militant organizations associated with both communities during the late 1960s.

Katarina Davis del Valle was an important actor in the National Chicano Moratorium's Committee's antiwar activities.[99] Born in 1951 and raised in the working-class Crenshaw district (South Central) of Los Angeles, Davis's family on her father's side had moved to California from New Orleans around 1917. Her paternal grandparents, who identified as African American despite their mixed ethnic and racial heritage, had been activists in both the Republican Party (then the party of choice of American Blacks) and the Pullman porters's union. Her father was born in Los Angeles; her mother in Vera Cruz, Mexico. Because of their complex racial origins, her father and his siblings as adults had opted for both "white" and "black" identities. Her father, Thurston Davis, who had attended UC Berkeley and had served in World War II, identified as African American despite his "Caucasian" features.

In this context of mestizo reality in urban Los Angeles, Cathy Davis, as she was known until the later 1960s, became involved in political activism in high school (St. Mary's Academy) where she founded "Students for Christian Awareness" and met organizers Fred Ross and Monty Pérez through tutorial programs in downtown Los Angeles and the UFW Safeway supermarket boycotts. As the American war in Viet Nam escalated, Davis del Valle began to counsel draft resisters and became increasingly active in student organizations such as UMAS, the Black Student Union, and MEChA. While attending Johnston College at the University of Redlands in 1969, she became involved with both the *La Raza* newspaper, where she met Eliezer Risco who urged her to change her name to Katarina, and with the National Chicano Moratorium Committee.

Upon moving to East L.A., she joined other women such as Gloria Chavez and Gloria Arellanes, a former Brown Beret, who were working out of Moratorium offices on Brooklyn Avenue. She attended the second Chicano Youth Liberation Conference in March of 1970 and was an organizer for the 1971 Vancouver meeting between Chicanas and North Vietnamese women. During preparations for the August 29, 1970, demonstration, for which she was one of two people in charge of security, Davis del Valle received a Western Union message of support and congratulations addressed to the Moratorium Committee and purportedly from Ho Chi Minh and the National Liberation Front. Her antiwar activities extended to the important GI resistance movement where she worked with Chicano GIs and with the anti-war newspaper *Military Intelligence*.

As she became increasingly committed to a Marxist-Leninist analysis of the war and of U.S. society in general, Davis del Valle experienced the tension in the Chicano Movement between sectarian nationalism and a more internationalist agenda. Because she did not learn of her father's African American heritage until she was in her thirties and therefore believed her own identity to be a mixture of Mexican and Caucasian, she was a vulnerable target for those Chicano activists who insisted on fabricated notions of racial authenticity and who argued that Marxism was a "white thing." Nevertheless, she would carry her belief in the international working-class movement into the post–Viet Nam war period, working closely with Dolores Huerta to establish the Coalition of Labor Union Women and spearheading the pro-Central America solidarity movement within the AFL-CIO during the conservative Reagan-Lane Kirkland administration. Today, Davis del Valle is Education Coordinator for the Western Region of the Service Employees International Union (SEIU) and directs an organizer's education project in Puerto Rico.

My second example is Mario Salas of San Antonio, Texas.[100] The son of a Lebanese mother and an African-Mexican father, Salas was born and raised in San Antonio where he attended Catholic grammar school and entered the segregated black Phillis Wheatley High School in 1964. His mother, who was an avid reader, had introduced him to a wide-range of European and American writings, including literary classics such as *Moby Dick* and works of socialist theory by Lenin and others. As a student at San Antonio Community College, Salas met members of the Student Non-Violent Coordinating Committee (SNCC) and quickly became a field organizer engaged in community programs based on Black Panther tactics such as free-breakfast programs. In 1972, he unsuccessfully ran for State Representative on the La Raza Unida Party ticket.

Salas's opposition to the war had begun in high school because of his own critical analysis and the example of Muhammad Ali. With the invasion of Cambodia in 1970 and the murder of four students at Kent State University by the Ohio National Guard, Salas became increasingly active, working with John Dauer and the San Antonio Coalition Against the War in Vietnam, a coalition of Brown Berets, Quakers, SNCC, and the GI Resistance Movement from Fort Sam Houston.

Throughout the late 1970s and early 1980s, Mario Salas paid attention to the social injustices he saw in his own community. Sectarian nationalist agendas made no sense to him in the context of his multiracial realities. When told by African American friends who had heard he was Chicano, "I thought you were black," he answered, "I am but that's not all I am." When told by Chicano friends who had heard he was African American, "I thought you were Chicano," he answered, "I am but that's not all I am." "I think I was blessed," Salas told me, "because both my parents were multicultural" at a time when the term had yet to be invented. In my opinion, Salas's pan-ethnic perspective has much to teach us about the limitations of narrow nationalism and the promise of multiethnic and internationalist projects.

As mixed-race activists in an unusually turbulent period of U.S. history, Katarina Davis del Valle and Mario Salas constructed their adult identities less on racial or ethnic categories than on an unwavering ethical and political commitment to social justice. They "theorized" gender, race, and class not in isolation but through the process of lived praxis in their communities. It behooves us, in the face of renewed forms of exclusionary "nationalist" and "race-based" identities and an expanding neo-assimilationist Hispanic class, to look carefully at the lives of these cultural workers and the lessons they can teach us about identity, resistance, and historical change.

In its broadest terms, the Movimiento cannot be understood solely as a "racial movement" designed to extract concessions from a racial state or even as the product of a collective response to institutional racism. In his book, Ian Haney López argues for the latter, claiming that at its core the Movement marked a shift from the Mexican American community's desire to be considered "white" to a Chicano/a project founded upon nonwhite identities. Haney López is certainly correct to say that the racializing practices of law enforcement and other state apparatuses played a significant role in the elaboration of insurgent agendas. In essence, this is what Dr. George I. Sánchez had argued in 1963 when he suggested that Mexican American identity turned in large part on the dominant society's treatment or mistreatment of the community.[101] Historian Edward J. Escobar makes a similar argument about the role of the Los Angeles Police Department and the radicalization of the Chicano Movement.[102]

It would be reductive, however, to claim that "race" was the Movement's primary determinant.[103] Even though middle-class organizations such as LULAC and the GI Forum had sought to align themselves with the category of whiteness during the post–World War II era, the vast majority of working-class Mexicans in the Southwest knew quite well that they were not white and did not desire to be white.[104] Certainly, activists such as Katarina Davis del Valle and Mario Salas negotiated a social landscape that cannot be limited to simple matters of "whiteness," nor can Tijerina's Indo-Hispano cultural nationalism be understood solely as a racial movement. As I have argued throughout, blanket assertions about the Movimiento will necessarily efface important regional, organizational, and ideological differences.

BLACK AND BROWN TOGETHER?

Yes, there is quite a bit of competition and conflict because they are both minorities trying to find a niche in this "White man's' society. I don't think they realize that if they work together they can get both of their goals accomplished.[105]

I conclude this chapter with an anecdote reproduced in a book by San Francisco Bay Area activist Samuel Martinez. Recounting his early years as a young Chicano in the criminal-justice system, he remembers: "It was my first day out of Juvenile Hall at the age of fifteen; the year was 1965. I had been encaged for a month with a 'roommate' who constantly tried to step on my neck to feel good about himself. He spoke with fury and rage, overacting his pride in who he was. 'I'm Black and I'm proud,' he would echo every day. 'Your people are wetbacks, you have nothing. At least we have Marvin Gaye, Smokey Robinson, and the Temptations.' So great was the frustration I felt that my only response was a 'Fuck you!' My response would always be followed by us 'going chest': we locked left hands and beat on each other with our right, or just beat on each other from the neck down. All this in silence, because if caught we could get more time for fighting."[106]

In a worst-case scenario, Martinez's description of two young men of color beating on each other in silence for fear of reprisal by those in power may become an apt metaphor for the situation of poor Black and Brown communities at the beginning of the twenty-first century. According to the U.S. Census Bureau, "Hispanics" surpassed African Americans as the nation's largest minority group in the year 2003, rising to 13.5 percent over 13 percent for Blacks.[107] In the state of California, demographic projections to the year 2040 suggest that the Mexican-origin population will increase from seven million to twenty-eight million while African American numbers will increase only slightly. At the same time, the influx of Mexican immigrants into the Deep South will, for the first time, put ethnic Mexicans in direct contact with the traditions and history of a region dominated until now by a black/white binary in terms of race relations. According to the 2000 Census, the increase in Latinos between 1990 and 2000 in North Carolina was 393.9 percent, in Arkansas 323.3 percent, in Georgia 299.6 percent, and in Tennessee 278.2 percent.

It may be the children of these immigrants, born and raised in the Old Confederacy, will determine to a considerable degree the future of any Chicano/a political project on a national scale. In cities like Houston, for example, where the influx of Latino immigrants during the 1990s completely realigned the political landscape, Black and Brown relations suffered from a mutual lack of knowledge and the persistence of long-standing stereotypes.[108] In Houston as well as cities such as Compton in southern California and Miami, African American leaders have had to factor Latino/a issues into their reform agendas in ways they never had to in the past.[109]

In January 2004, the *New York Times* published a front-page story that posed several important questions: "Does the ascendance of Hispanics mean a decline in the influence of blacks? Does it doom, or encourage, alliances between the two groups? Does the old formula for those alliances—shared grievances—have much meaning given the diversity of income and status within each group?"[110]

The reality of an ever-widening gap between rich and poor and drastic cuts in state and municipal budgets, a situation exacerbated by the regressive social and economic policies put in place by the Bush/Cheney administration, means the potential for infighting among the majorities of people of color deprived of equal opportunities will continue to be great. To what extent will progressive activists in both communities be able to ensure that coalitions and solidarity rather than "going chest" become the model for future Black/Brown relationships? Some progressive activists in the Latino community were so concerned about the potential for friction between the two groups that they published an "Open Letter to Our African American Brothers and Sisters" in which they promised to eschew artificially created rivalries.[111]

Former Chicano activist Nick C. Vaca, however, sees Black/Brown rivalries as the most likely scenario for the future. In his study of political conflicts in Los Angeles, Houston, New York, and Miami, Vaca argues that "natural" alliances between African Americans and Latinos no longer exist (if they ever did) and concludes that each community will necessarily pursue its separate agenda: "The reality is that a divide exists between Blacks and Latinos that no amount of camouflage can hide. For each analysis that finds that Latinos and Blacks have a 'natural' basis for mutual support because of a common history of suffering and oppression, there are others that find great antipathy between the two groups. . . . We have seen that in the real world the ostensible moral and philosophical bases for coalition politics have largely fallen apart because of competing self-interests."[112]

Vaca's argument is convincing, especially in the arena of electoral politics and the pursuit of local power and resources although recent developments in some areas of the South such as the Southern Regional Council's attempt to sustain Black/Brown coalitions in Georgia, suggest a more optimistic alternative. I would submit that it is precisely at the grassroots level, outside official party circles, that such alliances are more likely to emerge.

In the academic world there have been limited attempts to foster dialogue between the two groups. The exchange between well-known activist-scholar Cornel West and former UC Berkeley anthropologist Jorge Klor de Alva that appeared in the April 1996 issue of *Harper's Magazine* was unsatisfactory insofar as it focused too narrowly on dissecting ethnic and racial identities and labels and ended up reproducing some of the more antiquated racializing stereotypes. Cornel West, for example, when asked to explain the fact that many public institutions have a Black buffer or gatekeeping managerial class, asserted: "Blacks are more likely to register protests than Latinos are. That's what I mean by raising hell, you see. Black people are more likely to raise hell than brown people."[113] The specter of the sleepy and docile Mexican reappears here in the language of one of our most progressive African American intellectuals. What will be needed in the future are more carefully planned and better-executed conversations of this kind among young artists, thinkers, and activists from both communities.

In the next chapter, I will explore one university campus in the late 1960s where, despite cultural differences, Chicano/a and African American students united in an attempt to extend educational opportunities to previously excluded communities. As they struggled against the entrenched elitism of their institutional setting, these young people confronted both the divisive effects of regressive ethnic nationalisms and the open hostility of local and federal authorities. In spite of the extremely difficult conditions that surrounded them, the Lumumba/Zapata activists at the University of California, San Diego, sustained, if only for a brief moment, a Black/Brown coalition that can teach us much about the future.

CHAPTER SIX

—"TO DEMAND THAT THE UNIVERSITY WORK FOR OUR PEOPLE"—

The students are on campus making new demands that may
seem strident and impulsive to some but that have a core of
profound significance for the future of the ethnic groups and
for American society as a whole.
            —Dr. Julian Samora and Dr. Ernesto Galarza (1971)

IN APRIL OF 1969 ORGANIZERS at the University of California, Santa
Barbara mailed invitations to progressive educators across the state. A
conference on the status of Chicano/as in higher education was to be
convened by the local chapter of the United Mexican American
Students (UMAS) and the Chicano Coordinating Council on Higher
Education (CCHE) in conjunction with other interested parties, among
them members of the Educational Clearinghouse in Los Angeles such
as Gloria López and René Nuñez. Following close on the heels of the
historic Youth Liberation Conference in Denver hosted by the Crusade
for Justice, the Santa Barbara meeting would be described years later as
the founding moment of the Chicano/a student movement.[1]

By the beginning of the next academic year, activists had prepared
a list of "25 Resolutions on Chicano Studies." Calling for the creation
of Chicano Studies programs at every University of California campus,
the document insisted that such programs be "staffed and controlled by
Chicanos" and demanded that within five years Chicano faculty and
student numbers "be proportionate to the Chicano population
statewide or in the region the campus serves, whichever is the higher."
Resolution 9 added that "direct experience in the Chicano community
be required of all professional training in the University system."[2]

The historic meeting of April 1969 in Santa Barbara that produced
the Plan de Santa Bárbara also led to the establishment of the
Movimiento Estudiantil Chicano de Aztlán (MEChA), an umbrella
organization designed to unify and replace other student organizations
first in California and then across the Southwest. Participants at the
conference selected the name MEChA over another proposed name—
Chicano Alliance for United Student Action (CAUSA)—in order to

emphasize the symbolic power of the idea of Aztlán and to capture the Spanish meaning of *mecha* (spark).[3] At numerous campuses, there was local resistance to the proposed name change. At the University of California, San Diego, the campus that is the focus of this chapter, a debate lasted for almost two months before the existing organization, the Mexican American Youth Association (MAYA) changed its name to MAYA/MEChA and eventually to MEChA.[4]

In an attempt to negotiate between reformist, narrow nationalist, and revolutionary positions within the Movement, the participants at the Santa Barbara conference argued forcefully for the Chicano community's right to determine the nature of public universities. According to the framers of the Plan de Santa Bárbara, any attempt to dismiss university reform as a "white" activity, a stance adopted by some regressive nationalists, would alienate the student sector and nullify a significant aspect of the Movement's strength. It would also allow universities and colleges to continue their business as usual with regard to the Chicano/a community:

> Not all Chicanos in the movement are in agreement as to the strategic importance of the university to the liberation of the Chicano people. A leading argument against involvement with the university holds that the participation will only result in cooptation of scarce Chicano time, manpower, and resources; and that it will only serve to legitimize basically racist relationships between the Chicano community and gabacho society. According to this view, the university and other major institutions are essentially irrelevant to the process of Chicano liberation . . .
>
> The inescapable fact is that Chicanos must come to grips with the reality of the university in modern society. . . . How can the university contribute to the liberation of the Chicano community? In the long term probably the most fundamental contribution it will make will be by producing knowledge applicable by the Chicano movement. . . . The role of knowledge in producing powerful social change, indeed revolution, cannot be underestimated.[5]

The college campus, then, was to become one more site of struggle in the Chicano/a assault against marginalization and the unfulfilled promises of liberal democracy. The university as a site for the production and dissemination of knowledge would make it a key battleground for the future of ethnic Mexican people in the United States.

In this chapter, I will focus on Chicana/o participation in a broad-based coalition that implemented Movement strategies and objectives at one specific location in the Southwest. Two weeks before the historic meeting at Denver and a month before the Santa Barbara conference, Chicano/a and African American students at the University of California, San Diego (UCSD), campus had submitted their demands for a radical educational experiment they called Lumumba-Zapata College.

It is my contention that the UC San Diego experience embodied one of the most radical attempts by students and faculty of color to transform the elitist and Eurocentric university into an inclusionary and democratic space that reflected the concerns of traditionally excluded communities. I believe the archival evidence confirms that the Lumumba-Zapata activists were exceptional because they presented their demands during the earliest moments of the Chicano/a student movement and, perhaps more important, because they struggled to maintain a multiethnic coalition even as they negotiated the oftentimes glaring conflicts between sectarian nationalism and a more far-reaching internationalist agenda.

In the late 1960s opportunities in higher education for young people of Mexican descent were minimal. Spanish-surnamed enrollments in colleges and universities nationwide made up only 1.6 percent in 1968; in 1972 numbers had risen slightly to 2.3 percent with a majority in two-year community colleges. In the University of California (UC) system in 1968, "Mexican or Spanish American" students made up only 1.8 percent of the total number of undergraduates and 1.1 percent of all graduate students.[6] As Chicano/a activism increased across the Southwest, numbers slowly began to increase so that in the UC system by 1973 the percentage of Chicano/a undergraduates was 5.0 percent. Aggressive outreach programs and innovative curricular reforms initiated by Chicano/Mexicano faculty and students made significant inroads into the most exclusionary campuses. By 1974 and the waning of the Movement's intensity, however, numbers became stagnant and in some cases began a slow reversal downward to such an extent that a 1976 report prepared for the National Chicano Commission on Higher Education declared: "The future of Chicanos in higher education is . . . less bright today than it was at the beginning of this decade."[7]

The late 1960s and early 1970s were marked by a series of radical projects that challenged the traditional educational system in California. In March 1968, Chicana/o high school students throughout Los Angeles organized and participated in "blowouts" demanding major reforms. Similar events took place in Texas and elsewhere in the Southwest.[8] Later that same year, students at UC Santa Cruz demanded the creation of a Malcolm X college (administrators rejected their proposal), and the first Mexican American Studies program in California was founded at Los Angeles State College. In the San Francisco Bay Area, an autonomous Third World college was established in late 1969 after the strike at San Francisco State College and in solidarity with Los Siete de la Raza (see Chapter Five). On the UC Berkeley campus, the Third World Liberation Front strike was called on January 22, 1969, after negotiations with the administration for a Third World College and other reforms (including a Center for Mexican American Studies) broke down.[9] Composed of the Mexican American Student Confederation (MASC), the African American Student Union (AASU), and the Asian American Political Alliance (AAPA), as well as a White Student Strike Support Committee, the Berkeley coalition and its demands shared a number of characteristics with the UC San Diego effort.

More specifically, both groups demanded fundamental changes in the governance practices of the university, changes that would challenge the elite composition of the academic hierarchy in terms of decision making, curriculum, faculty hiring, and student admissions. In addition to the creation of autonomous ethnic-specific departments, the Berkeley strikers demanded: "That Third World people be in positions of power. Recruitment of more Third World faculty in every department and discipline and proportionate employment of Third World people at all levels ... throughout the university system."[10] It was precisely the attempt by students of color to intervene in the governance structures of the academy that would frighten liberal and conservative administrators alike.

Outside of the elite UC system, activists battled for Chicano Studies programs on a number of campuses in the California State College and community college systems. At the same time, radical reformers developed alternative educational projects. Bob Hoover and Aaron Manganiello founded Nairobi College in East Palo Alto and Venceremos College in Redwood City. Both colleges eventually received accreditation from the Western College Association.[11] At Venceremos

College, radical Chicana women established a day-care center, and promoted a sophisticated feminist and internationalist agenda: "Venceremos supports no separatist movements on any level. . . . We, as the women of La Raza, must dare to carry on the revolutionary tradition of Las Adelitas, who fought so courageously during the Mexican Revolution."[12] In Fresno, activist educators from the local Cal State campus founded La Universidad de Aztlán (UA), "a learning institution for us, who think of ourselves as Raza." Inspired by the pedagogical theory of Brazilian Paulo Freire, UA organizers argued: "Our people possess tremendous intellectual potential that must be fully developed, and which can only be developed in the case of a bilingual-bicultural context."[13]

Farther north, near Sacramento, Native Americans and Chicano/as created Deganawidah-Quetzalcoatl University (DQU) in 1971. According to DQU's mission statement, Chicano/as and indigenous people shared a common lineage ("*raza o parentesco*") as well as similar positions in a racialized educational system: "*Por esta y otras razones gran número de chicanos e indios han considerado la buena idea de comenzar programas de educación elevada designados a conocer las necesidades de su gente*" ("For this and other reasons, a great number of Chicanos and Indians believe it is a good idea to initiate programs of higher education designed to respond to the needs of the people").[14]

A key player at DQU was UC Davis professor Jack Forbes who had been one of the first scholars to promote the idea of Aztlán as the Chicano homeland (according to Forbes himself, he had introduced the term as early as 1962). In his explanation of why DQU was necessary, Forbes touched upon many of the issues driving Chicano/a demands for educational reform across the Southwest: "Experience has shown that no white-run, white-oriented college can adequately meet the needs of the Indian and Chicano peoples. . . . If one of the white colleges of the United States were to fully integrate its faculty, revise its curriculum, do away with meaningless requirements, and share its governing authority, then perhaps there would be little (or less) need for DQU. But such a thing is not happening."[15] Relying heavily on notions of race and nation, Forbes made the case that "every people needs its university." Native and Chicano peoples were no different.

From 1971 to 1973, the community organization Casa de la Raza operated as a K-12 school in Berkeley, California, before being shut down by the local school district (after the Office of Civil Rights applied pressure) because of charges of exclusionary admissions policies. The stated guiding principle of the Casa de la Raza curriculum was "carnalismo," although the term was never defined in a way that translated into practical curricular initiatives. The objective of the school's founders was to create an alternate system of education in opposition to what they called "the gabacho system" of individualized competition.[16] Another alternative school was created in Palo Alto—the Free University. Among its founders was Jamaican literature professor Keith Lowe, who will figure in the events in San Diego described in this chapter.

Calls for drastic educational reform came not only from the grassroots but also from the handful of Mexican Americans who struggled within the ranks of public school systems, university administrations, and the federal bureaucracy. The spring of 1969 was an especially active period in California. In addition to the Santa Barbara conference, there was a meeting of Association of Mexican American Educators (AMAE) in San Diego in March, the Mexican American Political Association (MAPA) sponsored the Third Annual Mexican American Issues Conference at Sacramento City College in April, and activists such as Anna Nieto Gomez and Monte Perez met at Cal State Long Beach to discuss recruitment and retention issues in May. At the San Diego conference, educators passed the following resolution: "That AMAE support the actions of the Chicano student movement of pursuing better education . . . encourage educator support of student movements in their individual chapters . . . denounce the use of unreasonable police force in educational institutions."[17]

The following year, Philip Montez, director of the Western Field Office of the U.S. Commission on Civil Rights, wrote:

A study was recently completed at UCLA, the main focus of which was the low aspiration level of the Mexican American. And they proved that it was so. . . . The universities which produce our scholars in the Southwest have failed in attempting to know the Mexican American. They continue to place the cart before the horse. They look at motivation and aspiration before they know what society has done to us. By providing superficial programs, the society will never have to acknowledge what it has done to a people/s culture in a supposedly democratic society. This indicates to me that in all the things we are trying to do for Mexican Americans nobody has accepted the fact that the system has done a poor job.[18]

Earlier in 1970, some of the most prestigious educators in the University of California system addressed a letter to UC president Charles Hitch as members of the president's Chicano Steering Committee in which they spoke openly of the "great dismay and anger among Chicanos inside and outside the University" because of "the deep gulf that separates your understanding of and sensitivity to Chicano needs from that of the UC Chicano community." Taking key terms from the Movement discursive repertoire, chairman Eugene Cota-Robles concluded: "What Chicanos are asking of the University is that it be responsible to us as a people seeking self-determination. The University cannot and will not continue being the exclusive domain of the dominant sectors of our society; it belongs to all the people, it must serve us. . . . The University has the means to meet its responsibility to the Chicano people of California; what it lacks is the will. We are confident that history will compel the University to honor its obligations to our people."[19] Picking up the mantle of José Vasconcelos, who as Minister of Education in Mexico in the 1930s had insisted that the university "work for the people," Chicano/a reformers were arguing for nothing less than a restructuring of the racialized and class-based system of higher education in California.

The Chicano educational-reform movement held that students and faculty would not only reform the university from within but also move off campus in order to make resources and skills available to surrounding communities. As Ysidro Macias, one of the key participants at the Santa Barbara event, argued: "Chicano Studies institutionalization seems to mark the present stage of activity and the future involves the concept of 'moving into the community' to provide services, such as breakfast programs, medical clinics, etc., but [it is] just as important to politicize the community as to the economic and political nature, with its inherent oppression, of the capitalist system in this country."[20] That the idea of Chicano/a university students teaching "against capital" in working-class Mexican barrios was at best utopian was not lost on Macias and others activists. Nevertheless, the revolutionary tenor of the times reinforced the notion that U.S. imperialism was under attack around the world and that radical Chicana/os could implement their critique of liberalism and contribute to the creation of a more democratic society.

THE "WHITE SCHOOL ON THE HILL"

There appears to be a general community impression that UCSD has cloistered itself away from the community and is not interested in serving all the community, and that entrance requirements for higher education in general are too restrictive.

—"Concept of an Urban College in San Diego" (1969)

How does a school like UCSD, all white, elitist and with both feet on the moon, so to speak—how does it get one foot into the ghetto areas of the Inner City?

—UCSD Chancellor William McGill to *San Diego Magazine* (1969)

The history of the UC San Diego campus might best be thought of as a perpetual struggle between an elitist conservative philosophy and a more benign form of liberal, yet no less elitist, pluralism. These two sides of the educational and policymaking equation were never mutually exclusive. In fact, those administrators most closely identified with Kennedy-style liberalism were often themselves the supporters and beneficiaries of a deeply antidemocratic elitism. It is the elitism of an institution like UCSD that even today continues to produce racialized outcomes in terms of student enrollments, curriculum, staff promotions, and faculty hiring. Elitism or "class racism" leads inexorably to institutional racism.[21]

In her history of UCSD, Nancy Scott Anderson describes the early debates about where to locate what she calls "the cathedral on a bluff."[22] Proposals to build the new university in closer proximity to downtown San Diego near Balboa Park were rejected, and the potential for an urban college accessible to working-class communities was lost. In 1958, when the La Jolla site was finally approved, the local culture in the seaside community some twelve miles north of the city was typical of many wealthy neighborhoods across the country. Casual racism directed at Latinos and Blacks was everywhere present in advertising and other forms of media while deeper forms of structural racism and anti-Semitism ensured that resources be kept out of the hands of "any person whose blood is not entirely that of the Caucasian race" (La Jolla property deed, 1959).[23]

Campus founder Roger Revelle had never envisioned anything quite like the political battles that would engulf the university in the late

1960s. Revelle's Cold War–inspired vision was that of the university as a detached and pastoral training ground for engineers and scientists, and he imagined a campus where only a small and select group of students would be shaped as leaders. In his view, this elite group would guide a much larger but less talented group into the future. The larger group would not be educated at UCSD but at the local state college.

According to Revelle: "In any region of large population there may be need for several institutions of higher education, some to handle large numbers of students, the others to concentrate on relatively small numbers of highly selected young people who will be seed beds for the future.... There is the need to give undergraduate instruction to a relatively small number of potential leaders, including especially scientific and technical leaders."[24] Revelle proposed that officials in the San Diego school system begin to identify local children with "IQs above 140" for admission to the new campus. In the context of the late 1950s, this meant that disenfranchised working-class people and people of color without access to decent schools were locked out from the very beginning. In effect, UCSD's history of "selecting" the privileged few, through artificially stringent and biased admissions criteria rather than educating in a democratic fashion, had begun.

The founding fathers of the La Jolla campus were intimately tied to the military-industrial complex. In fact, if local tycoon John Jay Hopkins, the head of General Dynamics, had not offered one million dollars to the UC system in 1953 for the establishment of a campus UCSD might never have been built. The earliest names suggested for the campus provide some insight into the original vision—Institute of Technology and Engineering, School of Science and Engineering. Many of the first faculty members shared the class-based biases of the surrounding community, yet key faculty, including the early chancellors, were liberals never completely at ease in the Republican stronghold of San Diego, where military culture combined with conservative politics to produce one of the most segregated and economically stratified cities in the Southwest.

It surprised no one among the city's elite, for example, that a retired general was editor of the opinion page of the local newspaper. What successive UCSD chancellors faced, therefore, especially in the turbulent Viet Nam war years, was a constant struggle to defend their concept of academic freedom against the intrusion of what they perceived to be the irrational forces of both the right and the left. As Chicano/a and Black students became increasingly radicalized, new challenges perplexed even the most well-intentioned administrators. For the most part, the legitimate issues of racism and the demands of Black, Asian, and Chicano/a students were simply beyond their comprehension.

Despite the elitist origins of the institution and its geographical distance from the urban core of San Diego, La Jolla was from the mid-1960s on among the most politicized campuses in the University of California system. One of the earliest incidents that aroused the ire of San Diego's conservative community was a demonstration protesting the U.S. invasion and occupation of the Dominican Republic that had taken place in late April 1965. A front-page editorial in the *San Diego Union* demanded that the university administration "suppress" all further protests, and the newspaper expressed a "deep concern with the failure of discipline at the University of California local campus."[25] The denunciations of UCSD's lack of "discipline" emanating out of the state's most conservative sectors would increase throughout the next decade. Chancellor John Galbraith, writing to fellow chancellor Franklin Murphy of UCLA about the Dominican protest, jokingly referred to UCSD's growing radicalism: "We don't take a back seat to Berkeley in anything."[26] Little did he know that the next few years would put his campus on the front lines of a full-scale revolution over the future of higher education.

Accustomed to a relatively docile Mexican and Mexican American community, San Diego city leaders were caught off guard when the Chicano Movement came to town. As local writer Harold Keen put it:

> The slumbering brown giant is beginning to stir, to cast off the Tío Taco (Mexican Uncle Tom) sombrero-topped stereotype of subservience and abject acceptance of an inferior destiny. The demeaning image of servility projected by the bracero and the wetback, the busboy and the laborer, the scared immigrant and the passive alien resident is being erased by a new breed that proudly calls itself *Chicano* and spans the generation gap. The young and the middle aged—the passionate, angry students and many of their reserved, deliberate elders—are joined in the Mexican-American revolution of self-awareness, self-respect and self-determination.[27]

By the time the nation emerged from the bright light of revolutionary desire and the violent reaction against it that was the Viet Nam war era, UCSD had been home to an active Students for a Democratic Society (SDS) chapter; the Independent Left (IL); the Associated Moderate Students (AMS), a conservative student group; the Black Student Council (BSC), later the Black Student Union (BSU); the Women's Liberation Front; the United Native Americans (UNA); the Asian American Student Alliance (AASA); a Chicana activist group (MUJER); the Mexican American Youth Association (MAYA), and later the Movimiento Estudiantil Chicano de Aztlán (MEChA). But the campus high on the hill in affluent La Jolla first catapulted into the national consciousness (and the crosshairs of local and national law enforcement) when philosophy graduate student Angela Davis followed her mentor Herbert Marcuse from Brandeis University to southern California in the autumn of 1967.[28]

When she arrived to pursue graduate studies in philosophy at UCSD, Angela Davis was immediately struck by the segregated nature of the campus. She later recalled: "Each day brought on a more profound dejection, for there were still no Black people on campus. . . . I roamed the campus, examined the bulletin boards, read the newspapers, talked to everyone who might know: Where are my people?"[29] Because of the extremely low numbers of African American students on campus, Davis realized that any political organization interested in addressing students of color would have to pursue a multiethnic coalition. In this respect, her thinking coincided with that of the original Black Panthers who, far from being sectarian nationalists as some historians have misrepresented them, were eager to establish alliances with other groups.

In his rebuke of Stokely Carmichael's narrowly nationalist agenda, Eldridge Cleaver had written: "One thing they know, and we know, that seems to escape you, is that there is not going to be any revolution or black liberation in the United States as long as revolutionary blacks, whites, Mexicans, Puerto Ricans, Indians, Chinese and Eskimos are unwilling or unable to unite into some functional machinery that can cope with the situation."[30] The original Panthers were particularly opposed to the isolation of Black college students within Black-only organizations or programs. In 1969, David Hilliard told an audience of San Francisco State College students: "The Black Panther Party is not going to support any BSU policy that asks for an autonomous Black studies program that excludes other individuals. . . . Let's have an organization that we call the Afro-American, Asian, Latin Alliance. Motherfuck the BSU because the BSU is too narrow. We recognize nationalism, because we know that our struggle is one of national salvation. But this doesn't hinder our struggle to make alliances with other people that's moving in a common direction, but rather it strengthens our struggle."[31]

Angela Davis held a similar position on the issue of coalition politics, and she began to act on that philosophy once she was in San Diego. After collaborating on the formation of a small Black Student Council, she made contact with the recently created Chicano/a student organization the Mexican American Youth Association (MAYA).

MAYA had first appeared at nearby San Diego State University in 1967 under the direction of its first chairman, Bert Rivas. According to one of its founding members, Israel Chávez, the UCSD chapter was formed in late spring of 1968 after the death of Martin Luther King, Jr.[32] By the end of the year, Chávez and other MAYA members, working with the Black Student Council, had staged a hunger strike to protest Governor Reagan's granting of virtual absolute power to the Regents and placing of limitations on guest lecturers, an official response to the temporary hiring of Eldridge Cleaver at UCLA.[33]

The newly formed MAYA/BSC coalition would soon dive directly into the struggle over higher education by intervening in the UCSD administration's plans for a new campus college. Basing the organizational structure of UCSD on the elite British system, the founders had divided the campus into separate "colleges" each with a distinct character. Planning for the third college was well under way when provost-designate Armin Rappaport asked students for input on possible ethnic-studies courses. Much to Rappaport's surprise, BSC/MAYA activists developed an elaborate program that eventually would derail the university administration's existing plans.

A number of BSC undergraduates, Angela Davis, and literature professor Keith Lowe, a native of Jamaica against whom the U.S. government would invoke the McCarran Act in 1969 in order to refuse him reentry into the United States, drafted the BSC's original document in which they called for a college to be named after Congolese revolutionary Patrice Lumumba. The objective of the new college, as Davis put it, would be to provide Black and Brown students with "the knowledge and skills we needed in order to more effectively wage our liberation struggles."[34] Working collectively, BSC and MAYA activists revised the original document a number of times. The opening line of the final draft presented to the campus administration on March 14, 1969, as the "Lumumba-Zapata College, BSC-MAYA Demands for the Third College, UCSD" read: "Contradictions which sustained America in the past are now threatening to annihilate the entire societal edifice." Accordingly, the students proposed a complete dismantling of the entrenched class racism of the La Jolla campus:

> At the University of California, San Diego, we will no longer ensure the undisturbed existence of a false institution which consistently fails to respond to the needs of our people. Despite the Chicano rebellions in the Southwest and the Black revolts in the cities, the University of California, San Diego, which is part of the oppressive system, has not changed its institutional role. The puny reforms made so far are aimed at pacifying the revolts and sapping our strength. We therefore not only emphatically demand that radical changes be made, we propose to execute these changes ourselves![35]

The small core of Chicano/a students at UCSD (numbering only forty-four in 1968) formed a tight-knit group made tighter because they were so few. Most of them would participate in the major activities associated with the Movimiento period—United Farm Workers's boycotts, the Chicano Moratorium antiwar marches and demonstrations in Los Angeles from 1969 through 1971, the Crusade for Justice's youth conferences in Denver, and historic meetings on educational reform in the University of California system. As we shall see, some of them were active members of the Brown Berets and even the Young Lords (the Puerto Rican youth group originally formed in Chicago), some eventually joined the Communist Labor Party, and virtually all of them participated in the local actions of the San Diego Chicano/a community such as the establishment of Chicano Park in 1970.[36] That same year, the UCSD Defense Fund was established in solidarity with radical causes ranging from Los Siete de la Raza in San Francisco, the incarceration of Angela Davis, and the Soldedad Brothers case. Chicano student Carlos Monge served as the fund's spokesperson. The journey these activists made from urban neighborhoods, the Imperial Valley, and other working-class and rural areas would put them on a collision course with the ingrained elitism of the La Jolla campus, with local and national conservative faculty, politicians, and journalists, and ultimately with local and federal law-enforcement agencies.

Throughout the Lumumba-Zapata episode, the Chicano/a campus community was divided along sectarian nationalist, internationalist, and socialist lines. Differences were often put aside in order to present a united front against the administration, but ideological divisions typical of Movement organizations of the period were real. Years later student leader Vince C. de Baca recalled: "The Lumumba-Zapata demands represented a consolidation of the internationalist perspective. There were Black nationalists and there were Chicano nationalists who wanted a Black or Chicano college, who didn't want to work with other ethnic groups. But there was a larger faction which was internationalist in perspective, which held the view that the best way to get anything through . . . was to work together, to submit one joint Black-Chicano proposal."[37] In their struggle to balance the agendas of the African American community with their own even as they were forced to negotiate with narrow nationalists within their own cohort, Chicano/a internationalists like de Baca, Monge, Martha Salinas, Maria Blanco, Israel Chávez, Milan Lalic Molina, Theresa Meléndez, Maria Elena Salazar, Alda Blanco, Yolanda Catzalco, Marta Lomelí, Barbie Reyes, and others walked a precarious political tightrope. According to de Baca: "We were considered *mayateros* [nigger lovers], internationalists . . . whereas these other people considered themselves Mexicans. They didn't even really want to consider themselves Chicanos."[38]

In a series of developments that took place during the 1971–1972 academic year, divisions had grown within UCSD's Chicano/a community. One group that had developed a "Third World Studies" major called for an internationalist framework within which students might pursue Chicano, African American, and other concentrations. These students met opposition from peers with a more narrow nationalist perspective who demanded control over any future program. Not unlike the suspicious appearance of "Black nationalists" at UCSD one year earlier, the presence of recently arrived militants promoting regressive nationalist positions raised considerable suspicion. Many of the original Lumumba-Zapata organizers noted that one of the leaders of the "nationalist" faction had developed a reputation as an "internationalist" who had clashed with nationalist students at other local colleges. Given the recent history of infiltration and provocation on campus, the aggressive style and actions of such figures contributed to the students' sense of being under attack.[39]

In the end, supporters of the Third World position succeeded in convincing at least some students to agree to their basic principles. As they wrote in the local MEChA constitution: "The ideology of MEChA is loosely one of Revolutionary Nationalism which will unite Chicanos and build a consciousness of the existence of an oppressive system, a system whose perpetrators victimize not only Chicanos, but the majority of the people of this country and the rest of the world."[40] The development of a more narrowly focused Chicano Studies program moved forward although not without its critics, who claimed that such a program would weaken ties of solidarity with other communities.[41]

At the heart of the internationalist contingent was Marxist literary critic Carlos Blanco Aguinaga (fig. 16). The son of a Spanish Republican family, Blanco had been raised in Mexico City and educated at Harvard. Arriving at UCSD in 1964, Blanco would become instrumental in guiding emergent Chicano radicalism on campus in his role as faculty advisor to MAYA and intellectual mentor to student leaders. Early in the Lumumba-Zapata episode, Blanco explained: "Lumumba-Zapata was not conceived as a 'coalition' to train Black and Chicano aspirants to their own bourgeoisies." But for some Chicano/a activists winning access to middle-class privileges was precisely their goal. Given the disjuncture between revolutionary and sectarian nationalisms that existed on the UCSD campus, Blanco would spend a great deal of time attempting to hold MEChA together. In February of 1970, he spoke to *mechistas* about the tensions between them and African American students as well as the divisions between "Third World types" and "chicanismo," urging them to put aside petty differences in order to ask the fundamental questions of "Who owns the wealth?, Who distributed the pie?, and From whom was it stolen?"[42]

Despite divisions within the Chicano/a campus community, the primary antagonist to the Lumumba-Zapata coalition was psychology professor and UCSD chancellor William McGill. Following the assassination of Dr. King, the BSC had approached McGill (then chair of the Academic Senate) with demands for an ethnic-studies curriculum. His response was to solicit faculty donations for a BSC library and establish a committee to study the viability of an African American studies program. After assuming the chancellorship in late 1968, McGill took liberal stances on a number of issues including the key issue of

16. Carlos Blanco Aguinaga, September 26, 1970. UCSD Mandeville Special Collections, Marshall College Provost.

academic freedom in his defense of Marcuse. But McGill's preparation for the radical change taking place on California campuses was insufficient. When asked by a student reporter why there were no curricular offerings that dealt with issues of race, he replied: "Don't you see that when you start talking about racism you are dealing with advocacy rather than the field of objective analysis."[43]

A prolific writer, McGill at one point drafted a document titled "Some Considerations on Black Student Demands for Education," in which he applied his training as a psychologist to the social movement developing around him. According to the chancellor: "the causes of unrest and character of the demands of the black students may be seen in a parallelism between the growth of persons and the emergence of cultures."[44] In other words, the students were acting like immature children or, to put it another way, they were still in the process of passing from a lesser stage of civilization to a higher one.

Not unlike most liberals of his generation, McGill could defend academic freedom against conservative attacks but simply could not understand a student movement whose agenda for educational reform was based in large part on a radical critique of institutional racism and racialized elitism.[45] Trapped in his academic disciplinary blinders, McGill cast himself as the understanding but stern parent who would defend the integrity of his "home" (i.e., the university) against attacks by partisan forces:

> At the same time, the "establishment" must be true to what it considers its true character, and not allow itself to be brow-beaten into invalid submission, which some teenagers are able to accomplish with their parents. It is apparent to this writer that the university has a valid challenge to alter its curriculum so as to include ethnic and cultural history which is a crucial part of the identity, not only of the black and brown communities, but of the white community as well. However, insofar as the black community wishes the university to be involved in the political activity resulting from the emergence of identity, it appears that this would be denial of the character of the university as being free from political control or of taking a partisan position in politics.[46]

The long-standing traditions of liberal pluralism and the university as a space free of the corruption of politics reassert themselves in McGill's meditation. The flaw at the very core of his thinking, however, was the notion that the Chicano/a and African American students who had decided to challenge the university's deep structures were children.

Soon after the assassination of Dr. King, the BSC had submitted a proposal calling for the restructuring of the Revelle College humanities sequence because of its "extreme ethnocentricity" and the establishment of an Institute of Afro-American Studies. Writing to the administration, the students asserted: "The course offering of the University of California, San Diego by its restriction to the study of European culture is an excellent example of the racist attitude—if it isn't white, it isn't worthwhile—that infects virtually every aspect of American culture."[47] Working through more traditional campus channels, biology professor Dan Lindsley proposed that the new third college be named for Dr. King and that the college focus its curriculum on race relations, enrolling high numbers of underrepresented students. By this time, however, planning for the college had been going on in official faculty committees for over three years. Nothing came of the Lindsley proposal.

Literature professor Andrew Wright chaired the original planning committee for the new college.[48] After historian Armin Rappaport was named college provost (and before radical students made their demands), he charged Wright with the establishment of programs that might bring university resources to disenfranchised communities in San Diego. Rappaport hoped to establish a "social-issues" major that would carry students directly to African American sections of the city. In 1968, he told an interviewer: "There have always been those who think that the University should be insulated from the outside and be an institution dedicated to pure reason and thinking. This is impossible today; we must bring our intelligence to bear upon the problems that face mankind."[49]

Rappaport began to seek advice on the future of the college from student leaders such as MAYA's Robert Carrillo, but Chicano/a and Black activists did not see much promise in what they perceived to be the administration's limited reform agenda. Carrillo told a local reporter: "UCSD is an ivory tower separated geographically and socially from the community. It is not in touch with reality, with the problems of poverty, the ghettos, or lack of opportunity."[50] Just a few weeks later, BSC and MAYA decided to intervene directly in the planning of the new college.

In a 1989 interview, MAYA member Joe Martinez, who in 1966 was one of the first Chicanos to enter UCSD, recalled that initially students had circulated two separate proposals—the African American plan for a "Patrice Lumumba College" and a less-developed Chicano/a plan for general curricular reform. One of the key Chicano activists, Vince de Baca, remembered that through a collective process the two proposals were merged and the name of Mexican revolutionary Emiliano Zapata added. According to de Baca: "In developing our plan we looked at many other colleges. We thought we would change not only UCSD but we saw ourselves as being in the forefront of progressive university education."[51] Central to the thinking of many student participants was the idea of self-determination or what in the 1990s would come to be called "empowerment," that is, the ability of formerly disempowered groups to determine their own futures by gaining access to resources and decision-making apparatuses.

One of the fundamental areas in which self-determination would play a key role was the definition of the group's collective identity. As BSC member Sam Jordan wrote just three months after the issuing of the students's demands: "Primary among the responsibilities of Lumumba-Zapata College will be the rejection of all white definitions concerning Blackness, Brownness, justice, rationality, beauty, etc. In their stead will be concepts and terminology embracing our overdue unification and

collective interests . . . made intelligible in the language of our people."[52]
Jordan's final point stressed the importance of avoiding overly abstract
and technical languages typical of university settings in order to maintain
close relationships with off-campus working-class communities.

According to one unfriendly account that described the proposal as
"a highly literate evocation of Marxist dogma," the students received
encouragement and direct help from a number of sources which
included local chapters of the Black Panthers, Ron Karenga's US organization, the Urban League, the NAACP, CORE, and the Citizens'
Interracial Committee.[53] But the demands, while decidedly antiracist
and anti-imperialist in nature, were not particularly Marxist, and there
is no reason to believe that the students and faculty were not completely
equipped to draft the document on their own. As we have seen,
Professor Keith Lowe, Angela Davis, and other students had written the
original BSC proposal for a Patrice Lumumba College while the final
draft of the Lumumba-Zapata demands was the product of a broad student coalition that included MAYA representatives.

Like most political and educational reform movements of the
period, the Lumumba-Zapata experiment had little to say about issues
of gender and sexuality. Given that the long and arduous process in
which feminists struggled to reeducate their male *compañeros* in the
Movement had only begun, it is unfortunate but not surprising that
men continued to disregard women's issues. As the editors of *Encuentro
Femenil* put it: "In 1969, there was a great eagerness to experience the
first Chicano studies classes. The women were very excited to learn
about their heritage both as Chicanos and as mujeres. However, the
women were very disappointed to discover that neither Chicano history, Mexican history, nor Chicano literature included any measurable
material on the mujer."[54]

In an important corrective to this fundamental omission in
Movement thought, Chicana activists pointed out that the Plan de
Santa Bárbara itself, which by 1971 was referred to as "the Bible" of the
Chicano/a educational-reform movement, did not address issues of
vital interest to women. A conference held at Cal State San Diego in
March of 1971 sought to rectify the problem by suggesting revisions to
the Plan that included "adequate representation" for women on all governing bodies, recruitment of Chicana faculty, and curricular changes
that developed courses on "la Mujer."[55]

On the issue of admissions, Lumumba/Zapata activists called for a 35 percent African American, 35 percent Chicano, and 35 percent "Other" ethnic breakdown, a demand that sent opponents of "racial quotas" into cardiac arrest and one that even MAYA faculty advisor Carlos Blanco called "utopian." For the students, however, this demand was necessary in order to "compensate for past and present injustices and to serve those most affected by institutional racism and economic exploitation."[56] In a like manner, the proposed curriculum emphasized a focus on the relationship between economically developed and underdeveloped nations. The suggested areas of study captured the concerns of students around the world during the Viet Nam war period:

1. Revolutions
2. Analysis of Economic Systems
3. Science and Technology
4. Health Sciences and Public Health
5. Urban and Rural Development
6. Communication Arts
7. Foreign Languages
8. Cultural Heritage
9. White Studies

In his role as chair of the Lumumba-Zapata curriculum subcommittee, Carlos Blanco proposed a course of study that was "humanistic" and designed to "offer the possibility for minority students to apply the critical and analytical tools of modern learning to the problems they face in their environment and to provide for White students an understanding of the problems involved in present-day society."[57] By the end of 1969, Chicano/as at UCSD were attempting to bring together an organization with community ties, called United Chicanos at San Diego, whose first objective would be the establishment of a high-ranking advisor to the chancellor on Chicano issues. Chancellor McGill rejected the idea in a January 21, 1970, letter, calling the demand for what he called a "super-Chicano" a step toward producing "professional Chicanos or career blacks." With a curious choice of words, he added: "I cannot bring myself, at this point in time, to relegate either community to this 'stoop-labor,' 'back-of-the-bus' role."[58]

By 1970 the San Diego campus "enjoyed" a national reputation for the most part due to the Lumumba-Zapata experiment. That same year, the

Los Angeles Times published a five-part series on the proposed third college and syndicated columnists on the right stirred the flames of conservative fear and outrage. On the UCSD campus, sociology professor Jack Douglas became the most persistent critic of the new college and a prolific writer to editorial pages, warning in an August missive: "They intend to kill the soul of the university."[59] When radical students heckled cartoonist Al Capp, creator of "Lil Abner" and a political raconteur in the 1960s, during his talk at UCSD in October, 1970, Capp added to the campus's notoriety: "I predict that there will be dynamite set off on that campus before the year is out. The 2 percent of the student body, which are animals, are the foulest bunch I have seen in the 288 campuses I have visited."[60] In an increasingly hostile environment, the survival of the new college was by no means assured.

But the point at which the Lumumba/Zapata activists struck deepest at the core values of academic hierarchy and elitism was the demand to democratize the day-to-day governing of the college on every issue affecting college life including the most jealously guarded domains of academic departments—admissions and faculty hiring. In a proposal that anticipated by some thirty years the reforms instituted after the elimination of affirmative-action programs in the late 1990s, the Lumumba-Zapata activists argued for automatic admission for the top 12 percent of all high school students and the rejection of economically and culturally biased entrance exams like the SAT. The objective in the final analysis was to "attack the race and class bias of the admission requirements of the University of California, to ensure a sizable enrollment of minority working-class students to give Lumumba-Zapata College its maximum effectiveness in the community."[61] In an even more quixotic move, they emphasized the antiassimilationist ethos of the Chicano and Black liberation movements, stating that they were not interested in recruiting students who "had come to terms with the system and thereby lost their identities with their communities."[62]

By the time the revised Third College plan was made public, even the previously hostile student newspaper, the *Triton Times*, heralded the college as a major innovation in higher education. Calling it "the most exciting educational experiment in America today," the paper's editorial board opined:

Why is Third College unique? Because for probably the first time an entire college is being constructed to serve the specific needs of

17. UC San Diego students
Percy Myers and Tony
Valenzuela, September 26,
1970. UCSD Mandeville
Special Collections,
Marshall College Provost.

18. Carlos Blanco Aguinaga, Joe Watson, Acting Chancellor Herb York, student Carlos
Monge, September 26, 1970. UCSD Mandeville Special Collections, Marshall College
Provost.

a particular community—the Black and Brown. It is not a college that will serve Blacks and Browns by molding them into the established white society. Nor is it a college that will pacify students with doses of Black and Brown studies. It is instead the beginning of the commitment on the part of the University to correct its oversights of the past. The Black and Brown students cannot be given too much credit in what they have succeeded in doing. However rash their initial actions and words may have seemed to members of the academic community, they made an entire institution stop to re-examine its basic goals for the first time.[63]

The writer's transformation of "Black and Brown" into a single "community" is in and of itself an indication of what was taking place on the ground.

Although it would flourish for only a short time, the BSC/MAYA coalition was a significant episode in the genealogy of African American and Chicano/a alliances in the Southwest. Vince de Baca described the deeper significance of the coalition as "a continuing on-going process to say 'let's rid ourselves of racism towards each other.'"[64] African American activist Percy Myers remembered the project engendering "a great deal of camaraderie, a great deal of love and support because we all knew that we were in a battle. And that crossed racial lines."[65] For a brief period of time between 1970 and 1972, the new college was indeed a bold experiment in multiracial organizing and the democratic reform of higher education. The first Dean of Students, Pascual Martinez, explained: "The essence of Third College, I feel, is the creation of a learning community that is concerned with the process of continual growth—where there is an effort to probe and to search for better ways of living for all human beings, particularly those formerly left out altogether."[66] As we shall see, however, internal pressures and external forces would ensure that the coalition that had created the college could not survive.

CO-OPTATION AND ELITISM TRIUMPHANT

Chicano student groups share an orientation similar to that of black students, and on occasion they cooperate and support each other on similar demands. . . . The alliance between black and brown students, however, has not been close, harmonious, or continuous.[67]

Historian Carlos Muñoz, Jr., points out that as the intensity of the Chicana/o student movement diminished, rivalries with Black students and administrators increased. With greater numbers of Chicano students on campus (although still relatively small compared to other groups) and hostile administrations and law-enforcement agencies on the offensive, the potential for a widespread democratization movement could not be realized. Muñoz writes: "MEChA engaged in power struggles with white liberal and Black administrators, whose overriding emphasis on the recruitment of Black students was perceived as slighting Mexican Americans. . . . Chicano influence contributed to bitter and intense conflicts between Mexican Americans and Blacks on several campuses, making viable coalition politics difficult, if not altogether impossible."[68] The dynamic on the UC San Diego campus would lead to a local version of the conflict described by Muñoz in which an African American faculty member played a key role in co-opting the demands of the most militant students. At the same time, COINTELPRO-type projects increased after 1970, even as clever administrators and law-enforcement agencies devoted their efforts to creating splits between what they perceived as "radical" and "moderate" students in order to destroy the reform movement.[69]

I have suggested the ways in which the posture adopted by Chancellor William McGill was an extreme form of liberal paternalism. I quote McGill again at length because his position captures the basic strategies used by university officials in order to eliminate the possibility of student empowerment and radical institutional reform:

> The students see management as proceeding from their Board of Directors. I see it as flowing down a chain of responsibility from the Chancellor's office to the Provost. Thus, we're going to have a struggle over the appointment of the Provost. I can't endanger the basic values of the academic community by appointing a man whose primary identity is with the struggle of minorities for liberation. His primary allegiance must be to the values of the academic community. Otherwise, Third College may be used as a base to attack the rest of the academic community. This could produce severe convulsions here. We've seen that problem at Cornell and Antioch, and to a certain extent at San Francisco State. I didn't spend last year in a fierce struggle with the community over appointment of a Marxist

professor [Marcuse] in order to give away management of the Third College to another element of the community.[70]

The fear that Lumumba-Zapata would become the site of a revolutionary critique of the entire institution was real enough from McGill's perspective. Rather than appointing a provost who would accommodate student-led reforms, he selected someone whose "primary allegiance," as he put it, would be to the existing academic hierarchy and thus to the status quo. That man had been the first African American professor at UCSD and in 1970 was one of only three Black professors on campus—the thirty-year old chemist Joseph W. Watson.

Among the BSC's choices for college provost had been Professor James Turner of Northwestern University in Chicago. In a letter to his predecessor John Galbraith, UCSD's Chancellor McGill described Turner as a "young black militant," and admitted that he had consciously delayed the appointment of the new provost with the hope that Turner would accept a job offer elsewhere.[71] Another candidate—Harland Randolph—had impressed everyone involved in the search including McGill, but Randolph opted to assume the presidency of a Washington, D.C., college. A small group of Chicano candidates had been mentioned but never seriously considered, including historians Jesus Chavarría (UC Santa Barbara) and Juan Gómez Quiñones (UCLA) as well as the "minority advisor" to the president of Stanford, Calexico-born attorney Luis Nogales.

As the search process dragged on, McGill made it clear that he preferred a provost drawn from the ranks of the UCSD faculty. According to Watson's recollection, Black students and colleagues pressured him into accepting the position, but in fact it was McGill and the administration that had the most to gain from Watson's appointment.[72] As McGill described Watson to UC president Hitch: "I have found him to be the kingpin in the administration's efforts to take Third College away from the militants and to put it under the cool direction of mature academic leaders."[73] Given the charged context in which the UC system was under attack from a variety of quarters, McGill felt confident that the Regents would approve Watson's appointment: "The timing of the June Regents meeting could not be better for me in view of the upcoming fiasco involving Angela Davis. They will be feeling guilty and seeking to seize on ways to demonstrate commitments to minorities. I intend to present them with an obvious and easy way to do it."[74]

Once Watson agreed to serve, the majority of the search committee members threw their support to him, yet even after the committee had agreed to back Watson MEChA activists, whose representative on the search committee had refused to sign off on Watson, made a last ditch effort to present several Chicano scholars as candidates for provost, among them Julian Nava, Rudy Acuña, and Eugene Cota-Robles.[75] The committee, however, did not act upon these nominations because they felt that they were already committed to Watson who officially became provost in July 1970.

The son of immigrants from the British West Indies, Watson was a firm believer in a bootstraps ideology of hard work and tenacity. Born in Harlem and educated at the prestigious De Witt Clinton high school in the Bronx and the City College of New York, he received his Ph.D. in organic chemistry at UCLA.[76] By all accounts including his own, Watson was a political moderate, yet during the turbulent Viet Nam war period he was quite capable of deploying a fiery rhetoric more closely associated with Black militants.[77] In May of 1970 on the heels of the shooting of two students in Mississippi and the killing of several unarmed African American men in Georgia, Watson contrasted the university community's reaction to these events to its response to the actions of the Ohio National Guard at Kent State: "This outpouring of outrage and protest over the killing of four White Students stands in stark, glaring contrast to the lack of reaction to the murder of three Black students in Orangeburg, South Carolina in 1968. It stands in contrast to the lack of outrage and protest against the killing of six unarmed Black men (all shot in the back) in Augusta, Georgia and two Black college students in Jackson, Mississippi by cowardly White police this week. Given the racist nature of America, it would be irrational to expect this country or the campus to break its routine to protest the murder of Black people."[78]

In response to sociology professor Jack Douglas's consistent criticisms of Third College, Watson told a reporter: "This campus has not had and does not now have a militant minority. . . . If some professor gets nervous when he sees more than one or two black males or Mexican American males together, that's another matter."[79] Watson's antiracist stance was clear enough but his political allegiance to radical student demands was inconsistent and not deeply rooted. His accommodation with existing power structures would contribute to the demise of the BSC/MAYA coalition and ultimately of the entire Lumumba-Zapata experiment.

What provided much of the fodder for the breakdown of the coalition were Watson's early decisions as provost of the new college. As we have seen, events could at times transform Watson's essentially conservative nature into more militant rhetorical displays, yet as the institutionalization of the college proceeded Watson's role became one of defusing the radical potential inherent in the original vision imagined by Black and Chicano/a students. The recruitment activities that had yielded higher numbers of underrepresented students would be the first casualty of Watson's retrenchment.[80] The number of so-called special action students, that is, students who lacked one or two minor requirements for admissions but who were admissible nonetheless, was cut back. Faculty hiring for the college was another sore point. As a line of candidates came to campus, Chicano/a students began to suspect that Chicano interests were not being served. Years later, Percy Myers recalled: "Chicano students did not think enough progress was being made in terms of attracting Hispanic faculty members. Some felt that Third College was going to be predominantly black in terms of the student body and faculty because of Dr. Watson's thrust."[81]

Finally, and perhaps most important, was the issue of student participation in the governing of the college. Throughout the fall term of 1971, it became clear to the Chicano/a activists that Watson considered the board to be little more than advisory to the provost. In a meeting of the college faculty and staff, Carlos Blanco suggested that everyone concerned "read the Lumumba-Zapata plan and the Santa Barbara plan as a basis for continuing discussion."[82] But the far-ranging democratic structures proposed in those documents included a level of student empowerment anathema to the founding principles of the La Jolla campus and to the traditional structures of the University of California system.

Increasingly dissatisfied with Watson's decisions, Chicano/a activists called for his resignation and began to stage demonstrations and pickets on campus. MEChA chairman Francisco Estrada demanded increased student representation on the college governing board and argued that the provost should not be allowed to hold veto power over the board's decisions. In a letter to the new chancellor, William McElroy (who replaced McGill in January of 1972), Estrada wrote: "We have lost all confidence in his [Watson's] ability to unite the community and to direct Third College in a progressive manner."[83] A "Chicano Position Paper on Third College" was disseminated explaining the various "policy failures" made by Watson: "We find that Chicano student admissions are falling behind, and that programs of special interest to Chicanos are not being developed. We find that the College is following an educational philosophy with which we do not agree."[84]

Among the faculty who signed the letter requesting Watson's removal were Latino/a professors Carlos Blanco, Arturo Madrid, Mario Barrera, Richard Escobedo, Faustina Solís, Gracia Molina de Pick, and Diego Muñoz.[85] Carlos Blanco summarized the Chicano position on governance in a tersely written statement: "Third College was created through the joint efforts of Chicanos and Blacks to serve the higher educational needs of Chicanos, Blacks, and other ethnic minorities. As such, College decisions must be made jointly by representation of all groups involved. The College cannot function justly if any one man or group has the absolute authority to make and carry out decisions that will directly or indirectly benefit any group or groups to the detriment of others."[86] The Chicano/as soon were joined by a broad sector of Third College students and faculty—the Asian American Student Alliance, United Native Americans, the White Caucus, and even some African American students who came under tremendous pressure from their own community to support Watson.

According to Vince de Baca: "There were Blacks who supported Watson's resignation and they were intimidated by Black nationalists. Some of them were personally visited and threatened."[87] The strict Black nationalist position was articulated in an article that portrayed Watson as a hero in the battle against "neo-colonialism" and denounced Chicano/a activists for working with whites: "Get the white man's approval before you start the revolution, is that the idea? Wasn't Third College built to throw off the chains and to wash out the brainwashing inflicted on Black and Brown people everywhere? Hey, take a look around and into yourselves Chicanos."[88] The BSU took a somewhat more moderate position supporting Watson against his adversaries: "We hold the belief that these charges brought against the Provost were begun and perpetuated by a bunch of incompetent, insensitive, and irresponsible faculty members. The faculty members have proven to care nothing about minority education. They are simply seeking an opportunity to use Third College as a soapbox for people to rhetorize [sic] and learn nothing that benefits the communities from which we come. These faculty members are advocates of student participation. We say that the ghettoes, barrios, and reservations in this country cannot utilize people with degrees in participation."[89] For all intents and purposes, the Lumumba-Zapata coalition was finished.

But the struggle to oust Watson continued. From Watson's point of view, ideological differences were at the heart of the dispute. Describing his opponents to Chancellor McElroy, he wrote: "The other philosophy, while accepting these educational and social goals, believes that they are grossly insufficient without having Third College function as a participatory democracy with a specific sociopolitical philosophy."[90] Watson threatened to resign and in fact did step down on May 25, 1972, only to withdraw his resignation a short time later. Seven African American faculty asked to be reassigned to other colleges rather than Third if Watson were removed. In a letter to the chancellor, they argued: "Overemphasizing the importance of participation in governance is a disservice to minority students."[91]

McElroy had supported Watson in a public statement on May 8, writing: "At this point I find insufficient evidence to support the charges against Provost Watson. He enjoys my full confidence and will remain as Provost."[92] As the controversy dragged on, McElroy told an *L.A. Times* reporter that there were not enough qualified minority students to attend UCSD and used the local San Diego media to threaten to close the college down.[93] Quite ironically, the factors that in effect saved Watson's career as an administrator had been sectarian Black nationalism, FBI provocateurs, and white university officials. In a dramatic final attempt to salvage the original concept of the college, a multiracial coalition of students staged a hunger strike to protest Watson's "dictatorial authority over the rights of the Lumumba-Zapata community."[94]

Radical Students under Siege

No useful purpose would be served by setting forth here the sickening recital of incidents of violence, destruction and disruption that has befallen our schools and colleges since the Berkeley rebellion of 1964.
—*California Legislature's Fifteenth Report of the Senate Fact-finding Subcommittee on Un-American Activities* (1970)

The valiant efforts to democratize the university were slowly co-opted as radical student groups struggled against the entrenched practices of an institution with a superiority complex and an administrative culture that retained some liberal elements but was all too willing to make concessions to San Diego's right-wing politicians. State Assemblyman John Stull, an Iowa-born career navy man, kept up a constant attack against UC student activists whom he called "the barbarians whom we have tolerated too long in our midst." Stull called for the abolition of the tenure system, the firing of UC president Charles Hitch, and the disciplining of professors Richard Popkin and Herbert Marcuse for being "hard-line revolutionaries, eager to overthrow the system."[95]

On the UCSD campus, sociology professor Jack Douglas joined forces with like-minded colleagues to create a "Save the University" committee that argued that the Academic Senate, having approved the Third College compromise plan, no longer represented the views of the faculty. Claiming to have seventy members at the height of its short-lived existence, the committee sent a seven-person delegation to meet with Governor Reagan on July 8, 1970, to demand that he "reverse the trend toward political activism" in the university system.[96] Conservative students on campus formed the Associated Moderate Students (AMS) and began to publish a newspaper titled *Dimension: A Journal of Moderate Opinion* in the fall of 1969. Openly parodying the Lumumba-Zapata activists, AMS members issued mock demands for a Joe McCarthy-Francisco Franco College in which "25 percent of the student body would be Polish, 25 percent Italian, and 25 percent Viking."[97]

Taking their cue from local informants such as Douglas, nationally syndicated columnists Rowland Evans and Robert Novak wrote in alarm about the "threat" of Third College that in their opinion was a "Frankenstein monster that may devour the seven-year old campus." Conservative writer Jeffrey Hart, who taught English at Dartmouth and had worked for both Governor Reagan and President Nixon, compared the college to a shark about to consume the university. According to Hart, "one terrorized scholar" had described Third College as "the most radical academic institution yet established within the United States." In a subsequent column, Hart referred to the college as "a staggering academic scandal" and "a mini-revolutionary enclave" that had been established "for minority-group students, such as Negroes, Mexicans, Orientals, Indians and so on [and whose] curriculum provides them with a diet of modern revolutionary and anti-Western works, apparently calculated to produce hatred for this country, for whites, and for Western civilization generally."[98]

But Lumumba-Zapata students, staff, and faculty struggling to create the new college faced obstacles more serious than the attacks launched by conservative politicians and media. Much closer to home, academic departments successfully resisted attempts to hire faculty of color for the college despite their impeccable qualifications. At a May 2, 1969, meeting of the Third College provisional faculty and BSC/MAYA representatives, which now included students Israel Chavez, Milan Lalic Molina, Joe Martinez, Vince de Baca, Angela Davis, and Ed Spriggs as well as faculty members Carlos Blanco, Joe Watson, and Fredric Jameson, the most pressing issue was understood to be breaking the departmental stranglehold on faculty hiring.[99]

Despite the low number of minority faculty in the professional pipeline, Lumumba-Zapata supporters actively sought out qualified Chicano/Latino and African American candidates. Their activities brought charges of "compensatory racism" and "underqualified faculty" from conservative adversaries.[100] According to the original student demands, the college Board of Directors was to "dispense and fill all FTEs [full-time faculty positions] and approve all administrative appointments."[101] But from the earliest days of the college's existence the intransigence of academic departments, the product of class racism, would prove too powerful to overcome. In March of 1970, Provost Watson wrote "in confidence" to Chancellor McGill about the problem: "I hear from mutual friends that you are worried about the fact that Third College is not being very successful in its recruiting of faculty. Your worry is more than justified: we are not being very successful and we too are getting desperate. . . . It would seem (objectively speaking) that there are people and departments on this campus who are trying to make Third College a failure. Institutionalized racism? It is all very sad and very depressing and it may be too late for our joint efforts to be productive."[102] Specifically, Watson described the process by which the Department of Mathematics had blocked the hiring of a talented Chicano mathematician, Richard Griego.

In addition to facing the hostile reaction to Third College by conservative faculty, politicians, and organizations such as the American Legion (in many cities a front for FBI covert operations), the Lumumba-Zapata organizers, like other Viet Nam war era militants, would have to cope with insidious interventions by law-enforcement agencies. The Nixon administration in particular viewed the universities as a primary site for

counterintelligence operations, and within a month after Nixon's inauguration the director of the CIA informed National Security assistant to the
president, Henry Kissinger, of the intelligence agency's domestic program
on student unrest: "In an effort to round-out our discussion of this subject, we have included a section on American students. This is an area not
within the charter of this Agency, so I need not emphasize how extremely
sensitive this makes the paper."[103]

In a memo delivered to White House assistant H. R. Haldeman in
July 1970, it was stated unequivocally that "the campus is the battleground of the revolutionary protest movement. It is impossible to gather
effective intelligence about the movement unless we have campus
sources."[104] By late 1970, African American student organizations had
become a primary target even in cities where there had been no previous
disturbances. Haldeman approved the following recommendation: "In
view of the vast increase in violence on college campuses, it is felt that
every Black Student Union and similar groups, regardless of their past or
present involvement in disorders, should be the subject of a discreet preliminary inquiry through established sources and informants." On
November 4, FBI director J. Edgar Hoover instructed the Bureau:
"Effective immediately, all BSUs and similar organizations organized to
project the demands of black students, which are not presently under
investigation, are to be subjects of discreet, preliminary inquiries." [105] In
the same directive, Hoover referred to a specific section of the FBI
Manual of Instructions, Section 87D, that described procedures for establishing intelligence-gathering operations in "institutions of learning."

The repertoire of FBI provocation on college campuses relied upon
the fabrication of false rumors and the discrediting of key activists
through charges of moral misconduct.[106] In March of 1972, an anonymous document appeared on the La Jolla campus accusing students
and faculty associated with Third College of a variety of behaviors
involving drugs, interracial sex, and homosexuality. Ostensibly written
by African American nationalist students, the broad sheet charged
Chicanos, "Brothers," and "Honkies" with committing various crimes
against Black interests: "Already these white, mexican faculty are giving
low grades to students who don't see things the way they are told. Black
students who don't go along with the politics are afraid to do anything
because Black females are involved with the white faculty." In short, "the
mexicans, orientals and whites have banned together in an effort to get

rid of all righteous Brothers on the campus."[107] The authors go on to urge readers (presumably all males, given the document's title—"If you have a pair of balls"): "Do what you can to stop this mess."

In retrospect, the document displays all of the characteristics associated with FBI provocation designed to destroy radical organizations and multiethnic alliances. Many of the students at the time understood the letter in this way. Writing in the Lumumba/Zapata newsletter, one activist called it "nefarious," "mysterious," and perhaps an "April Fool's Joke." On a more serious note, the writer reported: "Some found the poison pen letter a reflection of the nature of conditions which makes a krank [sic] feel that Third College is ripe for this type of provocation."[108] In fact, Governor Ronald Reagan's covert campaign against radical student groups had begun early in his first term. By the summer of 1969, his office was in touch with J. Edgar Hoover and local FBI agents in order to obtain support for his efforts. Herbert Ellingwood, Reagan's Legal Affairs secretary, reported to Hoover's assistants that "Governor Reagan is dedicated to the destruction of disruptive elements on California college campuses" by "hounding the groups as much as possible," using the Internal Revenue Service to harass activists, and mounting "a psychological warfare campaign" against them with the assistance of the Department of Defense.[109] On March 20, 1970, Reagan's office requested that each UC campus submit the names of faculty, staff, and students who were involved in campus political activities.[110]

Most of the students and faculty involved with the Lumumba-Zapata project took for granted the presence of undercover agents on the San Diego campus. Milan Lalic Molina recalled in a 1990 interview that a certain Paul Simms "was there only for the purpose of agitating the nationalist Blacks against the Chicanos so that things would fall apart."[111] In a January 10, 1972, meeting of the Third College staff, Dean Pascual Martinez confirmed the existence of campus police dossiers on activists that presumably were shared with local and federal law enforcement agencies.[112] Although in his memoirs former Chancellor William McGill denied sharing information with outside agencies, he had written to California state senator H. L. Richardson in July of 1969: "I have good liaison with local and federal authorities."[113]

The end result of local and federal covert operations directed against the students was the demise of the coalition. Vince de Baca recalled that by late 1972 "the college was divided, it was being torn apart. Violence was going on in the dorms. At one point there was a 'Mexican stand-off' in the dorms involving about 20 blacks and 20 Mexicans and whites, five to ten feet apart with weapons drawn."[114] By the end of 1973 the "success" enjoyed by law-enforcement agencies in the breakup of other Chicano Movement organizations, ranging from the Brown Berets to Tijerina's Alianza to the antiwar National Chicano Moratorium Committee, had been duplicated on the UCSD campus.

Despite the demise of the Lumumba-Zapata experiment, the ideals of the original multiracial and internationalist coalition continued to inform the actions of specific students and faculty. One Chicano student addressed the community in a two-page document entitled "Third World Unity": "If you think that you can achieve black liberation without achieving Chicano liberation or vice-versa or if you think that Africa will achieve complete liberation from imperialist oppression without Asia and Latin America achieving it also, then you have some learning to do because no one will ever be free from this white racist oppressive society unless every one of us is free."[115] As director of the Third World Studies program, Carlos Blanco summarized what he considered to be the necessary focus of the curriculum and the core ideal of the Lumumba-Zapata activists: "I take it that our emphasis is and must be that of the relationships between Third World peoples, in and out of the USA, and the highly developed Western societies . . . the major theme is underdevelopment and the complex relationship between indisputable economic underdevelopment, political freedom, and the intrinsic cultural validity of non-Western life."[116]

"MANIFEST IGNORANCE ABOUT CHICANOS"

In a 1972 study of the status of Chicanos in the university and college system prepared for the California Legislature's Joint Committee on the Master Plan for Higher Education, authors Ronald Lopez and Darryl Enos reported on their fact-finding visit to the UC San Diego campus:

> The attitude of the several students spoken to was one of profound pessimism. Their initial response was one of grim distrust. They felt no one had listened to them and the people with whom they had dealt, had dealt with them with duplicity. After a period of discussion, they began to openly express their

views that the university had reneged on its commitment or promise that the governance of the school involved their participation. They were disillusioned and bitter people who asserted that they were being treated with contempt and disdain. They also felt that their experience was a classical [*sic*] example of the extremes that the institution was willing to go to minimize the relevance of the institution to Chicanos.[117]

Although the report tends at times to pathologize the Chicano/a students at UCSD ("disillusioned and bitter people"), it is clear that the students had been trapped in an institutional power play they could not win. Lopez and Enos went on to describe the administration's understanding of the Lumumba/Zapata episode as weak and uninformed: "Their apparent ignorance of the profundity of the dejection among the students was disheartening. This is not to suggest that people were not aware of many of the problems but rather to represent their view that most of the students' problems could be solved if the students would concentrate on their studies and worry less about the operation of the institution."[118] In their summary statement addressing the UC, Cal State, and community college systems, Lopez and Enos concluded: "Certainly the most consistent and the most disappointing thing about the visits was the manifest ignorance about Chicanos."[119]

By the mid-1970s, UCSD's basic institutional character had reasserted itself. Provost Watson essentially had gutted the democratic reforms put forward in the Lumumba-Zapata proposal and had turned Third College into a traditional academic unit governed by faculty committees engaged in proceedings that rarely if ever are conducted in public.[120] Although a small Chicano Studies program was established in 1973 with Carlos Blanco as its first director, in subsequent years the minor gains made in that period were either frozen or rolled back, and the gap between the campus and San Diego's underserved communities widened as successive administrations catered to corporate and military elites. One anonymous writer complained: "The new programs and policy changes especially are against relevant education that was the initial purpose of Third College. The new program changes are just a current example of appeasement to the white academic establishment by administrators who work hand in glove with them in serving their interests and not those of Black or other ethnic students."[121]

By the time the freshman class of 1976 arrived on campus, some 60 percent of the student body at Third College was white. The proposed departments of Communication, Third World Studies, and Urban and Rural Studies yielded only one academic department—Communication—with the other two entities becoming programs without budgetary and hiring autonomy. The Communication Department itself operated for years under the threat of defunding despite large numbers of students wishing to major in the program. Faculty founders such as Herbert I. Schiller gave the department a decidedly progressive orientation, but administrators were determined to keep him and the program in check. By 1978, the kind of meaningful political struggles that had marked the campus earlier in the decade had turned into academic squabbles. Literature department faculty, for example, split into opposed camps over methodological differences with one camp sounding the alarm that the department was in danger of being taken over by "Marxists."[122]

Throughout the 1980s, the number of Chicano/a and African American faculty at UCSD steadily decreased. Some saw the establishment of a Department of Ethnic Studies in 1989 as a positive step away from previous exclusionary and elitist practices with regard to Latino communities, yet a decade later in 1999 the department counted only one tenured Hispanic professor on its faculty. As part of a national trend to depoliticize academic disciplines created during the post-Viet Nam war period, the state of UCSD's Ethnic Studies program was not unusual. One astute observer put it bluntly: "Today, Ethnic and Feminist Studies programs across the country are, for the most part, full members of the academy (while still experiencing discrimination), but as such have been required to abandon their radical agendas."[123] The reactionary backlash in California during the 1990s—UC Regents' actions SP1 and SP2 and Proposition 209 abolishing affirmative action in admissions—created a climate in which UCSD's antidemocratic tendencies were allowed to flourish.

The percentage of Chicano/a and African American undergraduate students at UCSD in 1992 stood at 8 percent and 3 percent, respectively.[124] In 1993, Third College was officially renamed Thurgood Marshall College.[125] At the end of Chancellor Richard Atkinson's administration in 1995, a coalition of students, staff, and faculty fought to create a Cross-Cultural Center after decades of administration opposition.

The founding of the Cross-Cultural Center was a small but symbolic victory against the forces of class racism.

In campus doctoral and medical programs between 2001 and 2002, Mexican Americans made up only 4.3 percent.of all Ph.D.s conferred and only 1.6 percent of all M.D.s.[126] In 2001, a group of Chicano/a faculty working with community activists in San Diego proposed a Chicano/a and Latino/a program. Although a faculty committee rejected the original proposal, a revised version was approved in 2002. Funding for the program was kept at a minimum and there appeared to be little chance that it would be able to alter significantly UCSD's long-standing institutional character.

For many of those involved in these activities, history seemed to be repeating itself. The core issues that motivated the Lumumba-Zapata militants thirty years earlier played themselves out again in a dramatically changed and much more conservative context. What remained constant were the elitist and exclusionary character of the UC San Diego campus and its close ties to Department of Defense or "Homeland Security" funding. UCSD's engineering and wireless communications departments, for example, enjoyed enormous endowments from Science Applications International Corporation (SAIC), a local company with major responsibility for the "reconstruction" of Iraq after the 2003 U.S. invasion and occupation.[127]

Another constant was the abiding influence of reactionary politicians in San Diego. On October 26, 2001, former mayor and right-wing radio host Roger Hedgecock substituted for conservative pundit Rush Limbaugh on his nationally syndicated program. A little more than a month after the atrocities of September 11 and a few days after the U.S. bombing of Afghanistan had begun, Hedgecock advised his national audience that he would be leading a prowar rally at the UC San Diego campus because "Angela Davis taught there" and because "the Marxist professors there had to be exposed." First time, history; second time, farce.

—CODA/PRÓLOGO—

and where, raza, are our heroes?
the heroes of Aztlán?
what became of that great nation
we were going to build?

　　　　　　　　　—Andrés Montoya, "Locura"

IT IS A COMMONPLACE among a majority of academic and nonacademic commentators on the Chicano Movement to minimize its contributions. In part, this is a result of the ease with which the entire period known as the 1960s can be caricatured and trivialized. The extreme break at the level of politics and culture between the Sixties generation and their parents—radicalism, sexuality, music, fashion, drugs—makes for simple stereotypes that can then be inserted into any discussion of the period even in contexts where they are wholly inappropriate or misleading.

To cite only one example: In an article on the thirty-first anniversary of the August 29, 1970, Chicano antiwar Moratorium march, reporter Raúl Vásquez wrote: "The loud, turbulent and psychedelic 1960s and 1970s in the United States eventually dwindled away quietly and soberly. Young radicals who once pounded the pavements demanding justice and revolution realized they had to grow up, get real jobs, and raise real families. . . . By the 1980s and 1990s most activists realized that the Revolution wasn't going to happen right away, and subsequently retired their pipes and headbands, trading them in for gin and tonics and baseball caps to cover their balding heads."[1]

Vásquez is not particularly hostile to the Movimiento, yet he willfully reproduces "Big Chill" clichés that reduce a powerful social movement to "pipes and headbands," and implies (yet again) that activists were foolish children who only needed to grow up.

The filter of thirty years of neoconservative retrenchment makes it easy to represent the activists of the Viet Nam war era as unsophisticated participants in a foolish play. The concluding section of F. Arturo Rosales's study of the Movement, for example, includes the following statement by Alfredo Gutiérrez: "The majority of activists were just having a good time. . . . All the gains we made in civil rights and political representation would have been gotten without all the shouting."[2]

It is unlikely that the Movimiento could have had any impact on traditional educational institutions, police misconduct, or the war in Southeast Asia "without all the shouting." More important, Gutiérrez's remark (and Rosales's tacit approval of it) echoes neoconservative efforts to rewrite the entire period of the 1960s as a period of mass hysteria and authorizes contemporary Hispanic dismissals of the Chicana/o Movement and social movements in general. "We're not in the 60s anymore" was a phrase heard throughout the 1980s and 1990s by anyone pursuing a progressive agenda with tactics thought to be overly militant. It continues to be heard wherever Hispanic brokers seek to usurp the last vestiges of grassroots power for which activists struggled during the Viet Nam war era.

Rosales admits that the Movement made significant contributions to the areas of "identity, the arts, intellectual traditions, popular culture, civil rights activism, political behavior, gender identity, and workplace defense," but adds: "This does not mean that a completely new paradigm emerged from the movimiento."[3] For Rosales, Movement activists created a somewhat more intense version of the political agenda that earlier Mexican Americans had proposed in the period between World War II and the death of John Kennedy, a kind of "radical liberalism." But by Rosales's own admission, the breadth of Movement issues and the depth of commitment displayed by its actors were substantially greater than those of previous generations.

In fact, the Movement marked a qualitative adjustment in the positions available to citizens of Mexican descent in the U.S. cultural and political landscape. Historian Ignacio M. García makes this point in a forceful way when he argues that the construction of a politicized ethnic identity was not the sole objective of activists. Nevertheless, as I have argued throughout this book, the elaboration of radical and collective Chicano/a identities, especially among Mexican American youth, was the foundation upon which all other agendas would depend.[4]

The neoconservative refrain about a "failed Revolution" has found its way not only into the popular media but also into academic scholarship on the Movement. Chicano historians cite one another, for example, in order to substantiate the claim that "The Chicano Movement . . . emerges as a moment of radical potential that never engendered a revolution and ultimately brought complacency."[5] By taking the Movement's rhetoric too literally and by refusing to acknowledge that a term like *revolution* signified differently according to specific organizations and agendas ("revolution" in the Plan de Delano, for example, is not the "revolution" of the August 29th Movement), academic writers concoct a rigged narrative in which the Movement cannot be portrayed as anything else but a "failure."

If we listen to social-movement theorists who define "revolution" as "an action prosecuted with the use of force in order to occupy the existing roles in the political structure of a state," we can say quite confidently that virtually none of the diverse sectors of the Movement (with the possible exception of marginal splinter groups) seriously proposed "revolution" and the taking of state power.[6] In this view, the use of the term *revolution* must be understood as an example of a movement's language exceeding its actual objectives and resources in a process in which an ideological trope "radicalized the image of action beyond its factual contents."[7]

As we have seen in Chapter Three, the Chicano appropriation of Cuban revolutionary icons and discourse did not signify a direct correspondence between Chicano/a and Cuban agendas but rather a series of ideological affinities and resonances. Alberto Melucci explains that in their emergent phase, social movements tend to rely heavily on discursive formations: "The less capacity for action the still weak and unorganized movement has, the greater will be the production of symbols."[8]

It is not so much that the "Revolution" did not take place or that those who were politically engaged in the Viet Nam war era simply "grew up," but rather that many Chicano/a activists took their political values into the life's work they chose to do whether it was in the professions, in community service, or on the shop floor. Although a Movement based on utopian visions and mass mobilization was less visible by the end of the 1970s, complacency and neoassimilationism were not universal. If by the turn of the century the concept of "Aztlán" had been dispersed into small and isolated pockets of resistance or dismissed and transformed by academic theorists into a nebulous gas of collective delirium or "desire," for others it had been reworked as a sign of empowerment in the face of nativist attacks against recent immigrants from Latin America or a reinvigorated institutional racism aimed at ethnic Mexicans in the United States.[9]

Lessons and Avisos

Nuestra meta es la lucha.
(Our goal is the struggle)
                    —*Poeta anónimo*

I have argued throughout this book that far from being a "failure" the Chicano Movement made substantive contributions on a number of levels. The elaboration of a radicalized collective agency for ethnic Mexicans in the United States was in itself a major accomplishment. Equally important were the Chicano/a critique of naive and uncritical patriotism, the exposing of the imperial foundations of U.S. foreign policy, and the Chicana rejection of both subtle patriarchal and openly sexist practices. As the Black Civil Rights Movement had done in the South and urban centers in the North, Chicano/a militancy exposed the legacy of white supremacy and the history of economic exploitation in the Southwest. Coalition building with Black activists in the United States and solidarity work around the world can be counted among the Movement's other accomplishments.

In practical terms, any mass mobilization of a large ethnic working-class sector of U.S. society cannot possibly "fail" given that such a movement will always force existing hegemonic structures to respond in order to maintain their equilibrium. Sociologist Steven Buechler tells us: "When movements enjoy even partial success, they create changes that tend to become institutionalized over time. Even when movements fail, they often leave institutional traces because of how the prevailing social order responded to the movement before its demise."[10] As is the case with all social movements, then, the Chicano Movement was a contradictory process of centrifugal and centripetal forces, of two steps forward and one back. But it was hardly a failure.

As we have seen throughout the preceding chapters, the Movimiento as a whole and the positions taken by its leading spokespeople were riddled with ideological contradictions. The tragic figure of *L.A. Times* reporter Ruben Salazar, killed by police on August 29, 1970, is exemplary in this regard. In one of his final columns, Salazar explained to *Times* readers why many young Chicanos refused to celebrate the Fourth of July, and quoted folk singer Joan Baez: "Once we get rid of the obsession with defending one's country, we will be defending life. . . . That's why I hate flags. I despise any flag, not just the American Flag. It's a symbol of a piece of land that's considered more important than the human lives on it."[11]

Salazar, while not condoning Baez's position, nonetheless chose to reproduce her comments. Less than two months later, in what was to be his final column for the *Times*, Salazar described the Nixon administration's business initiative for those whom Vice President Spiro Agnew was one of the first to label "Americans of Hispanic descent." Salazar reported that most Chicanos viewed the National Economic Development Association (NEDA) with some skepticism, yet ended his column with the following sentiment: "NEDA, then, will mean little until the government is serious about creating more Chicano capitalists—through good schools."[12]

In what was his last published sentence, Ruben Salazar, who according to many Movement activists had become increasingly sympathetic to their critique of U.S. liberalism, captures the core belief of the middle-class and assimilationist ethos that would come to prominence in the Reagan-Bush-Clinton decades. Ruben Salazar's desire that more "Chicano capitalists" be created in fact was realized under the hegemony of the "Hispanic" dispensation. The critiques of capitalism, liberalism, and traditional patriotism that had marked the most radical sectors of the Movimiento for the most part faded away with the end of the Cold War and the demise of the socialist bloc.

We can safely assume that the vast majority of Mexican Americans in 1970 shared Salazar's liberal stance. In all of its various manifestations, the Movimiento was the work of a minority of dedicated organizers and activists. Post-Reagan neoconservative Hispanics would point to this fact as "proof" of the Movimiento's irrelevance. Syndicated "expert" on Latino affairs Gregory Rodriguez, for example, declared: "You have to keep in mind how marginal these ideas were even at their height."[13] But radical movements for social change rarely if ever are conducted by a majority of the population. Scholars of anticolonial movements remind us: "Not all the members of the 'nation' take the same view of the matter; nationalism is usually a minority movement pursued against the indifference and, frequently, the hostility of the majority of the members of the 'nation' in whose name the nationalists act."[14] If narrow nationalist agendas were not widely accepted in Chicana/o communities during the Viet Nam war era, socialist and internationalist positions in general were even more marginal. Yet none of this negates the power that cultural nationalism had (has) to mobilize large groups of ethnic Mexican people or the positive changes produced by the diverse groups of Chicano/a activists drawn from the Movement generation.

That a racialized minority's passage into self-determinism, to use the language of the Movement period, is a traumatic ordeal was made painfully obvious in the tragic events of August 29, 1970. It is fitting perhaps that a moderate Mexican American professional from one of the most conservative parts of southern California (Orange County) came to symbolize this crucible. In retrospect y *con todo respeto*, we might say that Ruben Salazar died so that future moderates might be born. Despite the radical postures we have seen in the preceding pages, it is not surprising that what the Movimiento actually facilitated was the accelerated integration of Mexican Americans into the U.S. mainstream. With the hard work of making it more difficult to practice overt anti-Mexican racism already accomplished for them, Hispanics in the 1980s and 90s, ever wary of offending those who controlled resources and career opportunities, were free to "celebrate" their ethnic difference even as they submitted themselves to the pervasive hegemony of neoliberal "free market" economics and neoconservative politics. Today, corporate Hispanics may even perform a street-wise, Spanish-speaking identity in some contexts, but for the most part he/she is careful neither to challenge the continuing tokenism of the mainstream nor to concede that the majority of Latinos in the United States and their Latin American cousins continue to live with significantly limited life chances as compared to other groups.

In both the neoconservative and the neoliberal dispensations, the forces of reaction carefully co-opted and redeployed the language of the Brown and Black civil rights movements throughout the 1980s and 1990s. The campaign to eliminate affirmative action programs in California (Proposition 209), for example, invoked the language of Martin Luther King, Jr., about a "color-blind society," and essentially succeeded in shutting the doors of University of California campuses and professional schools to Chicana/o and African American students.[15] Corporate advertisers drew their now depoliticized imagery from the 1960s social-movement repertoire, from Apple Computer's "Think different" campaign featuring César Chávez and Bobby Kennedy to Cingular Wireless Corporation's sampling of Dr. King's digitalized image standing at the foot of the Lincoln Memorial in order to hawk cell phones. On a variety of fronts, the Hispanic market carried forth the ideology of "consumerism is liberation" to an increasingly self-satisfied Hispanic middle class.

In early 2001, the great Chicano elder and labor activist Bert Corona passed away. The editor of *Hispanic Business* magazine, Jesus Chavarría, had this to say about Corona's death:

> Corporate diversity, Internet access, and media presence—these are the issues of today, ones that never appeared on the radar screen when I spent time with Bert Corona in the late '60s and '70s. Although he has passed on, several of the organizations he founded—National Council of La Raza, Mexican American Legal Defense Fund [*sic*], and Hermandad Mexicana Nacional—have adapted to the times by tackling these issues. But the struggle will be engaged by the heroes and heroines closest to the battle—the CEOs, managers, job applicants, and college students who believe in economic progress.[16]

The notion that together corporate caciques, a buffer managerial class, and intimidated and pliable job applicants will create a coalition in the pursuit of "the struggle" to which Bert Corona dedicated his entire life is laughable. But "the struggle," as Chavarría redefines it, is no longer for workers' and immigrants' rights and economic justice, as Corona would have argued, but rather for an idea of "economic progress" that is tailored to the needs of a capitalist elite, their lackeys, and existing racial and economic formations.

It could well be argued that at the beginning of the twenty-first century, there simply is no other game in town. In most educational and work environments this is absolutely true. To push a Chicano/a agenda—to demand meaningful structural reform, to reject tokenism, to actualize a militant commitment to progressive change—is to risk being labeled strident, a malcontent, a dinosaur from the 1960s, or all of the above. In academic circles where Hispanic brokers cleverly make their way down calculated career paths, the charge of "nationalist" is hurled at those who dare to question the status quo. If by insisting that the current state of affairs in which the Chicano high school dropout rate is staggering, the number of Chicano/Mexicans in prison is a scandal, violence is perpetrated against undocumented Mexican workers everyday, and prestigious universities accept only a token amount of students from communities of color one is practicing "nationalism," then perhaps nationalism as a tool for organizing the disenfranchised has not outlived its usefulness.[17] When the most aggressive forms of white supremacy or immigrant bashing threaten Chicano/as and Mexicano/as as in the period leading up to the October 2003 California recall election or the vigilante actions aimed at undocumented Mexican workers in 2005, then perhaps "nationalism" is the most appropriate means of self-defense.

According to recent studies sponsored by the federal government, Latinos in the United States fall below other groups on almost every social and economic indicator. Although Latinos have a high rate of participation in the labor force, about 7 percent of Latinos with full-time jobs were still living below the poverty line in 2001 (compared to 4.4 percent of African Americans and 1.7 percent for whites). Among all private-sector employees in the United States, 41.5 percent are considered blue collar, but 63.5 percent of all Latino/as hold blue-collar jobs. In 2002, 61 percent of all workers in agricultural production were Latino/as, the vast majority of Mexican descent. While nearly 11 percent of non-Hispanic whites earned more than seventy-five thousand dollars a year in 2001, only 2 percent of all Latinos earned as much. In 2003 over 9.0 million Latino/a workers were living in poverty (an increase from 8.6 million in 2002) and 32.7 percent of all Latino/as lacked health insurance.[18]

With regard to the discursive representation of ethnic Mexicans, the work of critical pedagogue Lilia Bartolomé convincingly shows how the mass media and educational system reproduce the degradation of Mexican culture in the United States. Moreover, Otto Santa Ana's research reveals how media languages perpetuate racialized stereotypes of Latinos.[19] Given the persistence of institutionalized racism, one of the basic objectives of the cultural nationalist agenda—to counter racist practices by instilling pride in the Spanish language and Chicano/Mexicano history and to take control of the writing of that history—may be as important to the well-being of Chicano/Mexicano students in the twenty-first century as it was to their parents and grandparents. On this point, Ignacio M. García's concept of a "militant ethos," elaborated by Movimiento activists and still present among many Chicano/a youth today, will have to be continually reinvented according to changing social and historical conjunctures.[20]

I have maintained throughout this book that any simple transference of Viet Nam war era Chicano/a agendas and practices to the twenty-first century is bound to fail. Assertions such as "We need to go back to the Plan espiritual de Aztlán," I would argue, are not particularly helpful. In the new context, we are faced with a solidly entrenched Hispanic class, Hispanic sororities and fraternities on college campuses able to recruit more successfully than historically progressive and activist organizations such as MEChA, and other symptoms of the deeply conservative reality of the "Homeland Security" period in which we find ourselves. Any attempt to organize Chicano/a and mexicano/a communities for progressive change will be no easy feat. Add to this the presence of millions of undocumented and recently arrived legal immigrants (a continually recurring event in the U.S.-Mexican context) and the enormity of formulating a progressive Raza political agenda seems overwhelming.

If the majority of recent immigrants suffer indignities as racialized occupants of the lowest rungs of the economic ladder, only a handful of them will have an understanding of the widespread institutional racism that will affect their children's and their grandchildren's life chances in the United States. For those few who do comprehend the obstacles facing their families, the idea of a mass social movement attempting to democratize the public sphere and challenge assimilationist identities will be both foreign and frightening. The issue of education is illustrative. Faced with a public school system that continues to fail Spanish-speaking youth, working-class parents search desperately for alternatives. But rather than demanding that the public school system be reformed, many choose to abandon it altogether.

In November 2000, for example, school voucher advocates put Proposition 38 on the California ballot with the promise that a four-thousand-dollar gift to private schools would allow parents the freedom to choose where their children could be educated. Proposition 38 was organized by former Pete Wilson and Newt Gingrich operatives (Wilson was the Republican governor of California from 1991 to 1999; Gingrich was the Republican Speaker of the House from 1995 to 1999). Opponents argued that the measure was a stealth attempt to privatize the public schools whereas supporters of the measure referred to public schools as the "last vestige of socialism." Anyone who thought the Cold War was over was bemused by the rhetoric used by the far-right critics of public education who in one political ad compared the school system to a "Soviet-style bureaucracy."

On October 21, 2000, a pro-Proposition 38 rally was staged at Chicano Park, the San Diego, California, park created by grassroots artists and activists in the spring of 1970. The rally co-opted an array of Movement songs and trappings—indigenous drums, "*No nos moverán*," "*De colores*," and "Brown-eyed Children of the Sun." A well-known San Diego musician and his conjunto performed the songs (the group had played the same songs at a NO-on-38 rally just the day before). A former La Raza Unida Party activist spoke in favor of the initiative, arguing that the public school system had not worked for Chicana/os and that any alternative was preferable. A former César Chávez associate who founded Escuela de la Raza in Blythe, California, led the rally.

In a brief conversation with this writer after the event, the organizer argued that vouchers were the only way for Raza to gain access to decent schools. Neither the quality of those private schools, the schools' ability to prepare students for college, or the fact that the vast majority of Raza will not be in those schools seemed to concern him. In Chicano Park, the one space in San Diego most closely associated with the high point of Chicano/a activism, the cultural practices of the Movement were now deployed to further the cause of privatization. What such a move might mean was unclear. In a worst-case scenario, the abandoning of public education by Chicano/as could foreclose any future engagement with two important sectors of the public school population—recent Mexican and Latin American immigrant families who do not yet identify as Chicanos and the non-Mexican working class.[21]

What lessons can we draw from such a spectacle? That the neoconservative attack on the public sphere, including public schools, now includes former Chicano Movement participants is symptomatic of the current situation. The call during the Movement period for the creation of "Raza schools" had been transferred to an entirely new context in which the idea of school "choice" resonates for poor Latinos who have given up hope that public schools are able or willing to serve their children. The neoliberal complicity with the Reagan-Bush attack on economic-justice agendas and the apparent lack of a convincing progressive program to counteract it has produced a no-exit dilemma for working people. In an opinion survey of one thousand adults conducted July 9–11, 2001, by pollster Opiniones Latinas, 58 percent expressed a negative opinion of the public school system and 74 percent favored school vouchers.[22]

At the university level, Chicano/a Studies has become an accepted (although undervalued) area of research to such a degree that non-Chicano/a scholars are eager to work on Chicano/a materials.[23] In theory there is certainly nothing wrong with this development except insofar as the percentage of Chicano/a faculty continues to be small and their scholarship much more vulnerable to charges of "lack of rigor" and "too subjective" than that of their non-Chicano/a colleagues. The number of Chicano/a university administrators is infinitesimal, the result of blatant institutionalized racism according to one recent study.[24] Chicano/a faculty who practice local activism are especially susceptible to delays in promotion and salary increases even (especially?) where white liberal administrators and faculty promote tepid versions of "diversity."

"Diversity" in this corporatized context does not and perhaps cannot include significant structural reform. In many locations, a Hispanic buffer class ensures that militancy or even advocacy is quietly punished. On this issue, Malcolm X's remarks on the relationship between Black nationalism and the white liberal establishment are still illuminating: "Any other Black people who get involved are involved within the rules that are laid down by the white liberals. And as long as they are involved within those rules, then that means they're only going to go as far as the liberal element of the power structure will endorse their activity. But when the nationalistic-minded Blacks get involved, then we do what our analysis tells us is necessary to be done, whether the white liberal or anybody else likes it or not. So they don't want us involved."[25]

Martin Luther King, Jr., in 1967 had anticipated the danger that a growth in middle classes of color might produce an unbridgeable divide within historically disenfranchised groups:

> For any middle-class Negro to forget the masses is an act not only of neglect but also of shameful ingratitude. It is time for the Negro haves to join hands with the Negro have-nots and, with compassion, journey into that other country of hurt and denial. It is time for the Negro middle class to rise up from its stool of indifference, to retreat from its flight into unreality and to bring its full resources—its heart, its mind and its check-book—to the aid of the less fortunate brother. The relatively

privileged Negro will never be what he ought to be until the underprivileged Negro is what he ought to be. The salvation of the Negro middle class is ultimately dependent upon the salvation of the Negro masses.[26]

By referring to "the salvation of the Negro masses," Dr. King meant something more than "compassionate conservatism" and acts of individual volunteerism. Although his call to action certainly does not preempt traditional acts of charity, his emphasis toward the end of his life was on the need for radical structural change facilitated by the active participation of the newly formed middle classes of color.

The great author, educator, and organizer Ernesto Galarza argued in 1972 that the emergent class of Chicano/a professionals would have to choose between service to their community or careerism:

If these people go back into the community understanding that their superior knowledge and training puts a proportionately higher responsibility which means helping the community to understand the situations that it finds itself in and to bring to the community information that is not available to them . . . the Mexican moving into American urban society is moving into an extremely complicated culture. The community needs people who know their way around in it but if you learn your way around a complicated culture you can easily be tempted to exploit it on your own behalf and to make a career out of it. Careerism is one of the temptations and pitfalls that face the Mexican graduate student.[27]

Galarza's warning has gone unheeded for the most part. The hyper-professionalization and careerism he described became the driving forces behind most of the Hispanic success stories of the 1990s.

This is precisely what too many Chicana/o professionals, the Hispanic "Talented Tenth," if you will, have chosen to forget. Self-satisfied and at times openly hostile to their less-fortunate brothers and sisters, the successful Hispanic takes the notion of the "Me Generation" to new heights of self-absorption. As one reader of *Hispanic Business* complained: "I am a fifth-generation American of Mexican descent. I come from an upper-middle-income family that lived in a predominantly Anglo neighborhood. So I don't fit the stereotypical profile of a poor immigrant, the symbolic Hispanic fixture most often portrayed in newspapers and other media. Have the wants and needs of Hispanics like me slipped through the cracks? Do we count?"[28]

POLITICS AND PLEITOS

> We want radical change. Nothing short of radical change is going to have any impact on our lives or our problems. We want sufficient power to control our own destinies. This is our struggle.
>
> —César Estrada Chávez

Given this new conjuncture, we are compelled to speak of several Mexican American identities coexisting at once. The self-satisfied Hispanic professional elite, a lower middle- and working-class U.S. born and educated Mexican American sector that shares many of the values of earlier pre-Movement generations, a much smaller but multigenerational group of Chicano/a activists dissatisfied with lingering structural racism and inequalities, and high numbers of recent Mexican or indigenous-identified immigrants for whom the American Dream is very much alive.[29] There is more contact between the latter two groups than between them and the first group since Hispanic professionals are more inclined to insulate themselves and their families from working-class or immigrant problems and political agendas.

The evidence for a similar kind of fragmentation in the African American community is abundant, and has convinced one theorist of ethnic identity to claim: "Ethnicity does not provide the basis for communal heavens in the network society, because it is based on primary bonds that lose significance, when cut from their historical context."[30] Any future attempt to construct collective Chicano/a and Mexicano/a political projects in the United States will face a similar reality, that is, the commodification of ethnicity and its transformation into an individualized or lifestyle characteristic with very few if any political applications.

In an op-ed piece circulated over the Internet in early 2000, historian Rudy Acuña posed the following questions:

> What is the duty of the Chicano middle class to the barrios in matters concerning civil rights? Have we grown too complacent? Have we come to believe that equality and justice can be

gotten solely through the election of Mexican American elected officials? Or, even more sarcastically, is our contribution to the barrio measured by our individual success? Or, should the question be, do we have any duty to others once we make it?[31]

Given his history of activism and committed scholarship, Acuña's response to the second and final questions is certainly an affirmative one—Chicana/o professionals have grown too complacent and Chicana/o professionals do have a duty to others once they are financially secure. But the ethos of service and cross-class, pan-ethnic, or international solidarity has little resonance for the majority of the Hispanic professional class. Today, the progressive agenda implied in Acuña's queries strikes many as naive and quaintly old-fashioned.

I am not suggesting that the gap dividing Acuña from his detractors is a generational impasse. On the contrary, some of the most enthusiastic ideologues of the new class came of age during the Movement period. Consider once again the musings of Jesus Chavarría, editor of *Hispanic Business* magazine: "Hispanic influence has surpassed the limits of traditional power sources such as politics to enter the dynamics of the New Economy. Influence now implies an ability to forecast and ride toward the future, not a need to regulate it. Hispanic culture fits well with this confluence, lending substance to a hope for more influence in years to come."[32] In 2002, the art exhibit organized by actor Cheech Marín and funded by corporate backers stimulated a variety of negative responses to the question of whether or not Chicano/a artists had a political responsibility to their working-class sisters and brothers. The answer offered by artist César Martinez to an interviewer was painfully direct: "Fuck the people."[33]

In this view, Acuña's questions and his implied answers could have meaning only in some imaginary museum as an exhibit about a time and space where progressive or left-of-center politics once mattered. For Chavarría and Martinez, the end of politics has arrived and the "logic" of the market, deregulation, careerism, and casino-style stock-market speculation are the only values upon which an Hispanic future can be constructed. Hispanic fat cats need only predict business trends and "ride toward the future," apparently winging their way over the huddled masses of disenfranchised poor below. Chavarría's assertion that "Hispanic culture fits well with this confluence" can only be read as

Orwellian doublespeak. Martinez's follow-up reply left no room for doubt about his motivation and principles: "If artists are corrupted by money, then I would like a chance at getting corrupted."[34]

The Chicano Movement's rejection of traditional models of assimilation had at its core a fundamental contradiction. For most Chicana/o activists and organizations the objective was not so much a total rejection of U.S. society as it was to mount a series of critiques, ranging from reformist to revolutionary, that exposed the most negative features of that society and interrogated its unfulfilled promises. Very few believed that a socialist America was a possibility and few committed themselves to actively pursuing the physical liberation of occupied Aztlán. Most sought a stable footing within a United States that might offer them real democracy and economic opportunity. The issue, then, was for Chicano/as to practice continual acts of criticism and self-criticism in order to decide which aspects of U.S. society were to be adopted and which ones were to be rejected. Or as one Mexican observer described the Chicano/a dilemma: "*Es, en síntesis, usar dialéctamente las definiciones supraestructurales de la realidad como armas para la lucha contra una realidad que les fue impuesta*" ("In sum, it is to use dialectically the superstructural definitions of the status quo as weapons with which to struggle against the status quo that has been imposed upon them").[35]

It is not surprising, given his rich personal history and experience, that in 1971 Ernesto Galarza succinctly described the ongoing collective project known as the Movimiento:

> Does the Mexican-American community merely want to catch up with the Anglo-American culture? The question is important, and we had better be careful before we say yes. My experience—in farm labor, in academic work, in politics—has taught me a lot of things about the Anglo-American culture that I do not like. Its economic system, for instance, produces certain values and behavior that I don't want to catch up with. Mexican-Americans have an opportunity to discriminate between the different values, behavior, and institutions in the pervading culture, and we had better choose wisely.[36]

Thirty years later it is clear that a large number of Mexican Americans disagree with Galarza insofar as they have rushed to "catch up" with the values and behavior of rampant consumerism and careerism. While there are still some who on a daily basis opt to construct collective identities and alternative political projects, the entire question of "choosing wisely," as Galarza and Movement activists understood it, has so drastically shifted its meaning that the very idea of a renewed progressive Chicano/a social movement is increasingly difficult to imagine.

In colleges and universities where the Movimiento produced an array of Chicano and Ethnic Studies programs, the academic variant of Chavarría's and Martinez's cynical careerism has produced an Hispanic professional elite weaned on European high theory and driven by corporate values of celebrity and institutional "power" (however circumscribed that power might be). One of the most perceptive and trenchant critics of this new situation is Cherríe Moraga who, in a brutally honest appraisal delivered at the University of California, Irvine (one of the foundational spaces of the "theory revolution" of the 1970s and a contemporary assembly line for the production of "theory celebrities" through its Humanities Research Institute), reminded Chicano/a faculty and students: "The university allows a benign liberalism, even a healthy degree of radical transgressive thought, as long as it remains just that: *thought* translated into the conceptual language of the dominant class to be consumed by academics of the dominant class, and as such rendered useless to the rest of us."[37]

The uselessness of much cultural theory, I would argue, has less to do with the theory itself or even where it is reproduced but rather with the fact that too many Chicano/a academics have chosen to accept the Anglo American insistence on the separation of theory and praxis, scholarship and politics. They therefore lose contact with progressive struggles taking place off campus or even on campus. The culprits identified by Moraga as "foreign eurocentric sources" and "their theory" are only to blame if Chicana and Chicano intellectuals choose to parrot theoretical languages that are so abstract they can have no relevance to ongoing struggles because they are understood by only the most select academic cliques.[38] This does not mean Chicano/as ought to abandon those insights of progressive European and Latin American thinkers through which we might analyze contemporary conditions for Latino communities. On this point, I continue to believe that Audre Lorde's oft-repeated phrase: "The master's tools will never dismantle the master's house" is misleading. It would be more accurate to say:

"The master's tools in the hands of Raza who identify with the master will never dismantle the master's house."

THE MAJORITY MINORITY

We will never achieve such a [just] society until the structure of concentrated economic, social, and political power, and the inequalities it fosters, has itself been democratized.
—Carey McWilliams, "Once a Well-Kept Secret"

In January 2003 it was reported that for the first time the number of "Hispanics" in the United States had surpassed the number of African Americans.[39] This national trend, coupled with the changing demographics of a state like California in which Latino/as will constitute a majority within the next few decades, has accelerated the creation of "white fear" of a Brown planet but also a Black fear that the African American community may be displaced as the most visible representative of the civil-rights tradition. The kind of Brown/Black coalitions created by Tijerina or the students who struggled for Lumumba/Zapata College are hardly imaginable now, and even tamer electoral alliances between the two groups are difficult if not impossible to sustain given entrenched party-machine politics.

The 2001 mayoral election in Los Angeles, for example, pitted long-time Chicano activist and former speaker of the State Assembly, Antonio Villaraigosa, against Jim Hahn, the son of legendary county supervisor Kenneth Hahn. Rather than support Villaraigosa, whose policy positions coincided almost exactly with progressive Black agendas, Congresswoman Maxine Waters threw her support to Hahn and essentially labeled Villaraigosa a carpetbagger ("We still don't know who this man really is") despite the Chicano leader's over twenty-year involvement in Los Angeles politics. The majority of the African American voters followed Waters's lead, alchemizing an uncanny blend of Black and conservative-white votes and electing Hahn by a 53 percent to 46 percent margin.[40]

In 2003, Ward Connerly, who had led the drive in California to abolish affirmative action, stated openly that his efforts to pass a "Privacy Initiative" that would ban the keeping of statistics based on race (Proposition 54) were inspired in part by his anger about "Mexicans" benefiting from affirmative-action policies. In an interview with the *Washington Post*, Connerly stated: "In California, this is no longer about race . . . it's about ethnicity, and those of Mexican descent who will soon be a majority. They don't want to see those categories go. They want to see affirmative action policies remain so they can take advantage of them. They want to claim minority status when, in fact, they will soon be a majority in California. They want to hide behind the term 'Latino' and 'people of color,' but most of them check the 'white' box [on the census form] anyway."[41] What is most troubling about Connerly's ignorant and anti-Mexican statement is that some progressive African Americans share its basic premise—that given the opportunity Latino/as can (and will) always choose to pass as white.

In the discipline of cultural criticism, one of the more misleading formulations of the late 1990s perpetrated by influential academics was "California is the Mississippi of the 90s."[42] Not only did the phrase unintentionally reassert the Black/White paradigm of racialized social relations, it distorted the specificity of both historical struggles—the Jim Crow South in the 1950s and the reactionary backlash in multiracial California at the end of the century—and reduced the complexity of the California context to a different and in many ways simpler moment in the civil-rights crusade.

In part the result of the intellectual and political class's inability to come to terms with the new demographics, the "California is the Mississippi of the 90s" slogan missed the important point that, given recent migrations from Mexico to the Deep South, Mississippi or Georgia or North Carolina may in fact become the California or Southwest of the 2030s. As I have already indicated, the increase in Latinos between 1990 and 2000 in North Carolina was 393.9 percent, in Arkansas 323.3 percent, in Georgia 299.6 percent, and in Tennessee 278.2 percent. In Mississippi, the historical ground zero of the segregationist South, the number of Latinos more than doubled. Whereas in 1990 only nineteen of the state's eighty-two counties had two hundred or more Latino residents, by 2000 more than half or forty-eight counties had two hundred or more. And these numbers are probably too low given the census bureau's track record of undercounting Latinos.[43]

Right-wing ideologues are by no means timid about sounding the battle cry against what they take to be a real threat to the fantasy of a pure White America. In his best-selling *The Death of the West: How Dying Populations and Immigrant Invasions Imperil Our Country and*

Civilization, for example, Patrick J. Buchanan dredged up conservative rhetoric from the 1960s to convince readers that student organization MEChA was a serious threat to national security. MEChA, warned Buchanan, is "a Chicano version of the white-supremacist Aryan Nation . . . and is unabashedly racist and anti-American." Quoting freely from the founding fathers, but most approvingly from Teddy Roosevelt, about the dangers of ethnic identities, Buchanan wrote: "With their own radio and TV stations, newspapers, films, and magazines, the Mexican Americans are creating an Hispanic culture separate and apart from America's larger culture. They are becoming a nation within a nation."[44]

Not long after the terrorist attacks of September 11, 2001, anti-Mexican activists attempted to link the "Latino menace" to the threat of Islamist fundamentalism. In the on-line newspaper *World Net Daily*, Joseph Farah described a radical Chicano group called "La Raza" and warned his readers: "Activists who see themselves as 'America's Palestinians' are gearing up a movement to carve out of the southwestern United States—a region called Aztlán including all of Bush's home state of Texas—a sovereign Hispanic state called the República del Norte. The leaders of this movement are meeting continuously with extremists from the Islamic world."[45] Farah's charges were ridiculous but they revealed much about the close ties between the radical wing of the Republican Party and a reinvigorated racism.

By the time of the presidential election year of 2004, Harvard professor Samuel P. Huntington had bestowed an Ivy League imprimatur on the new nativism. In his book *Who Are We?: The Challenges to America's National Identity*, he argued that more than any other group "Hispanics" represented a grave threat to the nation. He cautioned his readers: "The cultural division between Hispanics and Anglos will replace the racial division between blacks and whites as the most serious cleavage in American society. A bifurcated America with two languages and two cultures will be fundamentally different from the American with one language and one core Anglo-Protestant culture that has existed for over three centuries."[46] Huntington's legacy to the future seemed to be little more than the pitting of one ethnic or religious group against another.

In this climate of hostility and fear-mongering, Latinos continued to educate their children and contribute to U.S. society. The fundamental changes produced by a conservative Republican administration's "war on terror" included a policy of preemptive military strikes such as the invasion of Iraq in 2003, a complete restructuring of constitutional rights at home, and the creation of huge budget deficits that promised to engorge Pentagon coffers while demolishing state and local support for education and social services. The concept of "Homeland Security" meant immigrant communities were increasingly subjected to surveillance and intimidation. Throughout 2004, for example, the newly formed Bureau of Immigration and Customs Enforcement terrorized Latino neighborhoods with a series of raids and detentions even as many young people from those same neighborhoods served in Iraq and Afghanistan. Ironically, the militarization of public school systems and limited life chances will guarantee a steady stream of Latino/a recruits into the lowest ranks of the U.S. armed forces.[47]

Faced with such an intimidating environment and a radically different context than that of the Viet Nam war era, Chicano/as and Mexicano/as will be ill served by relying too heavily on concepts, rhetoric, and practices devised by an earlier generation of activists. While drawing the appropriate lessons from the Movement, Chicano/a progressive agendas will have to be reconfigured in order to affect events and policies in a more dangerous and less hopeful historical moment. Although it may sound ridiculous, we can say with some certainty that the next thirty years will make the Viet Nam war period seem simple by comparison.

In short, ethnic and national identities in the United States have only begun the dramatic process of transformation whose ultimate conclusion we can only begin to imagine. Might the next Chicano/a insurgency take place far from the Southwest? Will the legacy of white supremacy together with discrimination in education and housing and economic inequality in general eventually lead to a new Chicano Movement deep in the heart of Dixie? What role will "long-distance" transnational Mexican and Central American nationalisms play as thousands of new immigrants maintain close ties to their country of origin? What forms will the anti-immmigrant backlash take in a state like California where demographic changes exacerbate long-standing nativism? Can new social movements arise in a nation where a lack of historical memory is enforced daily by the educational system and the corporate media?

In May 2001, an exhibit of Mexican, indigenous, and Chicano/a art opened at the Los Angeles County Museum of Art. Titled "The Road to

Aztlán: Art from a Mythic Homeland," the show sought to make a connection between contemporary Mexican American culture and the ancient Mexica people, that is, those groups that according to the codex displayed in the exhibit had migrated centuries ago from what is now the U.S. Southwest to Tenochtitlán, the capital of the Aztec empire. In the final room of the exhibit were copies of three Chicano Movement documents displayed under glass—the Plan de Delano, the Plan de la Raza Unida Party, and the Plan Espiritual de Aztlán. Artist Armando Rascón had labeled his piece "Three Documents of Independence," and the installation invoked sentiments that surround documents such as the U.S. Declaration of Independence in a setting designed to lend an air of sanctity and transcendence to texts that were in fact human creations produced in the heat of revolutionary historical change.

On one level, the presentation of the documents conveyed the sense that the complex social movement upon which the preceding chapters have tried to shed some light was now a museum piece to be contemplated by future generations. Now safely under glass, the Movimiento's ideals of self-determination, the militant pursuit of equality, and solidarity with progressive projects around the world no longer threatened the status quo. As I observed the reaction to the exhibit of young Chicanas and Chicanos born long after the events discussed in this book, however, it occurred to me that the Movement was far from dead. For as long as the majority of Mexican people in the United States are denied social and economic justice, Chicanas and Chicanos will need to learn the lessons of the Movimiento in order to fashion struggles for their own time and place.

Appendix

—"ANCIENTS AND (POST)MODERNS"—

IN HIS INTRODUCTION TO THE *Voices of a New Chicana/o History* collection, José Cuello attributes the use of an internal colonialism model to the "founders" of Chicano Studies.[1] In contrast, he tells us, the research of younger scholars grows out of issues of class, race, gender, and sexuality. While it is certainly true that the study of sex/gender relations and gay/lesbian issues did not figure in the work of early Chicana/o historians and cultural critics (in great part because social movements addressing these constituencies were only emerging and academic disciplines in these areas did not exist), one would be hard pressed to prove that the "founders" did not investigate questions of race and class.

The artificial division between the Chicano "ancients and moderns" outlined by Cuello is misleading and potentially damaging to any rapprochement that might take place between those professors on the verge of retirement and their successors. Put another way, established scholars have much to learn from their younger colleagues just as those beginning their academic careers may benefit from dialogues with *las/los veteranas/os*. I would add, however, that it is the responsibility of Movement activist/scholars, who as tenured faculty are in a position of institutional power (albeit limited in most cases), to be magnanimous and seek to understand the new research in its historical context rather than rejecting it out of hand.

I submit that the "shift" in the writing of Chicana/o political and cultural history as outlined in the *Voices* collection is not a shift at all, but rather an expansion of a relatively familiar social-history model to include previously uninvestigated subjects, e.g., women, the Mexican American middle class, gays, lesbians, and others. This expansion of the research agenda was a positive development for American Studies in general and for Chicana/o Studies in particular. The claim of an epistemological break in Chicana/o Studies is unconvincing. Even less convincing are arguments that the changes in Chicana/o history writing are due to a shift from "modernity" to "postmodernity." Given the theoretical innovations that swept through history and literature departments beginning in the 1970s, it is a rather curious choice to deploy what are essentially aesthetic categories in an attempt to explain "the new Chicana/o history."

This is exactly what Ramón A. Gutiérrez does, however, in his contribution to the *Voices* collection in which he reproduces many of the clichés associated with 1990s poststructuralist thought in the U.S. academy: "If the 'old' Chicano history depended on certitude, on objectivity, on disinterestedness, and on 'facts' gathered in a systematic and unbiased fashion to reveal the truth, 'new' Chicana and Chicano historical writings have been presented as 'readings,' 'positioning,' 'perspectives,' and 'constructions' of the past."[2] This sea change has occurred, we are told, because of three main challenges to traditional philosophical thought (philosophy collapsed here into "the militant nationalism of the Chicano Movement between 1955 and 1970 [*sic*]"): the feminist critique of universal "Man," the deconstruction of the Enlightenment notion of progress (i.e., modernity), and the exhaustion of a "proletarian" or Marxist paradigm. In Gutiérrez's account an uninterrogated "radical Chicano nationalism" functions as a cucui figure responsible for everything wrong about the "old history." He goes on to define "nationalism" as a position "further to the political left" than Marxism because it "eschews class struggle, assimilation, and civil rights activism." Gutiérrez presents Rudy Acuña as the foremost proponent of this position due to his expressed solidarity with Third World liberation movements and the presence of Paolo Freire and Frantz Fanon in his work.

How exactly are we to understand this conflation of diverse political and intellectual agendas? If the Movimiento was "nationalist" according to this definition, it would have "eschewed class struggle and civil rights activism" which the majority of Movement organizations certainly did not do. If Acuña were a "nationalist" according to Gutiérrez's idiosyncratic definition, what business did he have in expressing a strong internationalist position and a consistent interest in class struggle and civil-rights activism? Finally, how can a narrow nationalist and regressive political project be to "the left" of socialist programs?[3]

But the nationalists are not the only villains in Gutiérrez's account. In this rather murky pot of conceptual *menudo*, Marxists and feminists soon join the nationalists as those forces hostile to "postmodern understandings of identities."

The implicit attack on "feminists" here is bizarre given Gutiérrez's claim that gender studies were a positive corrective to the old history and because there exists a vast bibliography of feminist scholarship fully engaged in the development of "postmodern understandings of identities." The confusion is compounded by Gutiérrez's linking of the necessary feminist critiques of sexism and patriarchal structures in Movement organizations with the critique of "Universal Man," the latter a philosophical project undertaken by Marx and every other materialist thinker since at least the mid-nineteenth century. Gutiérrez carelessly conflates contemporary feminist projects aimed at unseating phallocentrism, redressing institutional gender inequities, and challenging everyday sexist behavior with older Marxist and anticolonialist attacks on universalism and abstract humanisms.

Whether the collapsing of categories in such an account of the Movimiento is willful or unintentional is not clear. The consequences, however, are dire for the historical record and for future generations of students. Among the more ironic consequences of Reaganism, institutional efforts to depoliticize Chicana/o Studies programs, and neoconservative attempts to rewrite and discredit the social movements of the Sixties are the ways in which revisionist discourse insinuates itself into accounts of the Chicano Movement. In his essay on the Brown Berets, for example, historian Ernesto Chávez describes "Chicanismo" as a part of the counterculture in order to argue that both were "a form of anti-Americanism that permeated United States society in the 1960s and 1970s." Chávez writes: "Anti-Americanism encompassed a disdain for American institutions and reflected a transition from Americanism to an anti-Americanism that resulted from the turmoil of the 1960s."[4]

Although Chávez later admits that for the vast majority of organizations that made up the Movimiento the critique of U.S. society was premised upon a fundamental belief that the promises of liberal democracy could be realized, his use of the unfortunate term *anti-Americanism* unwittingly reproduces the same charge made by conservatives against ethnic and antiwar movements during the Viet Nam war era and resonates with the reactionary revisionist accounts of the Sixties written in the decades that followed. The politically charged binary "Americanism/anti-Americanism" is deployed and left uninterrogated and therefore runs the risk of oversimplifying the complex ideological terrain that was the Chicano Movement.

Let me cite a more complicated example that combines the perceived generational anxiety I have discussed above with the imprecise presentation of political stances. In a curious act of self-definition, historian María Montoya opens her essay in the *Voices* collection in the following manner: "I have a confession to make: I was born in 1964. I was not alive when Oswald shot President John F. Kennedy. I was one year old when Cesar Chavez led his first strike."[5] Montoya presents her autobiographical fragment as if it were a secret that she has only now chosen to reveal; thus the "confession" made to those readers who apparently were expecting someone older, someone more progressive, perhaps someone "more Chicana."

The necessity for this kind of statement is not immediately evident unless one is familiar with debates in the discipline during the "politically correct" hysteria of the mid-1990s and the tremendous pressure felt by young scholars to distance themselves from the militancy of the Chicano Movement. But in Montoya's case there is more to her "confession" than mere generational rivalry or ethnic identification. She provides her reader with a description of her political education in the 1980s: "The rhetoric of 'equality' espoused by the far Right, who were eager to eliminate affirmative action programs, and not the liberal radicalism of the previous decade, shaped my youth. My role models were not liberals like Dolores Huerta and Corky Gonzalez [*sic*], but conservatives like Linda Chavez and Manuel Luján."[6]

It is not at all clear here if Montoya is merely describing the "Decade of the Hispanic" during which, by the historical accident of her birthdate, she passed into adulthood or if in fact she consciously chose as her "role models" reactionary figures such as Linda Chavez. For despite the paucity of high-profile Chicana/o progressives in the Reagan-Bush era, young Chicana/os certainly had the option to select alternative role models. After all, Dolores Huerta and César Chávez were still alive and continued to organize, Latino/a progressives were actively contesting U.S. policy in Central America, and Chicana feminists like Cherríe Moraga and Gloria Anzaldúa were busy writing groundbreaking texts. The notion that one's historical context alone can explain one's political commitments or lack of them is unconvincing unless one eschews responsibility for what Montoya calls "a very unromantic, apolitical coming-of-age tale." Put another way, the notion that the Sixties were "unique" should not be taken to mean that later periods are devoid of opportunities to contribute to a progressive agenda both inside and outside the university.

Montoya's dilemma is not surprising, however, and her personal history certainly should not be an issue for public debate. What is of some interest to Chicana/o Studies scholars is the way in which the perception that any historical period is "apolitical" insinuates itself into scholarship. Montoya's essay contains a number of suggestions with which I agree, e.g., the elaboration of comparative pan-Latino studies and the continued attention to issues of gender and sexuality. But in her effort to distance her work from that of earlier Movement scholars, she misreads the contemporary moment as one that lacks the pressing need for meaningful praxis: "The political urgency that marked so many of the early writings and the revisionist spirit in which those texts were written will begin to fade away as younger scholars search for a more academic voice in which to place their work."[7]

In the end, the question of what will become of Chicano/a Studies will be answered by the agency of future generations of scholars and students in their specific historical circumstances. As early as 1978, Elihu Carranza asserted the inevitability of new perspectives: "To have witnessed the birth of Chicano Studies programs and departments, some of which were forged in the crucible of strife, constitutes part of the historical past for many of us. A new generation of Chicanos whose history does not include the memories of those events perhaps cannot be expected to be concerned with the genesis or future of Chicano Studies."[8] We can read Montoya's appeal to "a more academic voice," therefore, as a desire to return to the strict separation made by the most conservative scholarly traditions between objective "science" and the terrible chaos of politics. Scholarship, she suggests, ought to be neutral.

Faced with a reinvigorated U.S. imperialism, the plight of indigenous people in Mexico, the situation of the Chicano/a working poor, the victims of police brutality and corruption, the thousands of incarcerated Chicano/a youth, the assault by military recruiters on Latino/a communities, the violence and death along the U.S./Mexico border, and the exclusion of Chicana/o students from prestigious universities and professional schools in Texas and California, the implication that at the beginning of the twenty-first-century Chicano/a Studies scholars need not feel a sense of urgency can only be understood as denial or evasion.

The claim put forward by some of the essays in the *Voices* volume that "scholarship is activism" and José Cuello's summary of their position that "entering and excelling in new fields of scholarship and competing in the academic marketplace is as important to furthering the cause of the community as going back to it personally" should give us some pause, given that many universities, including public universities, are increasingly designed to serve only their corporate benefactors.[9] In this new arrangement, "competing in the academic marketplace" means competing in a marketplace in which scholars working in disciplines considered to be without prestige, e.g., Chicana/o Studies, are either tokenized or put at an extreme disadvantage compared to their colleagues in the sciences, engineering, or even British literature.

In other words, scholarship alone will not change the structural arrangements in which the vast majority of Chicana/o youth are excluded from elite educational institutions and consigned to low-skill jobs or military service while the number of Chicana/o faculty is kept artificially low. Only a renewed militancy that challenges the class racism and elitism of the new privatized university will overcome these obstacles. It is not a question of "going back" to the barrio since many of our finest young scholars were never in the barrio. Nor is it an issue of "going back to the Sixties" or "going back to the Plan espiritual de Aztlán," positions I have argued against throughout this book. Rather, it is a matter of acting upon the political awareness that in our own time the vast majority of working-class Latina/os and their children continue to be denied the dignity and equal opportunity they have earned.

—NOTES—

INTRODUCTION

1. Quotation accessed at *http://www.rfkmemorial.org/RFK/rfk_quotes.htm* (June 4, 2004).

2. Oscar Zeta Acosta, *Revolt of the Cockroach People* (New York: Vintage, 1989), 68.

3. Santana himself did not receive widespread recognition from a non-Latino public until thirty years later when the "Woodstock generation" was well into middle age. The 1999 "discovery" of Santana by a non-Latino mass audience coincided with the expansion of "Hispanic marketing" into the music industry as a response to changing demographics and a temporary lull in industry profits after the stagnation of hip hop and rap.

4. Rodolfo Acuña, *Occupied America: A History of Chicanos*, 4th ed. (New York: Longman, 2000), 329. The influence of the predominantly white and middle-class counterculture of the 1960s upon the Chicano Movement has been a point of contention ever since the Movement period. In his 1968 campaign for governor of New Mexico, Reies López Tijerina included in his platform the following plank: "I promise to recognize and protect the rights of Hippies and of all those who want to maintain their own personal lifestyle." *El Grito del Norte* (September 16, 1968): 3. By 1974, however, Tijerina lamented the "widespread use of drugs, free sex, and the hippie movement that is perverting the morality of our children. *They Called Me "King Tiger": My Struggle for the Land and Our Rights* (Houston: Arte Público, 2000), 199. Writing in 1975, Edward Murguía saw a direct link between "hippie" and Chicana/o youth subcultures: "By questioning the competitive, stressful, purely materialistic, future-oriented way of life of their parents, counterculture youth have made the cooperative, peaceful, traditional, tribal way of life of Mexican Indian ancestors even more attractive to Chicano militants." *Assimilation, Colonialism and the Mexican American People*, Mexican American Monograph Series 1 (Austin: University of Texas Center for Mexican American Studies, 1975), 97.

In what I can only take to be a tongue-in-cheek improvisation on the hippie-Chicano connection, Luis Valdez offered the following observation: "[The hippies are] reacting against the sterile existence of the middle class . . . and they started doing it with a very Mexican thing—marijuana. You find many conservative Mexicans smoking marijuana. They were born to it; it's something that's been around for centuries." "Chicano Power," *Open City* (March 15–21, 1968): 11.

Elihu Carranza, on the other hand, looked back at the 1960s counterculture as a perilous trap for Chicano/as. If the dominant society had disciplined middle-class hippies for their questioning of the status quo, it had reacted much more violently against movements led by people of color: "If a man abuses his son for things the father preaches and the son practices, what can be expected for the stepson and the 'outsider'? It became evident to many Chicanos that there was no hope for them within a set of values the application of which always placed them *a priori* and arbitrarily at a disadvantage." *Chicanismo: Philosophical Fragments* (Dubuque: Kendall/Hunt, 1978), 17. In a pointed speech delivered to a group of predominantly white antiwar activists in 1971, Brown Beret founder David Sanchez reportedly asked "whether an age of Woodstocks would truly end the oppression of Third World peoples." "Peace Rallies: S.F. Last Month," *Third World* [UC San Diego] (May 7, 1971): 1.

Right-wing ideologues had predictable responses to the Movimiento: "At a time when students were revolting (both literally and figuratively), when Black militants screamed 'Burn, baby, burn!,' and a general disintegration of values within the social fabric occurred, Mexican-Americans, or, according to some, Chicanos, viewed the turmoil as an opportunity to cash in on a good thing." Manuel A. Machado, Jr., *Listen Chicano!: An Informal History of the Mexican-American* (Chicago: Nelson Hall, 1978), 97. Machado's book mounts a vicious attack on César Chávez and articulates an early form of an Hispanic probusiness and proassimilation ethos by combining a conservative agenda with arguments in favor of bilingual education and multicultural curricula.

5. Steven Buechler argues that the period referred to as "the Sixties" stretching from the late 1960s into the early 1970s was in fact a period of decline for U.S. hegemony, a decline signified most clearly in the Viet Nam debacle. Looking back from the present moment of unilateral U.S. military and economic domination, it would be difficult to sustain Buechler's analysis, yet I completely agree that the U.S. war in Southeast Asia marked all domestic social movements in one way or the other. According to Buechler: "If the Vietnam War makes sense only in the context of the ambitions of a global hegemonic power, and if the movements of the 1960s make sense only in the context of the Vietnam War, then the salience of global structures of power such as the world-capitalist system for understanding social movement activism is readily apparent." *Social Movements in Advanced Capitalism: The Political Economy and Cultural Construction of Social Activism* (New York and Oxford: Oxford University Press, 2000), 75.

6. Paul M. Sheldon, "Community Participation and the Emerging Middle Class," in Julian Samora, ed., *La Raza: Forgotten Americans* (Notre Dame and London: University of Notre Dame Press, 1966), 127.

7. Helen Rowan, "*The Mexican American*, a paper prepared for the U.S. Commission on Civil Rights (San Diego: n.p., 1968), 69.

8. Joan W. Moore with Alfredo Cuéllar, *Mexican Americans*, Ethnic Groups in American Life Series (Englewood Cliffs, NJ: Prentice Hall, 1970), 158. According to one account, a federal bureaucrat referred to Mexican Americans as "the most disorganized ethnic group in the country." Helen Rowan, "A Minority Nobody Knows" in John H. Burma, ed., *Mexican-Americans in the United States: A Reader* (Cambridge, MA: Schenkman Publishing Co., 1970): 298.

9. Moore, with Cuéllar, *Mexican Americans*, 149. For the second edition of Moore's book (1976), the section on the Movement written by Cuéllar was dropped and replaced by one written by Harry Pachón. Pachón's text focuses on electoral politics and is silent about the Movement's important links to Third World struggles (e.g., Cuba) that Cuéllar had described.

10. Homer Bigart, "A New Mexican American Militancy," *New York Times* (April 20, 1969): A1. In the same issue, the *Times* offered its readers the following false etymology: "Chicano is never used in Mexico, but in the Southwest it is considered a diminutive of Mexicano, or little Mexican."

11. Carlos Muñoz, Jr., *Youth, Identity, Power: The Chicano Movement* (London and New York: Verso, 1989), 5.

12. "The Chicano Cultural Project since the 1960s: Interview with Michael Dear," in Gustavo Leclerc, Raúl Villa, and Michael J. Dear, eds., *La vida latina en L.A.: Urban Latino Cultures* (Thousand Oaks, CA, and London: Sage Publications in association with the Southern California Studies Center of the University of Southern California, 1999), 23.

13. Gilbert G. Gonzalez and Raul A. Fernandez, *A Century of Chicano History: Empire, Nations, and Migration* (New York and London: Routledge, 2003).

14. For the classic statement on a generational break, see Juan Gómez Quiñones, *Chicano Politics: Reality and Promise, 1940–1990* (Albuquerque: University of New Mexico Press, 1990). Mario T. García argues for more continuity between 1960s activists and their predecessors in *Mexican Americans: Leadership, Ideology, and Identity, 1930–1960* (New Haven and London: Yale University Press, 1989). For a brief but complex analysis of the Movement's origins, see Armando Navarro, *Mexican American Youth Organization: Avant-Garde of the Chicano Movement in Texas* (Austin: University of Texas Press, 1995).

One early Spanish observer provided a succinct observation: "*Más que de evolución y transformación del comportamiento tradicional de los chicanos se puede hablar de explosión, de irrupción violenta de nuevas actitudes, perfectamente justificadas después de años y años de indignación silente y reprimida*" ("More than an evolution or transformation of traditional Chicano behavior, one can speak of an explosion, a violent eruption of new attitudes, perfectly justifiable given the many years of silent and repressed indignation"). Marcelino C. Peñuelas, *Cultura hispánica en Estados Unidos: Los chicanos*, 2d ed. (Madrid: Ediciones Cultura Hispánica del Centro Iberoamericano de Cooperación, 1978), 139.

15. *The Colonizer's Model of the World: Geographical Diffusionism and Eurocentric History* (New York and London: The Guilford Press, 1993).

16. I take the term *window of opportunity* to describe the postwar period from M. Shahid Alam, *Poverty from the Wealth of Nations: Integration and Polarization in the Global Economy since 1760* (New York: St. Martin's Press, 2000), 173 ff.

17. "*El mundo despierta y que todas las viejas afirmaciones no son ahora aceptadas por el solo hecho de haber sido escritas desde hace tiempo. Sino que se exige la ratificación práctica de lo que se afirma, la investigación de lo que se afirma y el análisis científico de lo que afirma. Y de esa inquietud van naciendo las ideas revolucionarias y extendiéndose por el mundo cada vez más.*" Ernesto Che Guevara, "Speech to the Seventh International Conference of Architects," Havana (September 29, 1963) in *Che Guevara habla a la juventud* (New York and London: Pathfinder, 2000), 101.

18. *Spectres of Capitalism: A Critique of Current Intellectual Fashions* (New York: Monthly Review Press, 1998), 40.

19. *The Break-Up of Britain: Crisis and Neo-Nationalism*, 2d ed. (London: Verso, 1981), 347. The direction in which nationalisms develop will depend on specific material and ideological conditions but, as feminist theory has taught us, they are always gendered in ways that tend to privilege traditional forms of masculinity. Anne McClintock, therefore, includes among her four elements of a feminist theory of nationalism: "investigating the gendered formation of sanctioned male theories" [and] "bringing into historical visibility women's active cultural and political participation in national formations." "'No Longer in a Future Heaven': Nationalism, Gender, and Race"

in Geoff Eley and Ronald Grigor Suny, eds., *Becoming National: A Reader* (New York and Oxford: Oxford University Press, 1996), 261.

20. Francisco "Güero" Estrada, "Prison Culture and the Chicano," *La Raza Magazine* 1 (1971): 56.

21. Ibid., 56–57.

22. Nairn, *Break-Up of Britain*, 348. In his discussion of Chicano and Puerto Rican nationalisms, J. Jorge Klor de Alva astutely wrote: "Nationalism as both an ideology and a material force can be either progressive or reactionary." See his "Aztlán, Borinquen and Hispanic Nationalism in the United States" in Rudolfo A. Anaya and Francisco Lomelí, eds., *Aztlán: Essays on the Chicano Homeland* (Albuquerque: University of New Mexico Press, 1991), 141.

23. Robin D. G. Kelley, *Freedom Dreams: The Black Radical Imagination* (Boston: Beacon Press, 2002), ix. Kelley adds: "To write another book that . . . merely chronicles the crimes of radical movements doesn't seem very useful." Another scholar of Black radicalism puts it this way: "It is popular in light of our contemporary awareness of the limits of the racial reforms of the 1960s to disparage the 'minimal acomplishments' of the black movement. Such criticism is both ingenuous and inaccurate." Doug McAdam, *Political Process and the Development of Black Insurgency, 1930–1970* (Chicago and London: University of Chicago Press, 1982), 232.

24. One of the few young scholars who has sought to explain the Movement's positive contributions is Marcial González who writes: "What was right about [Chicano] nationalism was its energy of opposition, its spirit of collectivity, and its insistence on radical change." "Critiques of Nationalism and Contemporary Chicano Literature," paper presented at the (Dis)placing Nationalism Conference, UC Irvine, May 1996.

25. "The Social Psychology of Collective Action" in Aldon D. Morris and Carol McClurg Mueller, eds., *Frontiers in Social Movement Theory* (New Haven: Yale University Press, 1992), 57.

26. Cherríe Moraga, *The Last Generation: Poetry and Prose* (Boston: South End Press, 1993), 148.

27. Ernesto Chávez, *"¡Mi Raza Primero!" (My People First!): Nationalism, Identity, and Insurgency in the Chicano Movement in Los Angeles, 1966–1978* (Berkeley: University of California Press, 2002), 120.

28. Again, my position is that the decline in Chicano/a militancy cannot be attributed to its "ideological bankruptcy." Rather, I would attribute the decline to the consequences of State repression and to contextual factors as stated in the following general principle: "The decline or withering of an extant cycle of protest is due in part to changes in the prevailing cultural climate that render the anchoring master frame impotent." David A. Snow and Robert D. Benford, "Master Frames and Cycles of Protest" in Morris and Mueller, *Frontiers in Social Movement Theory*, 149.

29. Alberto Melucci, *Challenging Codes: Collective Action in the Information Age* (Cambridge: Cambridge University Press, 1996), 324.

30. Arturo Santamaría Gómez, *La política entre México y Aztlán: Relaciones chicano-mexicanas del 68 a Chiapas 94* (Culiacán: Universidad Autónoma de Sinaloa, 1994), p. 313. Santamaría Gómez suggests that anti-Castro Cuban Americans were the chief proponents of Hispanic identities and politics. For a variety of interpretations regarding

Hispanic and related terms, see the special issue "The Politics of Ethnic Construction: Hispanic, Chicano, Latino . . . ?" in *Latin American Perspectives* 19 (Autumn 1992), and especially Suzanne Oboler, *Ethnic Labels, Latino Lives: Identity and the Politics of (Re)presentation in the United States* (Minneapolis: University of Minnesota Press, 1995).

31. Dr. King's remarks on the "Negro middle class" are in *Where Do We Go from Here: Chaos or Community?* (Boston: Beacon Press, 1968), 36.

32. Richard and John Valdez, "Ernesto Galarza Interview," *Chicano Journal* [UC San Diego] (May 5, 1972): 17.

33. Patrick Carey-Herrera, *Chicanismo: Hypothesis, Thesis and Argument* (Torrance, CA: The Martin Press, 1983), 48.

34. Mario Barrera, *Race and Class in the Southwest: A Theory of Racial Inequality* (Notre Dame and London: University of Notre Dame Press, 1979), 216.

35. Nely Galán is quoted in "Nely Courts Controversy," *Hispanic Business* (November 2000): 100.

36. Machado, *Listen, Chicano!*, 96. Machado's book appears to have been funded by Republican Party sources. Large sections of the book are drawn from conservative writer Patty Newman's *Do It Up Brown!*, an attack on the Chicano Movement funded by right-wing organizations in California such as Constructive Action, Inc. (founded in 1963 and bankrolled in part by Walter Knott of amusement-park fame) and the Campus Studies Institute of San Diego, a division of World Research, Inc. (training ground for 1980s neocon Richard Viguerie). Machado's previous research had been on the control of foot-and-mouth disease.

37. I am not referring here to feminist and lesbian/gay critiques of the Movement that were necessary correctives and unrelated to right-wing revisionism. My point is that the neoconservative project to discredit the entire period of the 1960s was facilitated in Chicana/o communities (and continues today) by Hispanic brokers. It was a historical coincidence that the most powerful Chicana and queer rewritings of the Movement appeared during the early years of the neoconservative onslaught.

38. Renato Rosaldo, *Chicano Studies, 1970–1984*, SCCR Working Paper No. 10 (Stanford: Stanford Center for Chicano Research, 1985), 27. Rosaldo favors Américo Paredes's moderate critique of traditional social science over Romano's "strident assault."

39. See Rodolfo F. Acuña, *Sometimes There Is No Other Side: Chicanos and the Myth of Equality* (Notre Dame and London: University of Notre Dame Press, 1998); and Elizabeth "Betita" Martinez, "Brown David v. White Goliath," *Z Magazine* (January 1996): 120.

40. Ben Ehrenreich, "Rolling Back the Years, or Blame It on Brokaw," *L.A. Weekly* (December 14–20, 2001): 22.

41. Ernesto Laclau and Chantal Mouffe, *Hegemony and Socialist Strategy* (London and New York: Verso, 1985), 1.

42. Melucci, *Challenging Codes*, 29. Melucci argues that social movements may be reduced to three fundamental characteristics: "A movement is the mobilization of a collective actor (i) defined by specific solidarity, (ii) engaged in a conflict with an adversary for the appropriation and control of resources valued by both of them, (iii) and whose actions entails a breach of the limits of compatibility of the system within which

the action itself takes place" (29–30). In general terms, all sectors of the Chicano Movement fit this definition individually as does the "Movimiento" in its totality.

43. Raymond Williams, *Marxism and Literature* (Oxford: Oxford University Press, 1977), 55.

44. The case of the Chicano/a adoption of Che Guevara is illustrative of this point. In my interviews with activists, they are often hard pressed to explain what about Guevara attracted them. As I will show in Chapter 3, this inability to articulate ideological affinities is not because Chicano/as merely romanticized Guevara or engaged in copycat actions ("Everybody had a Che poster") but because of the inherent difficulty in objectively analyzing emergent structures of feeling.

45. Michel Foucault, *The Archaeology of Knowledge and The Discourse on Language* (New York: Harper and Row, 1972), 65–66.

Chapter 1

1. Quoted in *Black, Brown and Red: The Movement for Freedom among Black, Chicano, and Indian* (Detroit: News and Letters Committees, 1972), 52.

2. Article II of the 1929 LULAC constitution quoted in Ruth S. Lamb, *Mexican Americans: Sons of the Southwest* (Claremont, CA: Ocelot Press, 1970), 116. Article II also contained a statement that would become more relevant as the militancy of the Chicano Movement increased: "We shall oppose any radical and violent demonstration which may tend to create conflicts and disturb the peace and tranquility of our country."

3. Hector P. García, quoted in "Tio Taco Is Dead," *Newsweek* (June 29, 1970); repr. in Edward Simmen, ed., *Pain and Promise: The Chicano Today* (New York: New American Library, 1972), 128–29.

4. Wolfgang Binder, *"Anglos Are Weird People for Me": Interviews with Chicanos and Puerto Ricans* (Berlin: John F. Kennedy-Institut für Nordamerikastudien Freie Universität Berlin, 1979), 73.

5. Telegram from César Chávez to Mrs. Martin Luther King, Jr., published in *El malcriado* (April 15, 1968): 5.

6. Quoted in Stan Steiner, *La Raza: The Mexican Americans* (New York: Harper and Row, 1969), 195.

7. Gerald Paul Rosen, *Political Ideology and the Chicano Movement: A Study of the Political Ideology of Activists in the Chicano Movement* (San Francisco: R and E Associates, 1975), 55. Rosen's study, in which he interviewed thirty-one activists in East Los Angeles during the period between October 1968 and April 1969, attempts to fit the Movement into established social-science paradigms with only limited success.

8. Juan Gómez Quiñones, *Chicano Politics: Reality and Promise 1940–1990* (Albuquerque: University of New Mexico Press, 1990), 104. The debate around the origins of the term *Chicano* has not subsided. I take the term to be an abbreviated form of the Nahuatl "Mexicano," the etymology agreed upon by most historians. Arnoldo Carlos Vento, however, calls this etymology "an impressionistic and simplistic theory," suggesting that "chicano" derives from the Nahuatl "çhikanni" or "person with great strength, both physical and spiritual." See Vento's *Mestizo: The History, Culture and Politics of the Mexican and the Chicano* (Lanham and New York and Oxford: University Press of America, 1998), 221. Manuel Rojas argues similarly that "chicano" comes from

the Nahuatl "chix-zanotl" or an elite group of men who were guardians of Nahua culture. *Joaquin Murrieta "El Patrio": Truthful Focuses for the Chicano Movement*, trans. Ilsa G. Garza (Blythe: La Cuna Aztlán, 1996), n.p.

9. "The Chicano Movement needs to be placed in the context of what I call the politics of identity or the identity problematic." Carlos Muñoz, Jr., *Youth, Identity, Power: The Chicano Movement* (London and New York: Verso, 1989), 8. Ignacio M. García implicitly argues against Muñoz when he writes: "Its [the Movement's] primary goal was not simply finding an identity, as some have argued, but rather liberating Mexican Americans from racism, poverty, political powerlessness, historical neglect, and internal defeatism. Identity became important to the process, but so did the development of progressive politics." *Chicanismo: The Forging of a Militant Ethos among Mexican Americans* (Tucson: University of Arizona Press, 1998), 133.

I submit that a radical political agenda in the Mexican American context would have been impossible without the simultaneous creation of Chicana/o identities. A refashioned identity was both constituted by and constitutive of progressive politics. The emphasis on a collective identity is crucial, however, in order to avoid the impression that isolated individuals were simply "finding themselves" or "acting out."

The conceptual confusion between collective and individualist projects was widespread in Movement writings. Jesús Chavarría, for example, wrote: "When someone said or wrote anything about being a Chicano or about Aztlán, for the most part, what they were really saying was 'I want to be me' or 'we must be ourselves.'" "Professor Grebler's Book: The Magnum Opus of a Dying Era of Scholarship," *Social Science Quarterly* 52 (June 1971): 14. [11–14] Chavarría's early focus on the individual is revealing given his later conversion to a philosophy of corporate careerism as editor of *Hispanic Business* magazine.

10. John Breuilly, *Nationalism and the State*, 2d ed. (Chicago: University of Chicago Press, 1994), 414.

11. Gloria Anzaldúa's words appear in Ana Louise Keating, ed., *Interviews/Entrevistas* (New York and London: Routledge, 2000), 43.

12. Alberto Melucci's definition of collective identity is helpful here: "In collective action, the construction of identity assumes the character of a process that must be constantly activated if action is to be possible" *Challenging Codes: Collective Action in the Information Age* (Cambridge: Cambridge University Press, 1996), 67.

13. "El Chicano," "¿Qué es el Chicano?," *La voz del pueblo* (April 1970): 2.

14. Ysidro Ramón Macias, "Plan de Political Action for Chicano Campus Groups," document produced at the Political Action workshop at the University of California, Santa Barbara conference, April, 1969; repr. in *El Pocho Che* 1 (April 1970): 42. Macias was a key member of the Third World Liberation Front strike at UC Berkeley, and was clubbed unconscious by police on February 26, 1969. He was also a member of Teatro Campesino and reportedly the originator of the name Movimiento Estudiantil Chicano de Aztlán (MEChA) at the Santa Barbara conference.

In San Diego, California, where Chicano/as were engaged in a fierce political struggle on the local University of California campus (see Chapter 6), columnist Neil Morgan wrote: "There's some apprehension on the UCSD campus over the name changed voted by MAYA, the Mexican-American Youth Association. The new name is MECHA, an acronym for Movimiento Estudiantil Chicano de Aztlan. But the word

"Mecha" in Spanish also means match, fuse or wick." *San Diego Evening Tribune* (September 25, 1969): B1.

15. Vicente Carranza, "Chicanos and the Future with Raza Unida Party," *Caracol* 3 (November 1976): 21. In his analysis of the Raza Unida Party, Juan Gómez Quiñones argues that some of the narrowest forms of nationalism were not nationalism at all but rather "*un fuerte componente de regionalismo chovinista y étnico que se hacía pasar por nacionalismo*" ("a strong component of chauvinistic and ethnic regionalism that was made to pass for nationalism"). "La era de los setenta" in David R. Maciel, ed., *El México olvidado: La historia del pueblo chicano* (Tomo II), Colección Sin Fronteras (Ciudad Juárez and El Paso: Universidad Autónoma de Ciudad Juárez and University of Texas at El Paso, 1996), 244.

16. "This is, I further propose, a peculiarly Texas marriage, born out of our particular history and not to be found, for example, in California, where the situation more closely resembles a battering relationship, with [governor] Pete Wilson as the truly dominant white male." José Limón, *American Encounters* (Boston: Beacon Press, 1998), 161–62.

17. F. Arturo Rosales, *Chicano!: The History of the Mexican American Civil Rights Movement* (Houston: Arte Público Press, 1996), 223.

18. "Generally, students from Northern California expressed a Third-World alignment. They adhered to a sketchy form of socialism and identified their cause not just with oppressed Chicanos, but with other racial minorities in the U.S. and colonized peoples throughout the world; Communist Cuba and China served as inspirations." Rosales, *Chicano!*, 178–79. As we shall see in my chapter on "Lumumba/Zapata College" at the University of California, San Diego, the distinction made here by Rosales between northern and southern California did not always hold.

19. Miguel Abruch Linder, *Movimiento Chicano: Demandas materiales, nacionalismo y tácticas* (Mexico City: Acatlán, 1979), 22–23. Abruch Linder astutely differentiates among Movement organizations: "*Mientras que Chávez se interesó básicamente en los trabajadores agrícolas y la Alianza, con sus elementos místicos y revivalistas, en demandar la devolución de tierras concesionadas siglos atrás, el carácter urbano de la Cruzada y su nacionalismo mezclado con una retórica revolucionaria de izquierda han sido más atractivos para una juventud que vive mayoritariamente en los barrios urbanos*" ("While Chavez basically was interested in farm workers and the Alianza, with its mystical and revivalist elements, was interested in demanding the return of land lost centuries ago, the urban character of the Crusade [for Justice] and its nationalism mixed with leftist revolutionary rhetoric has been more attractive to youth living primarily in urban barrios") (67–68).

20. Given the heterogeneity of contemporary social movements, Melucci has called for scholars to attempt the "de-reification of collective identity." The majority of insurgencies in the late twentieth century (and here I would include the Chicano Movement) "are not 'subjects' that act with the unity of purposes that leaders, ideologues, or opponents attribute to them. They are always plural, ambivalent, often contradictory" (Melucci, *Challenging Codes*, 78).

21. Ibid., 76.

22. Tom Nairn, *The Break-Up of Britain: Crisis and Neo-Nationalism*, 2d ed. (London: Verso, 1981), 339.

23. Quoted in Armando Rendón, "La Raza—Today Not Mañana," *Civil Rights Digest* (Spring 1968): 11.

24. Ibid.: 13. Academic observers of the Movement in the Southwest also predicted violence: "There is good reason to believe some elements of the new Chicano youth movement are fully capable of taking really violent action." Nancie L. Gonzalez, "Positive and Negative Effects of Chicano Militancy on the Education of the Mexican American," *Educational Resources Information Center Reports* (Albuquerque: Southwestern Cooperative Educational Lab, 1970), 18.

25. Ernesto B. Vigil, *The Crusade for Justice: Chicano Militancy and the Government's War on Dissent* (Madison: University of Wisconsin Press, 1999), 50. In 1970, a report by the U.S. Commission on Civil Rights confirmed what Chicano/a activists had been claiming—that people of Mexican descent received "unduly harsh treatment by law enforcement officers, that they are often arrested on insufficient grounds, receive physical and verbal abuse, and penalties which are disproportionately severe." *Mexican Americans and the Administration of Justice in the Southwest* (Washington, D.C.: U.S. Government Printing Office, 1970): iii.

26. Joan W. Moore with Alfredo Cuéllar, *Mexican Americans*, Ethnic Groups in American Life Series (Englewood Cliffs, NJ: Prentice Hall, 1970), 150–51.

27. "Communiqué from Chicano Liberation Front," *Los Angeles Free Press* (August 13, 1971): 5.

28. Memorandum from the FBI Los Angeles office to U.S. Secret Service, Los Angeles office, November 3, 1971, Chicano Liberation Front (CLF) file, no. 105–29512, U.S. Department of Justice, Federal Bureau of Investigation. This file names attorney Oscar Zeta Acosta as the "originator and apparent prime mover of the CLF" (5). A later FBI memo identifies Acosta as "the originator of at least the name CLF, but according to sources, is no longer associated with the group." Memorandum from the Special Agent in Charge, Los Angeles, to the Director, December 8, 1971, Chicano Liberation Front file, no. 105–29512, U.S. Department of Justice, Federal Bureau of Investigation.

29. "Chicano Revolutionary Party Platform and Program: What We Want, What We Believe," *La Chispa*, Oakland, California (January 1971): n.p. Las Gorras Negras or Black Beret organization in New Mexico declared: "We believe armed self-defense and armed struggle are the only means to liberation." "Black Beret Twelve Point Program" (1971); repr. in Gilberto López y Rivas, *The Chicanos: Life and Struggles of the Mexican Minority in the United States* (New York and London: Monthly Review Press, 1973), 162–67.

30. In Chapter 3, I will discuss the influence of the figure of Ernesto Che Guevara and the Cuban Revolution in general on the Chicano/a militant imaginary.

31. "Memorandum for the President;" repr. as "Text of the Moynihan Memorandum on the Status of Negroes," *New York Times* (March 1, 1970): A 69.

32. Richard Shaffer, "The Angry Chicanos, Deepening Frustration of Mexican-Americans Stirs Fears of Violence," *The Wall Street Journal* (June 11, 1970): A 1.

33. Ibid.

34. See Ernesto Vigil, *Crusade for Justice*; and Edward Escobar, "The Dialectics of Repression: The Los Angeles Police Department and the Chicano Movement, 1968–1971," *The Journal of American History* (March 1993): 1483–1514. .

35. Non-COINTELPRO operations were conducted against Native American, Asian American, and Arab American organizations during the Viet Nam war era. See Ward Churchill and Jim Vander Wall, *The Cointelpro Papers: Documents from the FBI's*

Secret Wars against Dissent in the United States, South End Press Classics Series, Volume 8 (Boston: South End Press, 2002).

36. "A Special Supplement: The Chicanos," *New York Review of Books* 19 (August 31, 1972): 15. Rudolph O. de la Garza criticized Womack in a letter to the editor to which Womack replied in *New York Review of Books* 20 (April 19, 1973): 42. Womack's phrase "only another ethnic movement" gained new life in the late 1990s when historians and museum curators began to refer to the Movimiento as an example of "identity politics." In my opinion, this grossly oversimplifies the Movement's ideological complexity.

37. Interview with Octavio Paz in *La voz del pueblo*, Berkeley, California (July-August 1971): 16.

38. Ibid.

39. Jorge Bustamante, "El Movimiento Chicano y Su Relevancia para los Mexicanos" in James W. Wilkie, Michael C. Meyer, Edna Monzón de Wilkie, eds., *Contemporary Mexico*, Papers of the IV International Congress of Mexican History (Berkeley: University of California Press, 1976), 534.

40. Breuilly, *Nationalism and the State,* 420. Although Breuilly defines nationalism as primarily a political phenomenon, he disagrees with Tom Nairn who emphasizes the importance of class struggle in nationalist movements. Nairn argues that nationalism arises among populations with a strong sense of disenfranchisement. As Breuilly summarizes Nairn's position: "Nationalism, which in a sense is a glorification of that population, provides a means of mobilising that population behind such political action. As the lines of economic division usually coincide with divisions of language, culture, race or religion, these can be employed to create a common identity to support such action" (412).

41. Nairn, *Break-Up of Britain*, 332.

42. Dionne Espinoza, "Pedagogies of Nationalism and Gender: Cultural Resistance in Selected Representational Practices of Chicana/o Movement Activists, 1967–1972" (Ph.D. diss., Cornell University, 1996), 34. See also Dionne Espinoza, "'Revolutionary Sisters': Women's Solidarity and Collective Identification among Chicana Brown Berets in East Los Angeles, 1967–1970," *Aztlán: A Journal of Chicano Studies* 26 (Spring 2001): 17–58. For an interesting analysis of "nationalism" and gender (using literary texts as evidence), see Montye P. Fuse, "Powerful Positionings: Intersections of Language, Ideology and Politics in African American and Chicano 'Nationalist' Narratives" (Ph.D. diss., University of California at Berkeley, 1997). My thanks to David G. Gutiérrez for bringing Fuse's dissertation to my attention.

43. Angie Chabram and Rosalinda Fregoso, "Chicana/o Cultural Representations: Reframing Alternative Critical Discourses," Special issue: "Chicana/o Cultural Representations: Reframing Alternative Critical Discourses, *Cultural Studies* 4 (October 1990): 205–6.

44. Espinoza, *Pedagogies of Nationalism and Gender,* 34.

45. In terms of the ways in which historians have tended to erase the ideological heterogeneity of organizations, Richard García's description of changes within the Crusade for Justice is interesting. By focusing on Corky Gonzales as leader of the Crusade, García argued that Gonzales's "extreme nationalism was then grafted onto a Marxist-socialist philosophy in the early seventies." While at the individual level this may have been the case, I would argue that what took place organizationally was less a

"graft" than the emergence of subordinated agendas already present. This would explain why a "nationalist" such as Gonzales could espouse an internationalist and anti-imperialist position against the Viet Nam war as early as 1966. See García's "The Chicano Movement and the Mexican American Community, 1972–1978: An Interpretive Essay," *Socialist Review* 40–41 (July–October 1978): 120.

46. Peter Cirilio Salazar, "The Social Origins of Chicano Nationalism: Class and Community in the Making of Aztlán, 1800–1920" in Reynaldo Flores Macías, ed., *Perspectivas en Chicano Studies I*, Papers presented at the third annual meeting of the National Association of Chicano Social Science (Los Angeles: UCLA Chicano Studies Center, 1977), 204–5.

47. A great deal of the confusion surrounding the term *Chicano nationalism* has its origins in the debate that took place in the late 1970s over the usefulness of the "internal-colonialism" model for Chicano history and whether or not the Movimiento was an anticolonialist movement of national liberation. For a representative example of this debate, see Fred A. Cervantes, "Chicanos as a Postcolonial Minority: Some Questions Concerning the Adequacy of the Paradigm of Internal Colonialism" in Macías, *Perspectivas en Chicano Studies I*, 123–35. By separating out the cultural component of the Movement and noting a shift from anticolonialist (or national separatist) to reformist agendas, Cervantes was able to argue: "The reformist thrust of progressive Chicano politics suggests that Chicano nationalism is not a very important political factor in and of itself" (131).

Another publication that contributed to an exaggerated emphasis on "nationalism" was Rudolfo A. Anaya and Francisco Lomelí, eds., *Aztlán: Essays on the Chicano Homeland* (Albuquerque: University of New Mexico Press, 1991). By focusing on the slippery signifier "Aztlán" and by reproducing imprecise usages of "nationalism," some of the authors in the collection posited unusual political divisions within the Movement. J. Jorge Klor de Alva, for example, opposed "cultural nationalist humanists" (i.e., literature and arts faculty) to "Marxist social scientists," while Rudolfo Anaya imagined rival factions composed of "cultural nationalists" and "political activists."

48. García, in "Chicano Movement and the Mexican American Community," characterized the "era of nationalism" as one based on "emotionalism and activism" and the "era of ideology" as one of "intellectualism and contemplation' (122). Despite what appears to be a rather artificial chronology, García himself warned: "These periods are not synchronic mechanical divisions, but diachronic overlapping processes" (124).

49. I first suggested that scholars may need to "denationalize" the Chicano Movement and begin to investigate the Movement's internationalist sectors in "Cultural Nationalism and Internationalism in the Chicano Movement, 1965–1975," a paper delivered at the National Association of Chicano and Chicana Studies conference, Portland, Oregon in March 2000.

The research of Maylei Blackwell on the genealogy of Third World women's organizing will be an important contribution. Blackwell limits the term *internationalism* to signify state-sponsored projects and uses *transnational imaginary* to describe networks of non-state-sponsored solidarity work.

50. Alex Callinicos, "Toni Negri in Perspective" in Gopal Balakrishnan, ed., *Debating Empire* (London and New York: Verso, 2003), 136.

51. Alicia Gaspar de Alba, *Chicano Art inside/outside the Master's House: Cultural Politics and the CARA Exhibition* (Austin: University of Texas Press, 1998), xiii.

52. Manuel G. Gonzales, *Mexicanos: A History of Mexicans in the United States* (Bloomington: Indiana University Press, 2000), 1. Gonzales complains bitterly about "denunciations and charges of backsliding from the old sixties militants who continue to dominate ethnic studies departments" (2), their "lack of objectivity" (4), and their portrayal of Chicana/os as "monolithic victim" (5). According to Gonzales, "Historians need to approach their subject in the context of objectivity" (5). Gonzales's account of the Movement is hardly objective. For a more balanced narrative (assuming "balance" is one's preference), see Matt S. Meier and Feliciano Ribera, *Mexican Americans/American Mexicans: From Conquistadores to Chicanos* (New York: Hill and Wang, 1993), especially 209–32.

Gonzales mounts an especially harsh critique of Rodolfo Acuña, whom Gonzales calls "an intellectual who has lost touch with the times" (4). Gonzales disapproves of Acuña's seminal *Occupied America* because it was "purportedly a history of Chicanos [but] was actually a history of Chicano-Anglo relations" (4). It is difficult to imagine how any serious history of Mexicans in the United States could not be "a history of Chicano-Anglo relations."

53. Refugio I. Rochín and Dennis N. Valdés, eds., *Voices of a New Chicana/o History* (East Lansing: Michigan State University Press, 2000). The analytical frame of the collection—"paradigm shifts"—is taken from Thomas Kuhn's *The Structure of Scientific Revolutions*, a book widely perceived in the 1970s to be a challenge to traditional understandings of historical change. In literature departments, Michel Foucault's theories of epistemological rupture and "archeology" quickly displaced Kuhn's influence. By the 1980s poststructuralist readings of history had challenged the very idea of linear narrative itself. As we might expect, in traditional history departments Foucault was viewed with extreme suspicion and even today is rarely invoked.

54. Ignacio M. García, "Chicano Studies since 'El Plan de Santa Bárbara,'" in David R. Maciel and Isidro D. Ortiz, eds., *Chicanas/Chicanos at the Crossroads: Social, Economic, and Political Change* (Tucson: University of Arizona Press, 1996), 195. García's decision to reproduce 1970s rhetoric ("poverty, political powerlessness, and a collective identity crisis") rather than updating his language in order to speak to contemporary forms of oppression exacerbated the sense that he advocated a "return" to a time long past.

55. Ibid., 196.

56. The most lucid commentary on the new corporate university is Bill Readings, *The University in Ruins* (Cambridge and London: Harvard University Press, 1996). As Readings taught us: "The University is no longer simply modern, insofar as it no longer needs a grand narrative of culture in order to work. As a bureaucratic institution of excellence, it can incorporate a very high degree of internal variety without requiring its multiplicity of diverse idioms to be unified into an ideological whole. Their unification is no longer a matter of ideology but of their exchange-value within an expanded market" (168). In other words, Chicana/o studies programs can be easily accommodated as one more choice for the student/consumer but can expect reprisals (e.g., budget and staffing cuts, consolidation into Ethnic or American studies, etc.) the minute it seeks to challenge or even question the institutional status quo. On the origins of the corporate

university, see also Masao Miyoshi, "Ivory Tower in Escrow," *boundary 2* (Spring 2000): 8–50; Christopher Newfield, *Ivy and Industry: Business and the Making of the American University, 1880–1980* (Durham: Duke University Press, 2003); Derek Bok, *Universities in the Marketplace: The Commercialization of Higher Education* (Princeton and Oxford: Princeton University Press, 2003).

57. María E. Montoya, "Beyond Internal Colonialism: Gender, Ethnicity, and Class as Challenges to Chicano Unity" in Rochín and Valdés, *Voices of a New Chicana/o History*, 192.

58. Francisco Santana, "The Race," in *Tristealegría: Poems* (Tempe, Arizona: Bilingual Press/Editorial Bilingüe, 1991), 7.

CHAPTER 2

1. Although not as central as Mexican and Cuban revolutionary heroes, the figure of Sandino would reappear in Chicano Movement discourse throughout the Viet Nam war period. Ernesto Vigil recalls that Nicaraguan poet Roberto Vargas distributed posters of Sandino at the first Chicano Youth Liberation Conference in March 1969, and lectured on his role in Latin American history. *The Crusade for Justice: Chicano Militancy and the Government's War on Dissent* (Madison: University of Wisconsin Press, 1999), 96.

2. It has been suggested to me that the activism of Betita Martinez was primarily with Black civil-rights groups and less with Chicano Movement organizations. While this may have been true early in her career, I would argue that she (and others) must be included in any inclusive rethinking of Chicano/a militancy in the Viet Nam war period, especially if we are to understand Chicano/a internationalist, Chicana feminist, and "leftist" positions.

3. Valdez said: "Our ideology is in this earth, this continent." Stan Steiner, *La Raza: The Mexican Americans* (New York: Harper and Row, 1970), 90. Several years later during the Lumumba-Zapata experiment at the University of California, San Diego (see Chapter 6), African American student leader Sam Jordan wrote a vigorous class-based critique of what he called "reactionary nationalism," pointing out to Chicanos who based their identity on a glorified Aztec past: "Moctezuma didn't pick maiz.... In this manner, we expose those who see the future in the past." "Letter to BSC/MEChA members and officers" (n.d.), UCSD MSC, Third College files (Dorn project).

4. Dionne Espinoza, "Pedagogies of Nationalism and Gender: Cultural Resistance in Selected Representational Practices of Chicana/o Movement Activists, 1967–1972" (Ph.D. diss., Cornell University, 1996), especially Chapter 3. In my opinion, Espinoza's research is the best to date on the ways in which the complex field of Movement discourses and practices was experienced by women activists.

5. Ignacio M. García writes: "Barrio activists were more concerned with racial discrimination and cultural genocide and regarded participation in international struggles to be political deviancy." *Chicanismo: The Forging of a Militant Ethos among Mexican Americans* (Tucson: University of Arizona Press, 1997), 86. As I hope to show, this is too sweeping a generalization. On pre-1960s Mexican American internationalist positions, see Ben V. Olguín, "Barrios of the World Unite!: Regionalism, Transnationalism, and Internationalism in Tejano War Poetry from the Mexican Revolution to World War II," in

Bill Mullen, ed., *Left of the Color Line: Race, Radicalism, and Twentieth-Century Literature of the United States* (Durham: University of North Carolina Press, 2003), 107–40.

It is useful to recall Juan Gómez Quiñones's point that some of the more narrow forms of "Chicano nationalism" were not nationalism at all but rather "*un fuerte componente de regionalismo chovinista y étnico que se hacía pasar por nacionalismo*" ("a strong dose of chauvinist and ethnic regionalism that was made to pass for nationalism"). "La era de los setenta," in David R. Maciel, ed., *El México olvidado: La historia del pueblo chicano* (Tomo II), Colección Sin Fronteras (Ciudad Juárez and El Paso: Universidad Autónoma de Ciudad Juárez and University of Texas at El Paso, 1996), 244.

6. On the NCMC, see George Mariscal, *Aztlán and Viet Nam: Chicano and Chicana Experiences of the War* (Berkeley: University of California Press, 1999); Ernesto Chávez, *"¡Mi Raza Primero!" (My People First!): Nationalism, Identity, and Insurgency in the Chicano Movement in Los Angeles, 1966–1978* (Berkeley: University of California Press, 2002); and the comprehensive study by Lorena Oropeza, *¡Raza Sí! ¡Guerra No!: Chicano Protest and Patriotism during the Viet Nam War Era* (Berkeley: University of California Press, 2005).

7. Ignacio M. García, *Chicanismo*, 171.

8. The complete poem is reproduced in Tino Villanueva, ed., *Chicanos: Antología histórica y literaria*, 2d ed. (Mexico City: Fondo de Cultura Económica, 1994), 340.

9. Antonio Gomez, "Un solo mundo," *Con safos* 3 (1970): 6.

10. Enriqueta Longeaux y Vásquez, "La santa tierra," *El Grito del Norte* (December 1970); repr. in Antonia Castañeda Shular, Tomás Ybarra Frausto, and Joseph Sommers, eds., *Literatura Chicana: Texto y Contexto* (Englewood Cliffs, NJ: Prentice Hall, 1972), 267–69.

11. Ibid., 268. See the collection of Longeaux y Vásquez's writings, *Despierten Hermanos! Awaken Brothers and Sisters!* , ed. Dionne Espinoza and Lorena Oropeza (Houston: Arte Público Press, forthcoming).

12. Gomez, "Un solo mundo," 5.

13. Reies López Tijerina, Interview with Elsa Knight Thompson, April 5, 1968; repr. in F. Arturo Rosales, ed., *Testimonio: A Documentary History of the Mexican American Struggle for Civil Rights*, Hispanic Civil Rights Series (Houston: Arte Público Press, 2000), 318. In a 1971 interview, Tijerina stated: "South America will become very close, close, close to Southwest bilingual people because they will need us in order to relate to the Anglo who is more becoming isolated by the world." *La voz del pueblo*, Berkeley, California (December 1971): 5.

14. "¡¡Cuídate, Méjico!!" (1979), in Rodolfo "Corky" Gonzales, *Message to Aztlán: Selected Writings*, ed. Antonio Esquibel, Hispanic Civil Rights Series (Houston: Arte Público Press, 2001), 224–25.

15. The Paz interview is in *La voz del pueblo* (July-August, 1971): 16.

16. Jorge Bustamante, "El Movimiento Chicano y Su Relevancia para los Mexicanos," in James W. Wilkie, Michael C. Meyer, Edna Monzón de Wilkie, eds., *Contemporary Mexico*, Papers of the IV International Congress of Mexican History (Berkeley: University of California Press, 1976), 535 and 541.

17. Gonzales, *Message to Aztlán*, 212–13.

18. Armando Rendón, *Chicano Manifesto* (New York: Macmillan, 1971), 307; 318. In a later essay, Rendón refers to "Hispanics" as a "built-in transnational people" and

asserted that for Chicano/as, "Out of an aroused nationalism has come, inevitably, a mounting interest in world politics." "Latinos: Breaking the Cycle of Survival to Tackle Global Affairs," in Abdul Aziz Said, ed., *Ethnicity and U.S. Foreign Policy* (New York: Praeger, 1981), 183. [183–200]

19. Vicente Carranza, "The Third World Struggle with a Chicano Perspective," *Caracol* 2 (September 1975/August 1976): 74.

20. Erin Texeira, "Justice Is Not Color Blind, Studies Find," *Los Angeles Times* (May 22, 2000): B1.

21. Gregory Rodriguez, *Los Angeles Times* on-line edition (August 20, 2000).

22. Chicano/a scholars began to use the term *cultural nationalism* at least as early as 1970. See Alfredo Cuéllar, "Perspective on Politics," in Joan W. Moore and Alfredo Cuéllar, *Mexican Americans* (New York: Prentice Hall, 1970), 148–56; repr. as "Cultural Nationalism in the Southwest" in Cuéllar, *Viewpoints: Red and Yellow, Black and Brown* (Minneapolis: Winston Press, 1972), 295–300.

23. "Plan espiritual de Aztlán," *Punto* 1 (March 1969). Quoted in Vigil, *Crusade for Justice*, 100.

24. Rodolfo Acuña, *Occupied America: A History of Chicanos*, 4th ed. (New York: Longman, 2000), 358.

25. The key texts documenting sexism in the Movement continue to be those written by contemporary Chicana activists. See Adelaida R. Del Castillo, "Mexican Women in Organization" in Magdalena Mora and Adelaida Del Castillo, eds., *Mexican Women in the U.S.: Struggles Past and Present*, Occasional paper no. 2 (Los Angeles: Chicano Studies Research Center Publications, University of California, 1980), 7–16; and the collected documents in Alma M. García, ed., *Chicana Feminist Thought: The Basic Historical Writings* (New York and London: Routledge, 1997).

26. I. M. García, *Chicanismo*, 105.

27. On the function of "la familia" in Movement culture, see Richard T. Rodríguez, *Reimagined Communities* (Durham: Duke University Press, forthcoming).

28. Espinoza, "Pedagogies of Nationalism and Gender," especially chapter 2. Espinoza convincingly argues: "The ambiguity of Chicano cultural nationalist philosophy in its nascent phase enabled strategic moments and modes of empowerment for women Berets, even as patriarchal and sexist cultural values permeated the milieu" (191). See also Espinoza's "'Revolutionary Sisters': Women's Solidarity and Collective Identification among Chicana Brown Berets in East Los Angeles, 1967–1970," *Aztlan* 26 (Spring 2001): 17–58.

29. A focus on individual behavior or single literary texts, e.g. Oscar Zeta Acosta and his *Revolt of the Cockroach People* (1973), can produce especially distorted representations of the Movement. Although the analysis of *Revolt* by Carl Gutiérrez Jones is an inventive one (filtered through Eve Sedgewick's theory of homosocial desire), it overly privileges Acosta's idiosyncratic conflation of Chicano activism and machismo/sexism and thus implicitly transforms a figure who was marginal to most Chicano organizations (Acosta) into one of the Movimiento's principal ideologues. *Rethinking the Borderlands: Between Chicano Culture and Legal Discourse* (Berkeley: University of California Press, 1995).

30. Vigil, in *Crusade for Justice*, writes: "Gonzales believed nationalism should, and would, transcend those factors that divided Chicanos. Leftists and many intellectuals at the youth conference, however, argued that 'La Raza' itself was divided into classes with

divergent interests, and that, at its worst, primitive nationalism could be racist. For them, nationalism alone would not transcend class privilege and bias. The *Plan* did not address these issues" (100).

31. Richard García, "The Chicano Movement and the Mexican American Community, 1972–1978: An Interpretive Essay," *Socialist Review* 40–41 (July–October 1978): 108.

32. David G. Gutiérrez translates "*Por la Raza todo, Fuera de la Raza nada*" as "For the [Chicano] people everything; for [non-Chicanos] nothing." *Walls and Mirrors: Mexican Americans, Mexican Immigrants, and the Politics of Ethnicity* (Berkeley: University of California Press, 1995), 185. As we shall see in this book, the focus on one's own community did not necessarily preclude many Movement organizations from working with non-Chicanos. Gutiérrez's translation was the one preferred by conservative pundits who attacked the Chicano/a student organization MECha during the late 1990s and early 2000s.

33. Nigel Harris, *National Liberation* (Reno: University of Nevada Press, 1990), 13. Alurista recalled in a 1981 interview: "The myth of Aztlán, as I saw it in the 1960s, was just a way to identify a people, a land, and a consciousness that said, 'Struggle. Do not be afraid.'" "'Mitólogos y mitómanos,' Mesa Redonda." *Maize* 4 (1981), 23.

34. Tomás Ybarra-Frausto, "The Chicano Cultural Project since the 1960s: Interview with Michael Dear," in Gustavo Leclerc, Raúl Villa, and Michael J. Dear, eds., *La vida latina en L.A.: Urban Latino Cultures* (Thousand Oaks, CA, and London: Sage Publications in association with the Southern California Studies Center of the University of Southern California, 1999), 29–30. [23–34]

35. Elihu Carranza, *Chicanismo: Philosophical Fragments* (Dubuque: Kendall/Hunt, 1978), 11. In a self-critical move not typical of contemporary essayists, Carranza argued that an essential part of the Chicano's "cultural revolt" was "an honest self-examination to determine what in his heritage must be cast aside and what is of value for this time" (12).

36. "Statement of the Revolutionary Caucus," Denver Chicano Youth Liberation Conference, in *El Poche Che* 1 (April 1969): n.p.

37. Ysidro Ramón Macias, "Plan de Political Action for Chicano Campus Groups," document produced at the Political Action workshop at the University of California, Santa Barbara conference, April 1969, in. *El Pocho Che* 1 (April 1970): 44.

38. Ibid. As we will see many times in this book, the issue of coalition building was a controversial one throughout the Movimiento period. In the same document, Macias argues: "If a coalition becomes too burdensome or conflicting with partners, a way out should be reserved for the Chicano group. . . . Subservience to any other group is not to be tolerated" (48).

39. Ibid. Later accounts have ignored these kinds of texts and have sought to portray coalition building as a tactic that did not arise until the 1980s. Gloria Anzaldúa, for example, claimed in a 1991 interview: "Our nationalism is one with a twist. It's no longer the old kind of 'I'm separated from anything to do with blacks or with Asians or whatever.' It's saying, 'Yes, I belong. I come from this particular tribe, but I'm open to interacting with these other people.' I call this the New Tribalism." In Ana Louise Keating, ed., *Interviews/Entrevistas* (New York and London: Routledge, 2000), 185. As I hope to

have shown in this chapter, many Movement organizations in the late 1960s and 1970s already were promoting cross-ethnic alliances and international solidarity.

40. Anonymous, "Nationalism Dangerous," *Third World* [UC San Diego] (January 27, 1971): 2.

41. Anonymous, "Chicano Nationalism Indispensable," *La vida nueva* 1 (April 30, 1969): 2.

42. Ibid.

43. Anonymous, "UC-MECHA Conference," *Prensa popular* [UC San Diego] 1 (November 26, 1973): 2. The author who summarized the UC Riverside conference reported that it had been disrupted by "infiltration and manipulation by the YSA-SWP groups" and declared: "Thus ends the history and the life of Mecha, an organization once valid in its action for the time but unable to change and accept the reality of the class nature of our society" (2).

44. Luis Pingarrón, "Cultural Nationalism: A Fight for Survival—The Language," *Chicano Student Movement* (August 1969): 3.

45. Frobén Lozada, speech delivered at California State University-Hayward on November 13, 1968. Quoted in Gilberto López y Rivas, *Los chicanos: una minoría nacional explotada* (Mexico City: Editorial Nuestro Tiempo, 1971), 93–94. A member of the Socialist Workers Party, Lozada had begun his activist career in the Civil Rights Movement, having participated in the march on Selma in 1965. After organizing in south Texas during the late 1960s, he became director of Latin American Studies at Merritt College in Oakland, California, and a candidate for the Berkeley school board in 1969. See *La voz del pueblo* (October 1970): 6.

46. La Simpática, "Viva La Raza!," *The Movement* (July 1969): 6.

47. Elizabeth "Betita" Martinez, "Viva La Chicana and All Brave Women of La Causa," *El Grito del Norte* 4 (June 5, 1971); repr. in A. García, ed., *Chicana Feminist Thought.*

48. Rodolfo Corky Gonzales, in *La voz del pueblo*, Berkeley, California (June 1971): 4.

49. I take the term *translocal* from Jan Nederveen Pieterse, who defines it as an "outward-looking sense of place" or a "global sense of place." It was this opening outward that accounts for attempts by Chicano/a activists to transcend narrow nationalism in order to form coalitions such as those discussed in my section on Tijerina (Chapter 5) and those which led to expressions of solidarity with Cuba, the Mexican student movement, and the anti-imperialist struggle in Viet Nam. See Jan Nederveen Pieterse, "Globalization as Hybridization" in Mike Featherstone, Scott Lash, and Roland Robertson, eds., *Global Modernities* (London: Sage, 1995), 61.

50. Anonymous, "Cultural Nationalism Indispensable," *La vida nueva* 1 (April 30, 1969): 2.

51. Rodolfo Corky Gonzales, "Message to El Congreso on Land and Cultural Reform" (1972), in Christine Marín, *A Spokesman of the Mexican American Movement: Rodolfo "Corky" Gonzales and the Fight for Chicano Liberation* (San Francisco: R and E Research Associates, 1977), 49.

52. Macias, in his "Plan de political Action," warned that some Chicano/as might "sell out the objectives of the student group if they feel they may profit from concessions offered by the establishment" (46).

53. Anonymous, "Cultural Nationalism Indispensable," *La vida nueva* 1 (April 30, 1969): 2.

54. John Ortiz, "On Ideological Conflicts, " *Regeneración* 2 (1971): 18.

55. Ibid.

56. Ibid.

57. Eldridge Cleaver, "Interview from Exile," *The Black Panther* (October 11, 1969); repr. in Philip S. Foner, ed., *The Black Panthers Speak* (New York: Da Capo, 1995), 108–17.

58. Personal communication from María Blanco (August 3, 2001).

59. Michael Abramson and the Young Lords Party, *Palante: Young Lords Party* (New York: McGraw-Hill, 1971), 68.

60. Interview with Cha Cha Jimenez, Chairman of the Young Lords, in *The Movement* (November 1969): 13.

61. Tony Martinez, "Basta Ya!," *The Movement* (November 1969): 3. The women of the Young Lords were notable for successfully reducing sexist practices in the organization. See the documentary by Iris Morales, *¡Palante, Siempre Palante!: The Young Lords* (New York: Third World Newsreel, 1996).

62. Abramson, *Palante*, 150.

63. Refusing to attend the meeting were Representatives Henry B. Gonzales and Eligio de la Garza of Texas. The *Washington Post* referred to conference organizers as a "Spanish coalition." See "Spanish Coalition Asks Probe of Alleged Police Gang Rape" (October 24, 1971): A3; and "U.S. Latin Coalition Plans Convention" (October 26, 1971): A2.

64. See Armando Rendón, "Latinos: Breaking the Cycle of Survival to Tackle Global Affairs," in Chris F. García, ed., *Latinos and the Political System* (Notre Dame, IN: University of Notre Dame Press, 1987), 188. The slow process of educating Chicana/o youth about the histories and cultures of other Latino groups has yet to bear fruit. In 2000, a Chicana student declared to a colleague of mine that she had little in common with Puerto Rican students because "they were never colonized like we were."

65. See Philip Vera Cruz, *A Personal History of Filipino Immigrants and the Farmworkers Movement*, ed. Craig Scharlin and Lilia V. Villanueva, 3d ed. (Seattle and London: University of Washington Press, 2000).

66. Anonymous, "Forging a United Front," *La familia de la Raza* (May 1, 1972): 20–21. Thirty years later, Chinese American essayist Richard Chang argued that Asian/Chicano political alliances had their origins in the material history of the Bering Land Bridge and the ancient civilizations of the Americas. "The Asian American Road to Aztlán," *The Orange County Register*, on-line edition (May 13, 2001).

67. Bob Garcia, "Chicano Appraises the Old Left," *Open City* (November 10–16, 1967): 13. The CP (USA) during the Viet Nam war period did in fact include members of Mexican descent. In Los Angeles, for example, CP members Lorenzo Torres and Evelina Alarcón operated the Instituto del Pueblo on the Eastside.

68. *Indicator* [UC San Diego] (April 16, 1969): 2.

69. See Oropeza, *¡Raza Sí! ¡Guerra No!*, 2005.

70. René Nuñez is quoted in "Chicano Speaks at Free Angela Teach-in," *La Verdad*, San Diego, California (April 1971): 5.

71. Thomas Martinez, "Chicanismo," *Epoca: National Concilio for Chicano Studies Journal* 1 (Winter 1971): 35–39. Martinez's essay contains an interesting argument that

"Chicano time" is a product of Chicano/a consciousness's lack of concern about the future.

72. Ibid., 37.

73. "El Gavilán," "Honkyism: A Satire," *El Chicano*, San Bernardino, California, (July 3, 1970): 3.

74. See *Fifteenth Report of the Senate Fact-finding Subcommittee on Un-American Activities* (Sacramento: Senate of the State of California, 1970), 66 ff.; and Acuña, *Occupied America*, 512, n. 149. By the early 1970s, Cruz Olmeda was a member of the August 29 Movement and the Labor Committee. At a May 18, 1974, meeting at the University of California, Irvine campus, Olmeda reportedly argued that Chicano culture would fully develop only in a socialist society. See *Prensa popular* (UC San Diego) (May 1974): n.p. Acuña points out that other Chicano community groups such as the League of United Citizens to Help Addicts (LUCHA) were opposed to any form of "Third World" internationalism and given to red-baiting. *Occupied America*, 381.

75. See Espinoza, "Revolutionary Sisters," on the formation of "Las Adelitas de Aztlán" after February 1970.

76. Ibid., 84.

77. "On the Black or White Revolutionary's Relation to the Chicano Struggle," *La Causa* 2 (March 1970): 7. The nationalist/internationalist split within the Beret organization was often played out in the pages of *La Causa* with Prime Minister David Sanchez representing the former position and Agustín "Chris" Cebada the latter. Although this article is unsigned, Sanchez may have authored it. See Espinoza, "Revolutionary Sisters," 145 n. 118.

78. "On the Black or White Revolutionary's Relation to the Chicano Struggle," 7.

79. Ibid.

80. Carlos Montes, "The Brown Berets: Young Chicano Revolutionaries," *Fight Back!* 6 (Winter 2003).

81. Corky Gonzales is quoted in *La voz del pueblo*, Berkeley, California (June 1971): 5. The belief held by some Chicano/a activists that socialism and communism were "white" systems was complicated by the Movement's fascination with the Cuban experiment. This dilemma forced writers to distinguish between "comunismo blanco" and its Chinese, Latin American, or African variants. See Anonymous, "Tercer Mundo," *¡Es tiempo!* (June 1972): 5.

82. R. García, "Chicano Movement and the Mexican American Community, ": 134 n. 8.

83. Ibid.: 120–21.

84. Excerpts from the *Papel Chicano* article and responses were published in *The Militant* (July 7, 1972): 16–17.

85. Ibid.

86. By the mid-1970s, a wide array of splinter "revolutionary" groups competed for the attention of Chicana/o youth with only limited success. Many of them, such as the August 29th Collective or August 29th Movement (ATM), had their origins in earlier nationalist organizations. Internal dissension with regard to political objectives and ideologies led one group of Los Angeles Brown Berets to form a Labor Committee for the Raza Unida Party that eventually became the core group for the collective. The ATM eventually formed the League of Revolutionary Struggle with three other collectives—

La Raza Workers Collective, which had grown out of the Los Siete de la Raza issue; the East Bay Labor Collective; and the Albuquerque Collective.

All of these organizations struggled to distinguish themselves from competing groups, a process that produced doctrinaire charges of collaborationism and reformism and an insistence on a "correct party line." See the essay by R. García, "Chicano Movement and the Mexican American Community"; Jorge Mariscal, "Left Turns in the Chicano Movement, 1965–1975," *Monthly Review* 54 (July–August 2002): 59–68; *Statements on the Founding of the League of Revolutionary Struggle* (Marxist-Leninist) (n.p: Getting Together Publications, 1978).

87. "Class Struggle Main Theme of Chicano Conference," *Prensa Popular* (March 5, 1974): 3.

88. A reevaluation of Chicano/a internationalism permits us to escape the false dichotomies posited in recent accounts of the Movement between the "locally political" and the "universally cultural" or the "extremes of nationalism and socialism." The binary "locally political"/"universally cultural" is presented in Elyette Andouard Labarthe, "The Vicissitudes of Aztlán," *Confluencia* 5 (Spring 1990): 79–84. The phrase "extremes of nationalism and socialism" is in F. Arturo Rosales, *Chicano!: The History of the Mexican American Civil Rights Movement* (Houston: Arte Público Press, 1997), 268.

89. José Angel Gutiérrez, *The Making of a Chicano Militant: Lessons from Cristal* (Madison: University of Wisconsin Press, 1998), 241. At the August 1973 La Raza Unida Party conference, delegates held discussions about the function of "nationalism" as "a tool to educate towards internationalism."

90. Arturo Santamaría Gómez, *La política entre México y Aztlán: Relaciones chicano-mexicanas del 68 a Chiapas 94* (Culiacán: Universidad Autónoma de Sinaloa, 1994), 60. Echeverría had met previously with Reies López Tijerina in order to discuss the land-grant issue. Echeverría's immediate successor, José López Portillo, continued to meet with José Angel Gutiérrez. In private, however, he reportedly argued that the Mexican government should not become involved with Chicano issues. See ibid., 106.

91. Armando Navarro, *La Raza Unida Party: A Chicano Challenge to the U.S. Two-Party Dictatorship* (Philadelphia: Temple University Press, 2000), 257–58.

92. Mario Cantú is quoted in *Prensa popular* 1 (January 29, 1974): 14.

93. Gutiérrez, *Making of a Chicano Militant*, 237–41. This brief section of Gutiérrez's autobiography is titled "Internationalizing the Chicano Movement." Within Chicano/a activist circles, there were competing definitions of "internationalism" ranging from solidarity with popular movements to high-level meetings with elected officials in foreign countries.

94. D. Gutiérrez, *Walls and Mirrors*, 19.

95. Tijerina is quoted in *La voz del pueblo*, Berkeley, California (December 1971): 5.

96. Acuña, *Occupied America*, 358.

97. Edward Muguía, *Assimilation, Colonialism and the Mexican American People*, Mexican American Monograph Series 1 (Austin: University of Texas Center for Mexican American Studies, 1975), 98–99.

98. According to historian Juan Gómez Quiñones, anticommunist and Cold War ideologies were especially strong in Mexican American communities during the Viet Nam war period: "Marxism invited denunciation and when this happened the widespread and

deeply ingrained phobia against it came into play." *Chicano Politics: Reality and Promise 1940–1990* (Albuquerque: University of New Mexico Press, 1990), 146.

99. David G. Gutiérrez, *CASA in the Chicano Movement: Ideology and Organizational Politics in the Chicano Community 1968–1978*, Working Paper Series 5 (Stanford: Stanford Center for Chicano Research, 1984), 18. Ernesto Chávez insists on the rigid opposition "nationalism/Marxism" in order to argue that the ultimate "failure" of CASA "stemmed in large part from its contradictory philosophy—a merger of nationalism with Marxist-Leninism." "Imagining the Mexican Immigrant Worker: (Inter)Nationalism, Identity, and Insurgency in the Chicano Movement in Los Angeles," *Aztlán* 25 (Fall 2000): 129. On CASA, see also Laura Pulido, *Black, Brown, Yellow, and Left: Radical Activism in Los Angeles* (Berkeley: University of California Press, forthcoming) and Arnoldo García, "Toward a Left without Borders: The Story of the Center for Autonomous Social Action—General Brotherhood of Workers," *Monthly Review* 54 (July-August 2002): 69–78; and E. Chávez, *¡Mi Raza Primero!*, especially chapter 5.

100. D. G. Gutiérrez, *CASA in the Chicano Movement*, 17.

101. See Bert Corona and Mario T. García, *Memories of Chicano History: The Life and Narrative of Bert Corona* (Berkeley and London: University of California Press, 1994), 94–96. Regarding the split within the CASA movement, Corona argues that while tactical differences existed between young activists and the founders there were no substantial ideological divisions: "There are some who claim that a major split erupted between the Young Turks in CASA, on the one hand, and myself and the older leadership in the Hermandad, on the other. This is simply not true" (312).

102. Malcolm X is quoted in *Malcolm X Speaks* (New York: Pathfinder Press, 1965), 115.

103. Antonio Gomez, "Un solo mundo," *Con safos* 3 (1970): 6.

104. Ybarra-Frausto, "Chicano Cultural Project since the 1960s, 31.

105. Jorge Bustamante, "Prólogo" to Reies López Tijerina, *Mi Lucha por la Tierra* (Mexico City: FCE, 1978), 23.

106. Myron Magnet, *The Dream and the Nightmare: The Sixties' Legacy to the Underclass* (New York: William Morrow and Co., 1993), 219.

107. For a brilliant critique of Rorty's thought, see Michael Billig, *Banal Nationalism* (London: Sage Publications, 1995). Billig points out that Rorty at times uses phrases such as "we Anglo Saxons" and "our pride in being bourgeois liberals."

108. George W. Bush, 2003 State of the Union speech, available at http://www.whitehouse.gov.

109. Cherríe Moraga, *The Last Generation* (Cambridge, MA: South End Press, 1993), 53.

110. Ibid., 62.

111. Teresa de Córdova poses the following important question: "While many of our writings are *anti-colonial*, many are not. While many challenge the essence of domination and oppression, many perpetuate it. Granted, our lives in the university are difficult, but they are also privileged. When do the explorations of our selves become self-indulgent; when are they truly *anti-colonial?*" "Anti-colonial Chicana Feminism" in Rodolfo D. Torres and George Katsiaficas, eds., *Latino Social Movements: Historical and Theoretical Perspectives* (New York and London: Routledge, 1999), 35.

Chapter 3

1. "The Return of Che!" from "A Bowl of Beings" in Culture Clash, *Life, Death and Revolutionary Comedy* (New York: Theatre Communications Group, 1998), 84. Chuy's whining response to Che's question "What is a Chicano?" is the hilarious, "I don't know," thus marking the inherent ambiguities that continue to cut across contemporary Chicano/a identities. Later in the skit, Chuy informs a dejected Che: "Don't forget, you inspired a whole generation of yuppies, and besides, you made a handsome silkscreen poster" (89). It undoubtedly would amuse the members of Culture Clash to know that during his time as a government official in Havana Guevara refused the luxury automobiles given to high-ranking functionaries and chose to drive a Chevrolet Impala, the automobile of choice among Chicano lowriders. See Pierre Kalfon, *Che. Ernesto Guevara, una leyenda de nuestro siglo*, trans. Manuel Serrat Crespo (Barcelona: Plaza and Janés), 369.

2. The original photograph from which the famous "angry Che" poster is taken was in fact shot on March 5, 1960, by Cuban photographer Alberto Díaz Gutiérrez (nicknamed "Korda") at a memorial service for the seventy-five victims killed in the bombing of the first foreign ship delivering arms to revolutionary Cuba. "Korda" himself reported: "*Casi me asusté, viendo la cara tan fiera que tenía*" ("I was almost frightened, seeing the fierce expression on his face"). Quoted in Kalfon, *Che*, 312.

3. Alfredo de la Torre, "El Grito" in *Caracoleando* (San Antonio: M and A Editions, 1979), 6.

4. It has been suggested to me that the widespread use of the Che image in Chicano political actions was simply the result of copycat activities, i.e., "Everybody was doing it." While I agree that all social movements reproduce a fixed repertoire of images, I would argue that we ought to investigate the reasons why those particular images are adopted in the first place and what they signify over time.

5. Antoni Kapcia , *Cuba: Island of Dreams* (Oxford and New York: Berg, 2000), 87.

6. Quoted in Cintio Vitier, *Ese Sol del Mundo Moral* (La Habana: Ediciones Unión, 2002), 210. Perhaps Guevara's most quoted words are the following: "*Déjeme decirle, a riesgo de parecer ridículo, que el revolucionario verdadero está guiado por grandes sentimientos de amor*" ("Let me say, at the risk of sounding ridiculous, that the true revolutionary is guided by great feelings of love").

7. Kapcia, *Cuba*, 211. Kapcia traces the ways in which the figures of José Martí and Che Guevara have been refashioned or "customized" even inside Cuba itself according to shifting political, economic, and generational currents.

8. Ibid., 25.

9. The letter was published in *El Grito del Norte* (June 1973). Composed in language typical of other Movement documents and not at all representative of Guevara's language, the spurious letter from Che claimed to have been written during Guevara's last campaign in Bolivia in 1967. Unfortunately, it refers to the May 1968 student rebellions in Paris and other events that took place after Guevara's death.

10. Luera was an active member of several Chicano organizations in Denver including the Crusade for Justice and Raza Association of Media Advocates. See Ernesto B. Vigil, *The Crusade for Justice: Chicano Militancy and the Government's War on Dissent* (Madison: University of Wisconsin Press, 1999), 371. Although this poem appeared in

1974, when Chicano/a militancy was waning, it captures well the discursive links between Cuba and Aztlán that persisted for some sectors of the Movement.

11. Anonymous, "Nationalism Dangerous," *Third World* (January 29, 1971), 2.

12. Bert Corona and Mario T. García, *Memories of Chicano History: The Life and Narrative of Bert Corona* (Berkeley: University of California Press, 1994), 186. Created in New Mexico in 1949, ANMA, although not a leftist organization, took a number of radical positions, e.g., opposing the Korean War and U.S. interventions in Guatemala and Iran, and found itself on the Department of Justice's subversive list described as a "Communist Party front."

13. William Gálvez, *Camilo, Señor de la vanguardia* (La Habana: Editorial de ciencias sociales, 1979), 130. Of San Francisco's climate, Cienfuegos wrote to his brother: "*Oye flaco esta ciudad . . . no vale nada o como diría un bato chicano no vale madre*" ("Look skinny, this city isn't worth a damn or as a Chicano dude would say it's not shit"). Gálvez, *Camilo*, 141. Information on Camilo Cienfuegos's experiences in California is scarce and has been relatively ignored by historians.

Although there is no record of Fidel Castro being in contact with any Chicano/a community, he briefly visited McAllen, Texas, on the U.S./Mexico border in September of 1956 where he met the former president of Cuba, Carlos Prío, in order to collect funds for the Granma expedition. See Tad Szulc, *Fidel: A Critical Portrait* (New York: Post Road Press, 2000), 366.

14. Peter Kornbluh, ed. *Bay of Pigs Declassified: The Secret CIA Report on the Invasion of Cuba* (New York: The New Press, 1998).

15. On the complex relationship between the Kennedys and Mexican Americans, see Ignacio M. García, *Viva Kennedy: Mexican Americans in Search of Camelot* (College Station: Texas A and M University Press), 2000. The *corrido* written by Arnulfo Castillo and reproduced in García's study captures the often idolatrous nature of the relationship: "John Kennedy has not died/God has taken him/And from heaven he is watching us/To better care for us."

16. Mario T. García, *Ruben Salazar, Border Corrrespondent: Selected Writings* (Berkeley: University of California Press, 1995), 66.

17. In the early 1960s, FBI and LAPD intelligence reported that "Communist front groups" such as the DuBois Clubs of America of Southern California were attracting small numbers of Mexican Americans. See *Thirteenth Report of the Senate Fact-Finding Committee on Un-American Activities* (Sacramento: California Legislature, Senate, 1965), 52. This report focuses primarily on "Cuban influence" over students movements at Berkeley, and prompted a rebuttal by Chancellor Clark Kerr: *Analysis of the Thirteenth Report of the Senate Fact-Finding Committee on Un-American Activities* (Berkeley: University of California Office of the President, 1965).

18. *Communist and Trotskyist Activity within the Greater Los Angeles Chapter of the Fair Play for Cuba Committee*, report and testimony of Albert J. Lewis and Steve Roberts (April 26 and 27, 1962). Committee on Un-American Activities, House of Representatives, Eighty-seventh Congress, Second Session (Washington, D.C.: U.S. Government Printing Office), 1525. During the week of the Playa Girón invasion, the *Los Angeles Times* gave extensive coverage to Cuban exile activity at their E. 35th St. office.

Gabaldón's bizarre adventures as an anticommunist crusader have yet to be chronicled. Working with the John Birch Society, the Christian Anti-Communism Crusade (funded in part by southern California amusement-park owner Walter Knott), and a group of Mexican falangists known as "Los Dorados," Gabaldón traveled throughout Mexico spreading his anticommunist message. See UCLA Special Collections, Collection 464: "Philip Kerby Papers," box 2, fld. 4. In the late 1970s, he traveled to Nicaragua to fight against the Sandinista rebels. As late as 1990, he continued to publish his right-wing beliefs: "It is difficult to understand the reasoning behind the actions of the Liberals. Some of these intellectually muscle-bound idiots must really believe that the indigenous people of the third world should be taught that they are under privileged only because of the 'Imperialist' United States." *Saipan: Suicide Island* (Saipan: Guy Gabaldon, 1990), 230–31.

19. Luis Valdez and Stan Steiner, eds., *Aztlán: An Anthology of Mexican American Literature* (New York: Knopf, 1972), 215; and F. Arturo Rosales, *Chicano!: The History of the Mexican American Civil Rights Movement* (Houston: Arte Público Press, 1997), 176.

20. Ibid., 217.

21. Carlos Muñoz, Jr., *Youth, Identity, Power: The Chicano Movement*, 7th ed. (London and New York: Verso, 1997), 52.

Valdez had also written a letter to his draft board in San Jose, California, in which he attacked Lyndon Johnson as "one insane Texan" and declared "I will not fight in Vietnam or the Dominican Republic." The letter was published in the Progressive Labor Party's periodical *Spark* and eventually found its way into Valdez's FBI files. César Chávez's FBI files contain a great deal of innuendo regarding Valdez. One resident of Delano interviewed by federal agents falsely claimed "Valdez had been in Cuba for a three month period about 1962 allegedly for training in revolutionary tactics." See http://foia.fbi.gov/chavez/chavez6B.pdf [140 ff.].

21. Elizabeth "Betita" Martinez, "Letter from Havana." *The Nation* (November 4, 1961): 358–61. In 1962, Martinez coedited with Howard Schulman and José Yglesias a collection of writings by the "League of Militant Poets" that included LeRoi Jones, Allen Ginsberg, Michael McClure, Nicolás Guillén, and others. The volume was titled *Pa'lante: Poetry Polity Prose of a New World.* Although the editors announced that *Pa'lante* was to be published three times a year, the sole issue was printed on May 19, 1962, "in honor of the death of José Martí."

23. On Carmichael's visit to Cuba, see Clayborne Carson, *In Struggle: SNCC and the Black Awakening of the 1960s* (Cambridge, MA: Harvard University Press, 1981).

24. Elizabeth Sutherland, *The Youngest Revolution: A Personal Report* (New York: Dial Press, 1969), 134. Martinez's retelling of her experience on the Isle of Youth was the only English-language account of that project until 2000. See Jane McManus, *Cuba's Island of Dreams: Voices from the Isle of Pines and Youth* (Gainesville: University Press of Florida, 2000).

25. Martinez , *Youngest Revolution*, 166–67.

26. Ibid., 189.

27. As a socialist and a feminist with extensive experience in the Black Civil Rights struggle, Martinez played a unique role in the Movimiento. A scholarly analysis of her role, which would teach us much about the conflictive ideological currents and sexist practices during the Movement period, has yet to be written.

28. Telephone interview with Betita Martinez, April 13, 2000.

29. Enriqueta Longeaux y Vásquez, "¡Qué linda es Cuba!," *El Grito del Norte* (May 19 and June 14. 1969): 12. For additional information on Longeaux y Vásquez's Cuban experience, see Dionne Espinoza, "Pedagogies of Nationalism and Gender: Cultural Resistance in Selected Representational Practices of Chicana/o Movement Activists, 1967–1972" (Ph.D. diss., Cornell University, 1996), 147–87.

30. Venceremos Brigades participants were closely monitored both by U.S. law enforcement and Cuban security agencies. According to the "Special Report" issued in June 1970 by the Interagency Committee on Intelligence (chaired by FBI director J. Edgar Hoover), U.S. *brigadistas* "must be considered as potential recruits for Cuban intelligence activities and sabotage in the United States"; repr. in *Hearings before the Select Committee to Study Governmental Operations with Respect to Intelligence activities of the United States Senate. Ninety-fourth Congress. First session. Volume 1, exhibit 1* (September 23, 24, and 25, 1975): Huston Plan (Washington, D.C.: U.S. Government Printing Office, 1976), 147. Passenger lists are reproduced in *Hearings before the subcommittee to investigate the administration of the internal security act and other internal security laws of the Committee on the Judiciary, United States Senate, Ninety-first Congress, Second session, Part 4 (June 10, 1970): Extent of subversion in the "New Left," Testimony of Charles Siragusa and Ronald L. Brooks* (Washington, D.C.: U.S. Government Printing Office, 1970), 645 ff.

31. *Brigada Venceremos* (Oakland: Brigada Venceremos, 1971).

32. Sandra Levinson and Carol Brightman, eds., *Venceremos Brigade: Young Americans Sharing the Life and Work of Revolutionary Cuba* (New York: Simon and Schuster, 1971), 235.

33. Ibid., 39.

34. Ibid., 379.

35. "Statement by Calderón—Repression on Chicanos," *Third World* [UC San Diego] (December 3, 1970): 1. The first issue of the internationalist student paper *Third World* appeared on November 4, 1970. Manuel de Jesús Hernández was editor-in-chief; Alda Blanco was managing editor.

36. raulrsalinas, *East of the Freeway: Reflections de Mi Pueblo* (Austin: Red Salmon Press, 1995).

37. Gonzales's remarks are in the *Congressional Record*, April 3, 1969: 8590, and *Congressional Record*, April 22, 1969: 9952.

38. José Angel Gutiérrez is quoted in Ignacio M. García, *United We Win: The Rise and Fall of La Raza Unida Party* (Tucson: Mexican American Studies and Research Center, University of Arizona, 1989), 139. Thirty years later, Gutiérrez posted the following on a San Antonio website: "Knowing that white America has not and does not recognize our welfare or destiny as intertwined, we must forge ahead with our own strategic plan, vision and timetable. We will not become an underclass to whites or blacks or Asians. We will seek and find our own public partners to meet destiny." "Latinos must join, shape the future," http://news.mysanantonio.com (June 29, 2003).

39. On MAYO and La Raza Unida Party, see I. M. García, *United We Win*; José Angel Gutiérrez, *The Making of a Chicano Militant: Lessons from Cristal* (Madison: University of Wisconsin Press, 1999); Armando Navarro, *Mexican American Youth Organization: Avant-Garde of the Chicano Movement in Texas* (Austin: University of Texas

Press, 1995); Armando Navarro, *The Cristal Experiment: A Chicano Struggle for Community Control* (Madison: University of Wisconsin, 1998); and Armando Navarro, *La Raza Unida Party: A Chicano Challenge to the U.S. Two Party Dictatorship* (Philadelphia: Temple University Press, 2000. During the second half of the 1970s, representatives of other Chicano groups such as the Centro de Acción Social Autónomo (CASA) traveled to Cuba. See Ernesto Chávez, *"¡Mi Raza Primero!" (My People First!): Nationalism, Identity, and Insurgency in the Chicano Movement in Los Angeles, 1966–1978* (Berkeley: University of California Press, 2002).

40. Vigil, *Crusade for Justice*, 283.

41. FBI document quoted in ibid., 284.

42. See Jorge Terrazas Acevedo, "A Marriage in Aztlán," *El Gallo* 2 (April 1969), 10; and Patricia Bell Blawis, *Tijerina and the Land Grants: Mexican Americans in Struggle for Their Heritage* (New York: International Publishers, 1971), 9.

43. The group Los Alvarados recorded the LP "El Movimiento Chicano" (1973) for the Escuela y Colegio Tlatelolco, Crusade for Justice, Denver, Colorado. It includes "Yo soy Chicano," "El corrido de Aztlán," and "Bella Ciao."

44. Dionne Espinoza, "'Revolutionary Sisters': Women's Solidarity and Collective Identification among Chicana Brown Berets in East Los Angeles, 1967–1970." *Aztlán: A Journal of Chicano Studies* 26 (Spring 2001), 18.

45. One anecdote from the Mexican context is especially revealing. In a dialogue between a young Mexican student and her mother, the figure of Che stands in for the widening gap between the student's generation and that of her parents. During the year between Che's death and the tumultuous weeks leading up to the Mexican government's massacre of students in Mexico City in October 1968, many such dialogues took place around the world. As reported by Elena Poniatowska, the conversation is both amusing and deeply suggestive of the radicalization of an international youth culture. Faced with a poster of Che on her daughter's wall, the mother exclaims:

—*¡Ay qué cosa tan horrible, ese hombre tan sucio, cómo tienes a ese hombre tan sucio en el lugar de los santos. . . . Hija, cámbialo, cámbialo . . .*

—*Mira mamá yo no me meto con tus santitos que tienes en tu cabecera y ésos los que no tienen cara de mariguanos, tienen cara de amujerados, así unas caras horribles tus santitos. . . . Yo no me meto con ellos. Te suplico que tú respetes a mi santito.*

("—Oh, what a horrible thing, that dirty man, how can you have that dirty man where the saints should be. . . . Daughter, move him, move him. Look, mom, I don't mess with the saints on your headboard, the ones who either look like pot smokers or sissies with their ugly faces. I don't mess with them so I'm asking that you respect my saint").

La noche de Tlatelolco (Mexico City: Era, 1971), 88.

In Mexican American homes across the United States parents heard their Chicano/a sons and daughters voice similar sentiments about the man who embodied their newly adopted ideals. Clearly, the meaning of Che in the Mexican context was nuanced by specific local traditions, especially the long-standing critique of U.S. interventionism. The Chicano Che was not identical to the Mexican Che. Nevertheless, for many Chicano/a and Mexican youth, Che signified a break with what they considered to be the accommodationist political posture of their parents' generation and their more militant hope for a just society.

46. Fidel Castro, Introduction to Che's Bolivian Diaries, *Ramparts* (July 28, 1968): 5.

47. On the relationship between African American progressives and revolutionary Cuba, see Van Gosse, *Where the Boys Are: Cuba, Cold War America, and the Making of the New Left* (London and New York: Verso, 1993); and Robin D.G. Kelley, *Freedom Dreams: The Black Radical Imagination* (Boston: Beacon Press, 2002). The radical Black press at times referred to Fidel Castro as a "colored leader" or even as "Black," an early episode of pan-American, people of color, solidarity (in the late 1950s!).

48. *The Black Panther* (December 27, 1969) quoted in Philip S. Foner, ed., *The Black Panthers Speak* (New York: DaCapo Press, 1995), 37. Panther leaders such as Huey Newton were well acquainted with Che Guevara's writings, especially the Bolivian diaries.

49. The presence of Che in Chicano-organized anti-Viet Nam war demonstrations was widespread. In the February 28, 1970 march in East Los Angeles, protesters carried the image of Che and chanted "Che, Che, Che Guevara." Della Rossa, "Chicanos Protest Murder." *Los Angeles Free Press* (March 6, 1970), 12. His image was used again in the historic August 29, 1970, march. In the aftermath of the police riot that day and the assassination of *L.A. Times* reporter Ruben Salazar, prosecutors at the official inquest referred to the image of Che. During the interrogation of Raul Ruiz, captured in David García's documentary *Requiem 29*, a prosecutor red-baited Ruiz, asking him specifically about a Che poster: "Isn't that Castro's man?" Ruiz's answer—"Che Guevara was a great hero to the people of Latin America. He struggled against oppression and injustice"—captured well Chicano/a feelings about Che. *Requiem 29* (Los Angeles: Visual Image, 1971).

50. John R. Chávez, *The Lost Land: The Chicano Image of the Southwest* (Albuquerque: University of New Mexico Press, 1984), 140. According to Betita Martinez, *nuevomexicanos* Juan Valdez and Baltasar Martinez, who later participated in the Tierra Amarilla courthouse raid, had actually traveled to Miami in the late 1950s in an unsuccessful attempt to join Fidel Castro in the Sierra Maestra (Personal communication with author, April 14, 2001).

51. David Kunzle, ed., *Che Guevara: Icon, Myth, and Message* (Los Angeles: UCLA Fowler Museum of Cultural History in collaboration with the Center for the Study of Political Graphics, 1997), 13. Che is quoted in Maurice Zeitlin's essay "Che and Me," in Kunzle, *Che Guevara*.

Martin Luther King, Jr.'s critique of violent revolution as a viable alternative for African Americans might just as easily have been applied to the Mexican American community. Dr. King pointed out that whereas Fidel Castro had enjoyed wide support from the Cuban people "[violent] American Blacks would find no sympathy and support from the white population and very little from the majority of the Negroes themselves." Martin Luther King, Jr., *Where Do We Go from Here: Chaos or Community?* (Boston: Beacon Press, 1968), 59.

52. Stan Steiner, ed., *La Raza: The Mexican Americans* (New York: Harper and Row, 1970), 110. With the establishment of a cooperative farming system in northern New Mexico, the slogan became "Che is alive and farming in Tierra Amarilla." In East Los Angeles, a mock headline in *La Raza* newspaper declared "FLASH! Che has been seen in Maravilla!" *La Raza* 1 (October 15, 1967): 5. When Tijerina suggested later that same year that the Cuban delegation might place the issue of the New Mexican land grants before the United Nations, he drew the immediate attention of the FBI. See Vigil, *Crusade for Justice*, 41.

53. Clark Knowlton, "Guerrillas of Rio Arriba: The New Mexican Land Wars." *The Nation* (June 19, 1968); repr. in F. Chris García, ed., *La causa política: A Chicano Politics Reader* (Notre Dame, IN: University of Notre Dame Press, 1974), 338.

54. Frank C. Brophy, "Reds Stir Mexican Americans," *The Review of the News, Report!* (October 2, 1968), 3. Brophy declared: "The Communists now seek to use Mexican-Americans in this area as a powerful adjunct of their Black Rebellion sweeping American cities" (1).

55. Ibid., 6; emphasis in original.

56. La Simpática, "Viva La Raza!," *The Movement* (July 1969): 7. The author added the following caution: "There may be some negative aspects to the 'Cuban mystique,' a mystique of 'Debrayism' which stresses the forming of a small tough band of fighters or engaging in adventurist activities, and neglects getting people organized and raising consciousness in day to day work—preparing the people for struggle."

57. Martinez was quoted in the article "New Mexico Revolt Grows," *Open City* [Los Angeles] (February 9–15, 1968): 11.

58. Quoted in Patricia Bell Blawis, *Tijerina and the Land Grants: Mexican Americans in Struggle for Their Heritage* (New York: International Publishers, 1971), 148.

59. Armando B. Rendón, *Chicano Manifesto* (New York: Macmillan, 1971), 110.

60. "Black Beret Twelve Point Program" (1971); repr. in Gilberto López y Rivas, *The Chicanos: Life and Struggles of the Mexican Minority in the United States* (New York and London: Monthly Review Press, 1973), 162–67. The English translation of López y Rivas's book (originally published in Spanish in 1971) received a negative review from Alberto Camarillo: "As a serious contribution to the literature on Chicano studies, *The Chicanos* cannot be considered a valuable addition." *Aztlán* 6 (Spring 1975): 126.

61. Roberto Vargas, *Primeros Cantos* (San Francisco: Ediciones Pocho-Che, 1971), 10.

62. Luis Omar Salinas and Lillian Faderman, eds., *From the Barrio: A Chicano Anthology* (San Francisco: Canfield Press, 1973), 45.

63. Guadalupe Saavedra's play *Justice* is repr. in Bernard Kukore, ed., *Drama and Revolution* (New York: Holt, Rinehart, and Winston, 1971); and the play is mentioned in Jorge Huerta, *Chicano Theater: Themes and Forms* (Tempe, Arizona: Bilingual Press, 1982), 157.

64. Arturo Silvano Bobián, David García, and Roberto "Chips" Portales, *and this is what we said* (Lubbock: Trucha Press, 1975), 43. Perhaps the most complete elaboration of the Che as Christ trope is Salvadoran poet Roque Dalton's "Credo del Che" which includes the stanza: "*Después le colocaron a Cristo Guevara/una corona de espinas y una túnica de loco/y le colgaron un rótulo del pescuezo en son de burla/INRI: Instigador Natural de la Rebelión de los Infelices*" ("And then they placed on Guevara Christ/a crown of thorns and a madman's gown/and to mock him they hung a sign around his neck/INRI: Natural Instigator of the Poor People's Rebellion"). Roque Dalton, *Poemas clandestinos* (New York: Curbstone Press, 1990), 49.

65. Juan Gómez Quiñones, Alurista, F.A. Cervantes, Mary Ann Pacheco, Gustavo Segade, eds., *Festival de Flor y Canto: An Anthology of Chicano Literature* (Los Angeles: University of Southern California Press, 1976).

66. Dorinda Guadalupe Moreno, *La Mujer—en pie de lucha ¡y la hora es ya!* (Mexico City: Espina del Norte, 1973), 230.

67. Salinas and Faderman, *From the Barrio*, 33. In a 1976 issue of *Caracol*, Max Martinez imagined a curious dialogue between Che and a Bolivian army officer shortly before Che's execution. According to the Bolivian major, Che and he are simply two sides of the same coin. The fact that the character of the major could be interpreted as sympathetic led Alfredo de la Torre to write a response in which Che exposes the major's lies. See Max Martinez, "Monologue of the Bolivian Major," *Caracol* 2(August 1976): 20–23; and Alfredo de la Torre, "Che Answers," *Caracol* 2 (September 1976): 17.

68. Roberto Luera, "Cuba: Tierra de libertad," *El Gallo* 7 (December 1974): n.p.

69. Elias Hruska y Cortés, *This Side and Other Things* (San Francisco: Ediciones Pocho-Che, 1971): 23. The influence of the Cuban Revolution was particularly strong in Chicano art produced in the San Francisco Bay Area. In 1970, the Galería de la Raza had mounted an exhibit of Cuban photographer René Mederos and in 1974 Chicano artist Juan Fuentes curated a Cuban poster exhibit at the San Francisco Palace of Legion of Honor.

70. raulrsalinas, *East of the Freeway*, 74.

71. Reyes Cárdenas, "If We Praise the Aztecs," *I Was Never a Militant Chicano* (Austin: Relámpago Books, 1986), 1.

72. Elizabeth Betita Martinez, "In Pursuit of Latina Liberation," *Signs* 20 (Summer 1995): 1019.

73. Viviane Forrester, *The Economic Horror* (Cambridge: Polity Press, 1999), 190.

74. José Esteban Muñoz, *Disidentifications: Queers of Color and the Performance of Politics*, Cultural Studies of the Americas, vol. 2 (Minneapolis and London: University of Minnesota Press, 1999), 14. Muñoz continues: "He [Che Guevara] also represents the entrenched misogyny and homophobia of masculinist liberation ideologies." It is not clear to me why the image of Che necessarily represents these things unless we read them into the image by reducing all liberation ideologies to their "masculinist" or narrow "nationalist" elements. I do agree with Muñoz, however, that Valentín's use of the Che image rearticulates the ideological field that usually surrounds it in a Chicano Movement context.

75. Artist Alex Donis's remarks and original image may be accessed at http://latinoartcommunity.org The painting was destroyed by vandals on September 15, 1997. My thanks to Professor Richard T. Rodríguez of Cal State University, Los Angeles, for bringing this image to my attention and to Alex Donis for allowing me to reproduce it.

The appropriation of the Che image by gay activists began early in the 1970s, especially in Europe. See the anonymous "Che Gay" (now housed in Amsterdam) in Kunzle, *Che Guevara*, 95.

76. Throughout the 1990s, the musical group Rage Against the Machine was essential for the maintenance of Guevara's memory among U.S. Latino/a youth. In the summer of 2001, the Sol Festival in Los Angeles raised over five thousand dollars for progressive organizations. In a festival-closing performance, Chicano musicians from Los Lobos and Ozomatli appeared on stage as the "Che Guevara All Stars."

77. James Petras, "Latin America: Thirty Years after Che," *Monthly Review* 49 (October 1997): 15.

78. Peter McLaren, *Che Guevara, Paulo Freire, and the Pedagogy of Revolution* (Lanham: Rowman and Littlefield, 2000), 8.

Chapter 4

1. Based on Chávez's own comments in which he insisted that he was a labor leader and not a Chicano Movement leader, several historians have argued that his connection to the Movimiento was tentative. Carlos Muñoz, Jr., for example, writes: "Chavez was a union organizer and lent his increasing prestige and astute leadership abilities only to farmworkers." *Youth, Identity, Power: The Chicano Movement* (London and New York: Verso, 1989). It is my contention that due to the immeasurable impact that Chávez and the UFW had on Chicano/a activism throughout the Movement period and his direct or indirect support of Movement sectors such as the anti–Viet Nam war National Chicano Moratorium Committee it would be misleading to isolate his efforts regardless of his own declarations.

Historian Ignacio M. García argues similarly that both Tijerina's Alianza and the UFW were essential to the broader Movimiento: "Some scholars argue that César Chávez's farmworkers' union and the Alianza were not part of the Movement because they never emphasized their *chicanismo*. I counter by saying that these two organizations were fundamental to the development of the militancy of the period." *Chicanismo: The Forging of a Militant Ethos among Mexican Americans* (Tucson: University of Arizona Press, 1998), 14. Manuel G. Gonzales artificially separates the Movimiento into "radical and moderate wings," and situates the UFW in the latter category. *Mexicanos: A History of Mexicans in the United States* (Bloomington and Indianapolis: Indiana University Press, 2000), 196.

2. Armando Navarro, *Mexican American Youth Organization: Avant-Garde of the Chicano Movement in Texas* (Austin: University of Texas Press, 1995), 23.

Tijerina's rhetoric in particular was dependent upon traditional forms of masculinity and homophobia. Referring to government agents who had threatened him and his family, he said: "Most of them are homosexuals now and very few men are found among them." Interview in the *Indicator*, University of California, San Diego (January 29, 1969): 4. Tijerina's use of homosexuality as a "charge" with which to dismiss his political enemies is reminiscent of the novels of Oscar Zeta Acosta. On the presence of homophobia in non-Chicano "New Left" organizations during this period, see Ian Lekus, "Queer and Present Dangers: Homosexuality and American Antiwar Activism during the Vietnam Era" (Ph.D. diss., Duke University, 2004). On Tijerina's rhetorical style, see John C. Hammerback, *A War of Words: Chicano Protest in the 1960s and 1970s* (Westport, CT: Greenwood Press, 1985); and Rudy Val Busto, "Like a Mighty Rushing Wind: The Religious Impulse in the Life and Writing of Reies López Tijerina" (Ph.D. diss., University of California, Berkeley, 1991).

3. F. Arturo Rosales, *Chicano!: The History of the Mexican American Civil Rights Movement* (Houston: Arte Público Press, 1997), 130–31.

4. David Gómez, "The Story of Ruben Salazar." In Livie Isauro Durán and H. Russell Bernard, eds., *Introduction to Chicano Studies*, 2d ed. (New York: Macmillan, 1982), 501.

5. I take for granted that scholars of the Chicano Movement agree that far from being a "monolithic" social movement (has there ever been such a creature?) the Movimiento was made up of diverse organizations with regional and ideological differences. One of the

goals of this book is to show how attempts to totalize the Movement under any one political language are reductive and therefore distort what was a complex tapestry of agendas and rhetorical strategies.

6. See Raymond Williams, *Resources of Hope* (London and New York: Verso, 1989).

7. Miguel Abruch Linder, *Movimiento Chicano: Demandas materiales, nacionalismo y tácticas* (Mexico City: Acatlán, 1979), 29; 78.

8. Carlos Blanco Aguinaga, "Unidad del trabajo y la vida—Cinco de mayo, 1971," *Aztlán* 2 (Spring 1971): 2. Indeed, in the earliest days of the UFW, Chávez often appealed not only to the workers's *mexicanidad* but also to his or her specific regional identity within the Mexican context. One participant in a rally during the grape strike in 1965 reported: "Speaker follows speaker as the enthusiasm of the crowd grows. 'Who is here from Jalisco?' César Chávez asks. 'Who is here from Michoacan?' A man from Tanguancícuaro rises: 'What have we to lose by going on strike?' . . . Men from state after Mexican state rise to pledge the aid of those from their part of the homeland, followed by cries of 'Viva Chihuahua! Viva Nuevo Leon! Viva Tamaulipas!'" Eugene Nelson, *Huelga: The First Hundred Days of the Great Delano Grape Strike* (Delano: Farm Worker Press, 1966), 27.

9. Manuel Castells, *The Power of Identity*, Volume 2 of *The Information Age: Economy, Society and Culture* (Oxford: Blackwell, 1997), 8.

10. Nelson, *Huelga*, 122.

11. Peter Matthiessen, *Sal Si Puedes (Escape If You Can): Cesar Chavez and the New American Revolution* (Berkeley: University of California Press, 2000), 113; emphasis in original. The new edition contains versions of some but not all of the materials in Matthiessen's 1969 *New Yorker* articles. See "Profile: Organizer-1," *New Yorker* (June 21, 1969): 42–85, and "Profile: Organizer II," *New Yorker* (June 28, 1969): 43–56. I have chosen several quotes from the original articles because of their more properly *testimonio* style, but I have included page references to both sources in those instances where material was either revised or reprinted.

12. *5 Plays* (Denver: Totinem Books, 1972), 61–62.

13. Nephtalí de León's words are in his *Chicanos: Our Background and Our Pride* (Lubbock, Texas: Trucha Publications, 1972), 43.

14. Anonymous, *El malcriado* 52 (n.d.): 22.

15. Early in his activist career, Reies López Tijerina was referred to as "Don Quixote." After the June 5, 1967, courthouse raid on Tierra Amarilla, however, one media outlet declared: "Don Quixote has become El Cid." Reies López Tijerina, *They Called Me "King Tiger": My Struggle for the Land and Our Rights*, trans. José Angel Gutiérrez (Houston: Arte Público, 2000), 102. On Chicano literary appropriations of the Don Quixote figure, see William Childers, "Chicanoizing Don Quixote: For Luis Andres Murillo," *Aztlan* 27 (Fall 2002): 87–117.

16. César Chávez, "Telegram to Mrs. Martin Luther King, Jr," repr. in *El malcriado* (April 15, 1968): 5.

17. That Chávez's masculinity signified an implicit critique of traditional forms of leadership was noted early on by perceptive observers. In their book on farmworker organizing in California, Henry Anderson and Joan London (daughter of Jack London) wrote: "He is challenging the long-standing, deeply embedded folkways which equate aggressiveness with manliness in the cultures of Mexico, the Philippines, the United

States—and in the culture of labor organizing itself. It is a breathtaking challenge." Joan London and Henry Anderson, *So Shall Ye Reap: The Story of Cesar Chavez and the Farm Workers' Movement* (New York: Thomas Y. Crowell Co., 1970), 184. Another account quotes Chávez as saying: "*La tradición mexicana de probar la hombría por la violencia es un error*" ("The Mexican tradition of proving one's manhood with violence is a mistake"). Tomás Calvo Buezas, *Los más pobres en el país más rico: clase, raza y etnia en el movimeinto campesino chicano* (Madrid: Ediciones Encuentro, 1981), 167. The study by Spanish scholar Calvo Buezas, who lived in California from 1972 to 1975, is the best analysis of the UFW written in Spanish.

18. César Chávez, "Creative Non-Violence," *Center Magazine* (March 1969): 27.

19. James Melvin Washington, ed., *A Testament of Hope: The Essential Writings and Speeches of Martin Luther King, Jr.* (San Francisco: Harper San Francisco, 1986), 661.

20. César Chávez, Interview with the *Observer* (May 1970): 1. Available at http://www.sfsu.edu/~cecipp/cesar_chavez.

21. Chávez told Peter Matthiessen in 1969: "I didn't know much about Gandhi, so I read everything I could get my hands on about him, and I read some of the things that he had read, and I read Thoreau, which I liked very much. But I couldn't really understand Gandhi until I was actually in the fast. Then the books became much more clear" (Matthiesen, *Sal Si Puedes*, 64; Matthiessen 2000, 187). Central to Chávez's understanding of the activist Catholic tradition were the figures of Father Thomas McCullough and Father Donald McDonnell, who founded a migrant ministry in the 1950s associated with the Spanish Mission Band and later the Missionary Apostolate. Father McDonnell exerted a direct influence over Chávez during his time in east San Jose, California. See London and Anderson, *So Shall Ye Reap*, 1970.

22. William Borman, *Gandhi and Non-violence* (Albany: State University of New York Press, 1986), 107. Chávez himself seemed to have practiced the fast according to this strict Gandhian interpretation, although many subsequent Chicano/a political actions have misunderstood the function of the fast and employed it as coercion. In their cartoon history, Lalo Alcaraz and Ilan Stavans perpetuate this misunderstanding by depicting Chávez on a fast saying: "I will not eat again until the grape growers concede." Lalo Alcaraz and Ilan Stavans, *Latino USA: A Cartoon History* (New York: Basic Books, 2000), 121.

During the Movimiento period, not all youth activists were convinced that the fast was an important strategy. In 1970, Ysidro Macias advised: "hunger strikes may be effective because of their sentimental value." Ysidro Ramón Macias, "Plan de Political Action for Chicano Campus Groups," document produced at the Political Action workshop at the University of California, Santa Barbara conference, April 1969; repr. in *El Pocho Che* 1 (April 1970): 47. According to Peter Matthiessen, some UFW members left the union specifically because of Chavez's use of the fast: "One dismissed the entire fast as a 'cheap publicity stunt.' The other, who had once been a priest, accused Chavez of having a Messiah complex. Both soon quit the United Farm Workers for good." Matthiessen, *Sal Si Puedes*, 56.

23. César Chávez, "Speech Ending Fast, March 10, 1968" (available on the California Department of Education website: http://chavez.scientech.com:8080/research). Many years later, upon ending a fast in August of 1988, Chavez explained: "The fast was first and foremost a personal act. It was something I felt compelled to do—to purify my own body, mind, and soul. The fast was also an act of penance for those in positions of moral

authority and for all men and women who know what is right and just. It is for those who know that they could or should do more." Richard J. Jensen and John C. Hammerback, *The Words of César Chávez* (College Station: Texas A and M University Press, 2002), 169.

24. César Chávez, "On Money and Organizing." Speech delivered in Keene, California, on October 4, 1971 (available on the California Department of Education website: http://chavez.scientech.com:8080/research).

25. Winthrop Yinger, *Cesar Chavez: The Rhetoric of Nonviolence* (Hicksville, NY: Exposition Press, 1975), 25. In his autobiography, African American leader Andrew Young recalls Chávez as "a small man with a soothing, spiritual presence" and "eyes that expressed the kind of loving determination with which the apostle Paul spread the Gospel." *An Easy Burden: The Civil Rights Movement and the Transformation of America* (New York: Harper Collins), 445.

26. César Chávez, Interview with the *Observer* (May 1970): 4–6. Available at http://www.sfsu.edu/~cecipp/cesar_chavez.

27. Yinger, *Cesar Chavez*, 196. This citation is from the "Sacramento March Letter." In documents such as these it is difficult to determine authorship since Chávez, Luis Valdez, Eliezer Risco, and others may have written the text collectively. On the practice of using multiple authors in the UFW and El Teatro Campesino, see Yolanda Broyles González, *El Teatro Campesino: Theater in the Chicano Movement* (Austin: University of Texas Press, 1994).

28. An anonymous reviewer for an earlier version of this chapter raised questions about the ways in which Chávez's hybrid masculinity, in a sense "feminized" by its indebtedness to religious traditions, might have worked to "hail" or attract women activists during the Movement period. This is an important issue that, in my opinion, deserves separate and multiple studies. For an important model for such research, see Dionne Espinoza, "Revolutionary Sisters": Women's Solidarity and Collective Identification among Chicana Brown Berets in East Los Angeles, 1967–1970, *Aztlán* 26 (Spring 2001): 17–58. Equally important are studies of the real-life ways in which farmworker women experience gender relations.

29. Washington, *Testament of Hope*, 291.

30. Ibid., 350.

31. Yinger, *Cesar Chavez*, 112.

32. César Chávez, "National Council Policy Statement," *Tempo* (Summer–Fall 1968): 9.

33. Yinger, *Cesar Chavez*, 87.

34. Gustavo Gutiérrez, *Teología de la liberación. Perspectivas*. (Lima: CEP, 1971).

35. Lisa Sousa, C. M. Stafford Poole, and James Lockhart, eds., *The Story of Guadalupe: Luis Laso de la Vega's Huei tlamahuiçoltica of 1649* (Palo Alto: Stanford University Press, 1998), 71.

36. According to Peter Matthiessen's eyewitness account, photographers staged the now famous 1966 tableau with RFK feeding Chavez (Matthiessen, *Sal Si Puedes*, 1969 ed., 68; 2000 ed., 195).

37. Evan Thomas, *Robert Kennedy: His Life* (New York and London: Simon and Schuster, 2000), 320.

38. "RFK Statement on Cesar Chavez, March 10, 1968," Collection JFK-RFK: RFK Papers, 1937–1968, JFK Library, Boston, MA (accessed at http://arcweb.archives.gov).

39. Quoted in Anonymous, "El poder Chicano," *La voz del pueblo* (December 1970): 5.

40. "César," in *El Chicano*, San Bernardino, California (January 12, 1970): n.p.

41. Elías Hruska-Cortés, "Recuerdos," in *La calavera chicana*, UC Berkeley (September 1973): 15.

42. Oscar Zeta Acosta, *Revolt of the Cockroach People* (New York: Vintage, 1989), 44.

43. Acosta, *Revolt*, 45. Acosta's scene captured the tone of actual events in which Movement leaders made the journey to Delano to consult with Chávez. In my personal conversations with Rosalío Muñoz, one of the founders of the National Chicano Moratorium Committee, he described a similar visit he made before deciding to refuse induction into military service.

44. Acosta, Revolt, 249.

45. Ibid., 250.

46. Ralph de Toledano, *Little Cesar* (Washington, D.C.: Anthem, 1971), 16–17. Toledano's writings bear many of the marks of COINTELPRO disinformation and so there is some reason to believe they were subsidized by government agencies. The FBI had begun to construct a file on Chávez as early as 1965, on the premise that "Communists" had infiltrated the UFW. In October of 1969, the Nixon White House requested a "name check" on Chávez. J. Edgar Hoover relayed the Bureau's information to Nixon aide John Erlichman. Some of Chávez's FBI files are available on-line at http://foia.fbi.gov/chavez.

47. Manuel A. Machado, Jr., *Listen Chicano!: An Informal History of the Mexican-American* (Chicago: Nelson Hall, 1978), 99. Machado's attacks on Chávez's character would be repeated twenty years later by opponents of a César Chávez state holiday in California. Despite a well-funded opposition, the holiday was officially established in 2000 and celebrated for the first time in 2001.

48. See, for example, Gary Allen, *The Grapes: Communist Wrath in Delano* (Belmont, MA, and San Marino,

: The Review of the News, 1966); W. E. Dunham, *Cesar Chavez* (Belmont, MA and San Marino, CA: The Review of the News, 1970); Susan Huck, *Little Cesar and His Phony Strike* (Belmont, MA and San Marino, CA: The Review of the News, 1974).

49. John Steinbacher, *Bitter Harvest* (Whittier, CA: Orange Tree Press, 1970). Steinbacher was a reporter for the local Anaheim, California, *Bulletin* whose writings predated by a decade the reactionary "family values" project of the Reagan-Bush era. The hero of Steinbacher's book on the UFW is a certain Alfred Ramirez, founder of a group called "Mothers Against Chavez" and California chairman of the Spanish Surname Citizens for Wallace (George Wallace was the former Alabama segregationist governor who ran for president as a third-party candidate in 1968). By the late 1990s and early 2000s, an even more virulent strain of antiliberalism was common currency. Right-wing hatred for centrist president Bill Clinton, for example, produced in southern California bumper stickers that read "Clinton=Socialism" [*sic*] or juxtaposed "Clinton" with a hammer and sickle. FOX News talking heads like Sean Hannity and Ann Coulter spoke incessantly about the "war against liberals."

50. Jensen and Hammerback, *Words of César Chávez*, 43.

51. Ibid., 85.

52. Quoted in David G. Gutiérrez, *Walls and Mirrors: Mexican Americans, Mexican*

Immigrants, and the Politics of Ethnicity (Berkeley and London: University of California Press, 1995), 199. Although he disagreed with the UFW on the undocumented-worker issue, Bert Corona later recalled: "Despite our differences with the United Farm Workers, we never had a major confrontation, even though on our side some people on the extreme left tried to provoke it." Bert Corona and Mario T. García, *Memories of Chicano History: The Life and Narrative of Bert Corona* (Berkeley and London: University of California Press, 1994), 249.

53. Navarro, *Mexican American Youth Organization*, 24.

54. raúlrsalinas, "Los caudillos," *La Raza* 1 (January 1971): 74.

55. Transcript of speech by Frobén Lozada delivered at Cal State University, Hayward (November 13, 1968). Copy in author's possession.

56. José G. Pérez, *Viva la Huelga!: The Struggle of the Farm Workers* (New York: Pathfinder Press, 1973), 13.

57. Antonio Camejo, "A New Ideology for the Chicano Party," in F. Chris Garcia, *La Causa Política: A Chicano Politics Reader* (Notre Dame: University of Notre Dame Press, 1970), 346.

58. Jesús Treviño, *Eyewitness: A Filmmaker's Memoir of the Chicano Movement* (Houston: Arte Público, 2001), 281.

59. Tony Castro, *Chicano Power: The Emergence of Mexican America* (New York: Saturday Review Press/E. P. Dutton & Co., 1974), 96–111.

60. Juan Gómez Quiñones, *Chicano Politics: Reality and Promise 1940–1990* (Albuquerque: University of New Mexico Press, 1990), 138. Elsewhere, Gómez Quiñones further criticizes the LRUP's position: "*La mesquina exclusión de César Chávez y de su sindicato fue espuria y ejemplo de la falta de visión de largo plazo. Se dejó fuera a una organización de estructura nacional, con una base de más de 70 mil trabajadores, con equipos organizados, considerable apoyo público y una fuerza que podía ser reconocida en elecciones tanto estatales como nacionales. Viniendo de donde venían, los cargos en contra de Chávez era hipócritas: trabajar con el Partido Demócrata y aceptar el apoyo de grupos no mexicanos*" ("The petty exclusion of Cesar Chavez and his union was mistaken and an example of the lack of a long-term vision. An organization with a national presence, a base of more than 70,000 workers, organized teams, considerable public support, and a force that could be deployed in state and national elections was cut out. Given where they came from, the charges against Chavez were hypocritical—working with the Democratic Party and accepting support from non-Mexican groups"). "La era de los setenta," in David R. Maciel, ed., *El México olvidado: La historia del pueblo chicano* (Tomo II). Colección Sin Fronteras (Ciudad Juárez and El Paso: Universidad Autónoma de Ciudad Juárez and University of Texas at El Paso, 1996), 247.

The troubled relations between the UFW leadership and leftists within the union itself have yet to be chronicled. See remarks by union cofounder Philip Vera Cruz in Craig Scharlin and Lilia V. Villanueva, eds., *Philip Vera Cruz: A Personal History of Filipino Immigrants and the Farmworkers Movement* (Seattle and London: University of Washington Press, 2000), 120.

61. In a speech at a Los Angeles antiwar rally in May of 1971, Chávez said: "It is hard for me because we in the farmworkers' movement have been so absorbed in our own struggle that we have not participated actively in the battle against the war." Quoted in

Jensen and Hammerback, *Words of César Chávez*, 63. When asked why he did not attend the 1968 Poor People's Campaign, Chávez answered that he could not abandon his responsibilities in California in order to travel to Washington, D.C. See Matthiessen, *Sal Si Puedes* (2000), 242.

62. Quoted in Matthiessen, *Sal Si Puedes* (1969), 66; Matthiessen, *Sal Si Puedes* (2000), 178–79. Many Movement activists, for whom indigenous histories and traditions had become a central part of their new identity, would have been disappointed by Chávez's favorable remarks in the same interview about the California mission system. See Matthiessen, *Sal Si Puedes* (1969), 65–66; Matthiessen, *Sal Si Puedes* (2000), 300.

63. Quoted in Matthiessen, *Sal Si Puedes* (1969), 69; Matthiessen, *Sal Si Puedes* (2000), 179. Chávez was always alert to the dangers of regressive ethnic nationalism. In 1971, he told an audience in Austin, Texas: "You know, one of the things that we have to be very careful [about] ourselves is that we struggle for our own *raza* and as we do our thing to protect ourselves, we have to constantly think that there are also other people, not necessarily Chicanos, who are in our same condition or even worse." See Jensen and Hammerback, *Words of César Chávez*, 57.

64. Corona, in Corona and García, *Memories of Chicano History*, 261.

65. Corky Gonzales, Interview in *La voz del pueblo*, Berkeley, California (June 1971): n.p. To the degree that radical organizations adopted an increasingly strident rhetoric threatening the use of violence, the mainstream media cast Chávez as a safe alternative and someone who could be reasoned with. In the April 1, 1969, issue of *Look* magazine, for example, readers were told: "At a time when many American radicals are saying that nonviolence—as an instrument for social change—died with Martin Luther King, Jr., it is reassuring to meet a man of faith who preaches compassion rather than bloody confrontation, practices what he preaches, and gets results." Anonymous, "Nonviolence Still Works," *Look* Magazine (April 1, 1969): 52.

Throughout the interview, Chavez's religiosity is emphasized. He praises Bobby Kennedy for his "*hechos de amor*, deeds of love" and eloquently states: "It may be a long time before the growers see us as human beings. . . . But we will win, we are winning, because ours is a revolution of mind and heart, not only of economics" (57). What one writer called Chávez's "tenacious idealism" sat in uneasy juxtaposition to traditional images of the union leader. See Cletus E. Daniel, "Cesar Chavez and the Unionization of California Farmworkers," in Daniel Cornford, ed., *Working People of California* (Berkeley: University of California, 1995), 401.

66. Abelardo Delgado, *The Chicano Movement: Some Not Too Objective Observations* (Denver: Totinem Publications, 1971), 17. According to Ernesto Vigil, Corky Gonzales "admired Chavez and praised his dedication to the farmworkers, but he—like Chavez himself—saw the latter mainly as a labor leader." *The Crusade for Justice: Chicano Militancy and the Government's War on Dissent* (Madison: University of Wisconsin Press, 1999), 10. Bert Corona, on the other hand, convincingly argued that the UFW deployed a form of *mexicano* nationalism that "complemented the stress on ethnic nationalism and ethnic revival in the sixties. . . . It was ethnic nationalism but it was interpreted through Cesar's earlier experience and consciousness which reflected a broader and more class-based approach." Corona and García, *Memories of Chicano History*, 248.

67. "It was the Chicano community that saw the struggle of the farm workers as its own struggle and formed the backbone of the [farm workers's] movement." Miguel Pendás, *Chicano Liberation and Socialism* (New York: Pathfinder Press, 1976), 7.

68. Matthiessen, *Sal Si Puedes* (2000), 109.

69. Rudy Villaseñor, "Chavez Gives Testimony for Gun Suspect," *Los Angeles Times* (November 26, 1970), Section 2: 3.

70. Pérez, *Viva la Huelga!*, 14. Pérez argued further: "The UFW is the closest thing today to the militant, socially conscious unionism of the CIO in the late thirties. It supported the movement against the Vietnam War when few labor leaders would go near it. The struggle of these oppressed workers and their attempts to link up with broader concerns of the working masses point in the direction of a new labor radicalism" (8–9).

71. Cháavez's spiritualized masculinity contradicts recent historiography and cultural criticism that casts the entire Chicano Movement as a hyper-masculinist orgy, as if Oscar Zeta Acosta not César Chávez were its primary inspiration. While there can be no doubt that the feminist critiques of the Movement carried out in the 1980s were necessary correctives to the sexist practices that characterized all organizations, arguments about the "origins" of the Movimiento that posit "emasculation" as its primary cause are misleading. A sense of "emasculation" among working-class men (of any ethnicity), the product of racializing capitalist formations, may produce a variety of pathologies ranging from alcoholism to domestic violence. In and of itself, however, "emasculation" cannot generate social movements. To argue that it can is to return to an older "pathological tradition" of social-movement theory, a tradition for the most part rejected by contemporary scholars. See William A. Gamson, "The Social Psychology of Collective Action" in Aldon D. Morris and Carol McClurg Mueller, eds., *Frontiers in Social Movement Theory* (New Haven and London: Yale University Press, 1992), 53–76. For a rather hastily constructed analysis of the Chicano Movement along these "pathological" lines, see Ramón A. Gutiérrez, "Community, Patriarchy and Individualism: The Politics of Chicano History and the Dream of Equality," *American Quarterly* 45 (March 1993): 44–72.

72. J. Craig Jenkins, *The Politics of Insurgency: The Farm Worker Movement in the 1960s* (New York: Columbia University Press, 1985), x.

73. César Chávez, Address to UFW's Seventh Constitutional Convention, September 1984. Available on the California Department of Education website http://chavez.scientech.com:8080/research.

74. César Chávez, Address to the Commonwealth Club of California, November 9, 1984. Available on the UFW website (ufw.org/commonwealth.htm) and in Jensen and Hammerback, *Words of César Chávez*, 122–29. Chávez added: "Our union will forever exist an empowering force among Chicanos in the Southwest. And that means our power and our influence will grow and not diminish. . . . The consciousness and pride that were raised by our union are alive and thriving inside millions of young Hispanics who will never work on a farm."

75. As early as 1968, Chávez had spoken about the unavoidable links between labor organizing and other struggles in the Southwest: "People raise the question: Is this a strike or is it a civil-rights fight? In California, in Texas, or in the South, any time you strike, it becomes a civil-rights movement. It becomes a civil-rights fight." Quoted in Jensen and Hammerback, *Words of César Chávez*, 33.

76. Address to the UFW's Seventh Constitutional Convention, September 1984, in Jensen and Hammerback, *Words of César Chávez*, 118.

77. César Chávez, "Lessons of Dr. Martin Luther King, Jr." (January 12, 1990). Available at http://www.sfsu.edu/~cecipp/cesar_chavez.

78. See "Chavez Blames Fatal Bus Accidents on Greed: 'inhuman treatment of farmworkers must end,'" *National Chicano Health Organization (NCHO) Newsletter* 3 (April 1974): 7 and Carl Ingram, "Farm Workers Celebrate Safety Law, Chavez Holiday," *Los Angeles Times* on-line edition (April 2, 2002).

79. Lesli A. Maxwell, "Davis Gives UFW Major Victory," *Sacramento Bee* on-line edition (October 1, 2002).

80. Dyson's colleague who denounces King begins boldly enough: "Fuck Martin Luther King. The nigga was the worst thing to happen to black people in the twentieth century." Michael Eric Dyson, *I May Not Get There with You: The True Martin Luther King, Jr.* (New York: Touchstone Press, 2000), 101.

81. On the situation for farmworkers in the 1980s and 1990s, see Rodolfo Acuña, *Occupied America: A History of Chicanos*, 4th ed. (New York: Longman, 2000); and Pat Hanson, "Migrant Farmers Suffering in Silence: California Groups Look at Problems and Solutions," *Hispanic Outlook in Higher Education* (June 3, 2002): 28–32. In his ground-breaking study of farm labor in the late twentieth century, Daniel Rothenberg writes: "The basic statistics regarding agricultural labor reveal an ethical challenge that raises questions about our professed belief that honest labor should be justly rewarded." *With These Hands: The Hidden World of Migrant Farmworkers Today* (Berkeley and London: University of California Press, 1998), xiii.

82. Rudolfo Anaya, *Elegy on the Death of César Chávez* (El Paso: Cinco Puntos Press, 2000), 26.

83. César A. (Teolol) Cruz, "Turning in Your Grave," unpublished MS (2002).

Chapter 5

1. Exchange between the Brown Buffalo and his brother in Oscar Zeta Acosta, *Revolt of the Cockroach People* (New York: Vintage, 1973), 188. Living in Mexico, the character of the brother speaks from a position far removed from actual events in the Southwest. The mistaken notion that Chicano/as were simply "doing what Blacks were doing" was shared by East Coast intellectuals and has been perpetuated in recent histories of the period.

2. *A Rap on Race* (New York: Dell, 1971), 122.

3. Martin Luther King, Jr., Interview with *Playboy* magazine (January 1965); repr., James Melvin Washington, ed., *A Testament of Hope: The Essential Writings and Speeches of Martin Luther King, Jr.* (San Francisco: HarperSanFrancisco, 1986), 364.

4. Martin Luther King, Jr., *Where Do We Go from Here: Chaos or Community?* (Boston: Beacon Press, 1968), 132.

5. According to some social-movement theorists, the Black Civil Rights struggle served as a frame for all subsequent movements: "One of the things that clearly linked the various struggles during this period was the existence of a 'master protest frame' that was appropriated by each succeeding insurgent group." Doug McAdam, "Culture and Social Movements," in Enrique Laraña, Hank Johnston, and Joseph R. Gusfield,

eds., *New Social Movements: From Ideology to Identity* (Philadelphia: Temple University Press, 1994), 42.

6. Celia Heller, *New Converts to the American Dream?: Mobility Aspirations of Young Mexican Americans* (New Haven: College and University Press, 1971), 15.

7. Nancie L. Gonzalez, "Positive and Negative Effects of Chicano Militancy on the Education of the Mexican American," *Educational Resources Information Center Reports* (Albuquerque: Southwestern Cooperative Educational Lab, 1970), 9.

8. Joseph Sommers, "From the Critical Premise to the Product: Critical Modes and Their Applications to a Chicano Literary Text" in Ricardo Romo and Raymund Paredes, eds., *New Directions in Chicano Scholarship*, Chicano Studies Monograph Series (La Jolla: University of California, San Diego, Chicano Studies Program, 1978), 69.

9. Leo Grebler, Joan W. Moore, and Ralph C. Guzmán, *The Mexican-American People: The Nation's Second Largest Minority* (New York and London: The Free Press, 1970), 584.

10. Joan W. Moore with Alfredo Cuéllar, *Mexican Americans*, Ethnic Groups in American Life Series (Englewood Cliffs, NJ: Prentice Hall, 1970), 151. Other scholars have argued that the Movement was a product of the Mexican American or World War II generation's activism: "The movimiento of the 1960s and 1970s was a direct consequence of successful organizational goals and efforts of the forties and fifties." Matt S. Meier and Feliciano Ribera, *Mexican Americans/American Mexicans: From Conquistadores to Chicanos* (New York: Hill and Wang, 1993), 218. As I suggested in the Introduction, however, the Movimiento marked a qualitative shift away from earlier Mexican American activism toward a militant critique of U.S. society and the unfulfilled promises of liberal democracy.

11. Bob Blauner, "The Chicano Sensibility," *Trans-Action* (February 1971); repr. as "More Than Just a Footnote: Chicanos and Their Movement" in Bob Blauner, *Still the Big News: Racial Oppression in America* (Philadelphia: Temple University Press, 2001), 166–67.

12. Ramón A. Gutiérrez, "Community, Patriarchy and Individualism: The Politics of Chicano History and the Dream of Equality," *American Quarterly* 45 (March 1993): 45. Historian Gerald Horne locates the African American "origins" of Chicano activism even earlier by confidently claiming: "There is little question that Watts 1965 had a catalytic impact on Mexican-American militance and the emergence of the Chicano movement." *Fire This Time: The Watts Uprising and the 1960s* (New York: Da Capo Press, 1997), 261. While the Watts rebellion undoubtedly influenced the political education of many young Latino/as in Los Angeles, including key members of the Brown Berets, Horne's assertion oversimplifies the complex genealogy of a social movement with diverse regional agendas.

13. José Limón, *American Encounters* (Boston: Beacon Press, 1998), 130. Some scholars made the claim as early as 1973 that the Movement was belated and imitative: "Impressed by the American public's initial support for Black civil rights and by the apparent concessions made to Blacks following the riots, some Native Americans and Chicanos began to emulate the Black model." Rudolph O. de la Garza, Z. Anthony Kruszewski, and Tomás A. Arciniega, eds., *Chicanos and Native Americans: The Territorial Minorities* (Englewood Cliffs, NJ: Prentice Hall, 1973), 2.

14. Manuel G. Gonzales, *Mexicanos: A History of Mexicans in the United States* (Bloomington: Indiana University Press, 2000), 196. Armando Navarro argues that "young Chicanos mimicked . . . the Black Power movement," but correctly adds: "This is not to say that all barrio youth organizations were carbon copies of Black Power groups." *Mexican American Youth Organization: Avant-Garde of the Chicano Movement in Texas* (Austin: University of Texas Press, 1995), 61. F. Arturo Rosales attributes Tijerina's early attempts at coalition building to his "emulating the Black civil rights movement." *Chicano!: The History of the Mexican American Civil Rights Movement* (Houston: Arte Público Press, 1997), 159.

15. Ian Haney López asserts: "These connections [between Chicanos and Blacks] operated so powerfully that some Mexican activists initially came to consider themselves effectively as black." *Racism on Trial: The Chicano Fight for Justice* (Cambridge and London: Belknap Press, 2003), 167. Haney López means Chicanos were "functionally black" vis-à-vis the judicial system. Beyond that narrow sphere, however, there is little evidence that ethnic Mexican militants adopted "black identities."

16. See, for example, the following characterization of Movimiento activists: "*Habían pecado de chauvinistas y pensando que su experiencia no tenía parangón con la de otras razas, dejaron de formar alianzas con otras minorías raciales que sufrían similares formas de opresión*" ("They failed due to their chauvinism and because they believed their experience was unique among the races they failed to form alliances with other racial minorities that suffered similar forms of oppression"). Ramón Arturo Gutiérrez, "El problema chicano," *Historia 16*, año II, 14 (June 1977): 109. As I show in this chapter, there is a great deal of historical evidence with which to refute such a claim.

17. In an earlier incarnation as a calypso singer, Nation of Islam leader Louis Farrakhan sang the following lines: "White man will say 'good morning' to [the] Spanish before [the] Negro . . . Negro will talk back, Spanish will obey." Quoted in Horne, *Fire This Time*, 103.

18. Blauner, "Chicano Sensibility," 171.

19. "Nosotros Venceremos: Chicano Consciousness and Change Strategies" (1972) reprinted in F. Chris Garcia, ed., *La Causa Política: A Chicano Politics Reader* (Notre Dame: University of Notre Dame, 1974), 223.

20. One of the few African American scholar/activists to address Black/Latino relationships, Marable has urged Black leaders to "transcend their parochialism." *Beyond Black and White: Transforming African-American Politics* (London and New York: Verso, 1995), 194–97. See also Elizabeth Betita Martínez, "Beyond Black and White: The Racisms of Our Time," *Social Justice* 20 (1993): 22–34.

21. According to one account, it was at the first Denver Youth Liberation Conference in 1969 that the artist Manuel Martínez first popularized the figure composed of indigenous and Spanish profiles and a frontal Mestizo or Chicano visage. See Marcelino C. Peñuelas, *Cultura hispánica en Estados Unidos: Los chicanos*, 2d ed. (Madrid: Ediciones Cultura Hispánica, 1978), 134.

22. Rodolfo Corky Gonzales, "Yo soy Joaquin." In a highly mannered discussion of the Gonzales poem, José Limón links it to Harold Bloom's theory of "the Counter-Sublime," and concludes by dismissing the poem in a depoliticizing act of self-deprecation directed at the critic's own generation: "Adolescent in its rebellious attitude toward

the father, 'I Am Joaquin' remains a primer for poetic and political adolescents, which we all were in 1969." *Mexican Ballads, Chicano Poems: History and Influence in Mexican-American Social Poetry* (Berkeley and Los Angeles: University of California Press, 1992), 129. Testimonials in the PBS series *Chicano!* attest to the positive impact exerted by Gonzales's poem on Chicano/a youth in the late 1960s.

23. George W. Grayson, "Tijerina: The evolution of a primitive rebel," *Commonweal* 86 (July 28, 1967): 465.

24. Ian Haney López overstates the influence of Vasconcelos on Movement thinkers: "In stressing mestizaje, Chicanos drew deeply on the racial ideas of José Vasconcelos." Haney López, *Racism on Trial*, 218. Haney López bases his assertion on one text by Luis Valdez, in which Valdez argues for the creation of a "new man." I would argue that Valdez's use of the term derives more from Che Guevara than Vasconcelos.

25. "José Vasconcelos and La Raza," *El Grito* 2 (Summer 1969): 49. García bases his discussion of Vasconcelos on John H. Haddox's laudatory study *Vasconcelos of Mexico: Philosopher and Prophet* (Austin: University of Texas Press, 1967). During the late 1960s and early 1970s Haddox was a scholar of Mexican philosophy at the University of Texas, El Paso, who encouraged his Chicano/a students to read the works of Vasconcelos. He published the interesting pamphlet *Los Chicanos: An Awakening People*, Southwestern Studies Monograph 28 (El Paso: Texas Western Press, 1970).

26. García, "José Vasconcelos and La Raza," 50.

27. Reies López Tijerina, *Mi lucha por la tierra* (Mexico City: Fondo de Cultura Económica, 1978), 377. See the abridged translation by José Angel Gutiérrez, *They Called Me "King Tiger": My Struggle for the Land and Our Rights* (Houston: Arte Público Press, 2000). The passage cited here does not appear in Gutiérrez's translation.

28. Michael Omi and Howard Winant, *Racial Formation in the United States: From the 1960s to the 1990s*, 2d ed. (New York and London: Routledge, 1994), 106.

29. Steven M. Buechler, *Social Movements in Advanced Capitalism: The Political Economy and Cultural Construction of Social Activism* (New York and Oxford: Oxford University Press, 2000), 137.

30. See Ruben Salazar's June 16, 1969 *L.A. Times* article on the Berets. Reprinted in Mario T. García, ed., *Border Correspondent: Selected Writings 1955–1970* (Berkeley: University of California Press, 1995), 212–19.

31. *Chicano Student Movement* (June 12, 1968): 5. See also Marguerite V. Marín, *Social Protest in an Urban Barrio: A Study of the Chicano Movement, 1966–1974* (Lanham: University Press of America, 1991), 101. For law-enforcement reports on Black/Brown alliances in Los Angeles, see *Hearings Before the Subcommittee to Investigate the Administration of the Internal Security Act and other Internal Security Laws of the Committee on the Judiciary, United States Senate, Ninety-first Congress, Second Session, Part 1: Extent of Subversion in the "New Left," Testimony of Robert J. Thoms* (January 20, 1970) (Washington, D.C.: U.S. Government Printing Office, 1970).

32. On Karenga and the US organization, see Scot Brown, *Fighting for Us: Maulana Karenga, the Us Organization, and Black Cultural Nationalism* (New York: New York University Press, 2003). On the conflict between the Black Panthers and US, see "The FBI's War on the Black Panther Party's Southern California Chapter," http://www.etext.org/Politics.

33. "Panthers Prepared!," *Berkeley Tribe* (July 18–24, 1969): 7.

34. Quoted in Marjorie Heins, *Strictly Ghetto Property: The Story of Los Siete de la Raza* (Berkeley: Ramparts Press, 1972), 58. Information about Los Siete de la Raza is taken from Heins, contemporary newspaper accounts and Research Organizing Cooperative of San Francisco (ROC), "The Lives of Los Siete," in Ed Ludwig and James Santibañez, eds., *The Chicanos: Mexican American Voices* (Baltimore: Penguin, 1971), 177–97. See also, Jason M. Ferreira, "All Power to the People: A Comparative History of Third World Radicalism in San Francisco, 1968–1974" (Ph.D. diss., University of California at Berkeley, 2003).

35. Heins, *Strictly Ghetto Property*, 161.

36. Mario Martinez interview in "Basta Ya!," *The Movement* (November 1969): 12. In the same interview, Mario Martinez stated: "Like I don't see no colors no more. I see and feel oppression, but I can't see the colors. Before I did. Before I was from El Salvador and everything else was different. But after you're here a while, this color thing fades away" (18).

37. Ibid.: 12.

38. Anonymous, "A Nuestros Hermanos," *El Pocho Che* 1 (April 1970): n.p. In his history of the Crusade for Justice, Ernesto Vigil tells the fascinating story of a certain "Juan Gomez" who appeared in Denver in the summer of 1969. "Juan Gomez" was in fact Gio Lopez, the seventh member of Los Siete who was in hiding. "Juan Gomez" disappeared a few months later. See Vigil, *The Crusade for Justice: Chicano Militancy and the Government's War on Dissent* (Madison: University of Wisconsin Press, 1999), 102–3.

39. "Angela Supports Denver Raza," *El Gallo* 5 (May 1973): 1.

40. Wolfgang Binder, ed., *"Anglos Are Weird People for Me": Interviews with Chicanos and Puerto Ricans* (Berlin: John F. Kennedy-Institut für Nordamerikastudien Universität Berlin, 1979), 100ff. In 2003, despite suffering from diabetes and confined to a wheelchair, Tijerina was still speaking out from his home in Mexico: "Bush and his masters are driving themselves into a hole . . . from which they will not be able to get out. . . . If the U.S. continues pushing for what he wants, they're going to end up exterminating a great part of humanity, just like they exterminated Hiroshima and Nagasaki." Adam Saytanides, "U.S. War on Terror Rankles Chicano Activist," *The New Mexican*, on-line edition (July 29, 2003).

41. For a useful summary of Tijerina's background, see David R. Maciel and Juan José Peña, "La Reconquista: The Chicano Movement in New Mexico" in Erlinda Gonzales-Berry and David R. Maciel, eds., *The Contested Homeland: A Chicano History of New Mexico* (Albuquerque: University of New Mexico Press, 2000), 269–301.

42. Ramón A. Gutiérrez argues that Chicano men marked the origins of Chicano history at 1848 while Chicana women preferred the date of 1519. Earlier in the essay, however, Gutiérrez says that Chicanos found "strength and inspiration in a heroic Aztec past" (45). Clearly, Movement activists drew upon both historical experiences of conquest as central to the elaboration of Chicano/a identity. See "Community, Patriarchy and Individualism: The Politics of Chicano History and the Dream of Equality," *American Quarterly* 45 (March 1993): 44–72.

43. Indigenous women's speech reported in "Alboroto y motín de México del 8 de junio de 1692," in Carlos de Sigüenza y Góngora, *Relaciones históricas* (Mexico City: Universidad Nacional Autónoma de México, 1992), 130.

44. Tijerina, *They Called Me "King Tiger,"* 9.

45. Ibid., 70.

46. Juan Roybal, "Corrido al Valiente Tijerina," *La voz de la Alianza*, Albuquerque, NM (July 10, 1970): n.p.

47. Alan Stang, "Reies Tijerina: The Communist Plan to Grab the Southwest, *American Opinion* 10 (October 1967): 6, 22.

48. Tijerina, *Mi lucha por la tierra*, 568.

49. Ignacio M. García, *Chicanismo: The Forging of a Militant Ethos among Mexican Americans* (Tucson: University of Arizona Press, 1998), 32–33.

50. "From Prison: Reies López Tijerina," in Ludwig and Santibañez, *Chicanos*, 219. Tijerina employed a variety of terms including *hispano, Latin, Indian, Indo-Hispano, Spanish American,* and *Chicano*.

51. Tijerina, *They Called Me "King Tiger,"* 37.

52. Tijerina, Interview with Elsa Knight Thompson, April 5, 1968, Pacifica News Archives, tape no. 155; transcript in F. Arturo Rosales, ed., *Testimonio: A Documentary History of the Mexican American Struggle for Civil Rights*, The Hispanic Civil Rights Series (Houston: Arte Público Press, 2000), 308–20.

53. Museum of New Mexico curator Frances Swadesh Early described some activities of the Alianza in a paper delivered at the 1968 American Ethnological Society. See her "The Alianza Movement: Catalyst for Social Change in New Mexico" in Renato Rosaldo, Gustav L. Seligmann, and Robert A. Calvert, eds., *Chicano: The Beginnings of Bronze Power* (New York: William Morrow, 1974), 27–37.

54. Tijerina, quoted in *The Movement* (August 1967): 6–7.

55. Richard Gardner, *¡Grito!: Reies Tijerina and the New Mexico Land Grant War of 1967* (Indianapolis: Bobbs Merrill, 1970), 208–9. Gardner's book on Tijerina, like that of Peter Nabokov, reproduces reported speech but does not cite sources. Nevertheless, both journalists lived in New Mexico and were in close contact with the Alianza leader.

56. Tijerina, *They Called Me "King Tiger,"* 101.

57. Edward Greer, "Unity Watchword at NewPol Convention," *Los Angeles Free Press* (October 6, 1967): 18. See also Vigil, *Crusade for Justice*, 39.

58. Patricia Bell Blawis, *Tijerina and the Land Grants: Mexican Americans in Struggle for Their Heritage* (New York: International Publishers, 1971), 99. Blawis's account is based on personal observation during her time spent with the Alianza and on contemporary newspaper reports.

59. Gardner, *¡Grito!*, 224. Although there is no mention in published accounts of Nation of Islam (NOI) representatives attending the meeting, a recent biography of Elijah Muhammad states that Tijerina had met with Muhammad, who agreed to sign the treaty and informed Tijerina of NOI's plan to take over "four or five states in the southeastern part of the country." Karl Evans, *The Messenger: The Rise and Fall of Elijah Muhammad* (New York: Vintage, 2001), 332.

60. Reported in *La Raza* 1 (October 29, 1967): 10. Father John Luce of the Episcopal Church of the Epiphany in Los Angeles supplied a bus for the delegates. See also Michael Jenkinson, *Tijerina: Land Grant Conflict in New Mexico* (Albuquerque: Paisano Press, 1968); and Gardner, *¡Grito!*, 209 ff.

61. Reprinted in *La Raza* 1 (October 29, 1967): 10–11. On law-enforcement accounts of the October 1967 Alianza convention, see *Hearings Before the Subcommittee to*

Investigate the Administration of the Internal Security Act and Other Internal Security Laws of the Committee on the Judiciary, United States Senate, Ninety-first Congress, Second Session, Part 1: Extent of Subversion in the "New Left," Testimony of Robert J. Thoms (January 20, 1970) (Washington, D.C.: U.S. Government Printing Office, 1970).

62. Blawis, *Tijerina and the Land Grants*, 100.

63. Nancie L. González, *The Spanish-Americans of New Mexico: A Heritage of Pride*, 2d ed. (Albuquerque: University of New Mexico Press, 1969), 103.

64. Leonard Brown, "Report from Albuquerque," *Los Angeles Free Press* (May 24, 1968): 35.

65. Blawis, *Tijerina and the Land Grants*, 65.

66. FBI report in Vigil, *Crusade for Justice*, 50; *Los Angeles Times* (February 19, 1968): A3. The *Times* reported the curiously precise number of "3,356." The L.A. *Free Press* put the number at 4,000; *Open City* at "more than 5,000."

67. John Bryan, "We'll Fight and Die Together," *Open City* (February 23–29, 1968): 3. A counterculture publication that moved from an early focus on rock and roll, drugs, and draft counseling to political reporting, *Open City* and its writers expressed a certain ambivalence toward Chicano Movement activities. Coeditor Bob Garcia, for example, reporting on an October 15, 1967, antiwar rally, wrote: "Last Sunday I joined 700 persons at what we all thought was going to be a peace rally at East Los Angeles City College stadium in the heart of the Mexican American community. But we soon found out that we were really at an Anglo hate rally." "A Chicano Peace Rally," *Open City* (October 18–24, 1967): 5.

68. Davis also criticizes Stokely Carmichael's speech at the Sports Arena meeting for espousing a hard nationalist line and dismissing socialism as white and European. See *Angela Davis: An Autobiography* (New York: Random House, 1974), 168.

69. Bryan, "We'll Fight and Die Together," 3.

70. Tijerina quoted in Della Rossa, "Tijerina and the Brown Berets: Making a Revolution, " *L.A. Free Press* (February 23, 1968): 20.

71. Bryan, "We'll Fight and Die Together," 3. The *Open City* account reported that East Los Angeles activist Moctezuma Esparza delivered a fiery speech in which he reportedly "screamed": "It's time for a street war, a war against the gabacho. He'll do us all in if we don't fight him together" (3). Federal law-enforcement agencies including the CIA, FBI, and military intelligence were all monitoring the meeting. According to one account, members of the 20th Special Forces Group (many of them active military returned from Viet Nam) had been issued photographs of individual radicals including the Brown Berets, and in some cases had been instructed to "eliminate" key leaders. See William F. Pepper, *Orders to Kill: The Truth behind the Murder of Martin Luther King* (New York: Carroll and Graf, 1995), 418–19.

72. Bryan, "We'll Fight and Die Together," 7.

73. Gerald D. McKnight, *The Last Crusade: Martin Luther King, Jr., the FBI, and the Poor People's Campaign* (Boulder: Westview Press, 1998), 20.

74. Interview with Elsa Knight Thompson, April 5, 1968, Pacifica News Archives, tape no. 155; transcript repr.. in Rosales, *Chicano!*, 310.

75. Ibid.

76. Maria Varela, "My Sixties Was Not Drugs, Sex, and Rock and Roll," unpublished MS. Copy in author's personal collection.

77. "The Poor People's Campaign" (Atlanta: SCLC, 1968). For an interesting analysis of the Poor People's Campaign, see Robert T. Chase, "Class Resurrection: The Poor People's Campaign of 1968 and Resurrection City" at http://etext.lib.virginia.edu/journals/EH/EH40.

78. Interview with José Yglesias, *New York Times Magazine* (March 31, 1967): 10.

79. The historic meeting called by Dr. King on March 15, 1968, included Chicano leaders Bert Corona, Reies López Tijerina, Rodolfo Corky Gonzales, and others. See Bert Corona and Mario T. García, *Memories of Chicano History: The Life and Narrative of Bert Corona* (Berkeley and London: University of California Press, 1994), 216. Dr. King's planned visit to Delano was postponed because of his decision to fly to Memphis in support of the garbage collector's strike. He was assassinated there on April 4.

80. Della Rossa, "Anglos No Angels," *L.A. Free Press* (April 19, 1968): 3.

81. There are numerous accounts of the Poor People's Campaign. An early one that portrays Tijerina as a "Southwestern rebel" who was "new to non-violence" but which is also critical of SCLC leadership is Charles Fager, *Uncertain Resurrection: The Poor People's Washington Campaign* (Grand Rapids: William B. Eerdmans Co., 1969). In his personal memoir, Ralph Abernathy fails to mention any Chicano leader by name, and portrays the Chicano/a and Puerto Rican delegations as too narrowly focused on their issues. Of the Chicano/as, Abernathy wrote: "They were clearly unhappy that we wouldn't abandon our agenda and concentrate on theirs. That night they drank heavily, played ranchero music [*sic*] on their guitars until three in the morning, and had to be visited several times by the national park rangers, who served as our official police force." *And the Walls Came Tumbling Down: An Autobiography* (New York: Harper and Row, 1989), 521.

In his recollections of the Campaign, Andrew Young wrote through a traditional black/white prism: "There was tension, not so much between black and white poor—their issues were largely the same whether rural or urban. But Hispanics and Native Americans brought issues that were entirely new to us—issues concerning language, treaties, and culture. One of the Hispanic leaders from New Mexico, Reis [*sic*] Tijerina, seemed more concerned about the Treaty of Guadalupe Hidalgo, which established the border between Mexico and the United States, than he was about poor people. Some leaders began agitating that their issues were being neglected." *An Easy Burden: The Civil Rights Movement and the Transformation of America* (New York: Harper Collins, 1996), 484. In a photograph included in Young's book, Tijerina is shown marching arm in arm with Abernathy and Young, but is misidentified in the caption as "Cesar Chavez."

Among the eyewitness Chicana/o accounts, the one by Los Angeles Brown Beret Gloria Arellanes is of special interest. Arellanes was the sole woman included in the Los Angeles Chicano/a delegation. She later became an important player in Chicano/a anti-war activities. See Dionne Espinoza, "Pedagogies of Nationalism and Gender: Cultural Resistance in Selected Representational Practices of Chicana/o Movement Activists, 1967–1972" (Ph.D. diss., Cornell University, 1996. See also Tijerina, *They Called Me "King Tiger"*; "Chicano Poor in Washington," *La hormiga* [Oakland, California] (August 8, 1968): 8–9; Blawis, *Tijerina and the Land Grants*, chapter 11.

82. Quoted in McKnight, *Last Crusade*, 108.

83. Ibid., 93. In the wake of September 11, 2001, it is interesting to note that FBI reports on the Poor People's Campaign included advisories about "black terrorists."

84. McKnight, *Last Crusade*, 92.

85. Not unlike most of the founders of the Black Civil Rights Movement, Rustin had a weak understanding of the Southwest and Spanish-speaking communities. In a 1967 article for the New York *Amsterdam News* in which he urged Blacks to form coalitions with other groups, he wrote: "In attempting to unify around common objectives, neither we nor they should allow cultural differences to stand in the way. There are deep and beautiful forms that the Spanish-speaking Americans hold dear, just as there are deep and beautiful cultural forms that we hold dear. True, our cultural differences are within the framework of American culture, whereas theirs are not. But there is one important contribution which their differences can make. Spanish Americans bring from their own historical backgrounds a tradition of revolutionary action against injustice which we can share." Rustin's claim that Mexican or even Puerto Rican histories are located "outside" the history of the United States was uninformed at best. See Rustin's "Minorities: The War Against Poverty" in *Down the Line: The Collected Writings of Bayard Rustin* (Chicago: Quadrangle Books, 1971), 201.

86. Ernesto Vigil explains that the decision of the Chicano leadership to remain at the Hawthorne School was in part due to the fear that Chicano agendas would be subordinated to African American agendas. See his *Crusade for Justice*, chapter 3. Vigil records four hundred members of the Southwest delegation; a SCLC memo quoted by Chase puts the total number of Mexican Americans at one thousand.

87. Della Rossa, "Poor People's Coalition," *La Raza* 1 (July 10, 1968): 7.

88. Della Rossa, "Anglos No Angels," L.A. *Free Press* (April 19, 1968): 19. By casting Robert Kennedy as essentially "rich and white," Tijerina ignored RFK's increased sympathies for ethnic-based agendas. Tijerina did not share the widespread admiration for Kennedy in the Mexican American community. He resented the fact that as U.S. Attorney General Kennedy had never responded to Tijerina's two attempts in 1963 to interest the Department of Justice in the land-grant issue, and felt that Kennedy had snubbed him at a 1968 meeting with César Chávez in Delano. See Tijerina, *They Called Me "King Tiger,"* 49.

Other Chicano/a activists, while publicly supportive of Kennedy, also harbored some resentment because of his campaign's refusal to contribute to the defense fund for the Chicano 13 (arrested in the March 1968 high school blowouts in Los Angeles). According to Carlos Muñoz, Jr., presidential candidate Senator Eugene McCarthy provided funds for the Chicano 13 while Kennedy did not. See "The Politics of Educational Change in East Los Angeles" in Alfredo Castañeda, ed., *Mexican Americans and Educational Change* (New York: Arno, 1974), 104.

89. "Reies Meets with Panthers," *La hormiga*, Oakland, CA (August 8, 1968): 6.

90. For an early characterization of the Alianza as a "cult," see Nancie L. González, "Alianza Federal de Mercedes," in Manuel P. Servín, ed., *The Mexican-Americans: An Awakening Minority* (Beverly Hills: Glencoe Press, 1970), 202. More recently, F. Arturo Rosales, in *Chicano!*, refers to the Alianza's "wild and meandering tactics, a reflection of Tijerina's state of mind [*sic*]."

91. Tom Nairn, *The Break-Up of Britain: Crisis and Neo-Nationalism*, 2d ed. (London: Verso, 1981), 340.

92. On January 24, 1969, for example, Tijerina told a group of students at the University of California, San Diego: "It's always a great satisfaction to see a few of these

so-called Chicanos in the universities. . . . My brothers pride themselves in calling them-selves Chicanos. They don't know that an anglo started calling them Chicano. They accept that but if I start bringing evidence to these youngsters, proofs, and prove to them that they are Indo-Hispanos they will say the anglo is the culprit." *Indicator* [UC San Diego] (January 29, 1969): 8.

93. Smith writes: "For an 'ethnocentric' nationalist, both 'power' and 'value' inhere in his cultural group. . . . My group is the vessel of wisdom, beauty, holiness, culture. . . . 'Polycentric' nationalism, by contrast, resembles the dialogue of many actors on a com-mon stage. . . . Other groups do have valuable and genuinely noble ideas and institu-tions." Anthony Smith, *Theories of Nationalism* (London: Duckworth, 1971), 158–59.

94. Blawis, *Tijerina and the Land Grants*, 169.

95. Zephyr Press reprinted Martinez's classic work *Letters from Mississippi* in 2002.

96. Clayborne Carson, *In Struggle: SNCC and the Black Awakening of the 1960s* (Cambridge, MA: Harvard University Press, 1981), 142.

97. *Personal Politics: The Roots of Women's Liberation in the Civil Rights Movement and the New Left* (New York: Vintage, 1980), 110–11.

98. Thanks to Maria Varela for sharing with me her unpublished manuscript "My Sixties Was Not Drugs, Sex, and Rock and Roll." I also conducted a telephone interview with Maria Varela on June 16, 2000. See also Gonzales-Berry and Maciel, *Contested Homeland*, 286–87.

99. The following information is based on an interview conducted with Katarina Davis del Valle on April 22, 1997.

100. The following is based on an interview conducted with Mario Salas on November 21, 1997, in San Antonio. In May of 1997, Salas was elected to the San Antonio City Council from the second district.

101. Sánchez made this point at a Mexican American youth conference held in April 1963 at Occidental College in Los Angeles. See Jack D. Forbes, *Aztecas del Norte: The Chicanos of Aztlán* (Greenwich, CT: Fawcett, 1973), 164. Ten years later, Mexican scholars Jorge Bustamante and Gilberto López y Rivas wrote: "There is a relationship between the constant repression and the radicalization of Chicanos in East Los Angeles. The political consciousness of Chicanos there has been raised by blows from the billy clubs of the police." "La Raza Unida Party in the Chicano Movement" (1973), in Gilberto López y Rivas, *The Chicanos: Life and Struggles of the Mexican Minority in the United States* (New York and London: Monthly Review Press, 1973), 156.

102. Edward J. Escobar, "The Dialectics of Repression: The Los Angeles Police Department and the Chicano Movement, 1968–1971," *The Journal of American History* (March 1993): 1483–1515.

103. "At root, I understand the Chicano movement as an effort to respond to the problem of race in this country." Haney López, *Racism on Trial*, 249. Haney López's study is a useful meditation on the impact of Movement-related court cases in Los Angeles, especially the Chicano 13 and the Biltmore 6. Despite his narrow focus on L.A., he makes sweeping generalizations about the entire Movimiento as a race-based social movement. Haney López's analysis of the criminal-justice system's relationship to the Movement in L.A. at times leads him to exaggerate the importance of figures such as attorney Oscar Zeta Acosta.

104. Despite making the white to brown shift the theoretical centerpiece of his study, Haney López admits that the "will to whiteness" visible among some Mexican American groups was not widespread: "The claim to be white stood at the center of many Mexican Americans' self-understanding. But this does not mean that all Mexicans from the 1930s to the 1960s emphasized white identity, or that whiteness held the same importance or meaning across the Southwest. . . . Los Angeles's Mexican population was more ambiguous about racial identity [and] there were fewer efforts to openly proselytize a white identity and generally less discussion of race itself." *Racism on Trial*, 79–80.

105. Anonymous forty-nine-year-old African American male quoted in Tatcho Mindiola Jr., Yolanda Flores Niemann, and Nestor Rodriguez, *Black-Brown: Relations and Stereotypes* (Austin: University of Texas Press, 2002), 57–58.

106. Roberto Vargas and Samuel C. Martinez, *Razalogía: Community Learning for a New Society* (Oakland: Razagente Associates, 1984), 58.

107. "Hispanics Now Largest U.S. Minority Group, Census Says," The Associated Press (January 21, 2003).

108. See Mindiola et. al., *Black-Brown*; and John D. Márquez, "Black Gold and Brown Lives: racial violence, memory, and collective resistance in Baytown, Texas" (Ph.D. diss., University of California, San Diego, 2004).

109. See my "A Chicano Looks at the Trent Lott Affair," Guest Commentary, *The Black Commentator* 25 (January 16, 2003) at www.blackcommentator.com.

110. Mireya Navarro, "Blacks and Latinos Try to Find Balance in Touchy New Math," *New York Times* (January 17, 2004): A 1. In early 2005, violence between Latinos and Blacks erupted in several Los Angeles high schools. See Earl Ofari Hutchinson, "Los Angeles School Brawls Expose Black-Latino Tension," Pacific News Service, on-line edition (April 27, 2005).

111. The letter was composed by Elizabeth Betita Martinez, who has figured prominently in these pages. See the letter at http://afgen.com/blacks_latinas.html.

112. Nick C. Vaca, *The Presumed Alliance: The Unspoken Conflict Between Latinos and Blacks and What It Means for America* (New York: Rayo, 2004), 186–88.

113. "Our Next Race Question: The Uneasiness between blacks and Latinos," *Harper's Magazine* (April 1996): 61.

Chapter 6

1. See the classic study Carlos Muñoz, Jr., *Youth, Identity, Power: The Chicano Movement* (London and New York: Verso, 1989), especially 78–84 and 134–41 on the Santa Barbara conference. According to one key participant, Jesús Chavarría, who at the time was an assistant professor of history at UC Santa Barbara, San Diego activist René Nuñez was the originator of the idea for a conference. See "On Chicano History: In Memoriam, George I. Sánchez 1906–1972 in Américo Paredes, ed., *Humanidad: Essays in Honor of George I. Sánchez* (Los Angeles: Chicano Studies Center, UCLA, 1977), 44.

2. "25 Resolutions on Chicano Studies," UC Chicano Conference, Santa Barbara, California (September 24, 1969). Author's collection.

In a 1971 article that summarized student objectives, members of Long Beach State College's Movimiento Estudiantil Chicano de Aztlán (MEChA) wrote: "The primary goal of Chicano student groups on college campuses is to make the colleges and universities serve the Chicano community. These institutions must become instruments in our struggle for community liberation from the political and socio-economic subjugation of institutionalized racism in U.S. society." "The Role of the Chicano Student," *Epoca: National Concilio for Chicano Studies Journal* 1 (Winter 1971): 18.

3. The word *mecha* had appeared in the UFW's Plan de Delano (1966): "*Nuestra peregrinación es la mecha, para que nuestra causa prenda, para que todos los campesinos vean su luz . . .*" (Our pilgrimage is the match that will ignite our cause for all farm workers to see . . ."). Richard J. Jensen and John C. Hammerback, eds., *The Words of César Chávez* (College Station: Texas A and M University Press, 2002), 21.

4. Barbara Galván interview with Vince de Baca, UCSD MSC, Third College files.

5. *El Plan de Santa Barbára, A Chicano Plan for Higher Education/Analyses and Positions by the Chicano Coordinating Council on Higher Education* (Oakland: La Causa, 1969), 77–78.

6. Ronald W. López, Arturo Madrid-Barela, Reynaldo Flores Macías, *Chicanos in Higher Education: Status and Issues*, Monograph No. 7 (Los Angeles: UCLA Chicano Studies Center, 1976). Since these figures included all Latino groups in the United States, the number of Mexican American students was far less.

7. Ibid., 160. The stagnation of the late 1970s produced only slight increases in the percentage of "Hispanic" graduates and undergraduates out of all students in degree-granting institutions—3.6 percent in 1976; 4.0 percent in 1980. By the end of the Reagan era (1990), numbers had risen to 5.8 percent. The 1990s brought substantial change primarily due to demographic increases. In 1999, the percentage of all "Hispanic" graduates and undergraduates out of all students in degree-granting institutions was still under 10 percent—9.2 percent. U.S. Department of Education, National Center for Education Statistics, *Status and Trends in the Education of Hispanics (2003)*, Table 208, 242.

8. On Chicano/a student activism, see Carlos Muñoz, Jr., *Youth, Identity, Power*.

9. A chronology of events at Berkeley is given in the pamphlet titled "Strike 1969" written and distributed by the Third World Liberation Front. Photocopy in author's personal collection.

10. "Strike 1969," 3.

11. Marjorie Heins, *Strictly Ghetto Property: The Story of Los Siete de la Raza* (Berkeley: Ramparts Press, 1972), 134. Primarily a Chicano-run project at the time of its founding in early 1969, Venceremos College was linked later to the Venceremos organization active in the Bay Area and at Stanford University. After the disintegration of the Revolutionary Union group in December of 1970, the membership of Venceremos expanded to include a wide range of organizations, changing the name of the *Venceremos* newspaper to *Pamoja Venceremos* in order to reflect a pan-ethnic agenda ("Pamoja" means "together" in Swahili). Los Angeles activist Katarina Davis del Valle worked briefly with Venceremos (see Chapter 5). On the congressional investigation of these Bay Area groups, see *America's Maoists: The Revolutionary Union, The Venceremos Organization*, Report by the Committee of Internal Security, House of Representatives, Ninety-second Congress, Second session (Washington, D.C.: U.S. Government Printing Office, 1972).

12. "On the Brown Women's Struggle! Statement from the Brown Women's Venceremos Collective," repr. in Gilberto López y Rivas, *The Chicanos: Life and Struggles*

of the Mexican Minority in the United States (New York and London: Monthly Review Press, 1973), 171–74.

13. Jack D. Forbes, *Aztecas del Norte: The Chicanos of Aztlán* (Greenwich, CT: Fawcett, 1973), 322.

14. "Universidad Deganawidah-Quetzalcoatl Course List," San Diego Historical Society, Mario T. García Collection, Box 2, fld. 28. Outside California other Raza schools included Colegio Jacinto Treviño in Texas, La Academia de la Nueva Raza in New Mexico, and the Crusade for Justice's Colegio Tlatelolco in Denver. See Charles Ornelas, Carlos Brazil Ramirez, and Fernando V. Padilla, *Decolonizing the Interpretation of the Chicano Political Experience*, Pamphlet Series No. 2 (Los Angeles: Chicano Studies Center, 1975), 29 ff.

15. "Why DQU? An Indian-Chicano University in 5082 A.C." (1972) in Forbes, *Aztecas del Norte*, 244. DQU lost its accreditation and closed its doors in 2005.

16. See *Casa de la Raza: Separatism or Segregation: Chicanos in Public Education*, Southwest Network Study Commission on Undergraduate Education and the Education of Teachers (Hayward, CA Bay View/Regal Printing, 1973).

17. Y. Arturo Cabrera, *Emerging Faces: The Mexican Americans* (New York: Wm. C. Brown Co., 1971), 81–82.

18. Philip Montez, "Will the Real Mexican American Please Stand Up," *Civil Rights Digest* (Winter 1970): 30 [28–31].

19. Letter from the UC Chicano Steering Committee to President Hitch (January 25, 1970): 2. UCSD MSC, Third College files (Dorn project).

20. Ysidro Macias, "Plan de Political Action for Chicano Campus Groups," document produced at the Political Action workshop at the University of California, Santa Barbara conference, April, 1969; repr. *El Pocho Che* 1 (April 1970): 43.

21. By "class racism" I mean a toxic brew of structural racism, racializing practices enacted by individuals (at times unconsciously), and a pervasive climate of elitist entitlement characteristic of traditional academic culture.

The research of Richard A. Ibarra shows that even on campuses with a critical mass of Latino/a and Black students elitism is a major obstacle to academic success: "Students encountered serious academic difficulties that were attributed more to the traditions of academic culture than to racism or sexism . . . Even in Hispanic serving institutions, where Latino student enrollment can range between 25 percent and 85 percent, conflicts with academic culture continue unabated and may even be exacerbated for many students and faculty." "At the Crossroads of Cultural Change in Higher Education," in *Strategic Initiatives for Hispanics in Higher Education*, The Hispanic Caucus, American Association for Higher Education (August 2, 2003): 55.

22. Nancy Scott Anderson, *An Improbable Venture: A History of the University of California, San Diego* (La Jolla: The University of California San Diego Press, 1993), 54–61.

23. In 1951 the director of Scripps Institute of Oceanography, Roger Revelle, had been forced to buy land for faculty housing so that Jewish faculty could be accommodated. In his eagerness to establish a UC campus in La Jolla, Revelle chose to discount local racist practices, and assured UC president Clark Kerr at a May 1958, meeting that racial discrimination was not a problem. When the city of San Diego transferred the "Pueblo lands" to the university, one local La Jolla group protested: "It will introduce

undesirable elements into the community. We can foresee an integration crisis in La Jolla schools when the children of these people apply for admittance." "Statement opposing the transfer of Pueblo lands," UCSD MSC, RSS 3, box 5, fld. 1.

24. "Letter to T. C. Holy from Roger Revelle, 5 August 1955," UCSD MSC, RSS3, box 4, fld. 12. In the minutes of a meeting of the UC Special Committee on New Campus Sites, one of the regents concurred with Revelle: "Regent McLaughlin was of the opinion that the University should concentrate on educating the intellectually elite rather than the great mass of students, which he believed the duty of the state colleges" UCSD MSC RSS 3, box. 6, fld. 9.

25. Edwin Martin, "Negro University Sets Standard for Discipline," *San Diego Union* (May 9, 1965): A2. In a letter to the editor, UCSD philosophy professor Avrum Stroll defended the demonstrators, and argued: "Rather than opposing the involvement of students in the political developments of our time, the university is duty-bound to encourage and foster such involvement if it is to do its proper job." Letter to the editor (May 8, 1965) in UCSD MSC RSS 1, box 249, fld. 5.

26. Galbraith letter to Chancellor Murphy (May 14, 1965), UCSD MSC, RSS 1, box 249, fld. 5.

27. Harold Keen, "The Death of Tío Taco," *San Diego Magazine* 22 (August 1970): 95.

28. The most thoroughly chronicled events related to radical politics on the UCSD campus had to with the controversy surrounding philosopher Herbert Marcuse, his subsequent rehiring, and the firestorm produced by the conservative reaction led by Governor Ronald Reagan. See McGill, *Year of the Monkey, Third College Twentieth Anniversary, 1970–1990* (La Jolla: UCSD Publications Office, 1990); and Paul Alexander Juutilainen's 1996 documentary *Herbert's Hippopotamus* (New York: Cinema Guild).

29. Angela Davis, *Angela Davis: An Autobiography* (New York: Random House, 1974), 152. Davis added: "Sometimes I would get in my car and, out of sheer frustration, drive into San Diego and head toward Logan Heights, where the largest concentration of Black people lived . . . trying to devise some way of escaping this terrible isolation" (152).

30. Eldridge Cleaver, Open Letter to Stokely Carmichael, published in *Ramparts* (September 1969); repr. in Philip S. Foner, ed., *The Black Panthers Speak* (New York: Da Capo, 1995), 104–8. Cleaver told Carmichael: "You were unable to distinguish your friends from your enemies because all you could see was the color of the cat's skin" (106).

31. Speech published in *The Black Panther* (December 27, 1969); repr. in Foner, *Black Panthers Speak*, 124–27.

32. Interview with Israel Chavez, UCSD MSC, Third College files (Dorn project).

33. Anonymous, "Regents Meet at UCSD—Reagan Likes OKd Resolution," *San Diego Free Press* (November 30-December 12, 1968): 3.

34. Davis, *Angela Davis*, 196. Over thirty years later, Davis's hope for the UCSD campus has yet to be realized: "The creation of the college would bring large numbers of Black, Brown and working-class white students into the university" (198). In 2004, African Americans made up about 1 percent of the total student body; Chicano/as 8 percent, this in a region where people of Mexican descent made up roughly 25 percent of the population.

35. *Lumumba-Zapata College, B.S.C.-M.A.Y.A. Demands for the Third College, U.C.S.D.* (March 1969): 2.

36. On the struggle for Chicano Park, see Marilyn Mumford's 1989 documentary *Chicano Park* (New York: Cinema Guild).

37. Randy Dotinga interview with Vince de Baca, UCSD MSC, Third College files. De Baca, a native San Diegan, had been an activist with the United Farm Workers and the Brown Berets. In 2005, he was chairman of the Chicano/a Studies Program at Metropolitan State College in Denver.

38. Barbara Galván interview with Vince de Baca, UCSD MSC, Third College files (Dorn project). Israel Chavez told an interviewer: "We wanted an international unity based on socialism and not national cultures." UCSD MSC, Third College files (Dorn project).

39. Details in this paragraph are from student Alda Blanco's notes taken at the UCSD MEChA meeting of November 3, 1971. Author's collection.

40. "MEChA Constitution (1971?), San Diego Historical Society, Mario T. García Collection, box 2, fld. 20. In a 1973 document, some UCSD *mechistas* critiqued the organization's narrow nationalist approach: "In the past MEChA has manifested a greater concern for the well-being of its own people. It seems that MEChA has never had any intentions of aligning itself with Third World movements within this nation. The ideal practice for MEChA to follow would be that of establishing viable relationships with Latin American movements (i.e., M.I.R.). Once being exposed to the working of groups within other nations, MEChA will be able to expand its knowledge and depart from its isolationist practices." UC San Diego's MEChA, "Analysis" (September 12, 1973), San Diego Historical Society, Mario T. García Collection, box 2, fld. 18.

41. See "Minutes of the UCSD Campus Relations Committee" (n.d.), San Diego Historical Society, Mario T. García Collection, box 1, fld. 2.

42. UCSD MSC, Third College files (Dorn project), Blanco files. In a letter to his predecessor Chancellor Galbraith, Chancellor McGill referred to Blanco as "one of our most formidable campus radicals during the past year." Letter to Galbraith (March 2, 1969), UCSD MSC, Chancellors's Archives, RSS 1, box 249, fld. 4.

43. "Freshman Chancellor Reveals Philosophy," *Triton Times* (October 11, 1968): 2.

44. UCSD Mandeville Special Collections, Chancellors's Archives, RSS 1, box 191, fld. 3.

45. On May 25, 1970, a group of UCSD faculty addressed a letter to UC President Hitch and the Regents protesting the firing of Angela Davis. In his cover letter to Hitch, McGill aligned himself with the faculty protest: "These men are not rabble rousers. They are the intellectual heart of the campus . . . I associate myself with the contents of the letter." McGill to Hitch (June 8, 1970). RSS 1, box 248, fld. 2.

46. RSS 1, box 191, fld. 3.

47. UCSD Black Student's Council, "Suggested Improvements in the Liberal Arts Curriculum at the University of California, San Diego," May 14, 1968. UCSD Mandeville Special Collections, Third College history project files. In April of 1968, the African American Student Union (AASU) at UC Berkeley had submitted a proposal for a Black Studies department.

48. I have reconstructed the chronology of events surrounding the creation of Third (Lumumba-Zapata) College from a number of sources including existing interviews with participants, newspaper and magazine accounts; McGill, *Year of the Monkey*; Marsha Harris and Michael Estrada, "The History of Third College" (1979 in UCSD MSC); Bob

Dorn et al., *Third College Twentieth Anniversary: Diversity, Justice, Imagination* (La Jolla: UCSD Publications, 1990); and Scott Anderson, *Improbable Venture.*

49. "Third College Plans to Involve Itself with Local Community, " *Triton Times* (June 14, 1968): 15. Rappaport also proposed "Operation Opportunity" in order to admit economically disadvantaged students, thereby "assuring that, when those doors [to the third college] are opened in 1970, youngsters from disadvantaged and culturally deprived environments will walk in side by side with the more typical UCSD students." Quoted in Judith Morgan, "UCSD Plan Offers a Break to Disadvantaged Students," *San Diego Union* (August 10, 1968): A 10.

50. "Black, Brown Studies Urged for UCSD," *San Diego Union* (March 26, 1969): B2.

51. Interviews with Vince de Baca and Joe Martinez, UCSD MSC, Third College files (Dorn project).

52. "Message: Liberation" (June 28, 1969), 6–7, in UCSD MSC, Third College files (Dorn project).

53. Harold Keen, "UCSD's Third World College," *San Diego Magazine* (September 1969).

54. Introduction to *Encuentro Femenil* 1 (1973): 3–7; repr. in Alma García, ed., *Chicana Feminist Thought: The Basic Historical Writings* (New York and London: Routledge, 1997), 114.

55. Anonymous, "Chicano Committee on Higher Education Conference," *Hijas de Cuauhtémoc* 1 (1974): 4; repr. in García, *Chicana Feminist Thought*, 164.

56. *Lumumba-Zapata College, B.S.C.-M.A.Y.A. Demands for the Third College, U.C.S.D.* (March 1969): 4. UCSD MSC, Third College files (Dorn project). A copy of the original demands with Carlos Blanco's handwritten comments may be found in the same location.

57. "Report of the Third College Planning Committee, Subcommittee on Curriculum" (May 19, 1969), UCSD MSC, RSS 1, box 106, fld. 1.

58. McGill letter to UCSD MEChA and United Chicanos of San Diego (January 21, 1970). Alda Blanco personal files.

59. Jack Douglas letter to the editor, *Los Angeles Times* (August 8, 1970): sec. 2, p. 7. Douglas's claims were often the product of his fertile imagination. In another letter to the *Los Angeles Times*, he labeled Third College students as unprepared for university work: "Though their courses are only about one-third as difficult as the regular courses, they have a failure rate twice as high" (May 16, 1971): G7. His faculty colleagues who supported the students, he told a local newspaper, were "like good German citizens who sat back while people went up the chimney." Alan Merridew, "UCSD Professor Says Opposition Results in 'Smear,'" *San Diego Evening Tribune* (June 3, 1971): A1.

60. Al Capp's remarks are quoted in Dick Betts, "Cartoonist Hits Campus Turmoil," *Santa Monica Outlook* (October 15, 1970): 13.

61. Anonymous, ""Progress on Lumumba-Zapata?," *Indicator* [UC San Diego] (May 14, 1969): 2.

62. "Minutes of Third College Planning Committee" (May 19, 1969), UCSD MSC, RSS 1, box 106, fld. 1. Faculty members on the committee included Carlos Blanco and Fredric Jameson.

63. "Third College—The Quiet Revolution," *Triton Times* 8 (November 25, 1969): 1. One year later, the *Triton Times* represented the college as one factor in international liberation movements and led with the frontpage headline "Third College: Hope for the Third World" (October 16, 1970).

64. Interview with Barbara Galván, UCSD MSC, Third College files (Dorn project).

65. Interview with Lisa Collins, UCSD MSC, Third College files (Dorn project).

66. Doug Wood, "Third College," *UCSD Contact* 2 (June 1971): 4.

67. Alfredo Cuéllar, "Perspective on Politics" in Joan W. Moore and Alfredo Cuéllar, *Mexican Americans* (New York: Prentice Hall, 1970), 148–56; repr. as "Cultural Nationalism in the Southwest" in *Viewpoints: Red and Yellow, Black and Brown* (Minneapolis: Winston Press, 1972), 295–300.

68. Muñoz, *Youth, Identity, Power*, 84–85.

69. Chancellor McGill recalled in his memoir: "The real achievers were the moderate minority students who knew what they wanted, and the fine, idealistic faculty at UCSD who transformed the strident ugliness of Lumumba-Zapata College into the fragile beauty of Third College, with all its hopes for a better world." *Year of the Monkey*, 153.

70. McGill quoted in Keen, "UCSD's Third World College," 175.

71. Turner accepted a job at Cornell University and never went to UCSD. In the letter to Galbraith in which he mentions Turner, McGill's tone was ominous: "There are dark clouds on the horizon for next year at UCSD. Our long struggle with minority students for control of Third College continues and once again trouble is very near the surface." August 7, 1969, UCSD MSC, RSS 1, box 249, fld. 4.

72. Various accounts of how Watson became provost are in Bob Dorn et al., *Third College Twentieth Anniversary*, 44–47.

73. Chancellor McGill to President Charles Hitch, May 20, 1970, UCSD MSC, RSS 1, box 29, fld. 5.

74. Letter to William Frazer, May 20, 1970, UCSD MSC, RSS 1, box 29, fld. 5.

75. The chair of MEChA in 1970, Nick Aguilar, recalled years later that as a body MEChA never voted on Watson's candidacy and Chicanos were not consulted on the appointment. Bob Dorn, et al., *Third College Twentieth Anniversary*, 47. MEChA did in fact have a representative on the search committee—Robert Carrillo. He apparently refused to support Watson's nomination. "Minutes of the Third College Provost Search Committee" (March 13, 1970), UCSD MSC, Third College files (Dorn project). Nevertheless, the minutes of a February 11 MEChA meeting and a February 12 meeting with Watson record that "MEChA ... supports the candidacy of Dr. Watson for Provost of Lumumba-Zapata College." Minutes of meetings in Alda Blanco, personal files. It appears that indecision and lack of a unified position on the part of UCSD Chicano/as facilitated the appointment of Watson as provost.

76. Diane Clark, "Young Professor Shapes Third College," *San Diego Union* (October 17, 1976): B1. Watson was quoted in this article as saying: "I grew up in an almost totally black environment. And although I can get along OK with whites, it's still not comfortable for me. I like to see black faces around."

77. In a 1989 interview, Watson offered the following comments on the conflict that transformed Lumumba-Zapata College into Third College: "I think it's fair to say

that there were ethnic group differences on the purposes of the college. I think some people viewed the college as an opportunity to do something radical in higher education. Others viewed it as an opportunity to educate more students in a traditional sense. I would say if you had to characterize me, I'm more towards the latter." Interview with Alex Wong, UCSD MSC, Third College files (Dorn project).

78. "To All at UCSD," statement signed by Joseph W. Watson (May 18, 1970) in UCSD MSC RSS 1, box 247, fld. 1. Two years later, following the shooting deaths of two Black students in Louisiana, Watson told a reporter: "The basic problem is that the black in the South and across the country is still not recognized as a person." "200 at UCSD Honor 2 Slain Dixie Students," *San Diego Union* (November 22, 1972): B3.

79. Watson is quoted in William Trambley, "Minorities College Called Too Radical; Regents to Decide," *Los Angeles Times* (October 11, 1970): B1.

80. The first group of Chicanos in 1965 was made up of just three students. Because of Chicano faculty- and student-initiated recruitment efforts, numbers rose steadily. From eighteen Chicano/as in 1967, the number climbed to forty-four the following year due in great part to the efforts of Ana Cárdenas, Eustacio "Chato" Benitez, Estelle Chacón, Carlos Blanco, and others.

81. Interview with Lisa Collins, UCSD MSC, Third College files. Biology professor Brian O'Brien had a somewhat harsher recollection: "Joe Watson tried to make sure that no radical people got tenure because it would denigrate black education to give them breaks." Interview with Anne Scott, UCSD MSC, Third College files (Dorn project).

82. "Minutes of Faculty and Staff of Third College" (October 4, 1971), UCSD MSC, RSS 1130, box 36, fld. 8.

83. Letter from MEChA chairman Francisco Estrada to Chancellor McElroy (1972), San Diego Historical Society, Mario T. García Collection, box 2, fld. 17. On February 14, 1972, Chicano/a students had welcomed the new chancellor to campus in a meeting during which they used the Plan de Sánta Barbara to call for reforms in admissions and staff hiring. Presenters included Chato Benitez, Maria Blanco, Patricia Nava, and Francisco Estrada. "Agenda for MEChA meeting with Chancellor" (February 14, 1972), San Diego Historical Society, Mario T. García Collection, box 2, fld. 17.

84. Anonymous, "Chicano Position Paper on Third College," UCSD MSC RSS 1130, box 27, fld. 7. In the same location, see also the documents "Where We Are Now" (May 8, 1972) written by the Lumumba-Zapata Steering Committee; and Jef [*sic*] Raskin, "To the Third College/Lumumba-Zapata Community" (May 9, 1972), which called for a compromise between Watson and his opponents.

85. Alan Merridew, "17 of 30 Third College faculty ask provost to quit," *San Diego Evening Tribune* (May 10, 1972): B1. Original letter dated May 1, 1972 in UCSD MSC RSS 1130, box 27, fld. 7.

86. UCSD MSC, Third College files (Dorn project).

87. Interview with Barbara Galán, UCSD MSC, Third College files (Dorn project). Fania Jordan, Sydney Glass, and Fred Barnwell were among the Black students who joined the group calling for Watson's removal.

88. Mr. James A. Trotter, "Watson Fights Neo-colonialism," *Black Voices* [UC San Diego] (May 1972): n.p. Trotter concluded: "For Chicano students to even imply a 'coalition' between the white caucus or white faculty is a farce in white racist America."

89. Anonymous, no title (on Black Students Union letterhead), n.d., UCSD MSC, RSS 1130, box 27, fld. 7. Shortly after his victory, Watson told an interviewer that the move against him had been led by "a faculty leadership, not a student leadership . . . essentially a white faculty leadership, not a Chicano faculty leadership. . . . The most forceful advocates of the opposing position were white faculty." Betty L. Padelford, "UCSD Third College Conflict Resolution," paper written for the U.S. International University Graduate program (July 13, 1972), 45.

According to a May 10, 1972, letter to McElroy from the coalition seeking Watson's ouster, the "white" professors who had been singled out by the BSU were Brian O'Brien, Will Wright, and Silvio Varon. The letter stated that both O'Brien and his wife had been subjected to threats and intimidation, apparently from Black nationalists. On May 30, Watson addressed a memo to "The Third College Community" "to request that we all maintain our commitment to avoid all forms of violence and intimidation in resolving our differences." Both documents are located at UCSD MSC, RSS 1130, box 27, fld. 7.

90. Letter to Chancellor McElroy, May 22, 1972, UCSD MSC, Chancellors's files, RSS 1, box 30, fld. 1.

91. *San Diego Union* (May 26, 1972): B6.

92. W. D. McElroy, "Statement" (May 8, 1972), UCSD MSC, RSS 1130, box 27, fld. 7.

93. McElroy told a local reporter: "If we can't solve these problems, one solution would be to dissolve it completely." Monty Norris, "McElroy Says Future of Third College in Danger," *San Diego Evening Tribune* (May 26, 1972): A1. MEChA reacted angrily to McElroy's statements: "The only place where it appears minority students are 'qualified' are the army and penal institutions. Minority students—indeed any student—who wished to attend UCSD should be allowed to enter. We must begin to open up to democratize the UC system." UCSD MSC, Third College files (Dorn project).

94. Among the hunger strikers were Chicana/os Martha Lomelí, Petra Gonzalez, Boris Larrata, Karla Padilla, José López, Richard Flores, Manuel Briseño, and Filipina student Marline Tuyay. "Support of the People" (June 5, 1972), UCSD MSC, Third College files (Dorn project).

95. Dave Stearns, "If I Ran the University—Stull," *Triton Times* [UC San Diego] (February 27, 1970): 1.

96. Charles Ross, "Moderate UCSD Teachers Organize," *San Diego Union* (July 9, 1970): A4.

97. *Dimension* 3 [UC San Diego] (November 10, 1971): 1. AMS students openly mocked Chicano faculty such as Arturo Madrid whom they red-baited as "Professor of Indoctrination (Ph.D., Havana U) . . . head mumbo-jumbo in Third College's "Third World Studies" program." *Dimension* 2 (September, 15, 1971): 2. Madrid went on to a distinguished career at the University of Minnesota, Trinity College, the U.S. Department of Education, and the Ford Foundation. The National Endowment for the Humanities awarded him the prestigious Charles Frankel Prize in 1997.

98. "Evans-Novak Report," *San Diego Union* (February 11,1971): B6; Jeffrey Hart, "Gulp: There Goes UCal La Jolla," *National Review* (October 6, 1970): 1046; Hart, "More Evidence of UCSD's Intellectual Apartheid," *San Diego Evening Outlook* (June 30, 1971): 5. Fledgling pundit Novak (who became a fixture on right-wing cable talk shows in the 1990s) actually visited the campus in February of 1971.

99. Minutes of meeting with BSC/MAYA representatives and Third College provisional faculty (May 2, 1969) in UCSD Mandeville Special Collections, Chancellor's Office, RSS 1, box 106, fld. 1.

100. Alan Merridew, "Third College Hiring Policy Stirs Storm," *San Diego Evening Tribune* (November 24, 1971): B1. On the charge of "compensatory racism" in faculty hiring, activists found an ally in acting chancellor Herbert York who told Merridew that if the university were to "absolutely ignore race and not do anything that compensates for it, then because there are still plenty of individuals who are racist in the negative sense, the average is going to come out negative. . . . It is correct, in my view, to compensate to a substantial degree."

101. On the question of admissions, the original demands stated: "The University of California admission requirements must not be used as an instrument for excluding minority students from or limiting their numbers in Lumumba-Zapata College." *Lumumba-Zapata College, B.S.C.-M.A.Y.A. Demands for the Third College, U.C.S.D.* (March 1969): 4.

102. Memo (not sent) from Provost Watson to Chancellor McGill (March 26, 1970), UCSD MSC, RSS 1130, box 35, fld 11.

103. Memorandum from Richard Helms to Henry Kissinger (February 18, 1969) in *Hearings before the Select Committee to study Governmental Operations with respect to intelligence activities of the United States Senate. Ninety-fourth Congress. First session.* (September 23, 24, and 25, 1975): Huston Plan, vol. 2, exhibit 65 (Washington, D.C.: U.S. Government Printing Office, 1976), 401.

104. "Domestic Intelligence and Gathering Plan: Analysis and Strategy," Memorandum from Tom Charles Huston to H. R. Haldeman (July 1970) in *Hearings before the Select Committee to study Governmental Operations with respect to intelligence activities of the United States Senate. Ninety-fourth Congress. First session* (September 23, 24, and 25, 1975): Huston Plan, vol. 2, exhibit 2 (Washington, D.C.: U.S. Government Printing Office, 1976), 196.

105. Executives Conference memo to Mr. Tolson (October 29, 1970) and Airtel from Director, FBI to SAC, Albany (November 4, 1970) in *Hearings before the Select Committee to study Governmental Operations with respect to intelligence activities of the United States Senate. Ninety-fourth Congress. First session* (September 23, 24, and 25, 1975): Huston Plan, vol. 2, exhibits 41 and 42 (Washington, D.C.: U.S. Government Printing Office, 1976), 317 and 323.

106. On the history of COINTELPRO, see Ward Churchill and Jim Vander Wall, *The COINTELPRO Papers: Documents from the FBI's Secret Wars against Domestic Dissent* (Boston: South End Press, 1990); Brian Glick, *War at Home: Covert Action against U.S. Activists and What We Can Do about It* (Boston: South End Press, 1989); and Alan Theoharis, *Spying on Americans: Political Surveillance from Hoover to the Huston Plan* (Philadelphia: Temple University Press, 1978). On federal and local law-enforcement attacks against the Crusade for Justice, see Ernesto B. Vigil, *The Crusade for Justice: Chicano Militancy and the Government's War on Dissent* (Madison: University of Wisconsin Press, 1999).

107. "If You Have a Pair of Balls," in UCSD MSC, RSS 1130. box 31, fld. 6.

108. Lumumba/Zapata newsletter (April 1972), San Diego Historical Society, Mario T. García Collection, box 2, fld. 16.

109. Memorandum from C. D. DeLoach to Mr. Tolson on meeting with Herbert Ellingwood, July 17, 1969. In the same meeting, Ellingwood reported to FBI agents that at one time Reagan had considered asking the California legislature to dismiss all eight chancellors of the UC system for their "palliative" treatment of student radicals. Memo available at http://sfgate.com/news/special/pages/2002/campusfiles.

110. UCSD MSC, Chancellors's files, RSS 1, box 246, fld. 3. In his memoir, Chancellor McGill reports that around 1969 "a vice president of the University of California was retained by the CIA to brief the agency on the nature of the New Left and the radicalization techniques employed by SDS." McGill, *Year of the Monkey*, 255.

111. Interview with Alex Wong, UCSD MSC, Third College files (Dorn project).

112. The existence of the UCSD student dossiers continues to be an unresolved mystery of the period. A committee chaired by MEChA member Nick Aguilar pursued the issue of secret files, but was unsuccessful in its attempt to gain access to them (if in fact they existed). In his memoirs, former UC president Clark Kerr refers to the "San Diego files" as "privately maintained files on alleged subversives, kept by a former FBI agent and available for a fee." *The Gold and the Blue: A Personal Memoir of the University of California, 1949–1967*, Vol. 2: *Political Turmoil* (Berkeley: University of California Press, 2003), 65.

113. Letter to H. L. Richardson, July 7, 1969, UCSD MSC, Chancellors's files, RSS 1, box 43, fld. 7.

114. Interview with Randy Dotinga, UCSD MSC, Third College files (Dorn project).

115. Ricardo Villareal, "Third World Unity" (June 1972?), UCSD MSC, MSS 1, box 96, fld. 4.

116. Memo from Carlos Blanco to Joe Watson, June 7, 1973, UCSD MSC, Third College files (Dorn project).

117. Ronald Lopez and Darryl Enos, *Chicanos and Public Higher Education in California* (December, 1972): Appendix B-3, n. 1.

118. Ibid., Appendix B-4.

119. Ibid., Appendix B-5.

120. On the changes at Third College in the years immediately after its founding, see Mario Barrera, "The Struggle for Third College at UC San Diego" in *Parameters of Institutional Change: Chicano Experiences in Education* (Hayward, CA: Southwest Network of the Study Commission on Undergraduate Education and the Education of Teachers, 1975), 62–68.

121. "Black Nationalism: Counter-revolutionary and Proud," *Prensa popular* [San Diego, CA] (March 5, 1974): 2.

122. Lanie Jones, "Faculty Takes Sides in UCSD Cold War," *Los Angeles Times* (November 26, 1978): sec. 4: p. 1.

123. Cherríe Moraga, *Loving in the War Years*, 2d edition (Cambridge, MA: South End Press, 2000), 173.

124. Over a decade later in 2004, the percentage of Chicano/a undergraduates at UCSD remained frozen at 8 percent. The number of African Americans had declined to 1 percent; the number of Asian students has risen from 19 percent in 1992 to 36 percent in 2004. "Undergraduates by Ethnicity," UCSD Office of Student Research and Information, Student Affairs (ugr8.ucsd.edu).

125. Over twenty years earlier in 1970, a Chicano/a proposal to name Third College after *L.A. Times* reporter Ruben Salazar, who was killed at the August 29 Chicano antiwar demonstration in Los Angeles, fell on deaf ears. See "Letter to Regents" (September 3, 1970), from UCSD Educational Opportunity Program coordinators Estelle Chacón, Nicolas Aguilar, and Javier Correa, UCSD MSC, RSS 1130, box 35, fld. 6.

126. "Degrees Conferred: Profile of Degree Recipients," UCSD Office of Student Research and Information, Student Affairs (ugr8.ucsd.edu).

127. Katrin Dauenhauer and Jim Lope, "Massive military contractor's media mess," *Asia Times*, on-line edition (August 16, 2003).

Coda/Prologo

1. "Where Are We Now?" *Eastside Sun* (August 30, 2001): 3. In the period leading up to the American invasion of Iraq in 2003, it was media common sense to disparage an earlier generation of antiwar activists: "Unlike the stereotypical scruffy, pot-smoking, flag-burning anarchists of the Vietnam era [*sic*], today's protests were joined by a wide segment of the political spectrum." Robert D. McFadden, "From New York to Melbourne, Cries for Peace," *New York Times*, on-line edition (February 16, 2003).

2. F. Arturo Rosales, *Chicano!: The History of the Mexican American Civil Rights Movement* (Houston: Arte Público Press, 1997), 268. Literary critic José Limón faults key Movimiento texts for being too close to "Anglo youth culture of the sixties" and implicitly reduces Chicano/a activism to petulant teenage behavior: "Adolescent in its rebellious attitude toward the father, "I Am Joaquín" remains a primer for poetic and political adolescents, which we all were in 1969." *Mexican Ballads, Chicano Poems: History and Influence in Mexican-American Social Poetry* (Berkeley: University of California Press, 1992), 129.

3. Ibid., 250.

4. See Ignacio García, *Chicanismo: The Forging of a Militant Ethos among Mexican Americans* (Tucson: University of Arizona Press, 1998); and Carlos Muñoz, Jr., *Youth, Identity, Power: The Chicano Movement* (London and New York: Verso, 1989).

5. Ernesto Chávez, *"¡Mi Raza Primero!" (My People First!): Nationalism, Identity, and Insurgency in the Chicano Movement in Los Angeles, 1966–1978* (Berkeley: University of California Press, 2002), 119. Chávez's study of four Movement organizations in Los Angeles opens with the claim that the Movement as a revolution "pales" compared to anticolonial struggles in the Third World and the Black Power movement. Chávez gets off on the wrong foot when he cites as his authority a song called "Revolution" by the musical group Los Lobos and proceeds to characterize a complex social insurgency on the basis of rock lyrics.

6. Alberto Melucci, *Challenging Codes: Collective Action in the Information Age* (Cambridge: Cambridge University Press, 1996), 365.

7. Ibid., 323.

8. Ibid., 350. In a similar fashion, the construction of a mythic Aztec past rooted in the concept of a "return" or "reconquest" of Aztlán far exceeded the actual objectives of most Chicano/a militants. Melucci adds: "A movement joins past and future, the defence of a social group with a demand for transformation. Symbols and cultural models are sought in the traditions of the group and the social movements that came before the movement now in formation" (351).

9. For one academic reworking of "Aztlán," see Rafael Pérez Torres, "Refiguring Aztlán," *Aztlán: A Journal of Chicano Studies* 22 (Fall 1997): 15–41. Cordelia Candelaria reminds us in her poem "On Being Asked to Explain Aztlán to a 'Manita'" that any provisional blueprint for a Chicano/a nation is a practical outline for political action, not a theoretical abstraction: "Aztlán is a model not a metaphysics. It's a model for the masses." In *Arroyos to the Heart* (Santa Monica, CA: Santa Monica City College and Lalo Press, 1993): 7.

10. Steven Buechler, *Social Movements in Advanced Capitalism: The Political Economy and Cultural Construction of Social Activism* (Oxford University Press, 2000), 70.

11. "Why Does Standard July Fourth Oratory Bug Most Chicanos?," *Los Angeles Times* (July 10, 1970); repr. in Ruben Salazar, *Border Correspondent: Selected Writings, 1955–1970*, ed. Mario T. García (Berkeley: University of California Press, 1995), 264.

12. "The Mexican-Americans NEDA Much Better School System," *Los Angeles Times* (August 28, 1970); repr. in Salazar, *Border Correspondent*, 266.

13. Reed Johnson, "The Many Masks of Aztlán," *Los Angeles Times* (June 3, 2001): E4.

14. John Breuilly, *Nationalism and the State*, 2d ed. (Chicago: University of Chicago Press, 1994), 405. Tom Nairn points out that in poor communities, one of the only tools for generating collective praxis is a core of dedicated activists, i.e., "a militant, inter-class community rendered strongly (if mythically) aware of its own separate identity vis-à-vis the outside forces of domination." *The Break-Up of Britain: Crisis and Neo-Nationalism*, 2d ed. (London: Verso, 1981), 340.

15. At the San Diego campus of the University of California (the subject of Chapter 6) out of all Ph.D.s granted in 2001–2002 only 4.3 percent were Mexican Americans; of all M.D.s granted at the School of Medicine only 1.6 percent were Mexican Americans (the numbers for African Americans were Ph.D.s 4 percent and M.D.s 0.0 percent. "Degrees Conferred: Profile of Degree Recipients," UCSD Office of Student Research and Information, Student Affairs (ugr8.ucsd.edu).

16. "Today's Heroes for Today's Struggles," *Hispanic Business* 23 (April 2001): 4. A former Movement activist who participated in the drafting of the Plan de Santa Bárbara, Chavarría stands as a perfect example of the cliché "Yesterday's radical is tomorrow's conservative." Following the spirit of Chavarría's corporate ethos, poet Gary Soto urged affluent Hispanic professionals to "try to achieve the social legacy" of César Chávez and Dolores Huerta not with acts of militant nonviolent activism but through philanthropy and charity. "The Boomitos' Next Challenge," *Hispanic Business* (September 2001): 64–65.

17. Mexican American high school dropout rates continue to hover between 30 percent and 40 percent. For first-generation immigrant students, the rate is over 60 percent. Between 1985 and 1995, the number of Latino/as in prison more than tripled. The percentage of California Chicano/a high school graduates eligible to apply for admission to the University of California is less than 4 percent. Latino/as make up only 3 percent of all Ph.D.s earned by U.S. citizens and only 2 percent of all university faculty nationally. Richard A. Ibarra, "At the Crossroads of Cultural Change in Higher Education" in *Strategic Initiatives for Hispanics in Higher Education*, The Hispanic Caucus, American Association for Higher Education (August 2, 2003): 54.

18. Data taken from the "Interim Report of the President's Advisory Commission on Educational Excellence for Hispanic Americans, September 2002 (www.yic.gov/

paceea/press/interim.html) and the U.S. Census Bureau report "Income, poverty, and Health Insurance Coverage in the United States: 2003" (www.census/gov/hhes/www/income.html).

19. See Donaldo Macedo and Lilia I. Bartolomé, *Dancing with Bigotry: Beyond the Politics of Tolerance* (New York: St. Martin's Press, 1999); and Otto Santa Ana, *Brown Tide Rising: Metaphors of Latinos in Contemporary American Public Discourse* (Austin: University of Texas Press, 2002).

20. García writes: "A Chicano militant ethos would be the collective defensive and offensive mechanism that the Mexican American community uses to combat racism, discrimination, poverty, and segregation, and to define itself politically and historically." *Chicanismo*, 4.

21. With public education for low-income families in shambles, the charter school movement continues to gain supporters in Chicano/a communities. In November of 2001, the first charter school (known as "Semillas del Pueblo") was proposed for East Los Angeles. The school received funding from the National Council for La Raza and endorsements from former Movement activists who are now university professors. Raúl Vásquez, "First Charter School in Eastside Nears Approval," *Northeast Sun* (November 29, 2001): A1. One of the ironies of the Hispanic charter school movement, including those schools that invoke some form of *chicanismo*, is the fact that many campuses welcome military recruiters and JROTC units.

22. "National Latino Poll Reveals Surprises," *U.S. Newswire* (July 25, 2001).

23. During the 1990s, Chicano Studies programs became popular in European universities. Selected Chicano/a artists and scholars were courted in Spain, France, and Germany. This development might well be positive if not for the tendency among some European scholars to exoticize "ethnic" communities they do not know well. A recent book published in Spain, for example, proclaims: "*El objetivo de este pequeño libro es incitar a los lectores a profundizar en su estudio de esta raza ancestral . . . pidiendo el respeto y la comprensión hacia un pueblo cuyos complejos matices lo convierten en una de las culturas más atractivas de nuestro planeta y espera concienciar a su público para que sea receptivo a los mensajes que esta Raza nos envía*" ("The purpose of this small book is to incite readers to study further this ancestral people . . . asking for respect and comprehension towards a people whose complex features make it one of the most attractive cultures on our planet and hoping that readers will be receptive to the messages that this People [Race?] sends us"). Raquel León Jiménez, ed. and tr., *Textos sobre el desarrollo del Movimiento Chicano*, Taller de Estudios Norteamericanos (León: Universidad de León, 2000), 59–60.

León Jiménez collapses several decades of Chicano/a history as if there were no distinction to be made between the Movimiento of the Viet Nam war era and the present. Texts such as the "Plan espiritual de Aztlán" are presented as recent writing, and because there is no contextualization offered Oscar Zeta Acosta becomes a contemporary of Gloria Anzaldúa.

24. Roberto Haro, "The Dearth of Latinos in Campus Administration," *The Chronicle of Higher Education*, online edition: http://chronicle.com (December 11, 2001).

25. *Malcolm X on Afro-American History*, 4th ed. (New York and London: Pathfinder, 1995), 53. As Malcolm pointed out, it is the nationalist impulse alone in the

face of institutional delay and diversion that insists on the urgency of social justice: "Black nationalism means: 'Give it to us now. Don't wait for next year. Give it to us yesterday, and that's not fast enough'" (79).

26. Martin Luther King, Jr., *Where Do We Go from Here: Chaos or Community?* (Boston: Beacon Press, 1968), 132.

27. "Ernesto Galarza interview," *Chicano Journal* [UC San Diego] (May 5, 1972): 17.

28. Joe Martinez, "Letter to the Editor," *Hispanic Business* 23 (July/August 2001): 12.

29. Many of the most recent Mexican immigrants now reside and work in the Deep South ranging from Arkansas to the Carolinas to Georgia and west to Mississippi. Most of these workers and their families will be cut off from earlier traditions of Mexicano/Chicano resistance in the Southwest. They will develop their own cultural and political identities in a social reality that is more rigidly black/white than was that of Chicano/a activists in the Southwest during the Viet Nam war period.

30. Manuel Castells, *The Power of Identity*, vol. 2 of *The Information Age: Economy, Society and Culture* (Oxford: Blackwell, 1997), 59.

31. "The Making of the Political Pocho." *La Voz de la Esperanza* [San Antonio] 13 (November 2000): 3. Also circulated on the Internet.

32. Jesus Chavarría, "From the Editor," in *Hispanic Business* (October, 2000): 6.

33. Bárbara Renaud González, "Targeting Chicano," *The Progressive*, on-line edition (July 2002). Even artists with a strong commitment to progressive change defended the exhibit. Richard Montoya of Culture Clash warned Renaud González in her article: "We are in the ghost-dance days of Chicanismo. There's only a few of us holding the banner. The movement is grinding to a halt."

34. Renaud González, "Targeting Chicano."

35. Jorge Bustamante, "Prólogo" to Reies López Tijerina, *Mi lucha por la tierra* (Mexico City: FCE, 1978), 22.

36. Ernesto Galarza, "The Task Ahead for Mexican Americans: Mexican Americans and the American Culture" in *Viewpoints: Red and Yellow, Black and Brown* (Minneapolis: Winston Press, 1972), 312.

37. Cherríe Moraga, *Loving in the War Years*, 2d ed. (Cambridge, MA: South End Press, 2000), 173. I agree entirely with Moraga's evaluation of the current state of Ethnic and Chicano/a Studies programs at most elite research institutions: "I have witnessed academic programs that emerged out of political struggle separate themselves from that struggle, even at a time when assaults against people of color and our right to education have escalated to the point of verifiable government-instituted racist paranoia" (186).

38. As Ernesto Che Guevara told a group of Cuban students in 1962: "*No dejen de ser jóvenes, no se transformen en viejos teóricos o teorizantes*" ("Don't stop being young, don't become old theorists or theory heads"). *Che Guevara Habla a la Juventud* (New York and London: Pathfinder, 2000), 20.

39. Scott Miller, "Hispanics Replace African Americans as Largest U.S. Minority Group," U.S. Department of State, International Information Programs (January 23, 2003). http://usinfo.state.gov/usa/race/diversity/a012303.htm

40. On Waters, see Harold Meyerson, "Powerlines," *L.A. Weekly* (June 1–7, 2001): 15. State Senator Richard Polanco's practice of *caciquismo* and his public opposition to

Villaraigosa facilitated Hahn's victory as did a media campaign directed against Villaraigosa funded by California Indian gaming tribes. See James Rainey, "Polanco Endorses Hahn as 'Best Prepared to Serve City,'" *Los Angeles Times* on-line edition (May 22, 2001); and William Booth, "Calif. Tribes' Clout Carries Political Risk," *Washington Post* on-line edition (October 1, 2003). Villaraigosa was elected mayor of L.A. in 2005.

41. Darryl Fears, "Calif. Activist Seeks End To Identification by Race," *Washington Post* (July 5, 2003): A01. Connerly's reactionary racial politics harkens back to the early Civil Rights era when organizations such as the Los Angeles-based United Civil Rights Coalition in 1963 refused to admit Mexican Americans.

42. See, for example, George Lipsitz, *The Possessive Investment in Whiteness: How White People Profit from Identity Politics* (Philadelphia: Temple University Press, 1998).

43. For a brief glimpse of how the dialogue between Chicano and Black activists might take shape in coming years, see the exchange on the *Black Commentator* website that began with my essay "A Chicano Looks at the Trent Lott Affair" (January 16, 2003) and continued in subsequent issues at www.blackcommentator.com/25/25_guest_commentary.html

44. Patrick Buchanan, *The Death of the West: How Dying Populations and Immigrant Invasions Imperil Our Country and Civilization* (New York: St. Martin's Press, 2002), 125–26. Media attacks against MEChA have been a staple of conservative rhetoric ever since the 2000 Census showed Latinos to be the fastest growing sector of the U.S. population. For an extreme example, see http://www.americanpatrol.org.

When Lieutenant Governor Cruz Bustamante ran for governor in the California recall election of 2003, anti-immigrant groups, the neoconservative press, and FOX pundit Bill O'Reilly attempted to discredit him for being a former *mechista* and more loyal to "Aztlán" than to California. See my article at http://www.counterpunch.org/marisca108302003.html

One on-line commentator lays the blame for MEChA's influence on college campuses at the doorstep of university administrators. Singled out for especially harsh criticism was University of California, San Diego, Vice Chancellor Joseph W. Watson (see Chapter 6) because he had defended a Chicano student newspaper's right to freedom of expression. David Orland, "The Road to Aztlan," *Boundless* webzine (October 10, 2002) at http://boundless.org/2002_2003/features.

45. Joseph Farah, "American's Palestinians" at www.worldnetdaily.com/news (November 15, 2001).

46. Samuel P. Huntington, *Who Are We?: The Challenges to America's National Identity* (New York: Simon and Schuster, 2004), 324.

47. See my "The Future for Latinos in an Era of War and Occupation," and "The Militarization of U.S. Culture," at jorgemariscal.blogspot.com.

APPENDIX

1. Introduction to Refugio I. Rochín and Dennis N. Valdés, eds., *Voices of a New Chicana/o History* (East Lansing: Michigan State University Press, 2000).

2. Ramón A. Gutiérrez, "Chicano History: Paradigm Shifts and Shifting Boundaries," in Rochín and Valdés, *Voices,* 91–114.

3. Historian Gerald Horne has argued: "The use of regressive nationalism as a tool against the Left is one of the oldest of elite tactics." "Blowback: Playing the

Nationalist Card Backfires" in Christopher Newfield and Ronald Strickland, eds., *After Political Correctness: The Humanities and Society in the 1990s* (Boulder: Westview Press, 1995), 85.

4. Ernesto Chávez, "'Birth of a New Symbol': The Brown Berets' Gendered Chicano National Imaginary," in Joe Austin and Michael Nevin Willard, eds., *Generations of Youth: Youth Cultures and History in Twentieth-Century America* (New York and London: New York University Press, 1998), 206. Chávez takes the term *anti-Americanism* to mean the rejection of the traditional repertoire of patriotic discourses and practices. The lack of precision in his argument, however, allows for the slippage into alternate and more pejorative meanings. He reproduces the term in a later article in which he argues that the Movimiento failed "to empower the ethnic Mexican community . . . because it conceptualized that group in a narrow manner." "Imagining the Mexican Immigrant Worker: (Inter)Nationalism, Identity, and Insurgency in the Chicano Movement in Los Angeles," *Aztlán* 25 (Fall 2000): 110. In his book, he repeatedly uses the term *anti-Americanism* without clarification. See *"¡Mi Raza Primero!" (My People First!): Nationalism, Identity, and Insurgency in the Chicano Movement in Los Angeles, 1966–1978* (Berkeley: University of California Press, 2002).

5. María Montoya, "Beyond Internal Colonialism: Class, Gender, and Culture as Challenges to Chicano Identity" in Rochín and Valdés, *Voices*, 183–84. Even in the Movement period when the Mexican American professional class was much smaller than it is today, some members of that class complained that an academic focus on working-class Chicanos deprived the Mexican American middle class of the attention it merited: "Social scientists have chosen to study that segment of the Chicano . . . population that Ralph Guzman refers to as 'quaint,' ignoring Mexican Americans who are middle class. The net result of this extraordinary scientific oversight is the perpetuation of very damaging stereotypes of the Mexican American." Edward Casavantes, ""Pride and Prejudice: A Mexican American Dilemma," *Civil Rights Digest* (Winter 1970): 23.

6. Rochín and Valdés, *Voices*, 184.

7. Ibid., 185.

8. Elihu Carranza, *Chicanismo: Philosophical Fragments* (Dubuque: Kendall/Hunt, 1978), 106.

9. Rochín and Valdés, *Voices*, 17. In her essay in the *Voices* volume, Lorena Oropeza asserts, "I am here to insist that scholarship is activism" (221), but then positively invokes the names of academics such as Cornel West and Rudy Acuña whose scholarly careers have been paralleled by an active engagement with local and national political struggles on and off campus. I would argue that while academic scholarship is indeed a social act (with extremely limited and deferred consequences in the nonacademic world) it is not activism.

Index